W9-AFM-503

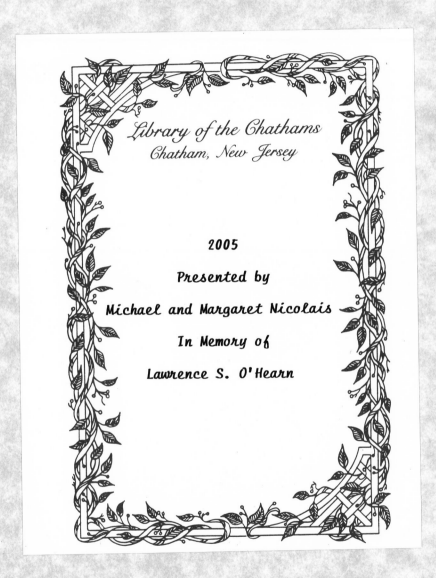

Library of the Chathams
Chatham, New Jersey

2005

Presented by

Michael and Margaret Nicolais

In Memory of

Lawrence S. O'Hearn

COMMAND AT SEA

Command at Sea

Naval Command and Control
since the Sixteenth Century

MICHAEL A. PALMER

HARVARD UNIVERSITY PRESS

CAMBRIDGE, MASSACHUSETTS

LONDON, ENGLAND

2005

Copyright © 2005 by the President and Fellows of Harvard College
All rights reserved
Printed in the United States of America

Library of Congress Cataloging-in-Publication Data

Palmer, Michael A.
Command at sea : naval command and control since the
sixteenth century / Michael A. Palmer.
p.   cm.
Includes bibliographical references and index.
ISBN 0-674-01681-5 (alk. paper)
1. Command and control systems—History.   2. Naval history, Modern.
I. Title.

VB212.P36 2005
359.3'3041'0903—dc22   2004054116

To William N. "Bill" Still, Jr.

Contents

Battle Maps

I will try to have a Motto,—
at least it shall be my watch-word, Touch and Take.

> —*Lord Horatio Nelson to*
> *Sir George Rose,*
> *17 September 1805*

A Regular Confusion

AT ABOUT 1430 on the first day of August 1798, as the British third-rate ship-of-the-line *Zealous* 74 cruised eastward along the Egyptian coast, a lookout in the masthead spied the topmasts of several large ships anchored in Aboukir Bay. After Samuel Hood, the captain of the *Zealous,* sent a glass aloft the man called down that he could make out a dozen-and-a-half large vessels, including what he thought to be sixteen ships of the line.[1]

Word of the sighting spread quickly through the British fleet. Commanders watched as drummers beat crews to quarters and the sailors and marines took their stations. Black gunports swung open and loaded cannon began to peek through the yellow, checkerboard sides of the British men-of-war. Crewmen cleared the decks of furniture and bulwarks and stowed below anything that a solid shot might splinter or that might get in the way during an engagement. On Hood's *Zealous,* sweating seamen "hove overboard" ten unfortunate bullocks, a bovine offering to Neptune.

On the flagship, the *Vanguard* 74, a troubled Rear Admiral Sir Horatio Nelson had yet to sit down to dinner. Since the escape of the French fleet from Toulon on 19 May, and the dismasting of the *Vanguard* in a storm off Sardinia the next day, Nelson had raced about the Mediterranean searching for the enemy. The British seemed always a step behind, or a step ahead. On 17 June Nelson reached Naples, where he learned that his quarry was at Malta. He hastened south to intercept, only to discover on 22 June off Cape Passero, the southeastern tip of Sicily, that the Knights of Malta had surrendered ten days before, and that the French had reembarked and departed on the nineteenth. Nelson, convinced that

I

his opponent was bound for Egypt, sailed eastward with all speed, trying to make up for the French fleet's three-day head start. Six days later the British were off Alexandria, but no Frenchmen were to be found. A disappointed Nelson sailed north for Alexandretta, only hours before the sluggish French came into view over the horizon. The next day the Gallic armada landed an army commanded by a young general, Napoleon Bonaparte, which quickly overran lower Egypt.

Nelson was distraught. "It is an old saying," he wrote in late July, " 'The Devil's children have the Devil's luck': I cannot find, or to this moment learn, beyond vague conjecture, where the French fleet are gone to." But he resolved to track down and destroy the enemy ships, even if they were "bound to the Antipodes." Time and again events frustrated his hopes. As the weeks passed without contact, Nelson's subordinates noticed that their commander exhibited signs of strain.[2]

He had good reason to worry. In England the news of the uncontested French passage of the Mediterranean and the landing in Egypt had the political hyenas scenting the blood of a faltering national hero. Thus far, in his first major independent command, Nelson had failed to live up to the high expectations of king and country. His Mediterranean misfire mortified William Pitt, the prime minister. The secretary of state for war, Henry Dundas, who along with Pitt was the architect of British strategy, wondered in a letter to Lord George Spencer how Nelson could explain his premature departure from Alexandria "after he got there in so auspicious a manner." Spencer, the first lord of the admiralty, had no answer, but hoped that Nelson "had a pretty good story to tell at least. His missing the French fleet both going and returning was certainly very unfortunate; but we must not be too ready to censure him for leaving Alexandria when he was there, till we know the exact state of the intelligence which he received on his arrival there."[3]

Spencer's more immediate concern lay with the course of future operations and their grand strategic impact on the affairs of the anti-French coalition. He lamented that Nelson's miscalculation off Alexandria had dashed British hopes for a "decisive" engagement in the Mediterranean. He assumed that Nelson would eventually run down the French fleet: but then what? "When he learns where they are," Spencer wrote, "it is likely enough that he will make some attempt on them; and perhaps if he finds (as he probably may) that they are not to be attacked in port without too great risk for his own ships, he will continue to block them up." But Nelson's squadron could not long remain on such a distant station and, ultimately, would have to withdraw. Bonaparte's Egyptian expedition had thus completely unhinged British strategy in the Mediterranean. The ramifications were being felt not only in Constantinople, the capital of the Ottoman Empire, but also in far-away Moscow, thereby imperiling Pitt's and Dundas's effort to put together an effective second coalition against France.[4]

Nelson, too, was aware of the consequences of the French invasion. He was strategist enough to appreciate the importance of Egypt, and he recognized that whatever his past heroics as captain and commodore, his failure as fleet commander to intercept the French before they reached Alexandria could short-circuit his career. He also knew that he could not maintain his force in the eastern Mediterranean, hundreds of miles from the nearest secure British base at Gibraltar. Thus there was little point in tracking down the enemy unless he was prepared to attack, whatever the circumstances. So when, on 28 July, he at last received firm intelligence placing the French at Alexandria, Nelson raced his fleet south, determined to gain either a peerage or a place of perpetual rest in Westminster Abbey.[5]

Once again he found disappointment. As the fleet approached Alexandria early on 1 August, the only ships in the harbor flying the tricolor flag of France were merchantmen. Nelson, who had eaten little and slept less over the past several days, was glum. So too were some of his captains, among them Sir James Saumarez of the *Orion* 74, who felt "utterly hopeless" and "out of spirits."[6]

All that changed with word that ships had been sighted in nearby Aboukir Bay. On the *Orion,* stewards were removing the dinner tablecloth when the watch officer burst into the mess and announced the sighting of the enemy fleet. "All sprang from their seats," Saumarez recalled, "and only staying to drink a *bumper* to our success, we were in a moment on deck." On the *Vanguard,* Nelson, after signaling at 1455 for his fleet to prepare for battle, finally sat down to dinner.[7]

For the French, reports of the early afternoon sighting of the English fleet precipitated acute anxiety, not excitement or the hoisting of "bumpers" to success. The French navy, unlike Great Britain's Royal Navy, did not consider victory in battle a prerequisite for a successful operation. Vice Admiral François-Paul Brueys d'Aiguilliers had successfully transported Bonaparte's army to Egypt and wished only to complete his mission with a safe return to Toulon.

Brueys nevertheless realized that the approach of the British made a

battle of some sort unavoidable, if not that day, then the next. At about
1500 he issued a series of orders to ready his fleet for action. He directed
that the armed parties sent ashore earlier in the day to dig wells—about
a third of his men—return to their ships, that hammocks be stowed,
and that the topsail yards be set. Brueys apparently considered the possibility of getting his fleet under way to meet the British at sea. But with
so many men ashore, his undermanned ships could not simultaneously
maneuver and fight effectively. Not that he had much faith in the seaworthiness of his ships or the seamanship of his officers and men. From
the start of the Egyptian expedition, he had expressed little confidence in
what he considered a poorly equipped and manned fleet. If there was to
be a battle, the French would fight at anchor.[8]

With his ships tucked into Aboukir Bay, geography, force, and time all
seemingly favored Brueys. In the age of sail, fleets at anchor possessed advantages that generally allowed them to drive off much stronger forces.[9]
Closely anchored together, the ships formed an almost impenetrable line
capable of concentrated fire, with one flank secured close to land and an
assault possible only from a single direction. Mooring (anchoring from
both bow and stern) and fixing springs (lines warped to the anchor cables
from the opposite quarter of a ship) allowed a man-of-war to pivot to
cover all angles of approach and support its neighbors. Anchored ships
also made more stable gun-platforms, and their crews were spared most
of the demands of working the vessel.

Furthermore, Brueys's fleet was nominally more powerful than his
enemy's. Nelson commanded thirteen 74-gun ships of the line, one 50-
gun fourth-rate, and a single 18-gun brig. Brueys's fleet included a 120-
gun first-rate ship of the line, three second-rate 80-gun ships, nine 74s,
and four frigates mounting between 36 and 48 guns.[10] In early July, assured by Bonaparte that the army would establish a battery of 40 guns to
cover the bay, the usually gloomy Brueys had responded that his position
in Aboukir Bay would be impregnable.[11]

Brueys also correctly calculated that it would be early evening before
the British reached the bay. For most sailing-age commanders, dusk was
too late in the day to initiate a battle, especially if their fleet was dispersed
in an order more suited to reconnaissance than to engagement. In the age
of sail, it took all day to fight what usually turned out to be an indecisive
action. What point could there be to beginning a battle at sunset? In the
dark, the visual signaling systems that commanders used to communicate
with their subordinates would be useless. Brueys assumed there would be
no battle until the morrow.

Brueys's position, in fact, was far from unassailable. Since the French men-of-war swung in the current from bow anchors only, without springs, their guns could not cover the large gaps—about three-quarters of a cable's length, or 450 feet—separating the ships. Nor was the 74-gun liner *le Guerrier,* Brueys's leading ship, anchored close enough to Aboukir Island, or his fleet to the five-fathom shoal of the bay, to prevent the British from passing the head of the line and running along the unprepared inshore side of the French armada.[12]

While Brueys's preparations for battle were appallingly inadequate, in hindsight his assumptions regarding the likelihood of an engagement were nevertheless rational. Whatever the shortcomings of his dispositions, they would only become apparent after the two fleets closed and the enemy conducted a reconnaissance. From a distance, his anchored position would appear secure. His opponent could not know that perhaps as many as a third of the French seamen were still ashore, or that the inboard guns were not ready for battle. And by the standards of the age, it was too close to nightfall for a battle to begin.

Brueys's problem was less the weakness of his position than the fact that Nelson was determined to attack. Nelson had written to Lord St. Vincent, the British naval commander in chief at Gibraltar: "You may be assured I will fight them the moment I can reach, be they at anchor or under sail." To prepare for that eventuality, during the long pursuit of Brueys, Nelson, whenever the weather permitted, ordered his captains to the flagship, where all became acquainted with his "ideas and intentions." Edward Berry, captain of the *Vanguard,* noted: "There was no possible position in which they [the French] could be found that he did not take into his calculation, and for the most advantageous attack of which he had not digested and arranged the best possible disposition of the force he commanded." In Berry's view, Nelson's "perspicuity" enabled him to present his ideas in such a fashion that his subordinates considered them "completely their own." As a result, "signals became almost unnecessary."[13]

Nelson's willingness, or more accurately eagerness, to fight without the use of signals was central to the undertaking at hand. As he told his captains, should they find the French anchored in a strong natural position, an immediate attack would be imperative lest the enemy have time to prepare. Given the torpid tempo of sailing-age engagements, that implied an action that, in part at least, would be fought in the dark. Thus, when the signal from Hood's *Zealous* confirming that the French were anchored in Aboukir Bay reached the *Vanguard* at 1441, Nelson needed

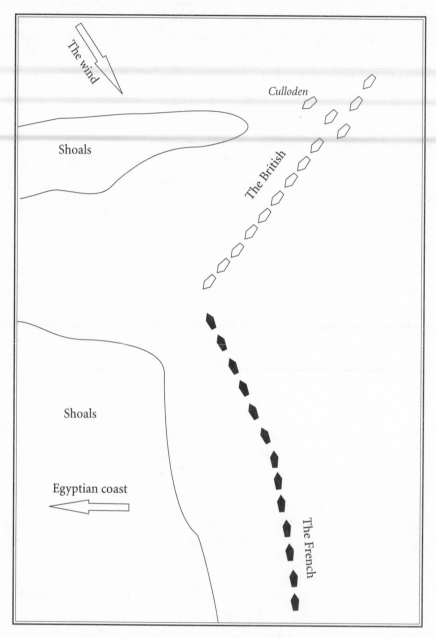

THE BATTLE OF THE NILE, 1 AUGUST 1798, CA. 1800

As Nelson approached the French fleet he made the signal to attack. Given the position of the enemy fleet and the direction of the wind, the British captains knew to concentrate their effort on the leading two-thirds of the French fleet. The downwind ships would be unable to intervene. Brueys, given the lateness of the day, did not expect an attack until the next morning.

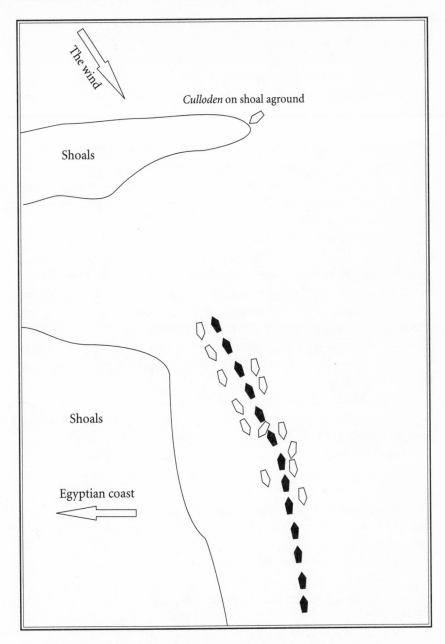

THE BATTLE OF THE NILE, 1 AUGUST 1798, CA. 2130
Captain Thomas Foley, commanding the leading British ship of the line *Goliath,*
noticed that the French ships were not properly moored and made the decision to
lead past the French line and to attack from the inshore side. The French, who did
not expect an attack, were even less prepared to have their line doubled.

no council of war with his commanders and less than fifteen minutes to evaluate the situation, to decide to attack, and to signal his fleet to prepare for battle. About ninety minutes later, as the British fleet closed, Nelson deduced that the French would not sortie. At 1622 he made signal 54: "when it may be necessary to anchor with a bower or sheet cable in abaft, and springs."[14]

Shortly before 1700 Nelson signaled again, this time to attack the enemy's van and center. With the French facing into the wind and the British approaching with the breeze at their backs, he wished to concentrate his attack against the leading two-thirds of the enemy line, yet another tactic he had discussed previously with his subordinates. The French rear, unable to sail upwind, would be helpless to intervene.[15]

As the British, still forming their line, worked their way around Aboukir Island, it slowly dawned on the French that the enemy meant business, an awareness that spread through Brueys's squadron about two and a half hours after Nelson's decision to engage. The dangerous weaknesses of Brueys's deployment then became evident, and not just to the French. The commanders of the leading British men-of-war could see that their enemy's ships were not moored. Nelson was among those who noted "that where there was room for an Enemy's Ship to swing, there was room for one of ours to anchor."[16]

Captain Thomas Foley, whose *Goliath* 74 led Nelson's line, made the same observation. On his own initiative, Foley, the only captain in the squadron with a chart of the bay, ignored the fire of the small battery on Aboukir Island as well as that of the two leading French ships, *le Guerrier* and *le Conquérant*, discharged a raking larboard broadside into the *Guerrier* as he passed, and then worked his way down the enemy's inshore side, intending to anchor opposite the gap between the two ships. But the *Goliath's* anchor was slow to drop, and Foley ended up opposite the *Conquérant* instead.

Samuel Hood followed Foley and, when he saw the *Goliath* miss its mark and sail past the *Guerrier*, "cut away the *Zealous's* sheet anchor and came to in the exact situation Captain Foley intended to have taken."[17] The next three ships in the British line—the *Orion*, the *Audacious*, and the *Theseus*—imitated their leaders, firing broadsides as they passed, and anchored inshore opposite the fifth, third, and fourth ships in the French line, respectively.

As they approached the battle, the officers commanding Nelson's leading ships faced difficult choices without direction from their commander in chief. They could either swing around the ships already in position and chance grounding or pass through the lines of fire of engaged British men-of-war, risking collision and friendly fire in the smoky confusion of battle. To avoid running aground, Saumarez took the *Orion* between the *Zealous* and the *Guerrier,* but then swung out and circled around the *Goliath.* Captain Davidge Gould, commanding the *Audacious,* took a shortcut through the French line between *le Guerrier* and *le Conquérant* but still had to pass between the latter and the *Goliath.* Captain Ralph Miller, in the *Theseus,* took the long way around the head of the French line and, rather than risk grounding, passed through two ongoing engagements.

Nelson decided that it would be foolish to take a similar risk with the flagship. The moment had come to begin doubling the French line—assaulting it from both sides. Captain Berry skillfully brought the *Vanguard* around and anchored opposite *le Spartiate* 74, which was already engaged on the inshore side by Miller's *Theseus.*

As the night darkened and a moderate wind swept the smoke of battle along the French line, confusion increased. Captain Thomas Louis's *Minotaur* 74 followed the lead of the *Vanguard* and anchored in a position abreast *l'Aquilon* 74. Captain Henry Darby, commanding the *Bellerophon* 74, who should have anchored opposite *le Franklin* 80, dragged an anchor and found himself alongside *l'Orient,* Brueys's 120-gun flagship. Shortly after 2000 the outgunned *Bellerophon's* mizzen and mainmasts went by the board. After a two-hour pounding, Darby ordered the "Billy Ruffin's" stern cable cut, and the ship slowly left the arena under what little sail could be set, before losing its topmast at 2100. Captain John Peyton brought the *Defence* into action off the starboard bow of *le Franklin,* filling the gap left by Darby. The *Majestic* 74 took up the next position in line, but Captain George Westcott anchored directly adjacent to *le Tonnant* 80, the ship immediately to the rear of *l'Orient.* The French 80-gun ship poured heavy fire into the *Majestic* and a French sharpshooter put a ball into Westcott's head, killing him. At about 2000 the *Majestic's* first lieutenant slipped the cable, drifted farther along the line until his ship was well positioned in the gap between *le Tonnant* and *l'Heureuse* 74, "and let go the best bower with a spring fast to it out of the gun room port."

As the rear ships of the British line approached the battle, the *Culloden* 74, commanded by Captain Thomas Troubridge, ran hard aground on the shoal east of Aboukir Island. Captain Alexander Ball's *Alexander* 74 cleared the shoal and cut through the French line between *l'Orient* and *le Tonnant,* taking an inshore position between the ships. At about 2030 Captain Benjamin Hallowell's *Swiftsure* 74 anchored opposite the gap between *le Franklin* and *l'Orient* and began a heavy fire into the French flagship. As Captain Thomas Thompson brought his undergunned fourth-rate ship *Leander* 50 into the fray, a shot from the *Orion* cut the cable of *le Peuple Souverain* 74, which drifted out of position. Thompson sailed into the gap between *le Peuple Souverain* and *le Franklin* and anchored. The *Leander* could thus rake its opponents with little risk of return fire.

By the time the *Leander* anchored, accurate and methodical British fire had dismasted the five ships of the French van and silenced their guns. *Le Spartiate* struck its flag to the *Vanguard* at 2030 after a two-hour pummeling, during the course of which a scrap of iron shot sliced into Nelson's forehead, loosing a flap of skin that fell over his one good eye, momentarily blinding him. Nelson, who seemingly always entered battle with a premonition of death, cried "I am killed! Remember me to my wife," and collapsed, only to be caught in mid-fall by Captain Berry. Fortunately, the bloody wound was not as bad as it looked. Once in the cockpit amid the dead and wounded, Nelson demanded that he "take his turn with the brave fellows."[18]

Following the destruction of the French van, attention focused on the center of the enemy line, where British and French ships dueled "within pistol shot"—a range of less than fifty yards. The British fire drove French crews from their guns. At about 2100 fire broke out in *l'Orient,* the French flagship. As Nelson had expected, the wind, still blowing along the line, prevented the five ships of Brueys's rear from coming to the aid of their commander. Confusion reigned as individual French captains, as well as the commanders of the van and the rear, accustomed to direction from their commander in chief, found themselves on their own as the battle raged around them. Nelson's "mode of attack" left the French paralyzed, confused, in "a stupor," locked in place, "peaceful spectators to the fight." As Rear Admiral Pierre de Villeneuve later admitted, "from the moment when the English ships doubled us by the head" the French squadron was doomed.[19]

Brueys nonetheless determined to continue the fight and refused to allow his flagship to strike, despite concentrated and effective gunnery from the *Alexander,* the *Swiftsure,* and the *Leander* designed both to spread the fire and to prevent its extinction. From the quarterdeck of the *Swiftsure,* observers could see Brueys, who had lost both his legs, "seated with torniquets on the stumps in an armchair facing his enemies, and giving directions for extinguishing the fire, when a cannon ball from the *Swiftsure* put a period to his gallant life by nearly cutting him in two."[20]

The fire on the French flagship blazed so fiercely that the ship made a "grand and awful spectacle" that illuminated everything in its vicinity. On Nelson's flagship, Berry sent a messenger below to advise his wounded commander in chief to come up on deck before *l'Orient* exploded. Nelson came to the quarterdeck and, aghast at what he saw, immediately directed Berry to launch the *Vanguard's* surviving boat to rescue those Frenchmen fortunate enough to reach the water. His example would not be followed. Those captains, both British and French, commanding nearest *l'Orient* thought only of the safety of their ships, not the deliverance of the French seamen. One by one, alarmed captains cut their cables to distance themselves from the French flagship before it exploded. The heat radiating from the ship was so intense that molten pitch ran down the side of the *Swiftsure*. Yet Captain Hallowell, unlike his neighbors, decided to stay put, convinced as he was that the force of the explosion would arc over his ship. He placed guards near the cables lest some petrified seaman try to cut them, although as a precaution he ordered the gun ports closed and the crew to the deck. At about 2200 the ship finally blew. Captain Miller wrote to his wife that such a sight "formerly would have drawn tears down the victor's cheeks, but now pity was stifled as it rose by the remembrance of the numerous and horrid atrocities their unprincipled and blood-thirsty nation had and were committing; and when she blew up . . . though I endeavoured to stop the momentary cheer of the ship's company, my heart scarce felt a single pang for their fate."[21]

The battle now entered its final stage. In an effort to escape, several French ships cut their cables and drifted toward their companions. In the confusion, Frenchmen fired on Frenchmen. Nor did Nelson's captains slacken their efforts, despite the damaged condition of their ships and the exhaustion of their crews. In the quest for a complete victory, they too cut their cables and drifted with the wind along the French line, marking out new victims for slaughter. Only Villeneuve's *le Guillaume Tell* 80, *le Généreux* 74, and a pair of frigates escaped the debacle.

When the sun rose on the morning of 2 August, revealing his fleet's handiwork, Nelson remarked, "Victory is not a name strong enough for such a scene." He had achieved something nearly impossible in late-eighteenth-century naval warfare—an annihilative victory. Moreover, as an astonished Lord Howe later said to Berry: "It stood unparalleled, and sin-

gular in this instance, that every captain distinguished himself." Howe
had been in the forefront of the development of visual signals, principally
as a means to control the movements of subordinates to ensure their participation in battle. Thus far, signals had failed to produce the desired results, yet Nelson, operating in the dark, had somehow brought his entire
fleet, less the grounded *Culloden,* into action. As a result, of the thirteen
ships of the line of the French Mediterranean fleet, only two remained
afloat and at large: seven had been captured, three others and a frigate had
been burned, *l'Orient* had blown up, and a second frigate had been sunk.
Though several of the British ships were severely damaged, all were re-
pairable. British losses totaled 218 killed and 677 wounded. French casualties, including prisoners, were ten times that number, with more than
5,000 killed or missing.[22]

THE CONTEST between Nelson and Brueys was not only a struggle between two men, two fleets, two navies, and two nation-states, but also,
and most important for this book, a clash between two very different
philosophies of command at sea.

Brueys was a child of his time, and his thinking embraced the naval
ideas of the age—the line ahead, the signal book, and order in battle. He
was the product of a country that for more than a century had led
Europe toward rationalism and an appreciation of science and the scientific method historians term the Enlightenment.[23] Throughout the eighteenth century, European naval circles increasingly espoused the idea that
scientific study could provide the answers to the difficult problems facing
mariners and naval warriors. The French excelled in this partnership of
government officials and academics and led the way in the study of navigation, cartography, shipbuilding, gunnery, tactics, and signaling. Frenchmen were the first to examine past sea battles in search of lessons to be
learned. The French made a science of navies and naval warfare, complete with manuals and signal books meant to bring order to sailing-age
battles formerly marked by disorder. And yet the French usually found
themselves victimized by their far less scientific but far more successful
British antagonists.[24]

Nevertheless, well before the end of the eighteenth century the French
scientific approach merged with British practical experience to establish
an analytic paradigm—a basic set of assumptions—within which naval
officers made rational decisions arrived at "via probabilistic calculations."[25]

All but a few naval commanders embraced this model and assumed that victory at sea could best be achieved by a fleet in a well-ordered line-ahead formation, executing preplanned maneuvers, at the centralized direction of a commander using well-developed systems of flag signals to communicate his wishes to his subordinates. The pervasiveness of the paradigm is evident: the fact that most sailing-age battles remained indecisive simply led to calls for ever more order and improved signaling systems.

Within this paradigm, Brueys's assumption that the British would not engage until the following morning was entirely reasonable. The apparent strength of the French position, the lateness of the day, and the debilitating impact of darkness on a system of command dependent on visual signals all ruled out an immediate attack.

But Brueys's opponent, Sir Horatio Nelson, was no child of the Enlightenment, no scion of the nobility, no dabbler in the sciences or the arts. He was, to quote a fictional nineteenth-century commentator named Sam Slick, a "cripple-gaited, one-eyed, one-armed little naval critter," a man who had been at sea since the age of thirteen, a man forever willing to risk defeat, and death, in a quest for glorious triumphs. Nelson's decisionmaking process was not analytic but cybernetic. He did not so much weigh the pros and cons of any particular engagement as wade into the enemy with a firm conviction that the key to victory was simple: "Lay a Frenchman close, and you will beat him."[26]

Nor did Nelson believe that commanders, however elaborate their signaling system, could direct naval battles. He acknowledged the value of sophisticated signaling systems for a fleet maneuvering under sail, but he believed that in battle signals would "either be misunderstood, or, if waited for, very probably, from various causes, be impossible for the commander-in-chief to make."[27]

As a leader, Nelson rejected the rational, scientific, material means at hand—signals—in favor of a method based on faith, in himself and his subordinates. His command style reflected less Enlightenment concepts than his upbringing as the son of the rector of Burnham Thorpe—a young man out of place in an age when others sought to bring order to chaos and to replace beliefs with understanding. His description of his meeting with his subordinates on his flagship before Trafalgar has more in common with Christ's last supper with his apostles than with a council of war. Nelson gathers his commanders about him, gives them his "touch," some cry, "and from Admirals downward, it was repeated—'It must succeed, if ever they will allow us to get at them! You are, my Lord, surrounded by friends whom you inspire with confidence.' Some may be Judas's; but the majority are much pleased with my commanding them."[28]

Nelson's years of service convinced him that the technical revolution in communications could not lead the way to true victory. He sought, in its stead, communion with his subordinates. During the pursuit of Brueys, Nelson met whenever possible with his captains so that all became acquainted with his "ideas and intentions." He believed the surest path to victory lay not through centralization, but through decentralization. He placed his trust, confidence, and faith in his subordinates. He chose to rely on the initiative of men who had, he hoped, absorbed from him an overall philosophy of battle. In a letter to Lord Howe after the victory at the Nile, he borrowed a phrase from Shakespeare's *Henry V* to describe these men: "I had the happiness to command a Band of Brothers; therefore, night was to my advantage. Each knew his duty, and I was sure each would feel for a French ship."[29]

Worse yet for Brueys, Nelson sought not order in battle, but disorder. In his quest for victory, he was willing not only to forgo the linearity of his fleet and of his decisionmaking, but also to embrace disorder, even the bedlam of a night action. Where others sought order, Nelson pursued chaos. Where others saw only disorder, Nelson saw a disparate form of harmony. In battle he hoped to "surprise and confound" his enemies. "They won't know what I am about," he told a friend before Trafalgar. "It will bring forward a pell-mell battle, and that is what I want." "On occasions we must sometimes have a regular confusion," he wrote in 1801, "and that apparent confusion must be the most regular method which could be pursued on the occasion."[30]

NAVAL HISTORY is rich in the study of commanders, but it is poor in the study of command. Recountings of the lives of the great admirals abound, but such portraits remain largely personal. Looking at these individual disquisitions together rarely reveals a common thread other than uniform and occupation. That thread should be the function at which these captains of the sea excelled—command.

Command, more specifically command and control (abbreviated C^2), is a relatively modern term, although the functions it defines are as old as conflict itself. For the purpose of this book, I have followed the official United States Department of Defense definition:

> The exercise of authority and direction by a properly designated commander over assigned forces in the accomplishment of the mission. Command and control functions are performed through an arrangement of personnel, equipment, communications, facilities, and procedures employed by a commander in planning, directing, coordinating, and controlling forces and operations in the accomplishment of the mission.[31]

In general I will refer to this process simply as command rather than as command and control, C^2, or the frequently used C^3, command, control, and communications.

As a history of command, this is a study not only of men but also of processes: organization, administration, technology, and individual and corporate decisionmaking. The commander is central to these proceedings, but his importance lies not in his biography but in how he exercised command.

Every commander throughout history has struggled with both the variables and the constants of warfare. Among the former are the technological advances evident in a comparison of the fleets of the twenty-first century with those of the wars of the French Revolution and Empire. Obviously, today's steam- and nuclear-powered vessels, tied together by a satellite telecommunications digital network, and striking with jet-powered aircraft and surface-to-surface missiles at targets tens, hundreds, or thousands of miles distant, contrast markedly with a wind-driven fleet, its commander signaling with flags and pendants, engaging its enemy with cannon and carronades at ranges measured in yards. But transcending time and technological change are the constants, including the principles of war (as they have been adopted over the decades by military organizations), the realities of war that Carl von Clausewitz termed "friction"— "factors that distinguish real war from war on paper"—and another reality identified by Clausewitz, uncertainty or the omnipresent fog of war.[32]

The scope of each chapter that follows was determined principally by variables—technology that not only reconfigured the forces to be commanded but altered the manner in which command was exercised. For the purpose of this work the strategic and operational application of the telegraph is more significant than the advent of steam power, and the use of ship-to-shore radio more important than the naval use of aircraft. Chapters provide background on the contemporary state of the art before examining historical examples of command. But my main thesis rests with the constants—particularly the fog of war.

Martin Van Creveld, in *Command in War*, argued that while uncertainty, as a constant, cannot be eliminated even by the most up-to-date technology, commanders have the option to shift its burden up or down the hierarchy of command. By centralizing control a commander can achieve greater certainty at the highest level—his own—but thereby increases the uncertainty in the lower echelons, where subordinates, denied initiative, often are left undirected. Decentralized systems accept greater uncertainty at the top, where commanders may be out of touch with events, but increase certainty at the nether levels of command. Van Creveld concluded: "These remarks seem to apply to all periods . . . and therefore appear to be independent of any specific stage of technological development. Nor, it is suggested, will their relevance be reduced in the future. So long as command systems remain imperfect—and imperfect they must remain until there is nothing left to command—both ways of coping with uncertainty will remain open to commanders at all levels. If twenty-five centuries of historical experience are any guide, the second way [decentralization] will be superior to the first."[33]

The study of naval command reveals that uncertainty is just as prevalent afloat as Van Creveld found it to be in his study of generalship ashore. As a result, decentralized approaches as exemplified by Nelson are on the whole superior to more centralized systems. Many naval thinkers have refused to accept the inability of technological advances to eliminate the fog of war, but there can be no doubt that during the past four centuries new communications technologies have failed to vanquish uncertainty at sea.

The world's military establishments recognize that key decisions are often based on selective data, for it is the function of training and doctrine—cybernetic systems—to provide a framework within which decisions can be made rapidly without requiring full-scale analytical processing. At the same time, militaries use analytical models at higher levels. For example, the U.S. Department of Defense defines the commander's estimate of the situation as follows: "A logical process of reasoning by which a commander considers all the circumstances affecting the military situation and arrives at a decision as to a course of action to be taken to accomplish the mission." For all the analytical emphasis, however, in practice preparation for higher command becomes an exercise in training and doctrine. Successful American naval commanders during the Second World War, such as Arleigh Burke, did not throw the manual of formal

doctrine, *Sound Military Decision,* overboard once the firing began; the
found that the analytical models had indeed provided them with a framework within which to make decisions. But they did not make those decisions in a deliberate analytic fashion. Burke noted that a decision that
would be reached after five hours of careful analysis in time of peace
would be made in wartime in five minutes. One assumes that such
lessons have not been lost on the modern navy and that few officers expect to conduct detailed studies during combat like those they carried
out at the Naval War College. The point is probably more overlooked by
historians, who are prone to ascribe rational, analytical models to human
decisions.[34]

ALFRED THAYER MAHAN, sea power's best-known theorist and advocate, began *The Influence of Sea Power upon History* with the Second Anglo-Dutch War of the mid-seventeenth century, "when the sailing ship
era, with its distinctive features, had fairly begun."[35] I begin a century earlier, in order to trace the evolution of concepts of command before 1660.
I do not include the age of galleys; only with the advent of the European
sailing navies did states seek to command the seas by destroying enemy
fleets. As John Francis Guilmartin, Jr., noted about the oar-driven fleets
of the Mediterranean in his classic *Gunpowder and Galleys:* "Mediterranean warfare at sea was not naval warfare in the orthodox sense, but . . . a
form of amphibious warfare in which the relationship of the fleet to the
shore was at least as important as its relationship to the opposing fleet."[36]

For the most part I follow doctrinal and other developments in command and control by examining the history of the dominant navies of a
given period—usually Great Britain's Royal Navy, the French navy during its heyday in the age of fighting sail, and later the navy of the United
States of America. I devote disproportionate space to the age of sail,
largely because of the relative absence of naval battles in later periods.
Nothing drives doctrinal development more than combat, and there was
plenty of that between 1650 and Trafalgar, but between 1805 and 1939
there were only a handful of major naval battles. The Second World War
was a major naval conflict by any measure, but during the half-century
that followed, while navies, particularly their aviation elements, were often busy, there were no major navy-versus-navy conflicts.

Nevertheless, sea power is a vital component of the nation-state, and despite incredible advances in technology future commanders can learn myriad lessons about the nature of their art from the careers of leaders such as Nelson. As a 1995 U.S. Navy doctrinal publication concluded: "Effective command and control relies on the shared understanding of separated commanders, an understanding that itself is based on doctrine, teamwork, and trust. No better example of this relationship is found than the Royal Navy's Admiral Horatio Nelson."[37]

CHAPTER ONE

Land Warfare Afloat: Before 1650

WE MAY CALL our planet Earth, but water covers more than seventy percent of its surface: man may be a terrestrial creature, but his environment is primarily aquatic. Small and large landmasses lie isolated, surrounded by great oceans that before the development of air transportation afforded the sole means of travel from shore to shore. The seven seas provide a global avenue for mankind, what Alfred Thayer Mahan termed a "great common," and in time of war give to conflict the widest scope.

Mahan's late-nineteenth-century view of the seas and concept of sea power have little relevance to premodern history. Certainly there were, as Thucydides suggested, states for which naval strength was "the foundation of empire." Athens was a sea power. Rome did rely, to some extent, on grain imported from Egypt. True thalassocracies were, nevertheless, the exception rather than the rule. The impact of sea power on ancient history cannot be compared to its influence on modern events.[1]

For millennia the oceans remained vast unexplored deeps capable of sudden changes of mood that could fool the unwitting mariner and in a moment swallow ship and crew. On land the passage of generations wore paths for others to follow, but men left only evanescent trails on the oceans' surface, no signs to mark the way, no totems of dominion. Travelers can still view the necropoles of the Egyptians, the temples and theaters of the Greeks, and the roads and aqueducts of the Romans. One finds no monuments to the glories of past navies while cruising the Mediterranean. Even the Rhodian colossus, one of seven wonders of the ancient world, disappeared beneath the waves. Only those who venture under the surface can find signs—the wrecked hopes of ancient voyagers—and know that long ago humans braved the sea-lanes.

Until the advent of steel ships driven by steam engines, mariners could only beg Neptune's forbearance while they passed. Only a fool, unversed in the vagaries of things marine, could believe that wooden ships driven by oar or sail could "conquer" or "command" the sea. Well into the nineteenth century the capacity of humans to kill their own while at sea paled compared with the hazards posed by the oceans themselves.

Ships built in the ancient period were too feeble to routinely take to the sea in any but fair weather. Longships—rowed galleys—were the state-of-the-art ships-of-war of the day, but they could not venture far. The classic Mediterranean galley had a freeboard too low to test even a moderate sea, and the oarsmen who filled the narrow, cramped hull forced frequent stops for food and water. The round, or sailing, ship could better manage rough seas, and its small crew and ample storage space gave it greater freedom of movement. But the roundship was difficult to sail, especially upwind, and it was hostage to breezes and currents in a way that the galley was not.[2]

Geographic ignorance and nescient navigational methods also handicapped ancient mariners. There were marvelous, though periodic, scientific advances. In the third century BC astronomers determined that the earth was a round sphere rotating on its axis as it revolved around the sun. About 240 BC Eratosthenes of Alexandria, the most versatile scholar of his day, calculated the size of the planet, overestimating it slightly but establishing the theoretical groundwork that allowed Columbus 1,700 years later to sail west to reach the east. In the second century AD Claudius Ptolemy, the most accurate of the ancient geographers, subdivided the world into fractions of a circle, marking his maps with what he termed lines of latitude and longitude.[3]

Despite these advances, science was of little use to the practical navigator. The outlines of regions, and an entire hemisphere, were yet unmapped. Maps were rare, expensive, and inaccurate, at least for the purposes of navigation. While astronomical devices existed, they were rarely taken to sea. Mariners had to rely primarily on their eyes to render crude judgments of the position of celestial bodies to determine latitude, and had no means, until the late eighteenth century, of ascertaining longitude. At best, captains owned coast pilots—what the ancient Greeks had termed *periplus*—that contained information on distances between ports, locations where ships could water, prevailing winds and currents, depth of water, and assorted geographic descriptions to aid mariners as they made their way along a coast. At the height of the Roman Empire,

some lucky captains may have possessed primitive charts of the Mediterranean.[4] But even after the appearance of functional navigational instruments late in the first millennium AD (the astrolabe and the magnetic
compass, imported from the Arabs and the Chinese respectively), most
European seafarers sailed or rowed near, if not along, the coast by their
wits, relying on years of experience, and praying for the clear skies that
allowed them to mark the positions of shore, sun, moon, and stars.

Lack of navigational tools did not prevent open-ocean navigation.
Phoenicians and Greeks in the Mediterranean, Arabs in the Indian
Ocean, the Irish and Norse in the North Atlantic, and the Chinese in the
Pacific all conducted open-sea cruises of great length and difficulty. But
the absence of instruments to guide mariners and the primitive state of
the shipbuilder's art combined to limit maritime activity to a season that
lasted little more than half the year.[5]

Evidence of the relative unimportance of the sea in the affairs of
nations can be seen in the nature of piracy. The pirates of the ancient
world, for example the Cretans, Illyrians, and Cilicians, sought their
booty ashore, not afloat. As Lionel Casson wrote in his history of seafaring:

> The ancient pirate, like his later brethren, chased and boarded merchant-
> men. But his stock-in-trade was not that; it was slave-running. And attack
> on the high seas was hit-or-miss: a pirate chief could not tell from the look
> of an ordinary merchantman plodding along whether it was carrying a
> load of invaluable silks and spices or cheap noisome goat hides. But a swift
> swoop on any coastal town was bound to yield, even if the place was
> too poor for plunder, a catch of human beings, of whom the wealthy could
> be held for ransom and the rest sold for the going price on the nearest
> slave block.

Not until after the Arab invasion of the seventh century AD turned the
Mediterranean into an embattled frontier between two cultures did the
activities of pirates gradually shift from raids against the shore to attacks
against shipping, most notably by the corsairs of the Barbary Coast of
North Africa. In northern European waters, where commercial development initially lagged behind that of the Mediterranean, piracy remained
associated with coastal raiding much longer.[6]

Only in the fifteenth century did a combination of scientific and technological advances—the magnetic compass and the astrolabe, better maps,
commercially available navigational charts, and ships of stronger con-

struction, superior design, and improved rigs—allow mariners to challenge, though by no means to conquer, the seas. Only then did open-ocean navigation become a regular, practical, and potentially year-round, though still dangerous, endeavor. Not until then did Europeans, somewhat serendipitously, find themselves in possession of a bundle of maritime technologies that would eventually allow them to dominate not just Europe but the world.[7]

In the interim, humankind's incapacity on the oceans limited the significance of sea power, even to those states with maritime pretensions. Commerce was seasonal, regional, and of marginal importance. Such limitations likewise circumscribed the significance of navies. Until the sea-lanes became a truly global common in the sixteenth century, interruption of activity on them was usually of minimal consequence, and the Mahanian concept of command of the sea was all but meaningless.[8]

The galley, be it of Greek, Roman, Byzantine, Arab, or Turkish design, was not an effective seagoing weapon system. Galley fleets were too unseaworthy and too logistically short-legged to act independently. As a result, well into the sixteenth century Mediterranean navies were still tethered to the shore. Galley fleets had limited radii of operations—five hundred miles at best—and that piloting along coasts, not sailing or rowing along a straight line from point to point.[9] At night, galley commanders preferred to back their ships onto a safe beach, where the crew could sleep and search for fresh food and water. A blockade of a distant enemy port was virtually impossible. Only if a friendly army held a nearby stretch of coast could a galley squadron attempt a blockade. Navies, leashed as they were, usually operated as flanking forces for the armies to which they were attached. Until the sixteenth century, naval operations were extensions of land warfare, more amphibious than truly naval.

The changes in ship design, navigation, cartography, and armament that occurred between the fourteenth and sixteenth centuries were not simply incremental steps in the evolution of sea power, but a collection of advances that engendered a maritime revolution. By the mid-seventeenth century the nature, scope, and scale of both maritime commerce and naval warfare had changed dramatically. Previously, only states with large and mighty armies—such as the Macedonians, Romans, Arabs, and Mongols—had been able to forge global domains. But now the world's new empires were maritime states more akin to Athens than to Rome. Sea power was no longer merely an adjunct to land power. "The sea," in the words of Fernand Braudel, had become "the gateway to wealth."[10]

That Europe's maritime empires all fronted the North Atlantic, a harsh, challenging sea, was no coincidence. Northern Europeans were never as enamored of the galley as their southern cousins. Northern seas, even coastal waters, were too rough for vessels with low freeboards. Many of the tides and currents of the English Channel ebbed and flowed more quickly than the best speed of a rowed vessel. The Vikings conducted most of their distant oceanic voyages, not in their rowed longships or war galleys, but in more functional sailing vessels.[11]

The harsh Atlantic environment forced northern Europeans to give more thought to the design and rigging of sailing ships, and to navigation techniques, than did the people of the Mediterranean basin. Often facing overcast or foggy conditions, northern mariners relied heavily on soundings and, when it became available, the compass. Eventually northerners developed several types of vessels notable for their seaworthiness, carrying capacity, range, and ability to sail upwind.

Northern shipbuilders enjoyed no monopoly on design improvements. Shipwrights in the Mediterranean also refined their roundships, not only by incorporating ideas imported from the north, but also through their own advances in construction techniques and rigging plans, advances northerners were more than ready to adopt. Shipbuilding know-how flowed freely between the Atlantic and the Mediterranean.[12]

Northern Europeans owed their maritime dominance over their southern neighbors, and ultimately over the entire world, to a pair of interrelated developments. First, northerners quickly adopted, by necessity rather than choice, improved roundships as war platforms; the Mediterranean states, both Christian and Muslim, did not. Second, the northern Europeans' continued refinement of the sailing man-of-war in the fourteenth and fifteenth centuries positioned them, unlike their southern neighbors, to take full advantage of the development of cheap iron cannon late in the sixteenth century.

Since the galley was never as satisfactory a platform for ship-to-ship fighting in rough northern waters as in the Mediterranean, as shipwrights constructed larger, more strongly built, more maneuverable roundships in the thirteenth century, states fronting the Atlantic began to incorporate the new vessels into their naval forces. The late-twelfth-century English navy, for example, consisted principally of assorted types of galleys, but by the early thirteenth century powerful roundships formed the core of English battlefleets. By the early fourteenth century galleys had all but disappeared from English orders of battle. In contrast, well into the sixteenth century Mediterranean navies clung to their battle-proven galleys, which continued to hold their own against roundships.[13]

As a result, northern shipbuilders had a three-century head start, not in the design and development of sailing ships as such, but in the refinement of the roundship as a fighting platform. While most sailing ships taken into the fleet in wartime were merchant vessels pressed temporarily into service, northern European states began to look to shipwrights to design and build sailing vessels specifically for wartime use. These new ships incorporated several prominent design features, such as towering fore and aft "castles," or fighting platforms, from which soldiers could hurl projectiles down onto their enemies. Gradually, the recognizable design of purpose-built sailing warships began to emerge.

Nevertheless, these early sailing men-of-war, even when armed with the primitive gunpowder weapons of the day, did not yet ensure technological superiority for northern navies beyond their home waters. Until the sixteenth century reliable cannon were too expensive to be used extensively, whether on land or on sea. States generally consigned their heavy guns to siege trains, of which the Muslim Ottomans, not the Christian Europeans, had the most powerful. Navies, both northern and Mediterranean, mounted only small numbers of heavy cannon, mostly brass or bronze, in the bows of their ships.

The costliness of the great guns masked the true nature of the technological changes taking place in the maritime world and lulled the Mediterranean powers into unwarranted complacency. As long as fiscal concerns limited the naval use of artillery, the galley was a viable fighting platform. Since bow-mounted guns fired forward, in battle they could be used more efficiently by the highly maneuverable galleys than by sailing ships. Thus in 1500 no one recognized that the war galley had reached the end of its long history of development; no one foresaw that the fighting roundship would continue to evolve as a weapons system for another 350 years; no one knew that by the end of the century the advent of cheap iron cannon would allow the larger, longer-ranged roundship to carry powerful broadside batteries to the four corners of the globe; no one suspected that the age of galley warfare was drawing to a close.

Cannon and sailing ships consummated their marriage unobtrusively. Only in the fifteenth century did ships begin to mount guns broadside. Not until 1501 did a Frenchman cut gun ports in the hull of a ship. Only a few men-of-war, such as the English *Harry Grace à Dieu* and the French *François,* mounted large batteries with numerous broadside cannon. And of the *Harry's* 141 guns, only 21 were heavy cannon, all brass and rather expensive.[14]

In the late sixteenth century the development by the English of cheap cast-iron cannon began to ensure the preeminence of the roundship over the galley. Cast-iron cannon weighed more than brass or bronze guns, did not last as long, and were more apt to explode. But new casting methods enabled English ironsmiths to produce large numbers of admittedly inferior but very inexpensive cannon. The use of both English methods and iron guns quickly spread throughout the navies of the north. As a result, northern Europeans possessed a monopoly on both the raw materials and the technological know-how to furnish enough guns to line the decks of their ships of war.[15]

Early in the seventeenth century the Mediterranean powers discovered that their navies were obsolescent, if not obsolete. Refinements could no longer make the galley a viable warship. The southern Europeans, Turks, Arabs, and the rest of the world had fallen behind the northerners, so quickly, so imperceptibly, and so far.

ATLANTIC EUROPEAN STATES did not wait until they achieved complete technical predominance at sea to begin their maritime expansion. In the fifteenth century, maneuverable, open-ocean-capable, long-ranged sailing merchantmen, armed with enough cannon to fight off galleys, navigated the seas and enormously expanded European commercial horizons.

The Portuguese were among the first to put the new technology to use.[16] Early in the fifteenth century they reached the Madeiras, the Azores, and the Canary Islands. By midcentury they had worked their way down the coast of West Africa as far as Senegal. In 1487 Bartolomeu Dias rounded the southern tip of the African continent—the Cape of Good Hope. Ten years later Vasco da Gama returned to the Cape, entered the Indian Ocean, and sailed as far as Calicut. By the end of the first decade of the sixteenth century, the Portuguese were fighting their way, not always with success, into the enclosed waters of the Red Sea and the Persian Gulf. In 1513 their first ships reached China, and in 1557 the Portuguese established themselves at Macao.

While the Portuguese ventured south, the Spanish sailed west, also in search of a route to the Indies. In 1492 Columbus found his way blocked by an unknown continent—an entire new world that Spain would soon dominate. In 1519 a small group of Spanish ships fought their way through the hazards of the waters at the southern extremity of South America—a passage since known by the name of the man who led the expedition, Ferdinand Magellan—crossed the Pacific, and reached the Philippines, where the natives killed the Spanish commander. A surviving ship eventually made its way back to Spain in 1522, thus completing the first circumnavigation of the globe.

Other European powers, most notably the English, the French, and later in the sixteenth century the Dutch, also sent their ships to the south, west, and east. At times these voyagers sought out new lands and new routes to the east, not already controlled by the states of the Iberian Peninsula. But often these maritime johnny-come-latelys played the role of parasitical challengers to the empires of the Spanish and Portuguese, especially in the Caribbean and the Indian Ocean. By the seventeenth century the European states not only had expanded their power and influence around the globe but also had hauled their old, and often new, antagonisms with them.

By the seventeenth century, too, the importance of sea power, broadly defined, had taken a quantum leap forward. Maritime trade, competition, and warfare had broken their regional bounds. Sea power, embodied in Columbus's discovery, had ended the division of the planet into two separate worlds. Sea power, and with it state power, had become global.

While the expansive and revolutionary character of modern sea power and naval warfare presented states with seemingly boundless opportunities, the new maritime empires also confronted entirely new sets of problems associated with command and control. At every level—administrative, logistical, strategic, operational, and tactical—those individuals responsible for naval and maritime forces faced dilemmas that had never before been encountered. Naval commanders, unlike their army brethren, could find few useful strategic and no tactical insights in the works of ancient historians. No earlier admiralty had ever directed transoceanic operations. No navy had possessed assets with the operational independence of the sailing man-of-war. No fleet commander had deployed wind-driven ships that moved along one axis but discharged their weapons along another. Nor had the scientific and technological advances that had altered the nature of sea power produced any new tools to command naval forces. For several centuries whatever advances occurred could only be the results of trial, error, and accident.

Atlantic Europeans quickly recognized the novelty of the situation they confronted. Their search for alternative seaborne routes to the Indies, and the methods they chose to manage distant undertakings, revealed a global thinking only possible in an age of enhanced maritime capabilities.

The Portuguese confronted the reality of the maritime revolution as they rounded the African cape and sought first markets and then dominance in the Indian Ocean basin. Portuguese commanders were quick to grasp the relevant geography of the region and identify all the choke points, where ships had to traverse narrow waterways: the Cape of Good Hope, the Bab el Mandeb at the entrance to the Red Sea, the Strait of Hormuz at the entrance to the Persian Gulf, and the Strait of Malacca through which the trade of India, the Indies, and eastern Asia passed. The Portuguese believed that if they could control these points, along with centrally located, fortified bases on the Malabar coast of India, they could destroy and disrupt local commercial traffic, divert the region's trade to their own routes, and outflank and economically undermine the Islamic powers, especially the Ottoman Empire.

The Portuguese developed and executed a three-phase strategy. First, they quickly disposed of the navies of the Arabs and other regional powers, winning a major naval engagement off Diu in 1509. Second, they conducted a series of raids to destroy local merchant shipping. Third, under the direction of commanders such as Afonso de Albuquerque, captain general and governor of India between 1509 and 1515, they attacked several critical strategic points: they seized the island of Socotra near the entrance to the Strait of Bab el Mandeb (1507), Muscat and the island of Ormuz in the Strait of Hormuz (1508), and the approaches to the Strait of Malacca (1511), but failed to capture Aden (1513) and Jiddah (1517). The ambitious and largely successful plan disrupted, but failed to halt, commercial activity along the Red Sea and Persian Gulf routes, and diverted a great deal of traffic to the new routes opened and controlled by the Portuguese.[17]

The Portuguese were nevertheless unable to consolidate their gains. Economic warfare did undermine the smaller local powers, such as the Mamluk regime in Egypt, but generally to the profit of their larger, more powerful Islamic neighbors, such as the Persians and the Ottomans. Portuguese successes induced the Ottomans to reinforce their southeastern sea flank; they checked the Portuguese at Jiddah in 1517. The Ottomans continued their naval buildup and launched several counterattacks, in the Red Sea in the 1530s and in the Persian Gulf in the 1550s. Despite some successes, the effort failed to break the Portuguese grip on the western basin of the Indian Ocean.[18]

Portugal's adoption of such an ambitious and bellicose maritime strategy, even though it could send no more than a handful of ships and a few thousand men to the region, demonstrated its faith in cannon-armed sailing ships. D'Albuquerque noted: "At the rumour of our coming the [native] ships all vanished and even the birds ceased to skim over the water." Another Portuguese governor general advised his king: "Let it be known that if you are strong in ships the commerce of the Indies is yours, and if you are not strong in ships little will avail you of any fortress on land." The keys, though, were not only ships but also cannon. "The Portuguese could have reached India without gunpowder," John Francis Guilmartin, Jr., wrote, "but they could never have maintained themselves there or brought their cargoes back."[19]

There was also a third key to Portuguese success: loyal and able commanders willing to act on their own initiative and monarchs willing to trust those they picked for command. Until the invention of the telegraph in the mid-nineteenth century, states had little choice but to grant commanders operating on distant stations wide powers, often including not only military but also diplomatic and economic responsibilities. Fleets or squadrons dispatched halfway around the world could not be controlled in the same manner as a fleet of galleys operating in concert with an army. Only on-scene commanders, such as d'Albuquerque, could direct the early-sixteenth-century Portuguese effort in the Indian Ocean. Portuguese officials in India were too far from Lisbon to receive or to seek direction or reinforcements. It took months to send correspondence back and forth between India and Portugal, and even longer to outfit and dispatch expeditions. Ships often departed for the Indies without knowing the fate of those which had sailed the previous year. The king had little choice but to appoint commanders he could trust and in whose abilities he had confidence. He would give such men general directions and substantial independent powers, and send them on their way.[20]

In the absence of communications, grand strategic command and control worked best if a state's political and naval leaders shared an understanding of naval capabilities and long-range national goals. Since no state had ever before conducted sustained naval operations on a global scale, the process of developing this understanding was empirical. Throughout the sixteenth century the Portuguese, and other Europeans, gradually grasped the revolutionary change in the nature of sea power and developed concepts to guide the use of naval forces.

By the end of the century, philosophy had moved beyond simple em-
piricism. In 1597 Sir Francis Bacon published a collection of essays,
among them "Of the True Greatness of Kingdoms and Estates." Bacon's
conception of sea power reiterated an old idea: "To be master of the sea is
an abridgement of a monarchy. Cicero, writing to Atticus of Pompey his
preparation against Caesar, saith, *Consilium Pompeii plane Themistocleum
est; putat enim, qui mare potitur, eum rerum potiri* [Pompey's plan is evidently
that of Themistocles; for he thinks that whosoever is master of the sea
will be master of the situation]."[21] But Bacon took the concept a step further, noting not only the general utility of naval power and its importance to insular England but also its global nature and its correlation with
the health of the state:

> But this much is certain, that he that commands the sea is at great lib-
> erty, and may take as much and as little of the war as he will. Whereas
> those that be strongest by land are many times nevertheless in great straits.
> Surely, at this day, with us of Europe, the vantage of strength at sea (which
> is one of the principal dowries of this kingdom of Great Britain) is great;
> both because most of the kingdoms of Europe are not merely inland,
> but girt with the sea most of their compass; and because the wealth of
> both the Indies seems in great part but an accessory to the *command of
> the seas.*[22]

To Bacon, and to many other Europeans, the connection between
sea power and state power had become self-evident; so, too, had the relationship between naval power and maritime trade. As a result, European
states with maritime interests developed regulatory policies, what the
English called "Navigation Acts," designed to harness maritime wealth
and power. As John G. B. Hutchins noted, "Since the beginning of the
modern commercial and industrial era in the fifteenth century, no industry has been more affected with a public interest and more continually
subject to regulation than has shipping."[23] The maritime empires of this
new age worked to combine economic, military, and diplomatic considerations in a comprehensive order—mercantilism, the modern world's
first national security policy. A core element of mercantilist policy was
the development of the factors, both physical and human, that contributed to the economic and maritime strength of the state.

IF BY THE SEVENTEENTH CENTURY Europeans had developed an
appreciation of the grand strategic nature of sea power, the same was not

true at the other levels of command—the strategic, operational, and tactical. At the strategic and operational levels there remained a tendency to try to manage naval warfare much as commanders controlled warfare on land. At the tactical level, commanders continued to employ their new weapons much as they had employed the old. The revolution in the technology of naval warfare was not accompanied by a revolution in naval tactics.

While it was clearly impossible to control operations in the Indian Ocean from Lisbon, within European waters commanders still often attempted to direct operations from a distance. The campaign of the ill-fated Spanish Armada well illustrates the problems of command and control inherent in geographically expansive naval campaigning.

Strategically, the determination of Spain's Philip II to destroy his chief Protestant and maritime rival—Elizabeth I of England—made sense. The problems the Spanish faced in the Netherlands, where the Dutch were in revolt; in the Caribbean, where the English chipped away at Spanish strength; and in the contest for the souls of Europe's rival Catholic and Protestant communities, could all seemingly be solved if England could be brought low.

Such a strategic goal necessitated an ambitious operational plan. "The Enterprise of England," as the proposed invasion was known, had long been a subject of speculative discussion. The attractions of the concept were matched only by the difficulties inherent in the undertaking. But in 1587 a variety of events conspired to transform the "Enterprise" from a scheme into a plan. Suddenly an invasion of England seemed part of "God's obvious design."[24]

At Philip's behest, his two ablest commanders—Don Alvaro de Bazán, marquis of Santa Cruz, the foremost Spanish naval commander of the day; and Alessandro Farnese, duke of Parma, the commander of Spanish land forces in the Netherlands—produced estimates of the necessary forces and sketched out preliminary plans for an invasion. Santa Cruz's proposal that he command a huge fleet of more than 500 ships, manned by 30,000 sailors, transporting 65,000 soldiers, ignored the financial and practical realities facing Philip. Parma's suggestion that a force of 30,000 infantry and 4,000 cavalry, under his command, traverse the Channel in 700 or 800 small boats, without a covering fleet, depended upon complete surprise, a factor Philip himself labeled "Hardly possible!" With two such proposals in hand, Philip might well have dismissed "The Enterprise of England" as a worthy but impracticable idea. Instead, as

Garrett Mattingly writes, "Out of the plans of his two ablest commanders Philip made a plan of his own."[25]

In the security of the monastery of San Lorenzo Escorial, Philip con-
cocted a new scheme. He decided that a powerful naval armada, though
one far smaller than that recommended by Santa Cruz, would sail from
Spain with a small land force and enter the English Channel. There the
armada would rendezvous with Parma's army, less than half the size
Parma had proposed, transported in small craft built or requisitioned in
the Netherlands. The army would cross the Channel, disembark, and begin the conquest of England.

Several practical problems marred what Mattingly describes as "a
complicated and rather rigid plan, without much allowance for mistakes
or accidents."[26] The amalgamation of two impractical plans did not ensure a positive result. Philip's design addressed neither Santa Cruz's concern about the need for an overwhelming naval force nor Parma's demand for troops and emphasis on the need for surprise. Philip skirted the
problem at sea by urging his naval commander to avoid combat. But,
without at least temporary Spanish control of the Channel, how could
Parma transport his army in small craft to England? The navy could escort the army across, but that would be an exceedingly difficult task in
the face of a strong English fleet. And how could Parma prepare such a
large force for the crossing without alerting the enemy? The English and
Dutch would certainly notice the assembly of hundreds of small craft and
any movement of the army toward the coast. There also were critical
questions concerning the rendezvous of the fleet with Parma's flotilla.
The Spanish possessed no deep-water ports where the Armada could
safely join up with Parma's transports. Thus Parma would have to make
his own way into the Channel to effect the rendezvous. But he controlled no naval force of his own, and swarms of small, shallow-draft
Dutch warships infested Flemish coastal waters.

Given these ambiguities and uncertainties, without an effective system
of command and control of Spain's naval and land forces, an invasion of
England was unlikely to succeed. Moreover, the command structure outlined, by default, in Philip's plan exacerbated the problems of command.
Santa Cruz's and Parma's proposals, whatever their weaknesses, had at
least embraced the principle of unity of command. Both men had envisioned a unitary invasion force, based in either Spain or the Netherlands,
descending upon England under the direction of a single individual.
Philip's plan involved the movement of two forces—one mostly naval

and the other mostly land; one coming from Spain and the other from the Netherlands—commanded by two men, neither of whom could command the other. Philip, in his spartan quarters in the Escorial, was both the head planner for the operation and the commander in chief, despite the fact that he was half a continent distant from Parma and would be just as far from his Armada as it entered the Channel. Since the king did not intend to accompany either Parma's army or the Armada, there was no prospect of his actually directing the operation once it began. In his absence, the commanders would be left to their own devices. As David Howarth noted: "This was the intrinsic reason why the armada failed: the king's belief that he could organize a huge operation of war without leaving his study, without consulting anyone, without any human advice, without allowing his commanders to discuss it . . . Especially, he did not understand seafaring or navigation—he had never embarked in a ship except as a passenger."[27]

Philip's plan manifested a lack of clarity, not a lack of flexibility. The king had good reason to draft a design that was elastic enough to account for myriad unforeseen circumstances. His on-scene commanders could best judge the situation as it developed. But those same commanders, if they were to operate effectively together, needed a directive written clearly enough to be understood *and* to be interpreted by both in the same fashion. They also needed some secure and reliable means of communicating from ship to shore.

Unfortunately for Philip, the campaign unfolded with his subordinates confused and virtually incommunicado. The Armada's commander—Alonso Pérez de Guzmán ("El Bueno"), duke of Medina Sidonia, who reluctantly accepted the position when typhus carried off Santa Cruz in February 1588—sailed from Spain in May expecting to rendezvous with Parma's force somewhere in the English Channel. Parma believed that Medina Sidonia's Armada would meet the transports at the coast and shepherd the army along the entire route to England. At no time during the planning or execution of the operation were Medina Sidonia (or before him Santa Cruz) and Parma able to communicate with each other in a timely and effective manner. In the planning stage, both Parma and the Armada's commanders communicated almost exclusively with the king, who alone understood, to the extent that anyone did, the entire situation. Medina Sidonia received only a single message from Parma, and that shortly before the Armada sailed. As Colin Martin and Geoffrey Parker commented: "Here was an extraordinary situation: the joint command-ers of the greatest amphibious operation in European history were not in effective contact with each other."[28]

From the start, problems of command and control plagued the Spanish effort. The Armada, in a series of inconclusive but demoralizing running battles with the English, fought its way into the Channel. Medina Sido-nia did manage to alert Parma to the approach of the fleet. But the Ar-mada's captain-general received little news from Parma, whose army was not yet prepared to strike out for England. As a result, when the Armada neared Calais and Parma's coastal encampments, Medina Sidonia faced not only the threat posed by the English navy but also a communications debacle that guaranteed the failure of an overambitious and ambiguous plan. As Howarth wrote: "If the two dukes had met for ten minutes, they could surely have sorted it out and agreed how to make an attempt, if it was to be made at all . . . But twenty miles of sea still separated them, and an even wider gulf of misunderstanding. The misunderstanding was mutual, and the fault for it lay far away in the secret rooms of the Escorial; for the king had given each of them false information, or no information at all, about the other." By the time Parma began what may have been a pro forma embarkation, the moment had passed. The Armada, weak-ened by battle, subjected to attacks by English fireships in an unprotected coastal anchorage, slipped its cables and headed eastward for the North Sea and hoped-for safety. Instead, the fleet's epic return voyage around the northern extremes of the British Isles turned a defeat into a naval disaster.[29]

The demise of the Spanish Armada cannot be attributed solely to problems of command and control. The tactical and operational ef-ficiency and aggressiveness of the English fleet, its commanders, and its seamen played the major role in the campaign. But poor planning, ques-tionable selection of senior commanders (namely Medina Sidonia, who considered himself ill-suited to the job), failure to appoint a commander in chief, nearly total lack of coordination, and poor communications contributed to the debacle. As Mattingly concluded: "It is hard to believe that even Horatio Nelson could have led the Spanish Armada to victory in 1588." Even if the Spanish had fended off the attack of the English fireships at Gravelines, for practical and logistical reasons Medina Sidonia could not have kept his fleet in place long enough to await Parma, as-suming the ground commander could even get his ill-fitted flotilla to sea

past the Dutch. A failure of coordination would have brought "The Enterprise of England" to an ignominious conclusion.[30]

THE DILEMMAS of command at sea at the strategic and operational
levels evident during the Armada campaign were no less severe at the
tactical level. Naval battles fought under sail before the mid-sixteenth
century more closely resembled contemporary land engagements than
they did the epic sea battles of the seventeenth and eighteenth centuries.

Two basic factors shaped naval warfare in the early sailing age: the long
history of naval warfare under oars, and the evolution of the sailing ship
as a fighting platform. The mêlée—in which crews boarded enemy ships
and engaged in hand-to-hand combat—had always been the principal
method of combat between fleets composed of galleys. For well-trained
crews, the ram, a variety of ranged weapons, and the infamous Greek fire
could occasionally be decisive weapons, but the mêlée determined the
outcome of most battles.[31] The reliance on the mêlée became even more
pronounced toward the end of the galley period. The beaked prow gave
way to the curved in the galley navies of the Byzantines, Italians, Ottomans, and Arabs as ramming became less common. Sailing ships were not
designed with ramming bows. Ships rammed each other in battle, but as a
prelude to boarding, not, except in rare cases, in an effort to sink an opponent. Nor did the development of more advanced ranged weapons—
the arquebus and cannon—alter battle tactics. Reload times were too
long and ranges too short. Since early sailing warships mounted only a
few cannon, galley-fashion to fire forward, commanders continued to
rely on the mêlée in battle.

The ad hoc nature of most early sailing navies reinforced reliance on
military—that is, land—tactics. Since no northern European state could
yet afford a large standing navy, in wartime monarchs impressed merchant vessels, and their small crews, into service. These trading ships were
refitted for combat. Workmen constructed raised structures on the forward and stern sections of the ships, giving them appropriately lubberly
names such as forecastle and sterncastle. When the ships were ready, an
army detachment arrived, led by a captain assisted by lieutenants, bearing
a commission from the monarch and orders to join the fleet. To command the fleet itself, the monarch appointed a trusted general, who
might or might not have had any experience at sea. Not surprisingly,
once afloat, landlubber lieutenants, captains, and generals sought to fight

their battles as they did ashore, relying on massed formations and the melée to sweep the enemy from the field.

Reliance on soldiers to fight on the monarch's ships not only delayed but also contorted the evolution of a naval officer corps.[32] A dichotomy developed between the army officers, who were responsible for doing the fighting on a man-of-war, and the ship's "petty" officers, who were responsible for handling the vessel. Even in Elizabeth's day, command of ships generally went "to noblemen and gentlemen, who often had little knowledge of the naval art."[33] Experienced seamen fortunate enough to work their way into positions of command, referred to in the seventeenth century as "tarpaulins," found themselves at a disadvantage in any political contest with the "gentlemen." Elements of this division in naval officer corps persisted well into the nineteenth century, for example in the staff-line controversy in the U.S. Navy.

The application of land tactics to sea battles was never a comfortable fit. Engagements ashore were chaotic and bloody enough, without the complicating factors of position relative to the wind, the state of the sea, and the inability to disengage from a melée that could turn sea battles into fights to the death. Accounts of the victory of England's King Edward III over the French off Sluys in 1340 illustrate the chaos and ferocity of naval engagements fought by ship-borne armies.[34]

While the chronicler noted the peculiar aspects of warfare at sea, his description of the fighting nevertheless reads like an engagement fought on land. The focus of the struggle, the ship *Christofer*, could just as well be a hill, taken in an assault and fortified by archers to ward off a counterattack. Forcing the enemy to fight looking into the sun was thought more important than holding the upwind—that is, windward—position, which would be deemed so critical in later naval battles.

Two centuries later, little had changed. There had been continued tactical evolution at sea, but principally because of general organizational advances in warfare. Generals still commanded fleets and arrayed their forces at sea as if they were armies on land.

The Spaniard Alonso de Chaves, who about 1530 published *The Seamen's Glass*, was one of the earliest authors to write about naval tactics. Because Chaves understood that his audience was not a corps of sea officers but soldiers confounded by the nature of warfare afloat, he attempted to explain naval tactics by using analogies to land warfare. The strongest ships, he advised, should be deployed in the center, as were men-at-arms ashore. Faster, lighter ships should cover the wings, as did cavalry ashore. The commander should control a centrally deployed heavy division, holding it in reserve as long as possible to allow him to monitor the progress of the battle. Yet another force, deployed behind the commander's, should bring up the rear of the fleet and could be dispatched to support any threatened flank or to reinforce success. Ships in all of these formations were to be deployed massed, in line abreast, prepared to fire their weapons during the approach and then to grapple and to board enemy vessels.[35]

Chaves, like the chronicler of the battle of Sluys, took into account some of the peculiarities of naval battles. The wind figured prominently in his instructions. So did seamanship, which he viewed as a force multiplier that could allow a weaker force to defeat a stronger one. He also noted the difficulties of commanding a naval force in combat. He exhorted the commander to avoid diving into the battle lest he lose control of the engagement. Instead, Chaves advised the commander to stay in the rear and to use the communicative means at hand—a handful of colored signal flags, raising and lowering the topsail, and the speaking trumpet—to send the fleet into battle and to direct the ships of the reserve to "give succour wherever the captain-general signals."[36]

As long as most ships' guns were mounted to fire forward and the mêlée remained the ultimate arbiter of victory, land-style tactics based on massed formations of ships deployed in line abreast made sense. During the fourteenth, fifteenth, and sixteenth centuries, at sea as ashore, infantry decided most battles; artillery was still too immobile, and too impotent, to dominate the battlefield. But late in the sixteenth century, as men-of-war began to mount their batteries broadside and the gun gradually became a potential ship killer, the need for a purely naval tactical system became obvious. Volley and charge tactics no longer worked, since the axes of a ship's movement and its fire now lay at right angles. Ships maneuvering in line-abreast formation could not use broadside-mounted guns effectively. But then again, the killing power of the new guns was limited.

The resultant confusion is evident in the tactics used during the Armada campaign. Despite developments in gunnery, the Spanish continued to deploy en masse and to depend on the mêlée to decide battles. The more maneuverable English avoided close quarters and relied on their gunnery. While English tactics appear more advanced, they were little more successful than those employed by the Spanish. The English had yet to devise a means by which their ships could maneuver in formation and fire their guns with effect. Elizabeth's ships sailed in figure-eight patterns, taking turns discharging their broadside batteries into the Spanish formations. This tactic, combined with the limited destructive power of the relatively light guns, was fine for harassing bewildered Spaniards but offered little hope of destroying an enemy fleet.[37]

To further complicate matters, the evolving naval tactical system stretched already inadequate methods of command and control. As the fleet began to deploy in something other than standard army-like formations—with a center, wings, and a reserve—two new problems arose. First, new concepts were needed to provide a doctrinal framework for commanders and subordinates. It was no longer sufficient to advise would-be admirals that the campaign they were about to begin could be understood within the framework of ground warfare. In 1588, for example, most senior Spanish naval officers, as well as King Philip himself, recognized the novel and asymmetrical nature of the tactical challenge the Armada would face in the Channel, with the English relying on maneuverability and long-range gunnery and the Spanish trusting to grappling, boarding, "valor," and "steel." But how could the less maneuverable Armada force the English fleet to fight at close quarters? The Spanish sailed without having devised a tactical solution to that problem. They simply hoped, or trusted in God, that favorable weather conditions or English mismanagement would allow them to fight at close quarters. As one of Philip's high-ranking naval commanders informed a papal emissary, "We are sailing against England in the confident hope of a miracle."[38]

Second, as fleets began to fight in looser formations and to rely somewhat more on maneuver, ship-to-ship communications became more necessary and also more difficult. Communicating in the midst of a sea battle fought under the old system had been far more complicated than communicating ashore. The standard method employed during a land battle—sending a staff officer with a message or riding oneself to a threatened sector—was fraught with hazard afloat, although well into the seventeenth century naval commanders did summon subordinates to the flagship during lulls in engagements. The use of speaking trumpets, never truly satisfactory, became even less so as distances between ships increased and the roar of ever larger and more numerous cannon drowned out auditory communication. Visual signals offered some hope of a solution, but were far too primitive and cumbersome to convey meaningful directions.

For the next three hundred years, until the advent of ship-to-ship radio, navies struggled to address these two fundamental problems of command and control. Gradually they developed coherent and comprehensible naval doctrines, what the Royal Navy would term its "Fighting Instructions." They also devised practical means of visual communication, culminating in the late eighteenth century with numerary signaling systems and telegraphic codes. These developments came piecemeal and never completely solved the problems. In the interim, naval commanders often fell back on more traditional methods. Well into the seventeenth century the Dutch, for example, less convinced than the English of the effectiveness of cannon, sought to ameliorate command and control and related tactical problems by fighting in tighter formations and relying on the mêlée.[39]

It is tempting to blame the "uncertain process" of the development of naval officer corps for the confused state of early-seventeenth-century naval tactics and command and control procedures. The evolution of naval thought did lag well behind that of military theory. But the retarded development of things naval was a direct result of the continued domination of naval commands by army officers whose experience was increasingly irrelevant to the problems they encountered at sea and to the revolutionary technical and practical challenges navies faced. As Nathaniel Butler advised in his "Dialogues," written about 1634: "Neither the whole of this age nor that which is past can afford any help or precedent; for we have none but those at Lepanto, and this was for the generality with galleys, which kind of fight hath a vast difference from that of ships."[40]

CHAPTER TWO

The Anglo-Dutch Wars

ON 18 MAY 1652 a Dutch fleet of about forty sail, commanded by Lieutenant-Admiral Maarten Harpertszoon Tromp, appeared off Goodwin
Sands, along the southeastern coast of England. An English squadron of
eight ships, commanded by Major Nehemiah Bourne, lay at anchor in
the nearby Downs, off Deal. Bourne watched as Tromp detached two
small vessels that quickly moved toward the anchorage and hailed the
English. The Dutch explained that they sought no trouble, only relief
from rough Channel weather. Despite such assurances, Bourne took no
chances. He ordered his ships cleared for action and sent a fast boat to
Rye Bay, where General-at-Sea Robert Blake commanded the main
English squadron of fourteen ships.[1]

Anglo-Dutch relations had been steadily deteriorating for years. While
the English had supported the Netherlanders during much of their
"Eighty Year War" for independence against the Spanish, the Hollanders
had become England's chief commercial and naval competitors, "indis-
putably the greatest trading nation in the world, with commercial out-
posts and fortified 'factories' scattered from Archangel to Recife and from
New Amsterdam to Nagasaki." In the English Channel and the North
Sea, the Dutch navy rivaled that of England. In the Baltic, the Dutch had
displaced the English commercially, gaining control over the lucrative
carrying trade as well as strategically important timber supplies. England's
Muscovy Company had been thrown out of Russia and suffered heavy
financial losses, in part because of the competition and machinations of
the Dutch. Personnel of the Dutch East India Company (the VOC)
quashed English attempts to develop trade in the East Indies in a series of
incidents that culminated in the infamous Amboyna massacre of 1623, in

which fifteen Englishmen of the East India Company were tortured and executed for allegedly conspiring to seize the Dutch fort at Amboyna.[2]

The English, alarmed by their seeming inability to compete with the Dutch, adopted tougher policies. The Commonwealth parliament passed the Navigation Act of 1651, England's first, principally to prevent the Dutch from totally dominating the carrying trade. Parliament determined to enforce the principle that the Channel was an English waterway, in which foreign ships were expected to lower their national flags as a sign of deference when confronted by English men-of-war. The English also asserted their perceived right to stop and search neutral ships for contraband. This policy risked war since the Netherlands, a small neutral engaged in an extensive carrying trade, supported the principle "free ships make free goods" and accepted an interpretation of contraband far narrower than that of the English. The Dutch also armed their merchant vessels, sailed them in convoys, and dispatched warships to escort them as they approached home waters. In fact, six days before Tromp appeared off the Downs, a small English squadron attacked a homeward-bound Dutch convoy escorted by three men-of-war, one of which had refused to lower its flag. No ships were searched and casualties were light, but tensions were high.[3]

Under Bourne's watchful eye, Tromp took his fleet southward and anchored in Dover Road. He refused to strike his flag to Dover Castle, which fired several shots in an effort to produce compliance. Tromp ignored the English reminders, calmly exercised his crews at their small arms, and anchored off Dover overnight.

The next morning Tromp awoke to see Blake's squadron coming up from Rye on a northeasterly course. The Dutch promptly raised anchor and made sail toward Calais. Tromp's squadron was now heading eastward, running between Blake's force to the south and Bourne's, now visible to the north.

Tromp, who appeared to have escaped a possible trap, suddenly reversed course and bore down on Blake. Who fired first is a subject of dispute, but within minutes the two squadrons had engaged. Bourne came up and led his squadron into the Dutch rear, trapping Tromp. The action continued throughout the day and into the night. The next morning Tromp was gone, defeated, though not decisively. The English lost no ships and captured two Dutch vessels, one of which later drifted off and was retaken.[4]

The engagement fought off Dover was a typically indecisive scrap.

Many aspects of it are obscure and subject to debate. But what is indisputable is that the battle began not as a result of state policies made in London or the Netherlands but because of decisions made by the on-scene naval commanders. Neither nation had yet declared war. In London there had been some last-minute fears, and corresponding hopes, that perhaps war should and could be avoided. The Dutch, who were winning the economic war, hoped to avert an armed struggle.[5] They sent Tromp into the Channel to protect trade from English attacks, not to provoke war. But by his actions, whatever their motivation, the lieutenant-admiral set in motion the final countdown to conflict. In early July the first of three Anglo-Dutch wars began, precipitated by an unwanted and unplanned action.

Armed ships at sea during periods of international tension held the potential to spark full-scale conflict. Unlike armies, deployed behind clearly defined boundaries, naval forces cruised the open sea and frequently encountered potential enemies. In the midst of a crisis, Tromp thought nothing of seeking shelter in English coastal waters, right under the guns of Dover Castle. As far as Blake and Bourne knew, he might have carried a declaration of war in his pocket, passed a few days before by the States General in Holland. Nor could Tromp know what the converging approach of the two English squadrons meant for his fleet, or for a Dutch convoy then making its way through the Channel. His decision to turn and attack Blake, whether it was rooted in a desire to incite a war, to preempt an English attack, or to safeguard the nearby convoy, was one taken in a fog of uncertainty generated by the inability of states to communicate effectively with naval forces operating at sea.

THE DUTCH AND ENGLISH FLEETS fought the first "official" battle of the war on 28 September 1652 off Kentish Knock in the approaches to the Thames estuary. The States General ordered a halt to the sailing of unescorted convoys and sent out a force of about sixty ships, commanded by Vice Admiral Witte Corneliszoon de With, to engage or otherwise occupy the English fleet to allow the safe passage of Dutch merchantmen through the Channel. Blake, commanding the main English fleet of sixty-eight ships, likewise hoped to destroy the Dutch in battle, after which the English would be able to bring their enemy's commerce to a halt and force an end to the maritime struggle.

The Dutch opened the engagement and initially held the upper hand.

Several ships from Blake's squadron ran aground on sandbanks in the estuary. Vice Admiral Sir William Penn's squadron, operating in the van with Blake's, had difficulty avoiding a similar fate. The leading English ships, even the ones that were grounded, nevertheless inflicted heavy damage and casualties on the attacking Dutch. Rather than press the assault on Blake and Penn, de With led his fleet to the south to attack the English rear, perhaps convinced that Blake's van divisions were now out of the fight. But Penn and his captains managed to make their way through the sand maze and fall upon de With's rear. By nightfall, after three hours of heavy combat, the Dutch retired. Despite the intensity of the fighting and the involvement of more than 120 men-of-war, the victorious English lost not a single ship, while the defeated Dutch had but two ships captured, one so riddled by shot that it later sank.[6]

Exaggerated reports of the success at Kentish Knock led the Council of State, which directed English naval operations, to disperse the fleet in an effort to gather more fully the fruits of victory. The Council detached several small cruisers to patrol the Channel. To cow the Danes, who had seized English ships and were all but allied with the Dutch, eighteen men-of-war sailed for the Sound, between Danish Sjaelland and Sweden. A dozen warships prepared to sail to the Mediterranean, where the Dutch outgunned a small English squadron.[7]

The Hollanders, however, were far from beaten. Within two months they had concentrated another fleet, this time of seventy-three ships. The States General placed Tromp in command and ordered him into the Channel "to do all possible harm to the English" and to cover the outbound passage of a large convoy.[8]

Tromp's fleet appeared off Goodwin Sands on 29 November 1652. Blake lay anchored in the Downs, his command reduced by detachments to thirty-seven sail. He nevertheless chose to risk an engagement and weighed anchor. Poor visibility may have hidden the true size of the force arrayed against him. In any case, once his ships were at sea, the wind, too strong to permit battle, prevented a return to the Downs and blew both fleets along the coast toward the southwest. That night they anchored off Dover. The next morning the wind slackened, and both the English and the Dutch continued their run to the southwest. As the ships neared Dungeness, where the coast jutted out into the Channel east of Rye Bay, Blake found himself pinned against the shore and forced to fight.[9]

This time victory belonged to the Dutch, although the spoils were trifling. Blake's fleet managed to slip the trap and make its way back to the Downs. Gunfire sank only three English ships. One Dutch ship exploded as a result of an accident on board. Tromp's ships licked their wounds for two days, shepherded the convoy of 400 merchantmen through the Channel, and cruised out into the Atlantic on the lookout for another large inbound Dutch convoy.

The defeat off Dungeness spurred the English government to action. The Council of State sent Generals Richard Deane and George Monck to join Blake in joint command of the fleet, now reorganized into squadrons. The Council concentrated all available ships, including those earmarked for the Mediterranean, in the Channel. The latter decision, combined with a crushing Dutch victory off Livorno on 4 March 1653, led the English to abandon the Mediterranean. But in home waters they quickly reasserted their control, forcing Dutch cruisers and merchantmen into port pending Tromp's return.[10]

In mid-February Tromp, commanding 81 ships, reentered the Channel escorting an eastbound convoy of about 150 merchantmen. South of Portland on the morning of 18 February 1653 the Dutch sighted a English force of 80 sail to the northeast bearing down on them. Tromp, responsible for the safety of the convoy, could have avoided a contest. According to the English commanders, "The Dutch Admiral might probably (if he had pleased to have kept his wind) [have] gone away with his whole fleet and we had not been able to have reached him with our main body." But Tromp, instead, turned toward the enemy in an effort to concentrate the bulk of his force against the English van, led by Blake and Deane, both of whom were in the *Triumph* 62. Thus began a running engagement often termed the "Three Days' Battle."[11]

This time fate favored the English. The fighting on 18 February was inconclusive, as Tromp shielded the convoy. But over the next two days Blake and Deane squeezed the Dutch against the French coast along the Pas de Calais, almost, but not quite, trapping Tromp. The wily admiral led his fleet, and most of the convoy, to safety through dangerous shallows where the deeper-draft English ships could not follow. Tromp avoided a crushing defeat, but at heavy cost. The Dutch lost between thirty and sixty merchantmen, although the English captured only four Dutch men-of-war. Five others sank, and two or three others may have been burned to prevent capture. English losses totaled one ship sunk, three disabled, and one lost through negligence.

Following the Three Days' Battle, an operational pause descended on the Channel. Both the English and the Dutch admiralties struggled to refit their fleets. Some of the English warships damaged in the battle off Kentish Knock had not yet returned to service. The Dutch, too, were hard pressed to repair all their vessels. English cruisers patrolled the Channel, while the Dutch merchantmen remained in port. Cromwell, now Lord Protector, and the States General pursued abortive peace negotiations.

THIS PAUSE provides an opportunity to examine the war's early battles, as did the Dutch and English commanders at the time. The Downs, Kentish Knock, Dungeness, and the Three Days' Battle were extremely chaotic affairs. Accounts written by participants in the last named, for example, included descriptions of ships and squadrons "charging" their enemies, firing guns to port and then to starboard. Ships boarded, and were boarded in return; some were captured, then recaptured. Captains discovered that they had sailed into the midst of an enemy formation, with ships to all sides, only to be saved when their compatriots "charged" into the pack. But the contemporary reports and letters are so confusing that their nature, more than any dearth of first-hand accounts, explains the inability of historians to reconstruct the engagements. The participants, even the commanding admirals, evidently had little sense of how the battles developed once the action began.[12]

Nevertheless, some tactical details are evident, and others can be inferred from the record. With large fleets (in some battles between sixty and ninety ships on each side), both Dutch and English commanders subdivided their forces into squadrons, each led by an officer who flew his personal flag from his "flagship." A fleet's senior subordinate commander, generally a vice admiral, commanded the lead, or van, division. The commander himself brought up the main, or center, portion of the fleet. Another subordinate, the rear admiral, commanded the rear division. Particularly large fleets sometimes included a fourth or even a fifth squadron. At times these divisions were further subdivided into smaller, more manageable formations. As in land warfare, subdivision facilitated maneuver and eased problems of command and control.[13]

The principal duty of the subordinate "flag" officers, as well as of the captains of individual ships, was to support each other, and especially their respective superiors. English instructions issued in 1650 called for the "relief and assistance" of any ship "over-charged and distressed." Tromp's instructions issued on 20 June 1652 stated: "Each captain is expressly ordered, on penalty of 300 guilders, to keep near the flag officer under whom he serves . . . The said superior officers and captains are to stand by one another with all fidelity; and each squadron when another is vigourously attacked shall second and free the other, using therein all the qualities of a soldier and seaman."[14]

Without a doubt, maneuvering as part of a squadron of from ten to thirty ships, each seeking to maintain its position relative to a commander who might change course in the midst of a confused battle and "charge" the enemy, was a true test of seamanship. The fact that relatively few ships were captured by boarding, the tactic preferred by the Dutch, or sunk by cannon fire, the tactic preferred by the English, suggests that individual ships were often unable to get close enough to an enemy vessel to grapple and board, or to fire their guns with effect. Substantial portions of these large, unwieldy fleets never came into contact with the enemy.[15]

The inability to bring the strength of a powerful fleet to bear on an enemy formation frustrated both English and Dutch commanders. The two fundamental constraints were obvious. First, warships moved along one axis and discharged their cannon along another. Second, with men-of-war ranged around a commander's flagship, only those on the periphery facing the enemy could fire their guns or hope to board. The solution to the first of these problems had to wait until the industrial revolution and the development of steam-driven ships with turreted guns. A possible solution to the second involved placing all the ships of a squadron in a line. In a linear formation each ship would have a clear line of fire, although a fleet so deployed would lack depth and be vulnerable to massed attack. Nor could a long line of sixty to a hundred ships execute any but the most basic maneuvers.[16]

While there is little evidence to prove the point, some of the more reflective senior English commanders must have deduced from their experiences in the first year of the war that a linear formation might be more effective than the old squadron-centered order of battle. Only the presumption that the English successfully employed some kind of linear configuration before the spring of 1653, either as a planned experiment or through some unintended development during an engagement, can explain the issuance of new instructions for the fleet that incorporated the line ahead as a standard formation in battle.[17]

To be sure, the line ahead was not an entirely novel formation. One of its earliest and best-documented combat uses occurred at the battle of Dunkirk on 16 September 1639. A small force of seventeen Dutch ships, twelve of them commanded by Tromp, deployed and fought in a close-hauled line ahead against a Spanish fleet of sixty-seven ships. Tromp reputedly told his commanders before the battle: "Work in such a manner that these our ships unite so closely, that by no chance will they allow any contrary force to penetrate between them."[18]

But Tromp's use of the line at Dunkirk was a tactical aberration, a desperate defensive measure to hold off a much larger enemy force. At the Downs on 21 October 1639, where Tromp commanded a heavily reinforced Dutch fleet of more than a hundred ships, he reverted to group tactics and the mêlée against the Spanish. The Dutch were still using such tactics when the First Anglo-Dutch War began, and there is no evidence that the English "stole" the idea for the line-ahead formation from their enemy. As Michael Lewis wrote nearly a half-century ago: "The First Dutch War produced one tactical innovation of the first importance—a real line-ahead. And there can be no doubt that it was the English, and not the Dutch, who produced it."[19]

On 29 March 1653 Blake, Deane, and Monck issued two sets of instructions: "For the Better Ordering of the Fleet in Sailing," and "For the Better Ordering of the Fleet in Fighting." Julian Corbett and Brian Tunstall, eminent historians of the development of naval tactics under sail, term these instructions "revolutionary." The new orders, which marked the beginning of a process of tactical and doctrinal development, were far from perfect. The signals by which a commander was to make his plans known to subordinates were primitive. The discharge of two guns "and putting out a red flag on the fore-topmast head" indicated an admiral's decision to engage. The instructions offered no guidance as to how commanders were expected to convey their intentions to the fleet once the battle began. Speaking trumpets, the dispatch of messengers in small boats, and sending up a general signal for a parley were still the chief means of communication in action. But the instructions were the most detailed and comprehensive yet issued for use by the English navy. They also marked the beginning of a new tactical system: the instructions for fighting directed that once an engagement began, "each squadron shall take the best advantage they can to engage with the enemy next unto them, and in order hereunto all ships of every squadron shall *endeavour to keep in a line with their chief*."[20]

WHEN OPERATIONS RESUMED in the spring of 1653, the use of linear formations and supporting doctrine was uneven. Nevertheless, the new approach to battle magnified the tactical superiority and operational capabilities of the English navy.

The Council, as it had after the victory off Kentish Knock, saw the Three Days' Battle as a signal to detach squadrons from the fleet to secure myriad objectives. Concerned about the situation in the Mediterranean, on 8 March the Council directed the admiralty to prepare twenty warships, manned by an extra four hundred seamen above their normal complements and six hundred marines, "to go into the Straits." The Councilors could not know, because of the time lag in communications, that four days earlier England's Mediterranean squadron had been destroyed.[21]

Deane and Monck, once they learned of the Council's intentions, advised against "this dividing" as "not very desirous." They suggested that the Mediterranean squadron probably was en route for England, and if not that it should be ordered home. The generals-at-sea wanted to keep the fleet's squadrons concentrated in English waters, where they could interdict Dutch shipping yet stay close enough together for mutual support once the enemy returned to sea. And return it would, Monck and Deane asserted, gently reminding the Councilors that they possessed intelligence to that effect.[22]

Fortunately for the English, the Council followed the generals' sound advice. When Tromp led the Dutch fleet to sea in early May, the English squadrons were able to concentrate quickly. For a month Tromp and the English generals groped about, vainly searching for the enemy in the Channel and the North Sea. Finally, at daylight on 2 June, the two fleets sighted each other near the Gabbard Shoal in the Thames estuary east of Harwich. Tromp commanded ninety-eight ships, Deane and Monck one hundred.

With a light wind from the north, the English ships stood toward the south in good order.[23] Because of the unexpected appearance of the Dutch to the southeast, Rear Admiral John Lawson, commanding the Blue or rear squadron, led the fleet. Behind him Monck and Deane, together in the *Resolution* 88, brought up the center or Red squadron. Vice Admiral Penn commanded the White or van squadron at the rear of the fleet. According to Dutch accounts, the three English squadrons appeared to form a crescent shape that threatened to envelop Tromp's fleet heading northward on a larboard tack.

The battle proper began at about 1100, with Lawson's squadron bearing the brunt of the Dutch cannonade. As the Red squadron came up and engaged, the first Dutch broadside swept the deck of the *Resolution* and killed Deane, leaving Monck, who was observing only the second naval action of his life, in command.

In midafternoon the wind shifted toward the east. Tromp seized the opportunity and sought to close the range and concentrate the bulk of his fleet against Lawson. Tromp managed to pass part of his fleet between the English Blue and Red squadrons, but before he could complete his maneuver, the wind began once again to blow toward the north and west. The English tacked and stood toward the north or northeast. Tromp had two choices: adopt a parallel course to the English and resume the gunnery duel, or turn to the south and try to disengage. With his badly shot up ships low on ammunition, facing a gunnery duel that favored the enemy, and confronting an English squadron of eighteen fresh ships led by Blake, Tromp stood toward the south. Whether he intended to retreat or simply to break off the action until the next day is unclear.

If Tromp hoped to disengage during the night, he was disappointed to find the English still in contact at dawn, although the morning wind favored the Dutch. As he had the day before, Tromp maneuvered to close the range, but again shifting winds intervened and the Dutch engaged in a gun battle. As Tromp stood to the southwest to disengage, this time successfully, the English harvested the fruits of their efforts—several crippled Dutch men-of-war.

Regarding command and control, the action fought on 2–3 June off Gabbard Shoal is important for two reasons. First, while the accounts of the battle are sketchy, the documents indicate that the English fleet was well handled, maintained the windward position through most of the action on the first two days of the battle, fought, at least at times, in something approaching a line-ahead formation, and forced the Dutch into a gunnery duel that they were unlikely to win. A participant reported: "Our fleet did work in better order than heretofore, and seconded one another." An anonymous chronicler noted that the English, "having the wind . . . put themselves in their order they intended to fight in, which was in a file at half cannon shot, from whence they battered the Hollanders furiously all that day." Second, unlike the earlier battles of the war, Gabbard was a crushing defeat for the loser. The English lost not a single ship and sustained only four hundred casualties. Tromp's fleet returned to Holland less nine ships sunk and eleven captured. The Dutch suffered about eight hundred casualties and left behind in the prizes a thousand men as prisoners. Worse yet for the Dutch, for the first time in the war the victorious fleet survived an engagement in fair enough shape to continue operations. By the end of the week the English were blockading the Dutch coast.[24]

Given the scale of the English victory, the natural tendency, at the time and since, has been to view the battle as "decisive."[25] But the Dutch were not finished. In the next two months they scraped together yet another fleet, this one of 125 ships. On 31 July 1653, 130 English men-of-war commanded by Monck met Tromp off the Texel in the battle of Scheveningen. In an extremely confused engagement, the fleets passed through each other several times. Tromp, like Nelson a century and a half later, fell mortally wounded by a musket shot. Despite the fact that the Dutch managed to fight in close, as they preferred, they lost, although how badly is a matter of dispute. The English fleet had only 2 ships sunk, although many others were severely damaged, and suffered about a thousand casualties. Dutch losses totaled between 19 and 40 ships, with an unknown number of killed, wounded, and missing.[26]

Monck, the victor, led his battered fleet back to England. As his ships were being refitted, he chose not to pursue a blockade throughout the winter but to wait until the spring, relying instead on cruisers in the Channel to harass Dutch trade. His decision was wise: in October a strong gale pounded the coast of the Low Countries, dismasting or destroying half of the surviving Dutch ships. The States General begrudgingly decided to negotiate, and on 5 April 1654 the First Anglo–Dutch War ended.

AFTER THE END of the war, Cromwell used English sea power to pursue aggressive policies against the Commonwealth's potential enemies. Blake led a new squadron to the Mediterranean to lessen the depredations of the Barbary corsairs, and to show the English flag in the Middle Sea. Without a declaration of war, Cromwell set in motion his "Western Design," an expedition to seize Hispaniola and begin encroaching on the Spanish empire in the New World. The joint (army and navy) operation failed miserably, although the English managed to capture Jamaica. When Spain responded with a declaration of war in March 1656, new English squadrons sailed for the Caribbean to raid the Spanish Main and a major joint expedition sailed south to strike the Spanish coast.

Although no major naval battles punctuated the Anglo–Spanish war, the conflict is worth noting. The failure of several army-navy amphibious expeditions accentuated the need for effective command and control

of such operations, a lesson ignored all too often over the next several
centuries. The winter blockade of Cadiz by an English fleet in 1656–
1657, a previously unheard of feat, marked a maturation of sea power.

Cromwell died in 1658, before the end of the war he had begun. England descended once again into political instability. Ultimately, General
Monck led his army to London and set in motion a chain of events that
led to the restoration of the Stuarts. King Charles II reached London on
29 May 1660 and quickly reasserted his royal authority.[27]

Over the next five years Charles worked diligently to bring stability to
England. His marriage to the daughter of the king of Portugal gave the
English an ally in the Iberian Peninsula and new bases in the Mediterranean at Tangier and in the Indian Ocean at Bombay. Charles, somewhat
reluctantly, also pursued an aggressive policy against the Dutch, whose
commercial successes again seemed to threaten English prosperity. Convinced that the Hollanders, after their defeat in 1652–1654, would go to
great lengths to avoid another war, Charles initiated what amounted to
an undeclared war along the Guinea coast of Africa and in North America, where in August 1664 the English seized New Amsterdam, which
they soon renamed New York in honor of the king's brother James,
Duke of York, who had been the force behind the expedition. The
Dutch responded forcefully to the English attacks, prompting Charles to
declare war on 4 March 1665.[28]

THE FIRST ANGLO-DUTCH WAR had highlighted the difficulties of
naval command and control at the strategic, operational, and tactical levels. Its major battles had been huge affairs involving between 100 and 300
ships, always chaotic, and never decisive. The frustrations inherent in supporting and controlling such large fleets in what often seemed a vain
quest for decisive victory led both the English and the Dutch to reassess
their naval policies.

Between the wars, admiralty administrations expanded, although the
English remained hostage to favoritism and graft and the Dutch to the
decentralization that reflected their political system.[29] The designs of
warships and merchantmen diverged even further. The standardization of
ship types continued. Naval officer corps took additional steps toward
professionalization. Both admiralties continued to purge, though not entirely, merchant captains from their navies and armed merchantmen from
their fleets.

The English and Dutch navies also refined their tactics and struggled with problems of command and control. Given the nature of the battles they had fought between 1652 and 1654, the relative effectiveness of line or group tactics, and gunnery or boarding, was unclear.

During the First Anglo-Dutch War, Dutch tactics had become increasingly linear, although the Hollanders had not adopted an actual line-ahead formation. Tromp, hoping to gain the wind gauge—that is, to get on the opponent's windward or upwind side—would lead his fleet into battle in a line, but would then use group tactics to swoop down on the English ships in an effort to grapple, board, and overwhelm the defenders. "The lack of any uniformity among the types of ships in the Dutch fleet," the historian Jaap R. Bruijn wrote, "would indeed have caused great problems with regard to a more strict and continuous order of battle." During the Second Anglo-Dutch War, the Hollanders' tactics were linear, but they still did not use the line ahead. In combat most ships were grouped in twos and threes. A contemporary observer, Armand de Gramont, Comte de Guiche, noted that such tactics—what later military analysts would call defense in depth—allowed the Dutch to repulse individual English ships that attempted to penetrate the line. Despite these advantages, the comte considered the English line ahead, which maximized offensive and defensive firepower, to be the superior order of battle, and one worthy of imitation by the French.[30]

English naval commanders, who between the wars had embraced the line, found that the use of the formation, while it enhanced order and ensured effective firepower, complicated control of the fleet in battle. At Gabbard in June 1653, the position of the English fleet relative to the Dutch and to the wind favored an approach and an engagement in line formation. Not so at Scheveningen in July, where the English reverted to a mêlée. That the English fleet paid a far heavier price for the latter victory than for the former reinforced the drift toward the adoption of the line. But how could a fleet so arrayed be controlled?

Maneuvering a fleet under the old tactical system had been relatively simple. When a fleet commander changed course, the ships of his squadron did likewise, and the subordinate commanders of the other squadrons followed suit, to be mimicked, in turn, by their subordinates. At Kentish Knock, for example, de With, after assaulting the English van, was able to change course abruptly and to lead his fleet to the south without difficulty.

Controlling the movements of a large body of ships arrayed in a line was a different problem entirely. How could the fleet commander, on his flagship in the center of the line, communicate his intentions to his subordinates commanding the van and rear divisions? And how could the commanders of the van and rear control their own formations? The prospect of having admirals lead their lines into battle involved enormous risk. In an engagement, flagships attracted enemy attention the way lights attract moths in the dark. Despite these risks, Admiral Sir Edward Spragge, commander of the English rear at the second battle of Schooneveldt in the Third Anglo-Dutch War, believed that division commanders had to lead their lines because inexperienced captains could not be expected to make the proper tactical decisions when maneuver became necessary. If a commander's flagship was in the center of the line, how could he direct the movements of his leading ship?[31]

The physical extent of the battlefield at sea also posed problems. A fleet of a hundred ships, even if arrayed in the old squadron formation, covered a good deal of ocean. Those same ships arranged in a line could easily extend beyond the visible horizon. In good weather, English captains were expected to keep at least a half-cable's length—304 feet—behind the ship they followed. This distance combined with the length of the typical ship—at least another 100 feet—meant that battle lines could extend for between seven and eight miles, assuming both good weather and good order. Unless visibility was good (and in the English Channel and North Sea visibility was rarely good), an admiral in the center of such an extended line might not be able to see either end. As Spragge noted in his journal after the second battle of Schooneveldt: "The line-of-battle . . . is so very long that I cannot see any sign the General Admiral makes."[32]

As if the problems of controlling one's own fleet were not daunting enough, there remained the question of an opponent's behavior. What if an opposing commander was less cooperative than Tromp and did not sail into the guns of an English line in an effort to bring on a mêlée? What if an enemy fleet accepted a gunnery duel and tried to maneuver to advantage? What if an opposing fleet, downwind from an English line, chose to disengage? In such cases, would a linear formation allow a commander to achieve results comparable to those attained by Monck off Gabbard Shoals?

Solving these problems required devising means by which to control a fleet in combat. There were two possibilities. Commanders could use visual signals to communicate their intentions to their subordinates. Unfortunately, the state of signaling systems in the mid-seventeenth century was primitive. The other possibility involved the use of prearranged instructions: doctrine. Experienced commanders could draw up rules specifying what action subordinates should take in given situations.

English fighting instructions issued on the eve of the Second Anglo-Dutch War relied on the latter approach. The new instructions included some additional signals, but doctrine became the principal means by which a commander could expect to control a large fleet arrayed in a line.

The third article of the new instructions did not mention the line, as it had under the Commonwealth, but the line ahead was still the prescribed order of battle. According to the new article, once the admiral made the signal to engage, "then each squadron shall take the best advantage they can to engage the enemy according to the order prescribed." Commanders were expected to lay out, before a battle, a specific order for each of the ships of the fleet. And that order, the additional instructions made clear, would be linear: "In all cases of fight with the enemy the commanders of his majesty's ships are to endeavour to keep the fleet in one line, and as much as may be to preserve the order of battle which shall have been directed before the time of the fight."[33]

The new instructions also attempted to take into account the different ways a battle might begin and to provide doctrine to guide subordinates' decisions. Assuming the enemies chose to fight (and there were no instructions to address the possibility that they might not), if the English fleet had the wind, the van would steer a course for the "headmost" of the enemy's ships. If the opposing fleet held the wind, the English ships would place themselves "in one line close upon the wind."

Once engaged, English ships were to fight in line. Captains were warned not to leave the line to render assistance to battered comrades whose ships fell out of formation, being admonished that "nothing but beating the body of the enemy's fleet can effectually secure the lame ships." Another article directed that no ships were to "pursue any small number of the ships of the enemy before the main [body] of the enemy's fleet shall be disabled or run." And in the event of a chase, the chasing ships were not to advance beyond sight of the flagship, and were to break off pursuit once darkness fell.

Some historians maintain that linear formations were destined to rob naval battles of their ability to produce decision,[34] but others portray the line as a reasonable response to the tactical dilemmas facing commanders.

Sir Julian Corbett argued that overly restrictive articles, and not the line as such, caused the inconclusiveness of fleet tactics as they developed in the eighteenth century. While indecisiveness may have been the ultimate result of the adoption of linear tactics, Tunstall points out that the motivation behind the initial issuance of the restrictive articles was nevertheless sound. English fleets of the mid-seventeenth century, comprising a hundred or more ships of myriad types commanded by captains of grossly uneven capabilities and temperament, cannot be compared to the smaller, well-ordered, well-disciplined, and well-led fleets of the next century. It had been common in the First Anglo-Dutch War for individual captains, some of whom were not naval officers but commanders of hired merchant ships, to break formation to go after a crippled enemy in a quest for glory or prize money. The authors of the revised articles were not seeking to stay an effective pursuit of a beaten fleet; they were simply trying to prevent the seaborne equivalent of looting in the midst of battle.[35]

Although the newly issued instructions relied principally on doctrine to ensure the effective command and control of a fleet, they also began an increased use of signals. Because of the still primitive nature of visual systems, their use was mostly confined to the approach to battle. The new instructions included signals for forming line ahead on a starboard or larboard tack, a maneuver that marked an advance in line-ahead tactics.[36] Other specified signals, for example the union flag at the mizzen peak of the flagship, indicated that "the admiral would have all the ships to fall into the order of 'Battailia' prescribed": that the admiral wished the van to tack first, the rear to tack first, the fleet to add more sail, or for the squadrons to chase.

The instructions circulated on the eve of the Second Anglo-Dutch War were a significant improvement over those issued during the previous war, but were still far from adequate. The doctrine and signaling systems with which admirals were to command their fleets were nonetheless rudimentary. There was a prescribed order of battle, with each ship given a designated place in the line, but the presence of small, slow merchantmen weakened the formation. At least one commander, Edward Montagu, the Earl of Sandwich, argued that the removal of the ships would shorten the line (by nearly three miles according to his calculation) and better concentrate the firepower of the fleet. But the merchantmen stayed, placed for their protection near the more powerful flagships, whose own safety should have been of primary concern.[37] Notwithstanding these shortcomings, in the spring of 1665 English commanders went to war with confidence in themselves, their ships, their subordinates, and their new fighting instructions.

The first major engagement of the war, fought off Lowestoft on 3 June 1665, seemed to justify that confidence. The English fleet opened the engagement in line. Throughout the morning the two fleets, each of more than a hundred ships, battled it out, reversing direction and passing each other time and again. The order of both fleets quickly degenerated. At one point Sandwich's squadron, by accident rather than by design, passed through the Dutch, breaking the Dutch formation in two. The Hollanders fought on and began to give way only when a powder-room explosion destroyed their flagship, killing Lieutenant Admiral Jacob van Wassenaer-Obdam, an army general appointed by the States General in the English fashion to command the fleet.[38]

The Duke of York, who himself was nearly killed when chain-shot swept the flagship's quarterdeck splattering him with blood and driving a piece of splintered skull into his hand, won his first victory at sea. The Dutch lost about thirty-two ships, of which nine were seaworthy enough to be taken to English ports as prizes. About four thousand Hollanders were killed or wounded and another two thousand taken prisoner. The English lost only a single ship, and suffered eight or nine hundred casualties, including prisoners.

"In spite of the victory there was a widespread conviction that it ought to have been more decisive." Many of the senior commanders, as well as some political leaders in London, believed that the fleet might have achieved a more impressive triumph had the pursuit continued throughout the night. The question was: Did the fault lie with the cautious Duke of York, or with the fighting instructions?[39]

Whether or not there developed at this time, as suggested by Sir Julian Corbett, two tactical schools among the senior English officers, one "inclined to formality" and the other to "hard fighting," greater aggressiveness did become a watchword in Charles II's navy.[40] With the prospect of renewed operations in the spring of 1666, Monck and Prince Rupert, the main fleet's joint commanders, were determined to seek out and destroy their adversary. The ultimate annihilative naval victory beckoned.

As the new campaigning season began, several factors complicated the strategic picture, weakened the position of the navy, and diminished the chance for a decisive encounter. That spring, first plague and then fire ravaged London, undermining naval administration and the economic

activity that supported the state. False rumors that the French, who entered the war in January 1666 alongside the Dutch, were bringing their
Mediterranean squadron to the Channel, led Charles to order Rupert to
lead his own squadron to the west to intercept.[41] As they had after Kentish Knock, the English committed a strategic mistake and divided their
fleet.

As Rupert sailed westward to intercept the French, Lieutenant Admiral Michiel Adriaanszoon de Ruyter's Dutch fleet of eighty-four ships
entered the Channel. Monck, commanding a reduced force of fifty-four
ships then sailing eastward from the Downs, sighted the Dutch at about
0900 on 1 June in mid-Channel between Ostend and Harwich. Despite
his marked inferiority, Monck attacked.

The ensuing action continued through 4 June, and thus became
known as the Four Days' Battle. It was one of the first sailing-age engagements that historians have been able to reconstruct with some degree
of detail and accuracy. A French commentator later wrote: "This fight
marks clearly the passage from former methods to the tactics of the end
of the seventeenth century. For the first time we can follow, as though
traced upon a plan, the principal movements of the contending fleets."[42]

The battle, marked by hard fighting and the arrival on the third day of
Rupert—who had heard the cannon fire in the distance and sailed to-
ward it with twenty of his fastest ships—ended in defeat for the English.
Considering the numerical advantage held during the first two days by
De Ruyter, the English were fortunate to escape as lightly as they did.
They lost seventeen ships, including nine captured. The Dutch lost only
four ships, but their badly battered fleet could not continue at sea and
had to return to port.[43]

The English navy hastened to refit, regroup, and prepare for a rematch
in the Channel. The admiralty strained to repair damaged ships and to
ready those newly constructed. The navy's senior commanders, perhaps because they believed that Monck's combative tactics had saved his
heavily outgunned fleet from destruction, issued revised, more aggressive
fighting instructions. A short set of additional instructions bearing Prince
Rupert's signature emphasized that all captains were "to endeavour the
utmost that may be the destruction of the enemy, which is always to be
made the chiefest care." Another article directed that if the admiral of the
fleet made a weft (a signal made by rolling, stopping, or fastening) in
his flag, the other flag officers were to do the same, "and then all the
best sailing ships are to make what way they can to engage the enemy,

that so the rear of our fleet may the better come up; and so soon as the enemy makes a stand then they are to endeavour to fall into the best order they can."[44]

Corbett suggested that articles embracing greater aggressiveness and a less than dogmatic adherence to the line anticipated "by a century the favourite English signals of the Nelson period for bringing an unwilling enemy to action, *i.e.* for general chase." But Tunstall argues convincingly that the contemporary intent of the order was to provide a means for the faster warships to avoid delays caused by the presence of the slower hired merchantmen. Moreover, a careful reading of the article indicates that captains were to re-form their line once the enemy turned and fought. The signals and instructions of Nelson's period referred to by Corbett sought not only to maintain contact but also to prevent an enemy's withdrawal from battle.[45]

English captains also received a completely revised set of instructions issued under the authority of the Duke of York, although the most important doctrinal changes appeared in the additional instructions. These new articles addressed the need "to keep the enemy to leeward," provided guidance for commanders of the van and rear divisions during engagements in which two fleets fought in parallel lines but while sailing in opposite directions, discussed the prospect of dividing the enemy fleet, and, finally, directed captains "to take special care that they keep their line, and upon pain of death that they fire not over any of our own ships."[46]

The additional instructions incorporated lessons learned in recent battles. Holding the wind gauge had long been a preferred tactic, but was now considered central to securing victory or avoiding crushing defeat. Directions as to what course commanders of the van and rear should follow during battles such as Lowestoft, where the English fleet lost its cohesion when it reversed direction after passing the Dutch, were essential. The advantages to be gained by "dividing" an enemy's line, as Sandwich had done accidentally at Lowestoft, had been the topic of much discussion, but commanders needed guidance as to what actions they should take once through the line. The recommended procedure was for the penetrating van division to return to its original course on the opposite side of the enemy line, while the center division stood on the same tack on the other side. The leading division(s) of the enemy fleet could then be assaulted, or what would become known as "doubled," from two sides, while the rear division supported either the van or center.

It is tempting to view the final instruction, to be complied with under "pain of death," as a step along the road to dogmatic adherence to the line and indecisiveness in battle. But the instruction embodied lessons learned. Ships falling out of line had fired over, or through, friendly ships, and not to good effect. The threat of "death" more than likely referred to such a risky and dangerous action and not simply to pulling out of formation.

Armed with a set of fresh instructions, Rupert and Monck (now the Duke of Albemarle) led an English fleet of eighty-one warships to sea late in July. Their hopes for a chance to recoup their reputations in yet another battle were soon rewarded. De Ruyter was out with eighty-eight men-of-war. The two fleets met on 25 July 1666, St. James's Day, not far from Kentish Knocks.

The battle began at about 1000 as the van divisions of the English and Dutch fleets opened the engagement in line. Later in the morning the center divisions joined the action, also in line. But Cornelis Tromp, the great admiral's son and commander of the Dutch rear, noticed a gap between the English center and rear. On his own initiative, Tromp pushed his division through the gap and forced a mêlée upon the English. The battle continued without cease until dusk. Tromp's ships fought well, capturing the *Resolution* 64. But accurate and steady English fire devastated De Ruyter's van and center divisions. The Dutch admiral used the onset of darkness to disengage.

The next morning, De Ruyter was clear, but Tromp found himself alone, still in contact with the English rear, and threatened with destruction by the entire enemy fleet. He reacted quickly and managed to save his squadron from annihilation. But the cost of defeat for the Dutch was high—twenty ships, four thousand killed, and three thousand wounded. The English lost only the *Resolution* and about three to five hundred men.[47]

In London, the politicians, outraged by the failure to destroy the enemy's fleet, or at least Tromp's division, stopped "bothering about the Dutch and turned their attention more and more to the in-fighting in domestic politics." Politicians tried to affix blame for the navy's shortcomings on their opponents. The various divisions within the navy, more political than doctrinal, went at each other mercilessly. With support for the war waning and with the royal treasury straining under the costs of maintaining a large navy, Charles decided to adopt a defensive military posture and to seek a quick diplomatic resolution to the conflict. At his direction, the admiralty did not refit the fleet for a renewed campaign in the spring. The English moored their larger ships in the Thames with many of their guns removed and crews reduced by a third or a half.[48]

In Holland, De Witt considered Charles's diplomatic overtures and naval de-escalation not as an opportunity to negotiate but as a chance to strike. He directed De Ruyter to develop a plan for an attack against England itself. In early June De Ruyter took the fleet, with more than sixty ships, into the mouth of the Thames. As detachments made their way up the river, Londoners were panic-stricken by the news: "The Dutch are in the Medway!" The Hollanders broke the boom (the chain of floating timbers stretched across the water to form a barrier) in the river, captured and destroyed magazines and naval stores at Sheerness, reached Chatham, and burned six of the English navy's largest men-of-war and scores of smaller vessels, both commercial and military. The Dutch also captured and returned to the Netherlands the Royal Navy's flagship, the *Royal Charles*. When the raid finally ended, the main Dutch fleet stayed to blockade the Thames.

With one strategic error, Charles threw away much, if not all, that his navy had achieved in two years of war. But his strategy did lead to a quick, if disappointing for the English, diplomatic accord signed at Breda on 21 July 1667.[49]

THE PEACE of Breda turned out to be a truce. Despite two bloody wars, unresolved issues still divided the English and the Dutch. But the principal and immediate cause of the renewed struggle was Charles II's ill-conceived concepts of realpolitik. Driven by a shortage of funds and a quest for glory, Charles allied himself with Louis XIV's France in a scheme, agreed to at Dover in May 1670, to crush the Dutch through the application of English sea power and French land power.[50]

The pretext for precipitating yet another war was the continued refusal of Dutch warships to strike their national flag when in the presence of English men-of-war in the Channel. In retaliation, Charles ordered his navy to attack a large Dutch convoy returning from the Mediterranean. In the Channel on 12–13 March 1672, a Royal Navy squadron conducted a completely unprovoked assault that even English historians term "invidious" and a "cold-blooded act of villainy."[51] Fittingly, the attack achieved only modest success and set in motion a series of events, among them a war that helped to undermine Stuart rule.

Allied strategy in the war was simple. The English navy, aided by a French squadron, would sweep the Dutch from the seas and blockade their coast. The French army, aided by a small English contingent, would invade and overrun the Netherlands. This seemingly sensible strategy nonetheless foundered. French successes on land drove De Witt from power but inspired the Dutch to rally around the Prince of Orange and generated sympathy among English Protestants who wondered why their king was helping the Catholic French. Such thoughts fed suspicion about the Stuarts' Catholicism and ultimate intentions regarding the religious future of their subjects.[52]

At sea, meanwhile, the English discovered that the Dutch navy was as resilient as ever. That fact, as well as the difficulty of operating a combined Anglo-French naval force, led to stalemate and indecision.

The Dutch did not publish formal instructions, but they had refined their tactics during and after the Second Anglo-Dutch War, dropping group maneuvers and adopting the line ahead. Before an engagement, Dutch commanders, like their English counterparts, wrote out specific orders of battle for their fleets. De Ruyter himself developed tactics to concentrate the Dutch squadrons against portions of an enemy fleet, as well as methods to break through a line.[53]

The English, who already possessed the most elaborate tactical doctrine, continued to revise their fighting and sailing instructions. The former expanded to twenty-six articles.[54] But the navy's commanders introduced no new tactical innovations. Nor did the four major battles of the Third Anglo-Dutch War—Sole Bay, the two battles of the Schooneveldt, and the Texel—offer much in the way of tactical insight; all were confused engagements fought along or very near the English or Dutch coast.

The Third Anglo-Dutch War ended on 9 February 1674 when the English signed a separate peace with the Dutch. Even Charles now realized that he had been fighting the wrong enemy, and Anglo-Dutch relations improved rapidly, most notably in 1677 when James's daughter Mary married the Dutch Prince William of Orange, with whom she would later rule England.

Given the indecisiveness of the four battles, there were few tactical lessons to be drawn from them. The most obvious was the difficulty commanding a fleet composed of different national forces. Accounts vary as to just how poorly the French squadron fought during the war. Certainly the English tried to blame all of their problems on their Gallic allies. But setting the hyperbole aside, the record is clear that the French squadron did not fight well at Sole Bay. Dispersing the French throughout the line, the procedure adopted in the two Schooneveldt battles, likewise proved unsatisfactory, leading Prince Rupert to reconcentrate the French in their own division. At the Texel, the French, as they had at Sole Bay, managed to drift out of the action, again prompting English recriminations.

That the French navy performed poorly in the war was obvious to the French themselves. Some ships fought well. But the fleet's commander, Vice Admiral Jean d'Estrées, was an army officer whose services were forced on Jean-Baptiste Colbert, the head of the French navy. Estrées's incapacity, combined with the difficulty of jointly operating fleets of different nationalities, training levels, and doctrines, undermined French performance. They did not understand English tactical methods and procedures—doctrine—and were often at a loss to know what to do. Similar problems continue to hound navies to the present day.[55]

THE ADOPTION of the line-ahead formation during the Anglo-Dutch wars was a critically important step in the development of naval tactics and doctrine. Most naval historians view it as a great leap forward. To Mahan, the development was long overdue, delayed by the persistence of "old traditions." To Clark Reynolds, the promotion of the line ahead was evidence of English tactical "superiority."[56]

Other historians take a different view. Russell F. Weigley wrote: "The Fighting Instructions regarded the difficulties of command and control in naval battles as so formidable that their proposed remedy limited officers' initiative so rigidly as to impose a nearly insurmountable obstacle to the development of a profession of naval officership—or for that matter, to decisiveness in battle and naval war." Weigley further argued: "Tactical expertise has tended to emerge first, with larger operational and strategic expertise built upon it. Because the Fighting Instructions stultified the growth of naval tactical skills as distinguished from seamanship, they also stultified professional growth in the higher levels founded upon tactics, in operations and strategy."[57]

It is all too easy for a historian writing three centuries after the fact to portray the English adoption of the line as something other than evidence of developing tactical skill and professionalism. But any attempt to understand late-seventeenth-century tactical developments must confine itself to the history of the three Anglo-Dutch wars. English and Dutch naval commanders were neither clairvoyants gathered around crystal balls looking into the future nor defense intellectuals assembled about a table theorizing about new tactical formations.

Mahan can portray the adoption of the line as a logical step, one obvious on an intellectual level, because his study begins in 1660 and thus does not cover the chaotic and frustrating battles of the First Anglo-Dutch War, which led pragmatic English commanders to adopt new tactics. Instead, Mahan's focus is on subsequent wars in which the line proved its worth, whatever the shortcomings of the men who applied it.

Weigley implies that the fighting instructions eased the problem of command but reduced the fighting power of the fleet. This may have been true in the eighteenth century, but the English experience in the Anglo-Dutch wars was exactly the opposite. Control of a fleet before the adoption of the line was simple: have captains mimic the leader. The English had to develop doctrine because linear tactics aggravated the problems of command and control. Why would the English, and later the Dutch and the French, accept such complications if the line lessened a fleet's effectiveness in combat? One might assume that the adoption of the line brought to an end an era of decisive battles. In fact, the battles of the first Dutch war fought before the adoption of the line not only were indecisive, with few ships captured or sunk despite the enormous size of the fleets engaged, but also left both victor and vanquished so shot up that neither could remain at sea. In the battle off Gabbard Shoal, the first fought in something approaching a line, the English won a significant victory, sinking and capturing twenty ships, and, most important, ended the engagement in fair enough shape to stay at sea and to follow up their victory with a blockade of the Dutch coast.

English commanders adopted the line because it enhanced fighting power despite its complication of command and control. The Dutch, French, and other navies followed the English lead for the same reason. English commanders did not begin to fight in lines because the advantages of the formation were obvious, but as the result of an evolutionary tactical process born of the experience of battle. Nevertheless, the course of naval warfare over the next century demonstrated that the adoption of the line ahead as the standard formation was a two-edged sword. As the quality of naval officers improved, the line ahead discouraged individual initiative and lessened the chance of decisiveness in naval battles.

But what were the alternatives? No tactical system could resolve the fundamental problem that sailing men-of-war moved and fought along perpendicular axes. The alternative to a linear formation was continued reliance on the pell-mell battle, during which a commander's ability to control the situation, as Blake, Monck, and Deane well understood, all but disappeared. The only commander in the entire history of naval warfare during the age of sail who managed to fight and to win pell-mell battles, repeatedly and by design, was Horatio Nelson. His genius for command was, though, well beyond the norm, and his trusted subordinates were long-term professionals with twenty years of service and a decade of wartime experience.

Nor is it fair to link the adoption of the line ahead to any "stultified professional growth" or lack of tactical acumen on the part of naval officers. Naval officers in the eighteenth century may have been guilty of fostering too strict adherence to the line. But if the line itself was the problem, the fault for its initial adoption does not rest with naval officers. The three men—Blake, Deane, and Monck—responsible for issuing the instructions of 29 March 1653 were not true seamen, by profession or choice, but experienced generals in Oliver Cromwell's New Model Army. Of the three, Blake had the most experience at sea, though with a checkered record of success and failure. He had also been badly wounded in the Three Days' Battle and probably was not the inspiration behind the instructions. Deane, whose forte was administration, no doubt liked the idea of more standard, formal instructions, but hardly seems a likely father of tactical innovation. Monck, an experienced army commander and artilleryman, who had just suffered through his first taste of naval command in a totally confused mêlée involving three hundred ships (including merchantmen), was the most likely advocate for the adoption of the linear formation that would provide as many vessels as possible with clear lines of fire.[58]

That an army officer may have been the chief proponent of the line should not come as a surprise. Cromwell's soldiers dominated the upper ranks of the English naval service. As Monck pursued line tactics afloat, his fellow generals ashore were also adopting more disciplined linear tactics. During the seventeenth century European armies gradually dispensed with massed pike formations, reduced the proportion of cavalry in their armies, and sought to maximize artillery and infantry firepower. For armies as well as navies, the era was one of tactical experimentation and frustration. Infantry battalions arrayed in straight lines could lay down deadly volleys, but were vulnerable to shock attacks, either by cavalry or, as was the case later in the eighteenth century, columns of infantry. The search for the proper balance between the line and the column remained a subject of doctrinal debate and experimentation until the end of the Napoleonic Wars.[59]

The failure of European navies to achieve "decision" in battle should not be measured against the strategic and operational capabilities, or lack thereof, of European armies. Other than Napoleon Bonaparte, no European commander of the seventeenth, eighteenth, or early nineteenth century routinely attempted to end campaigns in a single afternoon. Between 1650 and 1815, very few battles fought on land actually brought wars to a decisive end. And even if a quest for decisive, war-ending battle was a reasonable pursuit and worth the risk ashore, at sea the entire concept of decision through battle had little meaning. As B. H. Liddell Hart observed, "There is no *blitzkrieg* possible in naval warfare—no lightning flash over the seas, striking down an opponent." Few admirals, at least until the atomic age, ever held in their hands the power to win a war in an afternoon. At Trafalgar in October 1805, Nelson won what may well have been the most complete and annihilative battle in the history of naval warfare. Within a purely naval context, one might argue that Trafalgar was a "decisive" defeat for the French and the Spanish. But the war against Napoleon continued for another nine years.[60]

In that respect, the first and second Anglo-Dutch wars, being purely maritime struggles, were atypical. The historical record demonstrates that naval commanders and English and Dutch politicians did seek decisive victories that could end the war in a day. But that same record demonstrates just as clearly that the failure to reach a decision was not the result of the adoption of the line ahead. As a rule, the English navy achieved greater success, in terms of the destruction of Dutch ships and a post-battle ability to remain at sea, when it fought in a line than it did when it engaged in mêlées.

The indecisiveness of naval battles had less to do with the line ahead than it did the nature of naval warfare, or more broadly warfare in general. Navies simply do not possess the power to bring conflicts to a quick, decisive end. Mahan, the ultimate advocate of sea power, wrote of its "influence," not its decisiveness. More recently, Colin S. Gray has written of its "leverage."[61]

The development of naval tactics must be judged within the context of the realities of naval, not land, strategy and operations. The importance of sea power during the age of sail can only be measured within the context of prolonged struggle. Sea power, whatever its many virtues, could not deliver an expeditious victory. Decision at sea meant not the end of the war in an afternoon, but the destruction of an opponent's fleet as a prelude to the imposition of a blockade and the securing of freedom of movement for sea-transported ground forces. Neither of these ends was likely to yield quick results. Given the inability to achieve decision in battle, naval commanders' reluctance to accept the risks inherent in pell-mell battle becomes more understandable.

Thus the commanders' unwillingness to jettison a tactical system that failed to yield immediate results was not necessarily an example of professional stultification. Nor is there any evidence that naval officers' short-comings as tacticians handicapped the development of operational and strategic concepts. Portuguese commanders operating in the Indian Ocean in the sixteenth century demonstrated a grand strategic compe-tence comparable, if not superior, to that of contemporary land com-manders. English naval strategy in the First and Second Anglo-Dutch wars was well thought out, at least on the part of the naval commanders. Men such as Monck, Deane, and Blake did not write books on naval strategy and operations, but the clarity of their thought and understand-ing is evident in their correspondence.

Nevertheless, despite the tactical advances during the Anglo-Dutch wars, at the end of the seventeenth century naval officers were far less professional than their army counterparts. According to one historian, the reason for the disparity was that "Army officership descends from feudal knighthood; naval officership descends from merchant seaman-ship." This is, of course, an oversimplification. The men who first fought the king's ships were soldiers, not retread merchant seamen. Members of the royal family and army officers dominated the higher ranks of the English navy until the end of the seventeenth century. Jaap Bruijn, in his study of the Dutch navy, noted: "Since the days of the Sea Beggars (ca. 1570), it had not been uncommon for noblemen to command ships. At least one quarter of the Sea Beggars' captains belonged to the nobility." Of the seventeenth- and eighteenth-century navy Bruijn wrote: "Dutch naval officers and admirals have often been described as 'tarpaulins,' a label normally used in reference to common seamen and petty officers. There is little validity to that charge. With only a few exceptions, Dutch naval officers, certainly those reaching the rank of captain, belonged either to the higher or to the highest social classes in the cities and the countryside."[62]

The reasons why naval professionalism lagged behind that of the army are obvious enough. At the end of the seventeenth century naval officers faced imposing tactical dilemmas. They had to operate, in combat, the sailing man-of-war—the most sophisticated machine yet developed. They had to do so in an environment in which a mistake or ill fortune could lead to the destruction of the fleet by the elements. And they had to operate on a global scale. What should amaze us is not how far behind its army counterpart naval officership remained, but how quickly it had grown over less than a half-century. Captain John Smith's *Sea Grammar,* first published in 1627 and republished in 1652 as the First Anglo-Dutch War began, offered some general guidelines for war at sea, "because I have seene many bookes of the art of warre by land, and never any for the sea; seeing all men so silent in this most difficult service."[63] Although army officers had a head start of three millennia, naval professionalism was gaining fast.

CHAPTER THREE

At the Dawn of the Enlightenment

*T*HE TREATY of Westminster of February 1674 ended the Third Anglo-Dutch War, but the symbolic conclusion of the long naval struggle between England and the Netherlands came two years later. Despite England's withdrawal from the war, the Dutch and their Swedish, Spanish, and Imperial allies fought on against France. In a series of sea battles near Sicily, a combined Dutch-Spanish force dueled with the French Mediterranean fleet. On 8 January 1676 off Stromboli, one of the Lipari Islands in the Tyrrhenian Sea northwest of Messina, De Ruyter fought a successful running defensive battle against a stronger French fleet commanded by Abraham Duquesne. Three months later (on 22 April) the two fleets met again off the east coast of Sicily. In a vicious, sixteen-hour engagement that lasted until 2200, Duquesne's twenty-nine men-of-war pounded twenty-seven Dutch and Spanish warships off Augusta. Duquesne failed to destroy the enemy fleet, but in the course of the fighting De Ruyter fell mortally wounded. The battered Dutch-Spanish fleet sought refuge in the harbor of Palermo, but on 12 June Duquesne completed his triumph, virtually destroying the enemy fleet at anchor, sinking or burning ten ships.[1]

With De Ruyter's death and Duquesne's destruction of the Dutch Mediterranean squadron, France, already a recognized threat to the continental balance of power, had become a maritime rival to England. Jean-Baptiste Colbert, the secretary of the French navy, wrote to Duquesne: "His Majesty has at last had the satisfaction of seeing a victory against the Dutch, who up to now have always been superior at sea."[2] Louis's subsequent policies and intrigues toward England led to increasing Anglo-French hostility and a long struggle that ended only in 1815 with the defeat of Napoleon I at Waterloo.

Duquesne's Mediterranean triumphs marked the coming of age of the French navy and the culmination of a concerted policy to make France a major maritime power. Louis XIV ruled Europe's most centralized and modern nation-state. He fielded the continent's most advanced and capable army. And the "Sun King," at least for a time, wanted a navy to match.

Colbert was the central figure behind France's maritime buildup. As a young man he worked under the tutelage of Cardinal Jules Mazarin. After the cardinal's death, Colbert served as an adviser to the king, as comptroller general of finances from 1662 until his death in 1683, and from 1669 on as secretary of the navy. He believed that if his country was to be the preeminent European state, or, at the minimum, if Louis's comptroller was to keep the monarchy solvent, France had to become a thriving maritime power.

Colbert intuitively grasped the main elements of sea power, as broadly defined three centuries later by Mahan. He viewed trade as a generator of national income, colonies as a source of wealth, a merchant fleet as a necessity for an overseas empire, and a navy as an instrument of national policy. As a good mercantilist, he also understood the interconnections of these elements.

Colbert undertook a comprehensive national program to make France a formidable sea power. He established major naval bases, protected by modern fortifications, at Brest, Rochefort, and Toulon, established three naval academies, improved facilities at other ports, and supervised the writing of maritime and naval codes. He directed the strengthening of French colonial positions in North America and the Caribbean. He dispatched a French naval squadron to the Indian Ocean in 1666. The French seized permanent bases along the Malabar coast in 1670 and 1671, and in 1686 overran Madagascar. The French navy, which consisted of 18 warships in 1661, possessed 276 at the time of Colbert's death in 1683.[3]

While Colbert directed French naval policy, responsibility for the honing of the fleet as a fighting instrument on the eve of the War of the League of Augsburg rested in the hands of Anne-Hilarion de Cotentin, Comte de Tourville. In 1689 Vice Admiral of the Levant Tourville was a forty-seven-year-old veteran naval officer. He had commanded a ship that fought at Sole Bay, had served under Duquesne at Augusta and Palermo, and had fought in the campaigns against the Barbary corsairs of Algiers and Tripoli. Tunstall wrote that Tourville "did for the French navy, and ultimately for all navies, what *maréchal* Jean Martinet did for the army." In a matter of a few years, Tourville single-handedly advanced French naval doctrine well beyond that of England's Royal Navy.[4]

In May 1689 Tourville issued printed sailing and fighting instructions to the commanders of his fleet. Tactically, the instructions broke little new ground. Tourville completely embraced the English concept of the line ahead and the subdivision of the fleet into van, center, and rear. Doctrine, and a handful of primitive signals, remained the principal means of controlling the fleet in battle. But Tourville's instructions were the most comprehensive yet issued. A significant advance involved detailed sailing formations designed to enable a large fleet to change course, as a result of wind shifts or the sudden appearance of an enemy in an unexpected quarter, while retaining the capability to transpose quickly from the order of sailing into a linear order of battle. English sailing instructions would not rival Tourville's for comprehensiveness for another ninety years.[5]

Throughout 1689 and 1690 Tourville continued to issue revised and more elaborate instructions. Tunstall described one of the 1690 editions as a physically handy, "pocket size, thumb-indexed" manual. These instructions included even more detailed sailing directions for fleets of over a hundred ships organized in three or six columns, illustrated diagrams of sailing formations, and additional visual signals.[6]

The efforts of Colbert and Tourville made the French navy of the late seventeenth century a potent force. William Laird Clowes, historian of the Royal Navy, wrote:

> [By 1689] the young French navy had reached a pitch of development to which it had never previously attained, and to which it did not for many years attain again. The intelligence and energy of Colbert had created a splendid fleet, which was numerically, equal, if not superior, to the combined fleets of England and Holland; and the officers and men of the service had learnt experience in the best schools of the day, fighting at one moment with the Dutch against the English, and at another, with the English against the Dutch.[7]

Between the end of the Third Anglo-Dutch War and the beginning of the War of the League of Augsburg in 1688, the English navy, too, underwent steady improvement. The failures of the last two Dutch wars spurred both Charles and parliament to undertake a substantial naval expansion program. The remarkable Samuel Pepys, often considered the father of English naval administration, continued his reforms. He fought for the passage of the Act of 1677 that added thirty ships to the fleet, powerful vessels designed to fight in linear formations, henceforth termed "ships of the line." While the increase in the number of ships in the English navy between 1660 and 1688 appears nominal, the newer vessels were larger and more heavily armed and manned.[8]

Tactical and doctrinal innovation continued as well, but at a slow pace. The end of the Dutch wars and the seeming tactical superiority of the English navy made the need for continued doctrinal improvements appear less pressing. Individual commanders, for example Sir John Narbrough, who in 1678 led a fleet into the Mediterranean, and George, Lord Dartmouth, who commanded the fleet intended to prevent the landing in England of William of Orange in 1688, issued personalized revisions of the existing articles.[9]

Political turmoil in England did little to foster tactical development. The Duke of York, at times the commander in chief of the navy and a force behind innovative reforms, resigned in 1673 as a result of parliament's passage of the Test Act, designed to keep Catholics out of government office. Tension between monarch and parliament continued, with the former trying to secure, and the latter to prevent, James's accession to the throne. With Charles's death in February 1685, James II began his short reign. On 30 September 1687, William of Orange accepted an invitation to save England from the Catholic king's tyranny. William landed at Torbay with 14,000 men in early November. From a naval perspective, a cross-Channel operation launched in the late fall was an extremely risky venture. In fact, the first of William's attempts failed as the result of poor weather. As Richard Ollard remarked in his biography of Pepys: "The idea of a Channel campaign in November was as unthinkable as a hay-harvest in January." Nevertheless, the elements of surprise, good weather, and an English navy overwhelmingly sympathetic to the Protestant cause enabled William subsequently to conduct the first successful invasion of England since that of William the Conqueror in 1066. James lost political control and fled to France, where he accepted the protection of Louis XIV. William entered London in mid-December, and in January he and his wife, James's daughter Mary, jointly accepted the crown. In March James, with French naval support, landed in Ireland and began a partially successful attempt to raise the island in revolt. On 7 May, England and France went to war.[10]

Despite the political disorder, the English navy began what would come to be known as the War of the League of Augsburg in fair physical condition. But with new monarchs on the throne, new ministers running the government and overseeing the navy, and new commanders taking their places on the quarterdecks of the flagships, the service was psychologically unprepared for another prolonged struggle. The absence of continued tactical and doctrinal innovation exemplified the Royal Navy's lassitude. The fleet began the war armed with outdated sailing and fighting instructions. The main English fleet would fight its first major battle at Beachy Head in July 1690 under articles issued by the Duke of York in 1672 or 1673.[11]

THE FRENCH, too, were unprepared for war, even with Colbert's efforts. Ships were run down and undermanned. The bulk of the fleet was concentrated not in the Atlantic but in the Mediterranean, where it had been operating against the Barbary corsairs.[12]

Louis, facing warfare on the continent in the Low Countries and along the Rhine, as well as at sea against the English and the Dutch, adopted a somewhat complex strategy, in which the position of England, tied to the Netherlands by alliance and a shared monarch, was central. French strategy involved support for James in his effort to wrest all of Ireland from English control, the employment of a powerful fleet in the Channel to defeat the Anglo-Dutch fleet, and a ground offensive against the Netherlands. Ultimately, Louis hoped to invade England.

French strategy was judicious, but suffered from at least two of the problems that had undermined Philip's grand design a century earlier. First, French plans lacked clarity regarding the mission of the navy. Was the fleet supposed to seek out and destroy the Anglo-Dutch armada, or simply to fight as necessary to ensure the success of operations against Ireland? In other words, was gaining control of the English Channel, as a preliminary to an invasion of England, a primary goal? Second, since the strategy involved the coordination of land and sea forces in Ireland, the Netherlands, the Channel, the Bay of Biscay, and the Mediterranean, effective operational-level command and control was problematic.[13]

The English faced not only a more potent challenge in France but also a far more complicated strategic picture than they had during the war against the Dutch. France could not be blockaded as easily as Holland. Nor were the French as dependent on maritime trade. The English, tied as they were to the Netherlands, also faced a strategic dilemma. Sir Herbert Richmond noted:

The outstanding significance of this war was that, as it was the first in which the country was a member of a continental alliance, the statesmen were confronted with the problem which was to recur through the wars of the next century: the problem of whether England, as a maritime Power, could best help her allies by strengthening their armies on land or by weakening their enemy's resources at sea and over sea . . . These two alternatives gave rise to two schools of thought, the "continental" and the "maritime."[14]

Because of King William's ties to his native Holland, he was more a continentalist than a navalist. The king did not ignore the naval side of the war. He supported active operations in both the Atlantic and the Mediterranean against the French navy and trade. But the reality was that William and Mary had few strategic options. During the initial stage of the war, allied strategy was defensive and reactive. The defense of Holland against a French invasion and the need to defeat James's army in Ireland were paramount. But as the war progressed and the allies gained the initiative, it became apparent to contemporary critics that William was by inclination more a general than an admiral.[15]

The naval campaign in 1689 was indecisive. The allies failed to prevent the concentration of the French fleet at Brest. The French supported James in Ireland, but could not forestall English reinforcement of their garrison. Louis dissipated some of his naval strength by initiating a *guerre de course*—a war against allied commerce. But to counter the threat to their trade, the allies dispersed their own men-of-war. The two main fleets met only once, in May 1689 in Bantry Bay. Tactically, the battle was indecisive. The French claimed victory since they had held their own and had landed the troops and supplies to reinforce James. The English, having failed to lose, likewise saw their effort in a positive light. King William raised his commander, Admiral Sir Arthur Herbert, to the peerage as the Earl of Torrington.[16]

As the spring 1690 campaigning season began, the French held the initiative. Tourville left Brest in June with more than seventy-five ships. Torrington's Anglo-Dutch fleet numbered fewer than sixty. The English admiral proposed a strategy of delay, arguing that as long as he kept his "fleet in being" the French would not attempt an invasion, whereas if he risked battle and his fleet was destroyed, the enemy would be free to pursue whatever course they chose. At a council of war, however, Queen Mary ordered Torrington to sea to attack the French fleet.[17]

On 30 June the two fleets met in the battle of Beachy Head. For eight hours seventy-seven French men-of-war engaged fifty-six allied warships in the Channel south of Pevensey. Torrington fought cautiously, trying to prevent the longer French fleet from overlapping either end of his line. The Dutch squadron in the van engaged first and bore the brunt of the fighting. Late in the day the French center and van doubled the Dutch and threatened to destroy them. But the wind suddenly died. Torrington signaled his fleet to anchor and directed the fleet's boats to tow allied warships back into formation. Tourville was slower to recognize what was happening, and before the French could anchor they had drifted out of range and lost contact. Torrington disengaged that night, burning several vessels to prevent their capture, bringing his total loss to eight or nine ships.[18]

Fortunately for the English, Tourville did not follow up his victory. He had not lost a single ship, and his fleet, by his own admission, ended the battle in excellent fighting trim. Nevertheless, he pursued the English at a leisurely pace and then cruised about the Channel to little effect.

At Beachy Head, Tourville demonstrated his skill at controlling a fleet in battle, but he also made evident his failings as an operator and a strategist. Like many commanders in the eighteenth century, he lacked a killer instinct and was content to have beaten the English.[19] The frustrated French secretary of the navy labeled Tourville "brave de coeur, mais poltron de tête."[20] The French fleet returned to Brest without capitalizing on its great victory, while the English continued to reinforce their army in Ireland, where they defeated James at the battle of the Boyne.

The defeat at Beachy Head induced English commanders to look anew at their doctrine. The admiralty issued revised instructions that included twenty-seven articles. Tunstall considered the new issue noteworthy for two reasons. First, since they were distributed by the admiralty, rather than by a commander, the instructions were more official, and in a sense more binding. Second, they relied more heavily on a primitive signaling system to convey directions from the commander, and demanded less doctrinal interpretation on the part of subordinates.[21]

Despite appearances, the admiralty's sailing and fighting instructions remained quasi-official. In 1691 a revised set of instructions with thirty articles were issued under the name of Admiral Edward Russell, Torrington's successor as allied fleet commander. Corbett suggested that Torrington probably drafted the instructions, as well as the earlier set, since

Russell was relatively inexperienced. Corbett added: "That the point cannot be settled with absolute certainty is to be the more lamented because henceforth this set of Fighting Instructions . . . must be taken as the dominating factor of eighteenth-century tactics."[22]

Russell's instructions clearly illustrate the extent to which command of the fleet in battle was becoming centralized. Of the actions to be taken in Russell's thirty articles, twenty-four were initiated by visual signal. Only the eighteenth article—"If the admiral and his fleet have the wind of the enemy, and they have stretched themselves in a line of battle, the van of the admiral's fleet is to steer with the van of the enemy's and there to engage them"—allowed subordinates to take even limited action on their own initiative.

While the instructions further centralized control in the hands of the fleet commander, the means by which he could exercise that control remained extremely limited. Of the thirty articles, only six involved maneuvers that a commander could signal to begin, either by the entire fleet or by a specific division. There were only two signals, one for the fleet and the other for squadrons, to engage an enemy intent on keeping its distance. There was a single article for a general pursuit of a beaten enemy "put to the run."

The new instructions made battles less likely. Centralization of command denied subordinates latitude to exercise their initiative and to take advantage of opportunities that might arise. At the same time, the commanders responsible for controlling the fleet possessed few means to direct their forces. Noticeably absent was an instruction similar to that issued by the Duke of York, and in effect since 1672, "to divide the enemy's fleet."[23] If, as Corbett indicated, the revised instructions were "the dominating factor of eighteenth-century tactics," the Royal Navy was about to enter the next century confined by a doctrinal straitjacket. But such a view does little to explain why the English navy adopted such restrictive doctrine. Too many historians, including Corbett and even Tunstall, eager to interpret doctrinal development with an eye to the shortcomings of linear tactics in the eighteenth century, ignore the impact of recent operations and engagements on English commanders.

Taken together, Torrington's "fleet in being" strategy and the fighting instructions issued after Beachy Head mark a shift toward the defensive in English doctrine. The instructions of 1690 and 1691 do not represent an admiral's attempt to harness subordinates or prevent decision; they reflect the defensive mind-set of an anxious commander in chief. The queen, after all, forced Torrington to sea and into battle against his will. He led a mixed Anglo-Dutch force heavily outnumbered and out-gunned by Tourville's French fleet. For Torrington and Russell the development of doctrine to ensure the survival and cohesion of an inferior fleet, and not some quest for decisive victory, was foremost in mind.

The history of the Anglo-Dutch wars and the War of the League of Augsburg demonstrates that strategy shaped tactics as well as vice versa. Certainly, late-seventeenth-century philosophical concepts did find their way into the minds of some naval officers, and tactical and technical realities then, as now, had to be considered when developing strategy. But the relationship between tactics and strategy was two-way. In the Dutch wars the English employed an offensive naval strategy (except for the spring campaign of 1667 which brought De Ruyter into the Medway) that sought the destruction of the enemy's fleet and, accordingly, developed fairly aggressive tactics and doctrine. Conversely, during the War of the League of Augsburg, the English were forced to adopt a defensive strategy and developed a more defensive-minded tactical doctrine. Why would a naval force executing Torrington's fleet-in-being strategy require anything more than a cautious, defensive-minded, survival-oriented tactical doctrine?

ALTHOUGH the English and the Dutch had been battered during the first two years of the war, as the new campaigning season of 1691 began, their inherent maritime superiority became evident and the prospect of a more offensive strategy beckoned. The combined Anglo-Dutch fleet still numbered more than a hundred men-of-war. The French had not kept pace. Louis XIV's lack of enthusiasm for things naval deepened, and Colbert's successors lacked their predecessor's vision, determination, and administrative skills.[24] Tourville's fleet numbered seventy-two, five fewer than he had commanded at Beachy Head.

Tourville responded to the altered strategic picture with his famous *campagne au large*. He concentrated his fleet and led it into the approaches to the English Channel, where it attacked allied shipping. Russell's fleet sailed to intercept, but as it approached Tourville headed into the Atlantic, drawing the allies after him while avoiding an engagement. With the main allied fleet neutralized for nearly two months, French privateers preyed on English and Dutch merchantmen in the Channel. Tourville's strategy, while sensible, did not fit Louis's style of warfare. Louis's armies fought battles, conducted sieges, and undertook operations that had realizable and recognizable objectives. Supporters of the navy had trouble explaining to the king the benefits achieved by Tourville's *campagne au large*.[25]

Louis wanted victory, and in the spring of 1692 he believed the moment of decision had arrived. Convinced by James II that the English fleet was politically disaffected and pro-Stuart, Louis decided to launch an invasion of England. The king personally and secretly drew up his master plan. In April he ordered the Toulon squadron to sail for Brest to combine with the main fleet. Tourville would then lead the squadrons into the Channel before the allies could get to sea and concentrate, defeat the allied fleet should it appear, rendezvous with the army's transports concentrated near Cherbourg, and escort the armada across the Channel.[26]

In Versailles, Louis's strategic plan for an invasion looked sound. One can imagine the Sun King bending over maps, moving in his mind, if not on some board, his little fleets and armies. But his plan, much like Philip's "enterprise of England," contained no provision for what Clausewitz called "friction." What was Tourville to do if the English and Dutch fleets rendezvoused *before* the French fleet entered the Channel? Were the French to attack nevertheless? And how was Louis, intent on directing the operation from Versailles, going to communicate with Tourville once the fleet sailed from Brest?

According to early accounts of the battle, restated by Mahan, Tourville sailed "with a peremptory order from the king to fight when he fell in with the enemy, were they few or many, and come what might." But Clowes, in his history of the Royal Navy, asserted that the story of Louis's order was "without foundation."[27] Recent research indicates that both accounts are accurate. Initially, Louis did order Tourville to risk battle with a superior allied force. Louis wrote: "The contents of this Instruction are my will, which I desire to be carried out without any alteration." But when he learned that the rumors of disaffection among the English were unfounded and that the allied fleets either had already united or would soon do so, Louis issued new orders. Unfortunately for the French, the changed orders failed to reach Brest before Tourville sailed, as did fast corvettes sent to warn Tourville of the approach of the combined allied fleet.[28]

The French admiral, despite his orders to sail in April, delayed an extra week waiting for the Toulon squadron before he left Brest on 2 May.

Bad weather had slowed the progress of the eighteen ships of the Medi-terranean squadron, sixteen of which reached Brest in mid-month. On 12 May Tourville entered the Channel with forty-four men-of-war, slowly sailing eastward toward the Cotentin peninsula. In the early morning hours of 19 May, English scouts sighted the French fleet off Cape Barfleur. Tourville, had he chosen to, probably could have avoided action, but with his fleet holding the weather gauge, and with the king's orders in his pocket, he chose instead to risk an engagement. The allied fleet included ninety-nine English and Dutch warships.[29]

Throughout the day the enemies hammered each other. Tourville di-rected his fleet well and, despite his numerical inferiority, prevented the allies from effectively doubling either the French van or rear. But while he managed to stave off defeat, there was no chance of victory in the un-even fight. In the early evening the French disengaged. Neither side had lost a ship.

Unfortunately for Tourville, the allied fleet remained in fair shape and in good order, and it pursued him aggressively. Since Cherbourg could not shelter the French, Tourville sailed westward, hoping to weather, that is, to clear, the Cotentin and make for St. Malo. He led most of his force through the dangerous Race of Alderney, between the island of that name and the Cotentin's northwestern tip, but fifteen ships failed to make it through before the tide changed. Three French ships ran aground and were destroyed by their crews. Twelve were stranded in the lee of Cape La Hogue (Cap de la Hague), where they soon found them-selves trapped by the allied fleet. On 23 May 1692 Vice Admiral George Rooke led an attack by ships' boats and fireships against the twelve, de-stroying them all.[30]

The defeat was a major blow to the French. The weakest of the fifteen ships lost mounted sixty guns. Although they managed to rebuild their squadrons by the spring of 1693, a decade would pass before the French again fought another major fleet action against the English. Henceforth French strategy shifted geographically toward the Mediterranean, and philosophically toward the *guerre de course*.[31]

Command and control played a critical role in both French failure and allied success at Barfleur and La Hogue. At the strategic level, Louis's determination to plan and direct the operation from Versailles placed Tourville's heavily outnumbered fleet at great risk. Louis, whose appreci-ation of warfare at sea was limited, directed his squadrons as if they were armies. On land, a long march might weaken a ground force, but

weather rarely, if ever, caused the three weeks' delay that prevented the
Toulon squadron from keeping its rendezvous with the main fleet at
Brest. Louis's orders to Tourville were too restrictive and left his fleet
commander, a man far more knowledgeable about the vagaries of the sea
and the realities of naval warfare, few options. Nor, once the king recognized the inaccuracy of two critical assumptions on which he had based
his plan, was he able to dispatch new instructions to Tourville somewhere in the Channel. Tourville's well-developed doctrine and tactics
permitted him to control his fleet under very disadvantageous circumstances and almost avoid disaster. To escape the clutches of a force twice
the size of his own without losing a single ship was quite an achievement.
Likewise, while the restrictive English tactical doctrine, combined with
the leeward position, made a "decisive" battle a virtual impossibility,
it nevertheless enabled Russell to maintain the order of his fleet after
Barfleur, to conduct an orderly pursuit, and to take full advantage of
Tourville's misfortune at Cape La Hogue.

AFTER BARFLEUR, Tourville retained command of the main French
fleet, worked diligently to rebuild his shattered force, and continued to
revise his instructions. Tourville's "Signaux Généraux pour les Vaisseaux
de l'Armée du Roy" of 1693 included more than two hundred instructions. Tunstall termed the work "tactically limited, cautious and unin-
spired" with regard to combat, but in its comprehensiveness, "by far the
most elaborate body of instructions with signals to have appeared up to
that time." Tourville's instructions listed twenty-seven signals for sailing
close-hauled, twenty-one different orders of battle, and eleven signals for
chasing. The admiral even carried a printing press on his flagship so that
he could issue revised instructions and up-to-date orders of battle in a
clean, printed format.[32] It should be no surprise that Tourville's instructions were "cautious." Given the events of the previous year, the French
commander, like Torrington after Beachy Head, found himself on the
strategic defensive, concerned more about the continued survival of his
ships than about a quest for a knockout blow against a superior Anglo-
Dutch fleet.

Tourville had certainly not renounced the offensive. In May 1693,
commanding a reformed French fleet of approximately ninety warships,
he intercepted a well-escorted "Smyrna" convoy of four hundred merchantmen bound for the Mediterranean. The French overwhelmed Sir

George Rooke's twenty Anglo-Dutch escorts and captured two Dutch ships of the line and more than ninety merchant vessels valued, with their cargoes, at over £1,000,000.[33] The "disaster of the Smyrna fleet," Tourville's revenge for La Hogue, was the last major naval engagement of the War of the League of Augsburg.

EVEN BEFORE the treaty of Ryswick of September 1697 ended the war, Tourville took yet another step to further the effectiveness of the French navy. He directed the Jesuit priest Paul Hoste to write a treatise on naval warfare. Hoste, in his capacity as sometime chaplain, had served in French flagships since the Dutch wars. He had witnessed firsthand many of the greatest naval clashes of his day, including those of the Second and Third Anglo-Dutch Wars and the War of the League of Augsburg.

Hoste published his *L'Art des armées navales ou traité des evolutions navales* in 1697. He drew his lessons from the history of the last half-century, often from his own observations and the experiences of senior French commanders such as d'Estrées and Tourville, to develop a comprehensive overview of naval warfare. His work addressed the tactical advances of the English, Dutch, Spanish, and French fleets. He provided definitions of naval terms and discussed what he viewed as the principles of naval warfare. His illustrated treatise covered formations for sailing and fighting, orders of battle, fleet organization, movement, anchoring, and a variety of combat tactics including doubling and breaking an enemy's line. Hoste advocated not only line-ahead tactics but also restriction of the line to powerful men-of-war, or what were becoming known as ships of the line. The presence of smaller ships, he argued, weakened rather than strengthened formations. Hoste also reviewed the advantages and disadvantages of the windward and leeward positions. Unlike most French commanders of the next century, Hoste, like the English, considered the windward position the superior in battle. He also noted the shortcomings of current visual systems and toward the end of the book included his own scheme for signaling. His projected scheme, while far more elaborate than contemporary French and English systems, was impractical.[34]

While there was little that was revolutionary about Hoste's work, it was the first treatise on then-modern naval warfare, written at a time when other academics, including military specialists, were beginning to apply scientific principles and Enlightenment concepts to the world's complex problems. Hoste personifies the rationalist ideal: Jesuit training, use of history combined with personal experiences and observations, and the application of a scientific method. Hoste was French, and, as Carl L. Becker noted, while the Enlightenment was an international movement, France was "the mother country and Paris the capital." Hoste was not only a chaplain but also a professor of mathematics at the naval college in Toulon. In fact, at about the same time as his treatise on naval warfare, he also published his *Théorie de la construction des vaisseaux,* one of the first scientific efforts to develop a theory for ship construction. Becker also wrote of the Enlightenment world as one that had "emerged from barbarism into a civilized and ordered state." Along those same lines, Tunstall remarked that in his work Hoste "declared that without evolutions, fleets were like barbarians who waged war without knowledge and without order, everything depending on caprice and chance."[35]

Hoste was one of many seventeenth-century writers wrestling with the problems of what Michael Roberts termed "the military revolution." Azar Gat, in his study of military thought, notes that these authors based their work on "the accumulated strata of the doctrine of natural law, the neo-classical search for rules and principles in the arts, and Cartesianism, which together had dominated Louis XIV's France, stressing that reality was subject to universal order and to the mastery of reason."[36]

While Colbert's system of naval administration, Tourville's comprehensive instructions for the fleet, and Hoste's treatises on warfare at sea and ship construction placed the French in the forefront of naval science and professionalism, the question remains: Why did France not become the preeminent sea power of the eighteenth century? The English victories at Barfleur and La Hogue confirmed "English naval ascendancy," not that of the French.[37] English naval commanders, in spite of their inferior instructions, lack of professionalism, unscientifically designed ships, and absence of theoretical works, won the majority of the battles they fought. Not until the late eighteenth century did anyone in England bother even to translate excerpts of Hoste's work, nor did the Royal Navy's instructions begin to match the comprehensiveness of Tourville's. And yet the English won time and again. Good fortune is too simple an answer, for, as the Elder Moltke once wrote, "Luck in the long run is given only to the efficient." And the Royal Navy, however unenlightened, was efficient, or at least efficient enough to win.

AS THE NEW century dawned, the English Royal Navy continued to demonstrate its superiority over the French navy, as well as over other lesser naval powers. In May 1702 England declared war on France and the eleven-year European-wide struggle for the Spanish succession began.

At first the war at sea did not go well for the English. In August 1702 in the Caribbean an English fleet of seven ships caught but failed to destroy a much weaker French force of four men-of-war. But the fault was not with linear tactics. Several commanders were guilty of abject cowardice. The Royal Navy court-martialed, convicted, and shot two of the captains involved.[38]

The main campaign in European waters also floundered. In June 1702 Admiral Sir George Rooke led a combined Anglo-Dutch fleet of fifty ships, accompanied by transports with 14,000 troops, against Cadiz. The expedition reached the Spanish coast in August. The troops went ashore, but they were too busy looting and raping to capture the city. At a 16 September council of war, the allied commanders decided to reembark the army. Rooke, as directed in his original instructions, sent a detachment to the Caribbean and prepared to sail for England with the rest of his force.[39]

On 6 October, as Rooke, one of the most fortunate commanders in the history of the Royal Navy, made his way north along the Portuguese coast, he learned that a French fleet of thirty men-of-war escorting twenty-two Spanish treasure galleons from the Caribbean were in Vigo Bay, just north of the Portuguese-Spanish border. Rooke sailed north, according to some accounts against his own judgment, and reached Vigo on the morning of 8 October. A reconnaissance indicated that his quarry, far weaker than reported, had taken shelter well up the elongated bay, with the treasure fleet guarded by anchored men-of-war and artillery batteries ashore. The entire fleet could not make its way up the bay, but after another council of war, the allies decided to attack. Rooke would take fifteen English and ten Dutch ships of the line, as well as ten fireships, into the bay. The troops still with the fleet would land and eliminate the shore batteries.

The attack began on the morning of 12 October. In the face of an uneven and erratic wind, the allies pushed their attack home, both ashore and afloat. By nightfall nine French ships of the line and three frigates had been burned, either by the English and Dutch or by their own crews to prevent capture. Another six liners had been captured by the allies, along with eleven of the seventeen galleons in the bay. The remaining galleons had been burned. "Rooke," as Sir Julian Corbett would later write, "by the prompt daring of his officers, had gained one of the most complete victories in British naval annals."[40]

While Vigo Bay was not, obviously, a triumph of line-ahead tactics, Rooke's 1702 campaign along the Atlantic coast of the Iberian Peninsula nevertheless illustrates English understanding of the strategic and operational realities of command and control in the age of sail. During the wars of the last half of the seventeenth century against the Dutch and the French, the main English fleet had fought and cruised in the Channel, close to home, and within dispatch distance of London; the English deployed only small squadrons in the Mediterranean and even smaller detachments in the Caribbean. In the War of the Spanish Succession, the Channel was no longer the principal theater of conflict at sea. The main allied fleet operated far from home, off the Spanish and Portuguese coasts, and later in the western Mediterranean. Moreover, the movement of allied and Franco-Spanish forces between the Atlantic and the Mediterranean, as well as between the Caribbean and the Atlantic, played an important operational role. This interconnection between theaters had not been a factor in earlier wars.

Rooke's instructions took into account not only this global interrelationship but also the unpredictability of campaigns waged in distant seas. Whereas Philip at the time of the Armada and Louis before Barfleur had attempted to exercise centralized control over the operations of their forces, English monarchs did not issue orders to their commanders at sea, but broad instructions meant to guide, rather than to dictate, that left admirals with an enormous amount of both flexibility and responsibility. As Sir John Churchill, Duke of Marlborough, wrote to a fellow general: "The Sea service is not so easily managed as that of land. There are many more precautions to take, and you and I are not capable of judging them."[41]

The main English goal at sea early in the war was the capture of a secure base capable of supporting operations in the Mediterranean against the French at Toulon. Rooke's instructions listed Cadiz as the major objective of the campaign, but also included alternative goals, such as Gibraltar, Vigo, and Corunna. And if the attempt on Cadiz failed, Rooke was to dispatch a half-dozen men-of-war and two thousand troops to the Caribbean. Other commanders charged with responsibility for observing French naval forces, especially the English fleet off the island of Ushant watching Brest, were free, should the enemy escape, to sail in pursuit wherever necessary, whether the destination be the Strait of Gibraltar or the Caribbean. By 1702 naval strategy and operations had become global strategy and operations.

While general instructions helped to prevent debacles such as those that befell Medina Sidonia in the Channel and Tourville at La Hogue, they also permitted incompetent or uncommitted commanders to avoid taking action. Rooke, for example, had not favored the plan to attack Cadiz and probably did not do all he could have done to ensure the capture of the city. At the same time, the general nature of his instructions allowed him to conduct an alternative operation against the French and Spanish ships in Vigo Bay. Had Rooke sailed with more direct orders, akin to those issued to Tourville by Louis, Cadiz might well have fallen. Or, perhaps, the allies would have risked their army and their fleet in what was a forlorn hope. Given the nature of Rooke's instructions, he well knew that the responsibility for the decision was his and that failure could lead to his removal from command, perhaps even to an investigation, and possibly to a court-martial. In fact Rooke, after his triumph at Vigo, found himself called upon by the House of Lords to defend his conduct before Cadiz.[42]

In the naval campaign of 1704, the English again demonstrated the advantage of decentralized strategic and operational command and control. Allied plans, shaped by the strategic vision of the Duke of Marlborough, envisioned dramatic land and sea movements deep into the enemies' rear. Marlborough would lead his army to the Danube (where in August he would win his great victory at Blenheim). The main allied fleet would simultaneously enter the western Mediterranean and, if possible, seize Toulon with the help of an army from Savoy. As Winston S. Churchill wrote of his illustrious ancestor: "[Marlborough's] own eyes were constantly fixed upon the control of the Mediterranean and upon the Italian front. To have a good fortified harbour and naval base upon the coast of Spain, to pen the French fleet in Toulon, to take Toulon, to carry the war into France from the south, to sustain Eugene and the Imperial troops from the sea—these, apart from his own task of coping with the strongest French army, were his aims."[43]

Despite the importance accorded the Mediterranean theater, Corbett noted that Rooke's instructions were "framed in the best possible way. The portion of the far-reaching design that Marlborough wished Rooke to carry out was not forced upon the fleet. It was merely placed lucidly before the flag-officers that they might clearly perceive their place in the great whole so far as it could be safely disclosed. It was left to their judgment and loyalty to say how far the limitations of their art enabled them to carry into effect what the Government looked to them to perform."

Other options open to Rooke were to engage and to destroy the French
fleet if it should offer battle, to seize Cadiz, and to take the fleet to Barcelona and try to convince the Catalans to declare for the allies' candidate
for the Spanish throne—Charles III.[44]

Events quickly overtook the plan. When the duke of Savoy chose not
to play his part in the grand scheme, the capture of Toulon became an
impossibility. Rooke sailed instead to Barcelona, but there, too, met frustration. He then learned that the French fleet from Brest had entered the
Mediterranean. Rooke sailed for Toulon. There he discovered about
twenty heavy ships outfitting and also received intelligence that the
French fleet was bound for the Strait of Gibraltar. Rooke pursued, and off
Minorca sighted the French. The allied fleet included thirty-six English
and Dutch ships that had already been at sea for several months. The
French had thirty-two men-of-war. Given the rough parity in numbers,
Rooke knew that even a victorious battle might leave his fleet so battered
that it would have to withdraw from the Mediterranean to refit, while
the French had another score of fresh ships readying at Toulon. He also
knew that since the French Atlantic fleet had entered the Mediterranean,
the English commander responsible for watching Brest should have sent
a strong detachment south as well. Rooke decided not to press his pursuit
of the French, who showed little interest in fighting, and sailed instead
for Lisbon.

On 16 June Rooke reached Lagos Bay and there found Admiral Sir
Clowdisley Shovell with twenty-three fresh ships. Shovell, when he arrived off Brest and discovered the French fleet gone, had assumed that
they had sailed for the strait and led his entire command south in search
of Rooke. Flexibility in planning and initiative on the part of senior
Royal Navy commanders had brought about a concentration of naval
force the likes of which had eluded Louis XIV in 1691.

But to what purpose? Even with Shovell's reinforcement, nothing
could be attempted against Toulon. While at Lisbon, Rooke received
new orders from London to seize Cadiz, but without an embarked army,
even if the port could be taken, it could not long be held. After a council
of war, Rooke decided to sail into the strait to water his ships along the
North African coast, watch for the French, allow English diplomats and
Portuguese officials to try to scrape up an army, and wait on events.

In the strait on 17 July Rooke held yet another council of war, at
which the allied commanders suddenly decided to snatch Gibraltar, re-
portedly weakly garrisoned. The strategically located fortress-port had

been an object of English interest since the days of Cromwell. Rooke's 1702 instructions had listed Gibraltar as an alternate objective. And it is likely that Rooke and his fellow admirals and generals had the prospect in mind when they left Lisbon. Geography favored the enterprise. The actual fortress, the great "Rock," stood on the end of a narrow peninsula. English and Dutch marines landed at its base could isolate the fortress, which could then be reduced by the guns of the fleet. And, unlike Cadiz, Gibraltar could be held by the relatively small ground force Rooke could place ashore.[45]

The assault commenced on the morning of 21 July. Rooke's 1,800 marines easily isolated the fortress. The bombardment began the next morning and continued throughout that day and the next. The garrison commander surrendered on 24 July.[46] The French responded promptly to Gibraltar's capture and sent their combined Brest-Toulon fleet toward the strait. Rooke, who had reembarked half his marines, met the French off Malaga on 13 August. The fleets were well matched—fifty-one against fifty-one.

All day the two fleets, each arranged in line-ahead formation, pounded each other. The French fired high, into the masts and rigging of the allied ships; the English and Dutch fired low, into the French hulls. By the end of the day both fleets had suffered heavy losses and damage, but neither had lost a ship. On 14 August the two exhausted fleets repaired what damage they could. The next day the French sailed eastward for Toulon.[47]

While tactically inconclusive, Malaga proved to be an important engagement. The French, who fought an extremely cautious battle, were pleased to have avoided another Vigo Bay or Cape La Hogue. The allies, their ships fouled after six months at sea, short on shot because of the assault on Gibraltar, and with half their marines ashore, were happy enough to have driven off the French and to have protected their new base. Thus both sides could claim victory and attribute their success to a rather formal adherence to the line ahead.[48]

When Rooke's fleet left the strait to return home for the winter, the French and Spanish were given an opportunity to retake Gibraltar. In the spring of 1705, while a Spanish land force besieged the fortress, a French squadron of fourteen ships commanded by Rear Admiral Jean-Bernard Desjeans, baron de Pointis, blockaded it by sea. The allies sent Admiral Sir John Leake with thirty-five English, Dutch, and Portuguese warships to lift the siege and relieve the garrison. The two fleets met off Marbella on 10 March 1705. The French, clearly outgunned, ran. The English pursued and captured three French ships of the line and drove two others ashore where they were burned. Leake then sailed for Gibraltar and lifted the siege.[49]

The 1705 campaign demonstrated the difficulty the English faced operating in the Mediterranean without a secure base capable of harboring a large fleet through the winter. While in the future Gibraltar would become a major facility, at the time it remained a defensible but minor roadstead. Lisbon was too distant from the main French base at Toulon. Allied political and military leaders thus recognized that they needed a port in the western Mediterranean, but Toulon looked too hard to take, and Spanish and Italian ports were too exposed to French attack. Port Mahon, Minorca, seemed to offer an alternative.[50]

Nevertheless, Minorca was not an objective in the campaigns of 1706, 1707, or 1708. In 1706 the allied fleet spent its time shoring up positions in Catalonia and Italy. In 1707 the fleet laid siege to Toulon and pressed the French hard, but the Savoyard and Imperial armies expected to attack from landward never arrived. In 1708 troubles in the Italian peninsula brought the fleet into the Tyrrhenian Sea. Then Admiral Sir John Leake led a successful expedition against Sardinia.

Shortly thereafter, with the campaigning season rapidly drawing to a close and the bulk of the fleet facing yet another return trip to Lisbon and England, Minorca became the unordered objective of the fleet's operations. The Spanish king wanted the fleet to stay. Leake, too, understood the costs of having the fleet retrace its wake each fall and spring and had since his arrival in the Mediterranean discussed the possibility of seizing the island. Even back in London, the government, doubtful that Toulon could ever be taken, hoped that Leake could mount an attack against Minorca and was prepared to support success with measures "taken forthwith for the wintering of sixteen or twenty ships there, &c." Leake needed little prompting, reached Minorca and began landing troops on 25 August, and in less than a month secured the island.[51]

ENGLAND, or Great Britain as the nation can properly be termed after the Act of Settlement of 1 May 1707, had become a Mediterranean power, by grand design certainly, but not as the result of operations dictated from afar. The ability of the English to campaign successfully at such a distance from home, a range greater than that which had stymied the Spanish in 1588 and the French in 1692, illustrates the advantage of decentralized command and control at the strategic and operational levels during the age of sail.

But what of the tactical level? Was it true, as Mahan wrote, that the battle of Malaga marked the advent of the "degeneracy from the able combinations of Monk, Ruyter, and Tourville to the epoch of mere seamanship?"[52] Did the battle indeed wed the Royal Navy to strict adherence to the line and the "dead-hand" of the fighting instructions?

Malaga needs to be viewed within its proper context, and not as an isolated battle judged strictly on its tactical merits. Rooke's primary responsibility, given the rough parity of the fleets and the fact that his ships were badly fouled, short of ammunition, and without half their marines, was to protect Gibraltar, not to risk the fleet in the pursuit of a "decisive" victory. In other words, Rooke, like Torrington at Beachy Head, was on the strategic defensive and ought not to be judged harshly for failing to adopt a tactical offensive at Malaga. Certainly, after two years of campaigning, Rooke had cause to reason, as had Shovell since 1690, that "at sea, if the fleets be near equal, there must be great success to win a great victory, for by the time one is beaten that other generally is weary."[53] Rooke also understood that even the annihilation of the enemy fleet, an outcome that under the circumstances was highly unlikely, would not bring about an immediate French collapse.

While the action of 24 August 1704 was the largest set-piece naval battle of the War of the Spanish Succession, Malaga was not the only naval encounter of note. At Vigo Bay, the allied naval commanders—English and Dutch—displayed innovation by destroying a major enemy force anchored in a defended bay. It had been Rooke, after all, who had commanded the allied attack at La Hogue ten years earlier. While Leake's action at Marbella was hardly a major test of English tactics, he showed no hesitation to shed the line and chase down De Pointis's French squadron. Moreover, his personal instructions issued to the fleet before reaching Gibraltar, in which he outlined his plan for an assault on an equal number of French ships caught at anchor, read much like Nelson's scheme for attack before Aboukir Bay.[54] Against an enemy reluctant to give battle, and prone to run once engaged, the development of the skills necessary to cut out an enemy squadron in a bay or to destroy a fleet at anchor was at least as, and perhaps more important than, fleet-to-fleet tactics for encounters on the high seas.

Nor, as Tunstall points out, is there any evidence that in the immediate aftermath of the war senior British naval commanders felt encumbered by Rooke's instructions, or by the example of Malaga. In the summer of 1718 Admiral Sir George Byng brought a British fleet of twenty ships of the line into the Mediterranean to deter or, if necessary, to act against an expected Spanish invasion of Sicily and southern Italy. When Byng reached Naples, he found himself in a difficult situation: the Spaniards had already invaded Sicily but had not yet declared war against Britain, a possibility not foreseen in his instructions. He nevertheless decided to seek out and to destroy the Spanish fleet to prevent a further foray into Italy proper and to isolate the Spaniards already ashore in Sicily. As Mahan wrote, Byng displayed a "readiness to assume a responsibility from which a more scrupulous man might have shrunk."[55]

On 11 August 1718 the two fleets met off Cape Passero, the southeastern tip of Sicily. Byng's twenty-one powerful ships were well outfitted, manned, and led; the eighteen weaker Spanish ships of the line were not. Fortunately for Byng, the Spaniards fired first and saved him the trouble of starting the war. The British replied with a broadside and Byng sent up two signals—to engage and for general chase. By the end of the day Byng's captains had captured six Spanish ships of the line, including the flagship, and a frigate. Byng believed he would have won an even greater victory had his captains pursued individually and not ganged up in two and threes on the Spanish vessels.[56] Still, his victory gave Britain and its Italian allies the initiative, an initiative they would never lose in a relatively brief war (for the age) that ended in January 1720.

Cape Passero was an easy British victory, for as Mahan noted, Byng faced "a disorderly force, much inferior in both numbers and discipline."[57] But Byng exhibited impressive initiative at the strategic, operational, and tactical levels. He decided to attack despite the absence of a formal declaration of war. He shouldered the responsibility himself, noting that "a commanding officer should only call a Council of War to screen him from what he has no mind to undertake." Before the battle he issued written additional instructions announcing his intention "to attack and destroy the Spanish ships" before he knew their numbers or condition.[58] Byng hardly appears to be an example of an overly cautious commander or a tactical "degenerate."

While doctrinal innovation, measured by the development of the English fighting instructions, was far greater between 1652 and 1674 than between 1689 and 1713, comparisons between the two periods are meaningless. The belligerents fought thirteen major sea battles during the twenty-two years of the Anglo-Dutch wars. In all three conflicts the stakes for the maritime powers involved were high and the prospects of victory at sea frequently led both the English and the Dutch to run risks in the quest for a decisive stroke. The English and French fought only three major battles at sea during the twenty-four years of the wars of the League of Augsburg and the Spanish succession. At all three of these—Beachy Head, Barfleur, and Malaga—one of the fleets involved was clearly on the defensive and sought to survive, rather than to triumph. In none of the battles did any commander expect that his annihilation of the enemy fleet would lead to a quick end of the war. Given the nature of these battles, and their small number, we ought not to be surprised to discover that the development of English tactical doctrine slowed after 1674.

Fighting instructions were not the sole measure of tactical development. The refinement of the line as a combat formation continued. Admirals began to place other powerful men-of-war ahead and behind the centrally located flagships, both for greater protection and for massed firepower, and to position the ships of more senior and trusted captains at the all-important ends of the line, where most maneuvers began. Hoste's work marked the dawn of a new age in naval warfare in which tactics began to become "a science." Navies, albeit slowly, entered the era of the Enlightenment. In 1711 English naval commanders began to issue, along with the usual personalized additional instructions, separate signal books.[59] The increased, though still antediluvian, use of visual signals marked an important step in the evolution of naval command and control. Commanders, frustrated with doctrine, unwilling to place their trust in subordinates, began to look to a new technology as a means by which they might actually be able to direct, to conduct, to micromanage an engagement. A half-century would pass before truly serviceable signaling systems reached the fleet, but the first steps along the road to ever greater centralization had been taken, steps of far more importance than the publication of Admiral George Rooke's fighting instructions.

CHAPTER FOUR

The Conundrum of the Line Ahead

$\mathscr{B}$ETWEEN THE END of the Anglo-Spanish war in 1720 and that of the Seven Years' War in 1763, navies struggled with the pros and cons of the line ahead. To most contemporaries the line's virtues were clear enough. In 1745 a history of the operations of the British Mediterranean fleet during the first years of the War of the Austrian Succession (1741–48) noted: "A line of Battle is the basis and foundation of all discipline in sea fights, and is universally practised by all nations that are masters of any power at sea; it has had the test of a long experience, and stood before the stroke of time, pure, and unaltered, handed down by our predecessors as the most prudential, and best-concerted disposition that can possibly be made at sea."[1] And yet, while the line ahead may have been the most judicious method for the deployment of the ships of the era, it continued to pose difficult and at times seemingly insurmountable problems of command and control.

The experiences of the wars of the League of Augsburg and the Spanish Succession reinforced the view that doctrine was too rigid a formula for the successful direction of a battle. The prospect of drawing up a doctrinal manual that could address, clearly enough to be interpreted uniformly throughout a fleet, the myriad contingencies of naval engagements seemed impossible. So it was that the Royal Navy's fighting instructions drawn up after Beachy Head (fought in 1690) remained in force, with rather minor revisions, until the American Revolution.

This lack of revision of the fighting instructions led Sir Julian Corbett to label them, inaccurately, "permanent instructions." In fact, they had become often irrelevant instructions, as the effort to work out possible solutions to tactical problems devolved from the admiralty to individual commanders in chief who began to issue innumerable "additional" fighting instructions to the ships under their command and to seek alternative methods to address the conundrum of the line ahead.[2]

In the decades after 1720 the most significant tactical developments came in four areas. The first three accepted the line ahead as the formation of choice but attempted to tweak the system to improve fighting power. The fourth sought to identify situations in which a commander might safely depart from the line in the quest for a more complete victory. Most naval commanders recognized that an improvement in general tactical proficiency would enhance the line ahead as a fighting formation. More experienced captains, commanding well-trained crews, would be better able to execute maneuvers and to maintain high rates of fire from the ships' heavy guns, thus generating greater fighting power. The ability of British men-of-war in the latter part of the eighteenth century to sustain rates of fire more than twice those of their French and Spanish opponents explains much of the Royal Navy's success.

Other methods to enhance the effectiveness of the line involved several tactical maneuvers. Doubling, placing ships on both sides of a segment of an enemy's line, was an old method occasionally attempted, though rarely successful. The narrowing of the distance between ships—concentration—allowed a commander to focus the firepower of his own line against a portion of that of the enemy. Breaking the enemy's line, a maneuver first written into the fighting instructions during the Dutch wars but excised after Beachy Head, also reappeared in most "additional" instructions issued in this period. Many late-century writers and naval officers considered the breaking of an opponent's line the surest path to victory.

The continued development of visual signaling systems also offered commanders an increasingly effective means of controlling their fleets. After 1711 signal books became ever more elaborate. By the time of the American Revolution, the signal book had begun to supplant the fighting instructions as the principal means of fleet control.

The fourth method adopted to improve fighting power involved the actual suspension, or near suspension, of the line ahead. Most senior British commanders recognized that in certain circumstances, for example when a fleet held a clear quantitative and qualitative advantage (as Byng had possessed at Cape Passero), adherence to the line until the enemy fleet was actually put to flight was both unnecessary and likely to reduce the scope of the ensuing victory. On the whole, between 1739 and 1763, when operational finesse or sheer good fortune presented Royal Navy fleet commanders with such a clear-cut advantage, they were both willing and able to jettison the line, to order a "general chase," and to reap appropriate rewards.

While the history of naval warfare between 1720 and 1763 includes innumerable examples of mediocrity and failure, it is too simplistic to portray the era as one in which either the "dead hand" of the fighting instructions or the strictures of the line ahead held European navies in their grip. Nearly constant warfare and more frequent battles at sea, the same combination that led to innovation during the Anglo-Dutch wars, fostered tactical and doctrinal development. The problems were caused less by adherence to the line or to the fighting instructions than by an increasingly centralized system of naval command and control.

THE MAJOR DISAPPOINTMENT at sea for the Royal Navy during the War of the Austrian Succession came in the Mediterranean in February 1744 off Toulon. The British had already spent five frustrating years in the Middle Sea. They had not only failed to force the Dons to fight a major fleet engagement, but also failed to prevent a successful Spanish amphibious operation against the Italian peninsula. The British Mediterranean fleet was too weak for its many responsibilities both inside and outside the Strait of Gibraltar. Moreover, the British had to keep a wary eye on the "neutral" French who purposefully maneuvered their naval force at Toulon in a manner designed to complicate the Royal Navy's efforts and to aid the operations of the Spanish.[3]

With a political storm brewing in London, the pressures of command on Admiral Nicholas Haddock, the British naval commander in the Mediterranean, proved too great, and he suffered "a complete nervous breakdown." In March 1742 Haddock sailed for home and Rear Admiral Richard Lestock, who had brought out a reinforcing squadron from England, took over as acting commander. Lestock expected to be named fleet commander, but the admiralty gave the command instead to Admiral Thomas Mathews, a move that disappointed Lestock and placed in the senior positions of the fleet two men who were not on the best of personal terms. As William Laird Clowes noted: "That Mathews disliked Lestock cannot be gainsaid. Almost every naval officer of the day disliked Lestock."[4]

December 1743 found the British warily eyeing the French and Spanish at Toulon. Lestock's blockading squadron was at Hyères, the main fleet at Villefranche, between Nice and Monaco, and Admiral Mathews at Turin, where he was conferring with allied officials about the future course of the war. The admiral was overburdened by his many responsibilities, both political and military. And the latter, he discovered in Turin, were about to become even more difficult, since intelligence indicated that the French were preparing to enter the war, their Toulon squadron was busily outfitting, and their Brest fleet either was preparing to sail or had already sailed for the strait, a move that would give the combined Franco-Spanish fleet a clear superiority over the British.

Mathews returned to Villefranche in early January and in a few days had rejoined Lestock, now a vice admiral, and concentrated the fleet off Hyères. On 9 February the combined Franco-Spanish force of twenty-eight ships of the line began to form up in Toulon's outer anchorage. Mathews's twenty-eight liners likewise weighed, but then anchored in Hyères Bay. At dawn on the tenth, with the enemy, both actual and prospective, heading south in good order, the British again weighed amid confusion and fear that they were about to be trapped at anchor. But the enemy moved off and the British fleet gradually stood out on a starboard tack and made its way toward the south.[5]

Throughout the day Mathews tried to bring his fleet into line, but to no avail. According to the standing instructions, the van was supposed to lead if the fleet stood on the starboard tack, as it did early on 10 February. Accordingly, Lestock's ships raced south, trying to overtake Mathews's, which actually led the fleet. Then the wind shifted, and the fleet stood south on a larboard tack. The ships of Rear Admiral William Rowley's rear division were now supposed to lead, and made their way toward the van while Lestock's fell back through the formation, creating even greater disorder. Mathews, now with the wind gauge, nevertheless decided to initiate an engagement, sent up the signal for the line abreast, and stood toward the southwest and the enemy with the flagship. But in the light breeze the admiral's center division could only close the range gradually, while his van and rear were slow to mimic his movements and lay even farther to the east than they had before he had signaled his intent to engage. At day's end, he realized that no battle was possible and made the signal for the fleet to bring to, assuming that his subordinates would re-form a proper line, ahead and astern of his center division. Unfortunately, both Rowley and Lestock came to in place and the day ended with the British fleet in disarray.[6]

Dawn on 11 February found the British in possession of the wind gauge but badly formed for battle. Worse yet, as the two fleets resumed their run toward the south, the unfouled bottoms of the Franco-Spanish fleet allowed it to pull slightly ahead of Mathews's ships. Moreover, without a formal declaration of war, the French commander in chief, Lieutenant General Claude-Élisée de Court la Bruyère, was not about to halt for battle. He sailed intent on keeping his ships on the move in close order—360 feet apart. But while the French ships kept their stations, de Court's Spanish rear squadron did not and fell behind. Mathews saw his opportunity and decided to engage, since further delay would either allow the enemy to escape or lead the British fleet farther from Toulon, where a Spanish convoy bound for Italy awaited escort.[7]

At 1100 Mathews's flagship, the *Namur* 90, hoisted a red flag to the main—the signal to engage. There the flag flew for fifteen minutes until the admiral ordered it struck and replaced with the signal for the line. Mathews realized that he could not force a formal battle: van to van, center to center, and rear to rear. His center division was about two miles east and about a mile behind the French flagship. The British van was as far behind and another mile to the east. The leading ship of Lestock's rear division was almost two miles behind the last ship of Mathews's own force and more than three miles east of the enemy's rear. It was impossible for the British ships to both close the range and simultaneously make up the mile that they lagged behind their counterparts in the Franco-Spanish line.

Mathews, a veteran of Byng's victory at Cape Passero, nevertheless remained determined to engage, if not in a formal battle, then in an informal one. After conferring by speaking trumpet with Captain James Cornwall, who commanded the *Marlborough* 90 in the wake of the *Namur,* Mathews decided to make the best of his position and to focus his attack on the rear of the enemy line—the Spanish squadron. The *Namur* was over a mile ahead of the Spanish flagship, the *Real Filipe* 114, and Mathews judged that he could bear down and cut off the enemy's rear, which was lagging behind the French center. Lestock could then come up and finish the work, concentrating at least two-thirds of the British fleet against the enemy's weakest division. If the French reversed course and attempted to rescue their allies, Mathews would have achieved the general engagement he sought, without being drawn farther from Toulon.

Mathews's plan was excellent. It demonstrated tactical flexibility as well as a willingness to jettison the line and to risk a pell-mell battle, in which the French van and center might be able to overwhelm the British van while Mathews concentrated on the Spanish. But the crucial question was how his subordinates, especially Rowley and Lestock, would interpret their commander's actions. Interpretation would be the key, because the signal book was too limited to direct the movements that Mathews had in mind and his means of communication with Captain Cornwall—the speaking trumpet—would be of no use with the rest of a fleet meandering along an eight-mile-long line.

The inability of the British fleet to execute Mathews's scheme of attack was principally a failure of command and control. Mathews, while he admittedly lacked the tools to direct the battle, added to the uncertainty of his subordinates by his actions. Although he was bringing on a mêlée in what was basically a line-abreast formation, he left the signal for the line ahead flying from the flagship. Whether this was intentional, an oversight, or the result of the loss of his flag captain in the initial fusillade is unclear. What is certain is that neither Rowley nor Lestock fully understood what their admiral was attempting. Lestock, who earlier in the day had ignored two direct orders from Mathews to hustle into formation, showed no haste in the afternoon and reached the battle too late to do much good.[8]

While the commanders of the leading ships of Lestock's rear division sensed that they ought to bear down on the Spanish and join the engagement, with Mathews still flying the signal for the line and Lestock sailing south at his leisurely pace, they remained in formation.

Rowley, commanding the van, faced the most difficult dilemma. Under the nineteenth article of the fighting instructions, the job of the van in battle was to engage the enemy van. Given the distances involved, Rowley recognized that this could not be what Mathews wanted. Moreover, the commander in chief had made manuscript alterations to the instructions' first article that directed all ships to stay within a half-cable's length of each other. If Rowley's ships conformed to Mathews's movements, they would strike the head of the Spanish squadron, basically what Mathews intended. But there also was the tradition of flagships fighting flagships, which would mean in the circumstances that Rowley, in the *Barfleur* 90, should bear down on the flagship of the French commander in chief, the *Terrible* 74, located in the center of the enemy line. Rowley pursued this last course, although the four leading ships of his division continued to pursue the French van. As a result, Mathews's effort to concentrate the bulk of his fleet for a quick knockout blow against the Spanish squadron failed miserably. When the French van and center finally tacked at 1630 and went to the aid of their allies, Rowley's ships found themselves hard pressed and Mathews forfeited the few gains achieved earlier in the day. While both fleets suffered heavily, the sole loss was the Spanish *Poder* 60, captured by the British, recaptured by the French, recaptured yet again by the British, and later burned.

The battle of Toulon did little for the reputations of the senior officers involved. The French, Spanish, and British governments looked with disfavor on the conduct of their forces. The Spanish blamed the French for being slow to respond to Mathews's maneuver. The French countered that the Spanish had set themselves up for the attack by their lethargic sailing. In England, Mathews, Lestock, and eleven captains faced courts-martial. The Royal Navy dismissed Mathews and nine of the captains, although Lestock managed an acquittal.

The battle of Toulon reinforced the views of those, such as Lestock, who considered the line "the basis and foundation of all discipline in sea fights" and who attributed Mathews's failure to his deviation from the accepted norms of battle. No doubt Mathews's court-martial made it somewhat less likely that other commanders would act aggressively when faced with a situation akin to that which arose off Toulon. But clearly the British fleet's failure had little to do with the line ahead or with the "dead hand" of the fighting instructions. Mathews failed not because he departed the line and deviated from the instructions, two of the fifteen charges brought against him, but because he did so in the absence of any alternative means—direct or indirect—by which to manage the battle. And it was outrage and spitefulness, not the fighting instructions, that made Lestock so slow to join the engagement.

It is noteworthy that the first charge leveled against Mathews at his court-martial was that he had not held any councils of war, or other meetings with his commanders, either on a routine basis or between 8 and 11 February when the prospect of a battle was imminent. Unlike Nelson before Aboukir Bay, Mathews failed to discuss the possibilities of battle with his subordinates so that they might have some idea of what he was trying to accomplish. When Lestock visited the flagship the night before the battle, Mathews dismissed him with a curt wish for a good evening. As a biographer of Edward Hawke, who commanded one of the ships in Rowley's van division, wrote: "Mathews was to blame for not keeping his captains generally informed about the situation. There is no sign that he discussed tactical questions with them."[9]

The second charge brought by the court was that Mathews had not circulated substantive additional signals and instructions to his fleet. Because neither the standard fighting instructions nor the signaling system in use provided commanders with sufficient means to direct the fleet once the engagement began, it was already common practice for admirals to issue their own additional instructions and accompanying signals.[10] This Mathews failed to do, despite the fact that he had commanded in the Mediterranean for over two years. Was it reasonable for the admiral, who had neither taken his subordinates into his confidence nor issued additional signals or instructions covering his intended maneuver, to expect Rowley, whose *Barfleur* lay two miles ahead of the *Namur* and more than four miles from the *Real Filipe,* or the recalcitrant Lestock, whose *Neptune* was four miles to the rear and as many from the Spanish flagship, to respond to the situation in the same fashion as their commander in chief? The court ruled, reasonably, that it was not.

Although Mathews became a scapegoat whose dismissal seemed to strengthen the grip of the fighting instructions, the subsequent history of the war does not bear out that conclusion. Mahan may have been closer to the truth when, after attributing the fiasco to a lack of cooperation and experience to be expected in a first battle, he wrote of the "healthful reaction" that followed Toulon, a reaction that "woke up" the senior leadership of the Royal Navy.[11]

In fact, the Royal Navy's wake-up call had come earlier in the conflict, and had been ignored by Mathews. Admiral Edward Vernon, who commanded the British expedition to the Caribbean at the start of the War of Jenkins's Ear (1739–1742), was a man who spent much of his time thinking and writing about the myriad problems—from manpower to morale—facing naval officers. Vernon was quick to offer advice on naval policy, strategy, and tactics to anyone who would listen, from the king to a young American colonist named Lawrence Washington who, through the admiral's intercession in 1746, obtained a midshipman's warrant for his younger brother George. Vernon, who believed that his fellow officers gave far too little time to the study of tactics, issued to his subordinates a variety of well-thought-out additional fighting instructions and signals.[12]

Vernon was far from a formalist in his tactical approach. He wrote: "All formality therefore as matters are circumstanced only tends to keep the main point out of question, and to give knaves and fools an opportunity to justify themselves on the credit of jargon and nonsense." The most important of Vernon's additional instructions sought to smooth and to speed the transition from the order of sailing to the order of battle, the very problem that plagued Mathews at Toulon.[13]

Vernon doubted that commanders in chief could, in fact, control their fleets in battle. His additional instructions illustrated his willingness to place ever greater trust in the initiative of his subordinates. In one set of instructions issued to the captains of the fireships operating with his fleet in the Caribbean in 1739, he noted that since he was "apprehensive" about whether subordinates would be able "to discern such signals through the cloud of smoke we may then be in, I principally rely upon your prudence and resolution in observing where such services lie open for your execution." Vernon also directed that, in the event of an engagement against a smaller force, several of his ships would form a "Corps de Réserve." "As it is morally impossible to fix any general rules to occurrences that must be regulated from the weather and the enemy's disposition," he wrote, "this is left to the respective Captain's judgement that shall be ordered out of line to govern himself by, as becomes an officer of prudence and resolution, and as he will answer the contrary at his peril." But Vernon was not yet ready to abandon the line, or the signal book, and allow his entire fleet such freedom of action. Another instruction directed that in an engagement his frigates were to take up stations opposite the British line, away from the enemy, where they could repeat the commander in chief's signals.[14]

One of the senior officers who served under Vernon early in the war was Richard Lestock. While he was petty, troublesome, and unloved, and is usually portrayed as a die-hard advocate of the line, Lestock was aware of the shortcomings of the navy's instructions. A pamphlet published after Toulon that, if not written by Lestock, was inspired by him, noted: "Men in the highest stations at sea will not deny but what our sailing and fighting instructions might be amended, and many added to them, which by every day's experience are found to be necessary." The author went on to praise Vernon, "that provident, great admiral, who never suffered any precaution to escape him," for his innovations, innovations from which Mathews could have profited, had he been willing to accept advice and suggestions from a second in command he despised.[15]

As MAHAN SUGGESTED, the Toulon affair, far from hindering the development of British naval tactics, actually accelerated the process.

Within a month after taking command in the Mediterranean, Mathews's successor, William Rowley, who had commanded the van at Toulon, had issued fifty additional signals and instructions, many of which were based on those developed years before by Vernon.[16]

Another British commander who embraced the idea of developing additional signals and instructions was Vice Admiral George Anson. Named to replace Vernon as commander of the important Western Squadron in July 1746, the aggressive Anson eagerly sought battle with the French in an effort to erase the stigma of Toulon. He routinely drilled and exercised his fleet. Tactically, Anson, who as a young lieutenant had fought at Cape Passero, was, like Sir George Byng, willing to depart the line given the proper conditions, despite the example that had so recently been made of Mathews.[17]

On 3 May 1747 off Cape Finisterre, Anson's squadron of sixteen ships, including six of the line and fourteen men-of-war mounting more than 50 guns (totaling 938 guns), encountered a weaker French squadron of fifteen warships, only four of them mounting more than 50 guns (totaling 552 guns), escorting a convoy of thirty-eight merchantmen. Part of the French force was bound for Quebec, the rest for India. Anson, after sighting the French, sent up the signal for general chase, not with the intention of engaging, but as a maneuver to close the distance between the two fleets. At a range of about three miles, he made the signal for the line of battle abreast. He then conferred with his second in command, Rear Admiral Sir Peter Warren, who favored an immediate attack. Anson instead made the signal for the line of battle ahead. Somewhere between 1500 and 1600, as the British continued to close, still in line, the French commander signaled his fleet to retire. Anson promptly sent up the signal for a general chase and the race began. By the end of the battle, Anson's ships had captured the entire French squadron and eighteen of the thirty-eight merchantmen.[18]

Given Anson's overwhelming superiority, it is easy to overlook the importance of the battle off Cape Finisterre.[19] But to do so would be to neglect several important points. First, Anson, as well as Warren, evinced no concern about the example of Toulon or of Mathews's fate. Second, while Anson held a decided edge of about two to one in gun power, his Cape Passero–like tactics enabled him to convert that superiority into a crushing victory, unlike many other similarly situated naval commanders. At Barfleur in 1692, for example, Russell's English-Dutch fleet outnumbered Tourville's French force by more than two to one, but failed to capture a single ship. Third, Anson achieved his superiority of force not by accident but as the result of operational excellence and British conceptions of decentralized command. The admiralty's instructions charged the Western Squadron with myriad responsibilities: the protection of the Channel, the blockade of Brest, and the interception of any French detachments or convoys sailing from any of the Biscay ports to the Americas, the Mediterranean, or the Far East. Faced with such burdens, a commander of lesser caliber might have well dispersed his fleet from Ushant to Cape Finisterre, as the admiralty's instructions clearly permitted.[20] But Anson, on his own initiative, kept the bulk of his force concentrated and applied his strength at the right place and at the right time. Why belittle the tactical accomplishments of a commander who, through operational adroitness, brought a superior force to bear upon the enemy? Fourth, because of Anson's efforts before the battle, his fleet had achieved such tactical proficiency that his commanders were not confused by his unconventional tactics.

Anson, either shortly before or shortly after the battle, produced additional fighting instructions that incorporated the refinements introduced by earlier commanders and, in the event of an engagement against a smaller enemy force, "codified Byng's tactics at Cape Passero." On 14 October 1747, armed with a copy of Anson's instructions, Rear Admiral Edward Hawke intercepted yet another well-escorted French convoy off Cape Finisterre.[21]

Hawke's sudden rise to prominence was partly good fortune and partly the result of his aggressiveness. Hawke was the only British commander at Toulon to capture an enemy ship—the *Poder.* He had only recently been promoted to rear admiral and named as second in command to Sir Peter Warren, who had replaced Anson in command of the Western Squadron after First Finisterre. Warren, who was ill, was unable to return to sea and subsequently resigned his command, leaving the very junior Rear Admiral Hawke in charge. Like Anson, Hawke faced the difficult problem of covering the channel and the bay between Ushant and Finisterre with a modicum of force. The temptations to divide the squadron were great, as were the strains of maintaining the ships constantly on station. But Hawke was determined to retain a concentrated force, strong enough to avoid defeat should the main French fleet sortie, and powerful enough to overwhelm any French escorting squadron he might intercept along the convoy routes.

On the morning of 14 October off Cape Finisterre, Hawke's lookouts sighted a large convoy. The French escort consisted of eight ships mounting 538 guns. Hawke had fifteen ships, mounting just under a thousand cannon. But his superiority was less marked than had been Anson's in May. Individually, the French ships of the line were larger and more heavily armed than Hawke's. The British could easily have been outgunned in a close action. And it was to close action that Hawke wished to bring his fleet.

Hawke made the signal for general chase to close the range as quickly as possible. He then directed the fleet into a line ahead on the port tack, with the British parallel to but somewhat behind the French squadron. But, unlike what had happened at First Finisterre, the French, with their heavier ships and the wind gauge, did not break and run but formed line and awaited the British attack. Hawke, although his quarry had not yet "run" as required by the fighting instructions, signaled for general chase. His captains began to work their way along the leeward side of the rear of the French line, engaging the enemy ships as they passed. At least two of Hawke's captains, on their own initiative, clawed their way to windward and ran down that side of the French line, doubling the rearmost ships. By nightfall all but two of the French men-of-war had been taken. Nevertheless, the convoy, including a 64-gun East Indiaman, escaped.[22]

THE BRITISH EXPERIENCE of command and control at sea during the War of Austrian Succession was complex. Toulon was, judging by the number of ships engaged, the major battle of the war, and its inconclusiveness and Mathews's subsequent fate cannot be ignored. But the nature and scope of Anson's and Hawke's victories off Cape Finisterre in May and October 1747 hardly support the notion that Mathews's failure at Toulon and his court-martial and dismissal suspended the aggressive spirit of the Royal Navy. Looking at the history of tactical development during the war makes it clear that Toulon was an aberration. The trend toward decentralization that began with Vernon, but was ignored by Mathews, resumed under Anson and Hawke. They adopted many of Vernon's additional instructions and, unlike Vernon himself, were presented with opportunities to experiment with his revolutionary concepts of command.

Admittedly, both Anson and Hawke did so in settings where they had overwhelming superiority. In both the battles fought off Cape Finisterre only the extent of the British victory, not which side would triumph, was in doubt. The capture of twenty-one French ships-of-war in the two battles was a monumental achievement, a devastating blow to the French navy, and a clear demonstration that the British had developed a tactical system that enabled them to crush inferior enemy squadrons, something previously by no means assured. Cape Passero, and not Malaga, appears to have been the more important precedent for men such as Anson and Hawke.

Anson and Hawke, who were fully aware of the potential for tactical deadlock at sea, also were masters of the operational art. It was at the operational level of warfare where these two commanders struggled, successfully, to bring superior forces to bear upon the enemy. Both men, working under the rather general instructions issued by the admiralty, concentrated their forces and maneuvered them between Ushant and Cape Finisterre in efforts, not just to bring on an engagement, but to do so under the most advantageous circumstances. There is no special glory to be gained in fighting a bloody battle between equal forces, whether on land or sea. The two Finisterre battles were not just tactical victories, they were also demonstrations of successful naval campaigning at the operational level.

Despite Anson's and Hawke's successes, neither the Royal Navy nor any other European navy had solved the problems of command and control at sea by 1748. Decentralization and reliance on the initiative of subordinates had worked during the two Finisterre battles, but could the tactics employed in 1747 be used with equal success in larger engagements between fleets of similar strength? And in such an encounter, would any commander, faced with the prospect of defeat and dismissal should things go awry, have the fortitude to place the fate of his fleet, and his own career, in the hands of his subordinates?

The impulse toward centralization was not dead in European navies. Toulon not only spurred the development of decentralized methods but also stimulated further evolution of techniques to allow a commander to manage a battle by communicating directly with his subordinates. After the Toulon debacle, one anonymous writer suggested that a commander in chief fly his flag from a frigate, instead of a ship of the line, to which each ship in the fleet would send a small boat. In battle, these boats could carry the admiral's directions and subordinates' responses to and from the vessels of the fleet.[23] Most naval commanders of the mid-eighteenth century understood that such a system, akin to those employed ashore by armies, had no place at sea. No commander during the War of the Austrian

Succession appears to have attempted such a procedure (although a variant of the idea was tried during the American Revolutionary War, with little success). Commanders intent on directing their fleets in battle focused instead on the continued development of visual signaling systems.

As commanders such as Vernon, Rowley, Anson, Warren, Hawke, and others developed additional instructions, the corresponding number of signals in use rose. Keeping track of the available signals became an increasingly complex task. By the end of the War of the Austrian Succession, these developments had overtaken the signal book printed privately in 1717 by Jonathan Greenwood. In 1748 another private British publisher, John Milan, produced a new signal book that included the standard instructions, as well as many of the additional ones, arranged and displayed to permit quick and accurate recognition. Milan's was the first British signal book in which the various flags were numbered, a development regarded as one of the initial steps toward a numerary system.[24]

Not surprisingly, the French, who by the time of the War of the Austrian Succession had led the British in the "science" of naval warfare for a half-century or more, were the first to develop a true numerary flag system. French naval historians credit Admiral Bertrand-François Mahé de la Bourdonnais, the naval commander in the Indian Ocean during the war, with the development of such a system for his small squadron. His approach to signaling influenced subsequent developments not only in the French navy but in other navies as well.[25]

Despite evident advances in signaling, these systems did not yet offer solutions to the problems of command and control at sea. Mahé de la Bourdonnais's well-led squadron embarrassed, but failed to defeat, a smaller British force commanded by Commodore Edward Peyton off Negapatam on 25 June 1746.[26]

Admiral Sir Charles Knowles, one of the Royal Navy's more innovative commanders, fought an inconclusive battle with a Spanish squadron off Havana on 1 October 1748. Knowles relied heavily on signals to direct his seven-ship squadron during the engagement, but many of his flag signals were ignored, went unseen, or were misinterpreted. For example, as happened so often in the age of sail, the nominal "van" ships found themselves bringing up the rear, while the "rear" led the fleet. At a critical moment in the battle, Knowles wished his leading squadron to head more toward the Spanish line and made the appropriate signal. The ships that answered the hoist were those of the nominal van division, in the rear of the fleet. As the day wore on and the seven Spanish ships finally

broke formation and attempted to disengage, a frustrated Knowles signaled for a general chase, but without Anson's or Hawke's success. Only a
single Spanish ship was taken and another—the flagship—driven ashore,
where it was later burned. Knowles's inability to destroy the Spanish
squadron was due less to a failure of chase tactics than to his preference
for centralized control.[27]

Knowles, like Mathews, faced a court-martial on a variety of charges,
including cowardice, engaging before his squadron had formed up in
line, and failure to pursue effectively. The court acquitted the admiral,
who had at least won the battle and destroyed about a third of the Spanish squadron, including the flagship. But testimony at the trial indicated
that Knowles's penchant for centralization had prevented a much larger
victory. When he signaled for the general chase, his flagship was damaged
and could not join the pursuit. One of his captains put it succinctly:
"There being no other commanding officer than Admiral Knowles, and
he not conducting the action after dark, no captain without the Admiral's authority could take upon him to hoist the proper lights and take
direction of the squadron upon him, or else we should have been able
with great ease to have cut off [the Spanish] from the Havana."[28] Had
Knowles, before the battle, placed his trust in his captains and empow-
ered them to take action on their own initiative, the victory off Havana
would surely have been more overwhelming.

By the end of the War of the Austrian Succession, then, two distinct
philosophies of naval command and control coexisted in the Royal Navy.
Vernon, Anson, and Hawke epitomized the decentralizers, commanders who were willing to trust their subordinates. Lestock, Rowley, and
Knowles represented the centralizers, who increasingly looked to signals
or some other method of communication to allow commanders to manage battles. The question that remained unanswered was which approach
generated greater fighting power.

For the Royal Navy, the Seven Years' War (1756–1763) began in
much the same fashion as the War of the Austrian Succession—with a
disappointing major fleet action in the Mediterranean followed by an
embarrassing court-martial. Vice Admiral Sir John Byng's failure off
Minorca on 20 May 1756 is reminiscent of Mathews's 1744 encounter off
Toulon. The unfortunate Byng, tried, convicted, and executed for his
failure, was a man "caught in the meshes of the fatal System, and lost."

One historian blamed the line: "The stultifying sanctity of the line ahead had this time helped create not only another naval failure but a martyr."[29]

It is true that at a critical moment in the battle that called for a daring departure from the line ahead, Byng turned to his flag captain, Arthur Gardiner, and commented on the "misfortune" that had befallen Mathews at Toulon. But did Byng's failure off Minorca result from fear of what might happen to him if he departed the strictures of the fighting instructions and the line, or was it caused by his innate caution?[30]

The admiralty's instructions that sent the fleet to the Mediterranean reached Byng at Spithead on 1 April 1756. The instructions were typical for the British service of that day: drafted in a general fashion to meet a variety of contingencies, and heavily reliant on the commander's good sense and willingness to shoulder responsibility. The intelligence upon which the instructions were based was confused. To those in London, there appeared to be a real threat that the French would invade England. Thus the Western Squadron, commanded by Edward Hawke, had to be kept at peak strength, leaving fewer ships available for operations in the Mediterranean. Nor were the British certain about the role of the Toulon squadron in the French strategy. Intelligence revealed that the squadron and a large number of transports were preparing to sail, but to where? The admiralty believed that Minorca was the probable objective of the French effort, but the possibility remained that the expedition might be destined for service in North America.

Accordingly, the admiralty directed Byng to sail first to Gibraltar. There, he could determine what subsequent course to follow. If the Toulon squadron had passed the strait, he was to dispatch reinforcements immediately to Canada. If the French had not passed, he was to conclude that Minorca was in danger. In that case, Byng was to embark a battalion of troops at Gibraltar and "to go on without a moment's loss of time to Minorca, and if you find any attack made on that island by the French, you are to use all possible means in your power for its relief." If Minorca had not yet been attacked, Byng was to sail north and blockade Toulon.[31]

Byng sailed from England for the Mediterranean on 6 April unhappy with his command. He lamented to Augustus Hervey, one of his captains, that Lord Anson, the first lord of the admiralty, had held the best ships for his favorites (he apparently meant Hawke and the Western Squadron) and dispatched only the worst of the navy's men-of-war to the Mediterranean.[32] Byng commanded no storeships, fireships, hospital ships, or tenders. His fleet was also undermanned.

Byng's complaints about Anson were, to an extent, deserved, although it is noteworthy that Byng made no mention to Hervey of the admiralty's concern about a possible French invasion of England. But however justified Byng's disgust with the state of his fleet, his willingness to share his views with his subordinates could not but undermine their confidence. How well were officers and men who were told that theirs were the worst ships in the navy likely to respond in battle? Moreover, while Byng did not publicly voice doubts about the quality of his captains, they must have surmised that in their commander's mind, if Anson had not sent the best ships out with Byng, he probably had not sent the best officers either. In fact, Byng's lack of faith in his subordinates is evident in the organization of the fleet. Byng, who was seconded by only one other flag officer, Rear Admiral Temple West, divided the fleet into two rather than the usual three divisions, in part because he was unwilling to entrust a third division to any of his senior captains.[33]

Reaching Gibraltar on 2 May, Byng learned that the French had already landed on Minorca and were besieging St. Philip's Castle with an estimated 14,000 men. Worse yet, the governor of Gibraltar, Lieutenant General Thomas Fowke, was convinced that Minorca could not be saved and that it was useless and dangerous to strip a battalion of soldiers from the garrison of Gibraltar. Fowke convened his fellow army officers in a council of war and drafted an opinion advising against the detachment. This Fowke presented to Byng, acknowledging that if the admiral insisted, the troops would nevertheless have to go. Rather than accept responsibility for any ensuing trouble in Gibraltar by insisting on following the admiralty's instructions regarding the troops, Byng backed down, all but agreeing with the general's logic in the end. When the fleet finally sailed on 8 May, both Byng and Fowke had accepted the probable loss of Minorca.[34]

Historians who have examined the campaign as a whole, rather than just the battle that the French and British fleets eventually fought on 20 May, have concluded that Minorca was not irretrievably lost when Byng sailed from Gibraltar. The French troops on the island were suffering from disease, especially dysentery, and were heavily dependent on supplies arriving by sea from France. A composite battalion of British redcoats would not have been able to lift the siege of the castle, but troops deposited elsewhere on the island could have forced the French to divert troops from the siege. Nor was the presence near the island of a strong French naval squadron an insurmountable obstacle. Byng's primary objective was to lift the siege and relieve St. Philip's Castle. The destruction of the French fleet was not a necessary precondition. If Byng, while avoiding battle, could have interdicted the transport of supplies to the French army, the siege would have faltered. Faced with that threat, the French naval commander, Roland-Michel Barin, marquis de la Galissonnière, whose instructions directed him "to perpetually occupy himself" with the "preservation of the forces which His Majesty destines for this expedition," would have faced a Hobson's choice: risk the fleet to save the army, or jettison the army to save the fleet. Given the French penchant for defensive operations, forcing de la Galissonnière into an offensive engagement would surely have worked to British advantage. Thus the strategic situation confronting Byng did not force him to accept the tactical offensive. By doing so he made not only a tactical error but also a strategic blunder of enormous magnitude.[35]

Byng reached Minorca on 19 May. Early the next morning the two fleets sighted each other and prepared for battle. Byng's fleet consisted of thirteen ships of the line; de la Galissonnière's twelve. As the two lines neared, Byng held the weather gauge, thanks to a last-minute shift in the direction of the wind. The fleets passed each other on opposite tacks, the French heading toward the west-northwest, the British toward the south-southeast. Byng's choices were limited. Under the seventeenth article of the Fighting Instructions, as soon as the British van came abreast the French rear, Byng's fleet should tack, either in succession, starting with the rear ship, or simultaneously. Byng signaled his fleet to tack in succession, but delayed the maneuver so that his ships would approach the French line at an oblique rather than a right angle, and would be able to return fire as they closed the range. Such an approach was not entirely novel: in 1688 Lord Dartmouth had issued instructions to his fleet outlining just such a scheme.[36]

The nineteenth article of the instructions now took precedence: the British fleet was to engage in a formal battle van to van, center to center, and rear to rear.[37] But Byng had two problems. First, before the British tacked the two fleets had not been on parallel tracks and, as a result, the distance separating the two lines varied from about a mile at the British van to between three and four miles toward Byng's rear. If the fleet was to engage as a unit, and not piecemeal, Byng's captains would have to adjust their courses to compensate for the differing distances. Second, as his flagship, the *Ramilles,* bore down on the French, Byng noted that de la Galissonnière, who feared that the British planned to concentrate their attack against his rear, had thrown all aback, so that his ships were just making headway. As a result, Byng's van was rapidly pulling ahead of the French van, but was not closing the range between the two fleets. Twice Byng made the signal for the leading ship to turn a point to starboard, hoping its captain would get the hint to adjust his course and close on the French; twice the ship complied and turned a point, but no more. Byng gave up and continued to close the range with the enemy, hoping that his subordinates would surmise what he had in mind. Eventually the ships of the van did notice Byng's course change, but instead of timing their approach so that the entire fleet could join battle together, they ran down toward the French at about the same angle as their commander in chief. So the van engaged at greater distance than Byng had hoped, while the center and rear of the fleet were still out of range.

Nevertheless, as was so often the case in the age of sail, when opposing ships did engage at anything that could be described as close range, effective British gunnery drove French ships out of formation. Several of de la Galissonnière's ships dropped off to leeward, but with the signal for the line still flying from the *Ramilles,* none of the British captains were able, or willing, to follow up their success. They remained in line, with no opponent to engage.

Between 1400 and 1500 the sixth vessel in the British line, the *Intrepid* 64, had its foremast shot away and lay crippled, blocking the path of the following ships. Byng had two options: he could lead his line to leeward of the *Intrepid,* bearing down on the French; or he could pass the damaged ship to windward, which would lead his center and rear away from the enemy. Captain Gardiner wanted to take the *Ramilles* to leeward, but Byng refused. "You see, Captain Gardiner," the admiral replied, "that the signal for the line is out and that I am ahead of the *Princess Louisa* and [the *Trident*], and you would not have me as Admiral of the Fleet run down as if I was going to engage a single ship. It was Mr Mathews's misfortune to be prejudiced by not carrying his force down together which I shall endeavour to avoid."[38]

With this cautious decision, Byng not only gave up his chance for a close, and potentially victorious, engagement, but also presented de la Galissonnière with an opportunity for a counterstroke. As successive British ships worked their way to windward around the *Intrepid,* a gap opened in the British line and Byng's van lay exposed. If de la Galissonnière could direct his center and rear to windward, Byng's van would be doubled. Fortunately for the British, de la Galissonnière failed to take advantage of the situation before Byng once again closed up his line. "The maintenance of a rigid line," a French naval historian noted, "was still considered as the supreme goal of naval tactics." With the day growing late, and no prospect for victory in sight, the French disengaged, ending the battle.[39]

For several days after the engagement, Byng remained off Minorca repairing his fleet. He made no attempt to aid, or even to communicate with, the garrison at St. Philip's Castle. The French, licking their own wounds, kept their distance and did not resume the fight. Then on 24 May Byng convened a council of war—but what followed was more a council of fears. Byng presented five carefully phrased questions. Would another naval action relieve the island? The answer was no. If the French were driven off, could the British fleet lift the siege? It could not. Should an accident befall the fleet, would Gibraltar be endangered? It would. And would not yet another attack on the French endanger the fleet? It would. That being the case, should not the fleet proceed to Gibraltar? So it should. And so it did, leaving the garrison without hope of relief.[40]

In fact, Byng would not have had to risk another battle to hinder the French siege of St. Philip's Castle. The British were well positioned to conduct a campaign against French communications. And the 14,000 French soldiers on Minorca could not have been easily transported to Gibraltar in the presence of Byng's fleet. The most dangerous course was to allow the French to secure Minorca, thus freeing their army for an operation against Gibraltar. Many French historians lament their country's failure to capitalize on the victory at Minorca, a triumph that ultimately gained them little more than a name for a celebratory egg and vinegar-based sauce—mayonnaise.[41]

The reports of Byng's failure to relieve Minorca reached London on 14 July. Everywhere that summer of 1756 the British seemed to face defeat. In North America the French, who the previous summer had ambushed and destroyed Major General Edward Braddock's expedition near Fort Duquesne, followed up their victory with successful attacks against Forts Oswego and George. In India the pro-French Bengal nawab captured Calcutta and placed his prisoners, who had been promised quarter, in the infamous "Black Hole." These setbacks angered the British public, fostered the search for a scapegoat, and undermined the position of the prime minister—Thomas Pelham-Holles, Duke of Newcastle. Since Braddock and the commander of the Calcutta garrison were dead, much of the opprobrium for the war's failures fell on Byng and the government. Irate mobs burned and hanged the admiral's effigy. Newcastle was more than willing to see the public's anger focused on a man he considered a "cowardly admiral" who deserved "trial and condemnation." But if Newcastle hoped that such a sacrifice might save the ministry, he was soon disabused. The king asked the Duke of Devonshire and Sir William Pitt to form a new government. Newcastle's political demise did little to improve Byng's position. The new ministers, who had railed against the incompetence of their predecessors and fed the anger of the mob and of the king, were poorly positioned to plead for clemency for Byng once he was convicted by the court-martial.[42]

Byng's death ought not to obscure his failures as a commander in chief. And those failures ought not to be attributed to rigid adherence to outdated instructions. Julian Corbett commented:

> Few actions have been so misconceived in their tactical significance as [Minorca]. It has been studied almost entirely to see whether Byng did or did not deserve his hard fate, and the unhappy admiral has been stamped as an unfortunate bungler hide-bound in the stereotyped "Fighting Instructions," and without a spark of tactical initiative. That he was a man devoid of the character that makes a great commander is certain, but the idea that he was not a scientific tactician fully in touch with the developments of his time is as certainly an error. The injustice done to him in this way is no doubt due to the belief that naval tactics at this time were stagnant, and Byng has been used to personify that stagnation. But we have only to examine the battle closely with the new lights that are available to see that tactics were developing on normal and continuous lines of progression, and that Byng himself was in the forefront of that movement.[43]

Why then was Byng court-martialed? The reasons had less to do with his tactical shortcomings than with his strategic failings: he died not because he lost the battle, but because he failed to do his utmost, as instructed, to relieve Minorca. The trial focused on his tactical handling of the battle because "there was no Article of War on which he could have been brought to book" for having failed to relieve the garrison. Nevertheless, Byng's handling of his fleet was not entirely hidebound nor stereotypical. His opening maneuver was an intelligent revision of the standard instructions. Corbett wrote that Byng, "instead of adhering pedantically to the stereotyped method of the old Instructions, did attempt a modification of considerable merit." But, as Michael Lewis noted, the concept, "though not new . . . was old enough to be unfamiliar, and, not being in the Permanent Instructions, was liable to be misunderstood by the average Captain."[44]

There were fresh ideas aplenty in the minds of British naval officers, including John Byng. But if a commander expected, or hoped, to depart the standard instructions during the course of a battle, he had to share his ideas beforehand with his subordinates, as Vernon, Anson, and Hawke had done. This Byng failed to do. From the start of the campaign he expressed dissatisfaction with his fleet and his officers. Note his unwillingness to trust any of his senior captains to command a third squadron, a decision that did little to bind him to the men he led.

Perhaps Byng's principal misfortune was that he commanded Britain's Mediterranean fleet in the Royal Navy's opening engagement of the Seven Years' War. It is tempting to attribute Byng's failure at Minorca and Mathews's at Toulon to restrictions imposed by the line ahead and the fighting instructions. But the most obvious common denominator that can explain, not only the two defeats, but also subsequent British successes, is that Toulon and Minorca were both "first battles"—initial engagements in which, historically, events rarely go according to plan.

BYNG'S DEFEAT at Minorca, like Mathews's at Toulon, led not to more stultifying sanctification of the line ahead, but instead to the continued evolution of tactics and novel approaches to command and control. Most British and French commanders tried to fine-tune their fighting instructions to permit superior efficiency in battle, albeit with limited success. The French pioneered advanced signaling systems, although their use in battle failed to compensate for the lack of fighting power often manifested by French ships, commanders, and crews.[45] The admiral who achieved the greatest success of the Seven Years' War continued in the tradition of Admiral Vernon. Edward Hawke, the victor at Second Finisterre in 1747, remained a man willing to depart the line and to further decentralize command in battle.

Both Anson and Hawke continued where they had left off at the end of the War of the Austrian Succession. Anson, who in 1758 commanded the Channel fleet, issued additional instructions including one alerting his subordinates to the possibility that in the midst of an engagement their commander might "haul down the signal for the Line of Battle," in which case every captain was to "use his utmost endeavours to take or destroy such Ships of the enemy, as they may be opposed to, by engaging them as close as possible, and pursuing them if they are driven out of their Line."[46] Hawke, who replaced Byng in the Mediterranean in July 1756, adopted a similar approach to command and control. After taking over the squadron, he addressed his senior captains, among them Augustus Hervey, who later recalled: "Then [Hawke] made us a fine speech that he was determined to run close up to [the French], and that the honour of our country required we should do our very utmost to destroy these ships and he did not doubt that we should, with a great deal of all this sort of stuff." The following year, Hawke, commanding British naval forces in the ill-fated Rochefort expedition, formalized his ideas for close action. Crossing out the old article thirteen for engaging the enemy in the prescribed linear order of battle, he instead instructed his subordinates to engage the enemy "as close as possible" and not to fire until within "pistol shot."[47]

In May 1759 Hawke succeeded Anson in command of the Channel fleet and went further yet. In an additional instruction he informed his captains that after leading the fleet into action at fairly close range, he would make the signal to engage and then "haul down the Signal for the Line," at which point his subordinates were to engage the nearest enemy ship, as closely as possible, sink or destroy it, then move on, "as you shall judge most necessary, to join the closest battle at hand." These alterations of the "permanent" instructions were not the actions of an apostate. Hawke first altered article thirteen when Admiral Edward Boscawen, one of the lords of the admiralty, was serving as second in command of the fleet; Hawke's second alteration occurred at a time when he assumed that Anson, another lord of the admiralty, would soon arrive and take command. As Ruddock Mackay, Hawke's biographer, wrote: "It can hardly be doubted that the amended form of Article XIII had been approved by the Admiralty."[48]

Hawke was not a tactical innovator. He did not pen naval tracts replete with diagrams of formations for attack and retreat. Nor did he develop magnificently organized and illustrated signal books. Hawke was a command innovator who increased the fighting power of his fleet by rejecting centralization. He won battles by combining his belief in British tactical superiority at close range with an inclination to depart the line ahead and a willingness to share his tactical conceptions with his subordinates. That Hawke failed to secure a place comparable to Nelson's in the pantheon of naval heroes may have been the result of little more than "the failure of any French admiral to stand up to him in an unambiguous fashion."[49]

Hawke's victory at Quiberon Bay on 20 November 1759 provides an example of naval command and control at the strategic, operational, and tactical levels. The very fact that Hawke was able to keep his fleet concentrated and battle-ready at sea in the late autumn was a command achievement of the first magnitude.

Despite their "victory" at Minorca, the French suffered a string of defeats in the early years of the Seven Years' War. While the Prussians, with limited financial and military support from London, did their best to check Louis XV's armies on the continent, the British blockaded and raided the French coast, attacked French commerce, and began to isolate and harvest France's colonial possessions. "The year 1758 had teemed with military misfortunes for maritime France," the French naval historian Georges Lacour-Gayet wrote. "To the repeated descents of the English on coasts of the Saintonge, the Cotentin, and Brittany, had been added the loss of Louisbourg, which portended that of Montreal."[50]

Louis XV, much like Philip II two centuries earlier, recognized that the strategic center of his opposition lay in England. "The course of events led one," Lacour-Gayet noted, "to the idea of a landing in the British islands; because it was the true means to revenge ourselves with a single stroke, and to finish the war."[51]

While the invasion plan had many fathers, the French foreign minister, Étienne-François, duc de Choiseul, was its driving force. The final plan was rather complex. The Toulon squadron would escape the Mediterranean and race north to Brest to join up with the main French fleet. This combined force would sail back to the south and rendezvous along the Breton coast with a flotilla of transports carrying an army of 20,000 men commanded by the duc d'Aiguillon. The invasion fleet would proceed to the Firth of Clyde and land the troops in Scotland. The battlefleet, comprising thirty-five to forty ships of the line, would then proceed around the northern tip of the British Isles into the North Sea. Simultaneously, a smaller force would conduct a diversionary raid against Ireland. These moves, the French expected, would draw the Royal Navy in pursuit and away from the main thrust: the transit by a second force of 20,000 men, commanded by the Prince de Soubise, from Ostend to Malden in Essex. Once ashore the prince's army would be but a short march from London.[52]

The French plan appeared impressive on paper, but it was virtually condemned to failure by the absence of any effective means of command and control at the operational level, as were the earlier invasion schemes hatched in Madrid and Paris by Philip II and Louis XIV. As

Sir Julian Corbett noted, while the French devised their plan in a "thoroughly scientific spirit," it was, nevertheless, "a soldier's plan." French naval historians have also been critical, one terming the plan "chimerical," another "too complicated." Moreover, Corbett wondered, if the French considered their fleet, while encumbered with a convoy, powerful enough to contend with that of the British, why not just seek an engagement in an effort to gain, if only temporarily, command of the sea to clear the way for all the invasion forces?[53]

In addition to the command and control obstacles inherent in the plan and the philosophical shortcomings of Louis XV's naval strategists, the French faced practical problems. The principal difficulty was to unite, in spite of likely Royal Navy opposition, their Mediterranean and Atlantic naval forces at Brest, a task that had been a stumbling block in the 1689–1690 campaign and was now complicated by British possession of Gibraltar. Worse yet, for logistic reasons, the French could not concentrate both their fleet and the duc d'Aiguillon's army at Brest. The units assigned to the duke assembled in the Morbihan, while the troop transports designated to carry the army to the Clyde gathered in Quiberon Bay. Assuming the French could even unite their two squadrons, the fleet would have to escape the British blockade twice—first at Brest, and again at Quiberon Bay.

As events developed, the Royal Navy frustrated the movements of both the French Mediterranean squadron and the Brest fleet. The only element of the invasion plan that succeeded was the diversionary landing in Ireland.

Admiral Edward Boscawen sailed on 14 April to the Mediterranean to join the British squadron blockading Toulon. At that time the admiralty possessed no clear intelligence indicating that the French were serious about invading England.[54] When Boscawen joined the squadron of thirteen ships of the line and a dozen frigates in May, he established a close blockade off Toulon and cruised aggressively against French commerce. But without a nearby supporting base because of the loss of Minorca, Boscawen could not maintain his fleet off Toulon and eventually had to retire to Gibraltar to refit.

When Boscawen reached Gibraltar on 3 August new orders from the admiralty awaited him. The French were planning to invade England and the Mediterranean squadron would probably play a part in that plan. According to Boscawen's new instructions, if the Toulon squadron escaped the British blockade, he was to leave seven ships of the line and frigates in the Mediterranean and to sail for England with the rest of the squadron.

Boscawen faced a difficult choice. The admiralty clearly hoped that he could keep the French Mediterranean squadron in Toulon. Ought he, then, to sail posthaste to that port to reestablish a close blockade? What if the French had taken advantage of his absence and had already sailed? If so, there was a good chance that the British squadron would pass its quarry en route and would reach Toulon only to find the harbor empty, while the French sailed through the Gut—the Strait of Gibraltar—and into the Atlantic. Boscawen chose instead to remain at Gibraltar with the fleet and to deploy his frigates in a patrol line guarding the approaches to the strait.

Boscawen made the correct decision, because he could not have reached Toulon before Admiral M. de La Clue Sabran, commanding the French Mediterranean squadron, left the naval anchorage with ten of the line, two 50-gun ships, and a pair of frigates on 5 August. La Clue intended to sail southwest from Toulon and then to hug the North African coastline, timing his approach to enter the Strait of Gibraltar at night. While he hoped he could evade the British, La Clue doubted that his long-blockaded squadron could maintain its order along the entire 1,700-mile cruise to Brest. Accordingly, he instructed his captains, assuming the squadron avoided interception, to put into Cadiz after clearing the strait.

La Clue approached Gibraltar on the afternoon of 17 August. One of Boscawen's frigates sighted the squadron off Ceuta and rushed to warn Boscawen. It was evening, about 2000, when the scout reached Gibraltar. Boscawen and many of his senior officers were at a dinner ashore; many captains had parties of men on the Rock; and most of the ships had their sails detached from the yards and stowed below (unbent). The sight of his own flagship unmooring and preparing to sail alerted Boscawen to the emergency. By 2200 he was under way with eight of the line. By 2300 they were leaving the bay. "It was a splendid feat of seamanship," Corbett wrote, "such as only seamen who know the Rock can fully appreciate. In less than three hours a fleet of the line, moored in a difficult harbour, with sails unbent and the admiral absent, had got to sea at night. It would be hard to surpass it in all our annals."[55] While the British were too late to prevent French passage through the strait, Boscawen headed west hoping to intercept the French as they turned toward the northwest on a course to weather Cape St. Vincent, the southwestern tip of Portugal.

As La Clue's squadron cleared the strait, he noted that his ships were still in remarkably good order and decided not to stop at Cadiz but to continue toward Cape St. Vincent. He slowed the flagship to allow his squadron to form up and made the appropriate night signals. But fearing that his ships' lights might serve as beacons for the British, he extinguished the stern lights on the flagship and the others followed suit. Shortly thereafter, the five ships of the line and three frigates of the French rear guard, having either failed to see or misunderstood La Clue's signals, lost contact and sailed toward Cadiz.

Boscawen, with eight ships of the line in hand and Rear Admiral Thomas Broderick's additional five about an hour behind, pursued La Clue's main body throughout the night. The next morning British lookouts sighted seven French ships of the line about thirty miles from Cape St. Vincent. The French sighted the English as well, but mistook them for their own rear guard. La Clue slowed to allow the ships to catch up, but as the day grew brighter, and Broderick's ships became visible as well, La Clue became concerned. He directed that a private signal be made to the unidentified vessels. When the signal went unanswered, he recognized his mistake and made for Cape St. Vincent.

Boscawen, although Broderick was still a good distance off, knew he had to engage the French before nightfall. At about 0800 he made the signal to chase and the race was on for the cape. At about 1430 the leading British ship finally engaged the sternmost of La Clue's men-of-war. As additional ships reached the battle, they doubled the rear of the French squadron. While this tactical concentration was effective, Boscawen, with Broderick's ships also coming up, knew that he held a marked numerical advantage and, to make the victory complete, needed to engage the French van as well. But there was no appropriate instruction in the book and Boscawen's signals to individual ships to make more sail were not understood by their captains.

In the confused and vicious fighting, the French handled their ships fairly well. In the afternoon engagement the British captured only a single French vessel. A second French man-of-war, hard pressed, broke away from the engagement and escaped, ultimately to the Canaries. A third did likewise, heading to Rochefort. La Clue and his four remaining ships escaped and continued on course throughout the night. But as the sun rose the next day, La Clue, now heavily outnumbered, found himself trapped along the Portuguese coast. With his flags flying, he ran his flagship onto the rocks. One of his captains followed his example, and the other two anchored along the Portuguese coast, hoping that the British would either respect Portuguese neutrality or be deterred by the cannon of a nearby coastal battery. The British paid little heed to legal niceties or

Portuguese marksmanship. Royal Navy parties burned the two French ships on the rocks and captured the two anchored in Lagos Bay.

Initially Boscawen was unsure of the extent of his victory, for he could not account for seven of La Clue's ships of the line. But the French Mediterranean squadron was finished as an effective fighting force, and as a component of the grand plan for an invasion of England.

The defeat at Lagos did not put an end to the French invasion plan. Hopes for success now focused on the Brest fleet commanded by Marshal (Vice Admiral) Hubert de Brienne, comte de Conflans. Although Conflans had doubts about the prospects of a successful campaign, Louis XV and his ministers directed him to break out of Brest, sail to Quiberon Bay, chase off the small British squadron observing the transport fleet, rendezvous with the transports, and then escort the armada to the Clyde. But to carry out these orders Conflans would have to outwit one of the Royal Navy's most aggressive and skilled commanders—Admiral Sir Edward Hawke, the victor of the second battle of Cape Finisterre.

Despite the high stakes and the fact that Hawke's fleet, unlike Boscawen's squadron, was deployed within dispatch distance of London, the admiralty refrained from micromanaging Hawke's operations. "Once the campaign was under way" the editor of the admiral's papers noted, "Hawke communicated the way in which he proposed to conduct it. In nearly every case his proposals were accepted."[56]

When the campaign began in May 1759, French intentions remained unclear to the British, and so did the best course of action for the British fleet arrayed against the main enemy fleet at Brest. Should Hawke operate from a safe English Channel anchorage such as Plymouth, Torbay, or Portsmouth, or maintain a close blockade from Ushant, a small island just northwest of Brest? A distant blockade would help keep the fleet battle-ready, but would permit the French to escape Brest almost at their leisure. A close blockade would make a French escape from Brest more difficult, but would impose a potentially exhausting strain on Hawke's ships and crews.

Hawke determined to "keep a strict watch" over the French ships at Brest, establishing a punishing close blockade of the French navy's main base.[57] When the outlines of the French plan became clearer, and the enemy's transports began to concentrate in the Morbihan, Hawke detached a small squadron commanded by Captain Robert Duff to keep a close eye on that force as well.

Throughout the spring, summer, and fall, Hawke kept his fleet off

Ushant, rotating ships back to England to refit and revictual, while frigates kept watch on the French. When the westerly winds blew especially hard, he led the fleet to the safe anchorage at Torbay, knowing that those same winds made it impossible for the French to leave Brest. As soon as the winds relented, Hawke returned to sea as quickly as possible to resume his watch off Ushant, lest the French use the opportunity to escape. He maintained this routine, in spite of the threat posed to Duff's ships first by La Clue and later by a French West Indian squadron that Hawke knew was on its way back to France and might make landfall anywhere in the Bay of Biscay. Had La Clue's ships evaded Boscawen or the West Indian squadron made landfall off the Morbihan, the French might have trapped and destroyed Duff's ships in Quiberon Bay.

But the French West Indian squadron sailed to Brest, where its arrival set in motion the final implementation of the invasion plan. Driven by a strong westerly gale that had forced Hawke's fleet back to Torbay, the French Caribbean squadron entered Brest on 7 November. Conflans, aware that the squadron's ships would need refitting and that Hawke had been driven from his post, stripped the arriving ships of their veterans, dispersed the men throughout his ships, and prepared to break out of Brest as soon as the wind permitted. On 14 November the winds finally shifted more to the east, allowing Hawke to leave Torbay and head for Ushant. But on 17 November, before the British regained their station, Hawke learned that "the same wind which carried us from Torbay carried Conflans from Brest." Hawke later wrote that "the instant [he] received the intelligence" he deduced that the French would head for Quiberon Bay and "directed my course thither with a pressed sail."[58]

As Hawke assumed, Conflans was headed south—for the Morbihan, where he had to link up with the transports in Quiberon Bay. When the French reached the approaches to the bay late on 19 November, Commodore Duff's squadron was taking on stores, oblivious to the danger. Fortunately for the British, Hawke had sent the frigate *Vengeance* ahead to alert Duff. When lookouts spotted the frigate's warning signals, Duff ordered his ships to slip or cut their moorings before they were trapped in the bay. The commodore headed west to join Hawke.

At dawn the next day Duff sighted a fleet, but it soon became apparent that the ships were French. His position was perilous. Conflans, hoping to crush the small enemy squadron, pursued, with his flagship, *le Soleil Royal,* leading the way. But shortly before 1000, though the heavier French ships were gaining, Conflans signaled an end to the chase. His lookouts had spotted more sails to the west, which could only be those of the enemy's main fleet.

Hawke's ships had fought their way through the stormy night toward Quiberon Bay. At dawn on 20 November Hawke, unsure of his position and well aware of the dangers of a lee shore, sent Captain Richard Howe in the *Magnanime* ahead to find the coast while the fleet's other frigates scouted ahead for the enemy. At about 0830 the frigate *Maidstone* signaled that it had the enemy in view. Hawke pressed on, in gale-like conditions, his ships carrying far more sail than their French counterparts in the forty-knot wind.

From the moment he first sighted Hawke's fleet, the French commander had no intention of risking a battle. Destroying Duff's weak squadron was one thing; accepting battle with Hawke's fleet another. Conflans, even before he left Brest, "had resolved to avoid a general battle." Lacour-Gayet noted that Conflans "thought only of placing his whole squadron in safety, although it was not appreciably inferior in number." The fleets were fairly evenly matched: twenty-one French ships of the line against twenty-three British. But, as Conflans himself later wrote, conditions caused him "to take the route to the Morbihan, since the wind, given our position, would not allow me to put into any other place, and I believed that if I entered [Quiberon Bay] first with twenty-one vessels, the enemy would not dare to challenge me there, despite his superiority, that itself would hamper his movements in such a confined place." Conflans ordered his ships to form in line behind the flagship as he led them into the bay toward the planned rendezvous with the transports.[59]

When Hawke saw the French begin to edge toward the entrance to the bay, he considered the movement an attempt to disengage, sufficient cause under the fighting instructions for a commander of his temperament to order a chase. A white flag with a red cross soon flew from Hawke's flagship, and three cannon made their reports. By signal flag, Hawke directed his seven leading ships to form in a line and to engage the French before they could round the Cardinals, rock outcroppings at the southwestern entrance to the bay. With the remainder of the fleet, Hawke raced to join the fray. Thanks to the superior seamanship of Hawke's crews, the British closed the range. At about 1430 Hawke heard gunfire ahead as his leading ships engaged the French rear. His flagship promptly ran up a red flag—the signal for "every ship in the fleet to use their utmost endeavour to engage the enemy as close as possible."[60]

Hawke's decision placed Conflans in a difficult position. His fleet was strung out along a line eight to ten miles long, and slightly more than half of the fleet had yet to weather the Cardinals and enter the bay proper. To further complicate matters, just as the British engaged, the wind, which had been blowing from the west-southwest, shifted to the west-north-west, and the French could no longer hold their course to the north as they rounded the Cardinals. Conflans's rear division faced disaster.

But Hawke wanted more than a partial victory. While his van engaged the enemy rear, he led the rest of his fleet into the bay. Most of the British ships had no charts, the weather was atrocious, visibility was poor, and the situation was confused, but Hawke reasoned that the French knew where they were going and that as long as the British men-of-war remained close to the enemy ships, they would be at no greater risk than the French ships they pursued. The ensuing action was without doubt one of the most forbidding battles in the annals of maritime warfare. Eighteenth-century naval engagements were horrific enough without men having to confront the prospect of death at the hands of the elements. High winds made navigation and maneuver difficult. Sailors strained to work the guns on the canted decks of badly heeling ships of the line, whose lower gun decks, nearly awash, were mostly shut tight to lock out tons of seawater that could send even a large man-of-war to its destruction.

When Captain Augustus Keppel's *Torbay* 74 began its duel with Captain Armand-Guy de Coetnempren de Kersaint's *Thésée* 74, both commanders ordered their lower-deck guns run out despite the heavy weather. Water poured through the open gunports as the British gunners released their broadside into the French ship, but Keppel quickly and deftly swung the ship into the wind to reduce the heel while his men closed the ports. Kersaint, not to be outdone, mimicked Keppel's maneuver, but the ocean cascaded in through the open gunports. *Le Thésée* filled and capsized before Kersaint and his crew could react. Of his 650 men, only 22 survived.[61]

At about 1700, with nightfall approaching, both commanders recognized that the battle would soon have to end. Hawke concluded that further pursuit would be foolhardy, and the signal to anchor replaced that to engage on his flagship. But Conflans, eager to escape, sought to make his way out of the bay under the cover of darkness. In the confusion, one of his own ships crashed into the port side of his flagship, *le Soleil Royal* 80. Not long after the two had fended off, yet another French liner smashed into the flagship's starboard side. As Hawke's modern biographer, Ruddock Mackay, noted: "Conflans had had his fill of seamanship for one day. He dropped anchor." Unbeknownst to the French commander, several of his ships had nevertheless escaped and only eight were still in the bay.[62]

When dawn broke the next morning, le Soleil Royal lay anchored in the midst of the British fleet. Seven other French men-of-war were anchored inshore. Hawke knew he had a chance to crush his enemy; Conflans knew he faced defeat.

Unfortunately for Hawke, the wind blew even harder than it had the previous day. When the crew of Conflans's flagship cut her cable, Hawke directed the Essex 64 to pursue. But the wind blew both vessels onto the rocks. Hawke had no choice but to remain at anchor and to watch helplessly as the other seven French ships of the line, as well as all of Conflans's frigates, lightened ship by jettisoning their guns and attempted to escape over the bar into the Villaine River. All managed the feat except for one, la Inflexible 64, which was wrecked. Not until the following morning did the weather improve sufficiently to allow Hawke to resume his attack. But by then there was little left to do. The British salvaged what they could from the two ships they had lost on the rocks and burned the two stranded French men-of-war, including Conflans's flagship.

Quiberon Bay was not a "decisive" victory. The bulk of the French fleet survived the battle. The French lost seven ships—two sunk, one captured, and four wrecked. Hawke had two ships wrecked. British casualties totaled between 300 and 400; French about 2,500. But during the campaign, including losses at Lagos and Quiberon, the French had lost a dozen ships of the line. Moreover, Hawke's triumph ended the immediate prospect of an invasion of England and rendered the French fleet hors de combat for the next year. The defeat of the French navy's two main squadrons also ensured that the British would be able to complete their conquest of Canada without fear of intervention. As Lacour-Gayet wrote, Quiberon Bay was "the tomb of the French navy during the reign of Louis XV."[63]

Many have discounted the lessons of Lagos and Quiberon. Castex wrote that the battles "teach us nothing about the subject of the line. They were, moreover, combats of a very particular aspect, of the hunter and the hunted." True enough. But from the perspective of command these were important battles, not because of the willingness of the British to abandon the line, but because both Boscawen and Hawke relinquished control once the battles began. In this Hawke foreshadowed Horatio Nelson. "Hawke's captains had developed such a highly aggressive spirit throughout the long blockade," Tunstall noted, "that they did not require special signals to urge them on." Admittedly, Hawke possessed both quantitative and qualitative advantages, but other British admirals often held similar advantages but failed to exploit them.[64]

CHAPTER FIVE

The Advent of Numerary Signaling Systems

*I*N THE WAKE of the Seven Years' War there transpired one of the great enigmas in the history of naval warfare: Great Britain's victorious Royal Navy looked to its oft-defeated French antagonist for guidance. British naval officers turned their backs on the successful improvisational command styles of Vernon, Anson, and Hawke and embraced the highly centralized visual signaling systems pioneered by the French. The British did have a great deal to learn from the "scientific" French. The latter were far more advanced in a variety of areas, including ship construction and what could be termed ocean science. Many British officers considered French warships superior in design and construction to comparable English models. But during the three decades after the Seven Years' War, while British naval officers exhibited little interest in the ship-construction manuals published in Brest and Paris, they devoured French tactical manuals and signal books, despite the fact that in terms of fighting the Royal Navy, whatever its shortcomings, had demonstrated time and again its inherent and marked superiority.

Why such an attraction? The Royal Navy's civilian masters and senior commanders were, for the most part, children of the Enlightenment to whom the more "scientific" approach of the French held a natural appeal. And for a handful of high-placed admirals, most notably Richard Lord Howe, frustrated by the shortcomings of the fighting instructions and unnerved by the risks taken by men such as Edward Hawke at Quiberon Bay, the development of state-of-the-art signaling systems offered the comfortable prospect of centralized control from the quarterdeck of the flagship.

By the middle of the eighteenth century an abiding conviction in the power of reason had taken hold, not just in Paris, but throughout much of Europe. In Britain an Enlightenment "attitude of mind" was evident, and not just in the upper class, as the American colonists demonstrated in 1775. Enlightenment concepts had taken root in Britain and, as the historian N. A. M. Rodger noted in *Wooden World*, "the Navy, considered as a society in miniature, was very much a microcosm of British society in general."[1]

Given this intellectual environment, it is not surprising that British admirals looked across the Channel for solutions to their problems. Since the late-seventeenth-century pioneering works of Admiral Tourville and Father Hoste, the French had led Europe in the development of a rational, "scientific" approach to naval warfare. Throughout the eighteenth century French scientists and naval officers penned numerous treatises on things maritime—hydrography, ship construction, navigation, gunnery, and maneuver. A Royal Navy captain, Richard Kempenfelt, observed in 1780 "what an extraordinary genius prevailed amongst the French . . . to push up everything to the summit of perfection." He added:

> I say they had no sooner effected this prodigy of forming a navy without the apparent requisites, than they had the quickness of discernment immediately to see (what we have never been able to see yet) the great advantage that would result in sea fights from a system of naval tactics . . . They judiciously perceived that military tactics might be adapted to naval tactics in the arrangement and evolutions of fleets. They set to work about it, and completed it so well as to exhaust the subject, and so were as astonishingly rapid in perfecting the disciplines and manoeuvres of a fleet as they were in forming one.[2]

While there can be no argument that the navy of France was more militarily formal and "professional" than that of Great Britain, that "professionalism" did not necessarily translate into success. Raoul Castex, one of the harshest critics of the French navy of the age of sail, noted the paradox that the navy's repeated failures of the eighteenth century coincided with "an intense and well-intentioned effort, aimed at the improvement of the institution of the navy, and with a view toward which all zeal and talents were focused." "It is necessary to conclude *a priori*," he wrote, "that the application brought to the theoretical study of maritime questions was an exercise in a very special sense, speculative or scientific, distanced from the realities of war."[3]

The French Académie de Marine, for example, established in Brest in the 1750s under the direction of Sébastien-François de Bigot, vicomte de

Morogues, was not a school, but a society of scientists, academics, and naval officers, analogous to the Académie Française. The writings of the members of the Académie de Marine reflected scientific and Enlightenment methods at work. The French naval historian Georges Lacour-Gayet claimed that the efforts of the academy's members prepared the French navy for its "victories in the American war." But Castex linked the work and the personnel of the academy to the naval debacles of the Seven Years' War. Morogues was one of the architects of the invasion plan that led to the disastrous defeats at Vigo and Quiberon. To Castex, the work of the academy remained isolated from the more important problem facing the French navy: its inability to win battles. Of 274 academy papers identified by Castex, only 2 dealt with strategy and tactics, the same number as concerned agricultural topics.[4]

The notion that the French navy had achieved Kempenfelt's "summit of perfection" was rooted in the logical attractiveness of French methods and manuals rather than in a more empirical study of their performance in battle. As Admiral Pierre-André de Suffren, one of the most aggressive French naval commanders, wrote: "A military ought to distinguish itself by its actions, not by its writings."[5]

Nonetheless, enlightened British naval officers were drawn to the outward forms of French professionalism, while they attributed the shortcomings of the French navy not to its manuals but to its officers' character, or lack thereof. What these British officers failed to understand was that the French developed their well-thought-out tactical concepts and supporting visual signaling systems to serve a fleet that generally fought on the defensive.

IN THE DECADES following the Seven Years' War, British printers began to translate and publish French texts, including those of Father Hoste; Mahé de la Bourdonnais, a pioneer in the development of numerary signaling systems; Morogues; Jean-François de Cheyron, chevalier du Pavillon; and Jacques Bourdé de Villehuet. Kempenfelt himself, "convinced that the best immediate course for the Royal Navy was to copy the French system of signals," translated some of the works of Mahé de la Bourdonnais into English. As the Royal Navy's commanders digested these imported works, they began to experiment with, and ultimately to adopt, modified versions of the numerary signaling systems preferred by the French.[6]

Early naval signaling systems linked individual flags, differentiated by placement, to individual responses. For example, a green flag at the mizzen peak indicated that the fleet was to weigh, whereas the same flag at the fore peak might indicate that the fleet was to close its order. As the number of signals grew over the decades, the number of flags grew as well, until the British by the late eighteenth century were using as many as forty or fifty flags. Numerary systems, in contrast, used a basic set of ten flags, each representing a number from 0 to 9. Hoisting the three flags for 2, 7, and 5, for example, indicated #275 in the signal book. Thus ten flags could display a thousand signals. Additional flags were used as repeaters and designators, but the numerary system could convey far more information with fewer than half as many flags as older systems.

Admiral Richard Lord Howe was in the forefront of this transition. As a junior officer during the Seven Years' War Howe demonstrated an early interest in visual systems and issued signals of his own to the small squadrons he commanded. For Howe, Hawke's victory at Quiberon Bay demonstrated not the effectiveness of his chief's decentralized approach to command, but rather the need for a system of signals to control the movements of the fleet. After the war, Howe served as one of the lords of the admiralty and chose as "the great object of his study" the development of "a system of signals" for the Royal Navy.[7]

In the more than a decade of peace that followed the Seven Years' War, French and British naval commanders had little opportunity to experiment with new instructions and signaling systems in combat. As a result, much of the work remained theoretical. The French, in fact, took a step backward, adopting in 1773 not Mahé de la Bourdonnais's true numerary system, but instead a somewhat confusing arrangement developed by Pavillon. The British likewise struggled with their instructions and signals. During maneuvers in the summer of 1768 they tested a few new evolutions supported by an expanded system of signaling. In the meantime, Howe, working ashore, refined his ideas and about 1770 sent his first full set of signals to the printer.[8]

These peacetime developments broke little new ground. The revised instructions adopted by Royal Navy admirals, including those issued by Howe, codified the tactics employed by commanders such as Hawke. Tunstall considered Howe's 1770 work a "conservative production" that gave "official sanction to instructions with which the navy had been familiar for twenty years or more, while actually excluding some of the more useful."[9] Nevertheless, the limited experience gained in the late 1760s and early 1770s taught the British that visual signaling systems markedly improved the maneuverability of the fleet under sail. One major question remained unanswered: Would the system work in battle?

In the Royal Navy, the movement toward greater centralization of command accelerated with the start of the American war in 1775. While the rebellious colonists posed no major naval challenge to the British fleet, the admiralty had to concentrate a larger force in North American waters to support the operations of the army ashore, to blockade the coast, to safeguard maritime lines of supply, and to hunt down cruisers and privateers. In 1776 the command of this fleet went to Howe.

On the very day he reached New York—12 July 1776—Howe issued a new set of signals and instructions that has been called "one of the most important documents in the whole history of naval tactics." Howe's instructions were revolutionary in that the signal book, and with it a highly centralized approach to command and control, displaced the fighting instructions, though still unofficially. Henceforth signal books would increasingly dominate British naval tactics. "It was the indefatigable hand of Lord Howe," Sir Julian Corbett remarked, "that dealt [the fighting instructions] the long-needed blow and when the change came it was sweeping."[10]

Howe's "Signal Book for the Ships of War," while still not numerary, was a comprehensive tactical system in which the author appended an explanatory book of instructions to the now more important signal book. The instructions clearly demonstrate that Howe had one of the Royal Navy's keenest tactical minds. They were more flexible than those they replaced and became even more so as he revised his manual. Adherence to the line ahead remained, although certain instructions allowed individual captains to depart the line and even to act on their own initiative.[11]

Howe, despite his commitment to signaling systems, never turned his back entirely on the experience he had gained under Hawke. Unlike contemporaries such as Admiral George Brydges Rodney and Kempenfelt, Howe searched for a design that would leave some initiative to his subordinates. In fact, as he experimented with signals over the next twenty years, he allowed an increasing amount of initiative to his captains. As early as July 1777 he issued a set of "additional instructions" to his fleet. In the first article he admonished his officers that too "strict adherence [to signals] may on many occasions be found prejudicial to the service; by restraining captains from taking advantage of the favorable incidents which may occur in the progress of a general action; it is the object of these instructions to facilitate the means of improving such opportunity by an authorized deviation from those restrictive appointments." For example, in the eighth article of the instructions Howe "permitted" his captains, when coming to close action with the enemy, to take station either to windward or to leeward "as they see most suitable for boarding or closing with them at advantage to disable them more speedily."[12] By implication, ships availing themselves of this "opportunity" would have to pass through the enemy's line. Howe later formalized this concept in his 1790 signal book and employed, with mixed success, just such a maneuver at the Glorious First of June 1794.

The most important, if often overlooked, aspect of Howe's contribution to naval tactics was that he placed near-total responsibility for the control of the fleet in battle on the shoulders of the commander in chief. While the fleet was now better able to undertake a given evolution, under Howe's centralized scheme that evolution could begin only if the commanding admiral made the appropriate signal. But what if, as Vernon had asked nearly forty years before, circumstances prevented the commander in chief from properly judging the situation, or, worse yet, from making a signal? There also was the question of interpreting the instructions that explained the signals, a problem that dogged Howe throughout his years in command. Brian Tunstall, after praising one of Howe's instructions, admitted: "If there is some doubt about this interpretation, it arises from Howe's own wording which, though somewhat clearer than his worst utterances, is nevertheless ambiguous." Not that Howe was the sole offender. The British naval historian John Knox Laughton wrote in his introduction to the papers of Lord Barham: "It is not going too far to assert that nine-tenths of the miscarriages and blunders made in the eighteenth century arose out of the inability of the commanding officers to give an intelligible order, or of the commanded to understand one if given. Howe was, of course, an extreme instance of this."[13]

Another set of problems facing Howe involved the interrelated elements of space and time, critical factors recognized long ago by Vernon. Given the slow speed of ships under battle sail, was there enough time in a day to arrange one's fleet in a formal order, maneuver into a position of advantage, and then fight a battle to conclusion?

Two years passed before Howe had an opportunity to test his new system in combat. In the spring of 1778 France intervened in the American war and in April dispatched its Toulon squadron, commanded by Vice Admiral Charles-Hector Théodat, comte d'Estaing, to North America with a dozen ships of the line and five frigates. The French reached the Delaware in July and sailed north to New York, where Lord Howe's outnumbered fleet lay moored near Sandy Hook in a strong defensive position. D'Estaing chose not to press his advantage and instead sailed farther north to Rhode Island where he agreed to cooperate with American ground forces in an attempt to besiege a British garrison on Conanicut Island.[14]

Alerted to the French move, Howe, now reinforced, sailed north in pursuit and arrived off Narragansett Bay on 9 August. Still at a disadvantage, though not in the number of ships as much as weight of broadside, he was not prepared to assault the stronger French fleet at anchor. Fortunately for Howe, d'Estaing, alarmed by the enemy's unexpected arrival, cut his cables and headed out to sea.[15] Howe pursued, willing to risk a battle beyond the confines of the harbor. Throughout 10 August Howe maneuvered his outgunned command in an effort to gain a favorable position. As night fell, both fleets were heading south.

At daybreak on the eleventh, British lookouts could see the French to windward, about three miles distant. Howe switched his flag to the *Apollo* 32. From the quarterdeck of the frigate, which sailed throughout the day in a somewhat exposed position between the two fleets, Howe made the signals for his ships. All morning and well into the afternoon the two forces maneuvered until the day grew late, a gale began to blow, and the French disengaged. Because of the high seas, Howe was unable to return to his flagship and spent the night in the *Apollo,* which lost her fore and sprang her mainmast in the gale. The admiral awoke the next morning to find that he had lost contact, not only with the French, but also with most of his own fleet.[16]

For Howe, who had already decided to resign his command, the campaign proved to be a disappointment. His arrival off Rhode Island and d'Estaing's questionable decision to abandon his position in Narragansett Bay secured Howe's principal objective—the relief of Britain's 6,000-man Rhode Island garrison.[17] But the admiral had also hoped to destroy the French squadron, and to prove the value of his new system of signals.

Howe drew several lessons from the experience, although he might well have drawn others. His instructions seemed to work well enough and the fleet responded to his signals. His plan to control his force from a frigate, a scheme that had been tried during the 1768 maneuvers,[18] was an innovative idea, attempted later in the war by other British and French commanders. While Howe himself never again commanded from a frigate, he remained convinced of the efficacy of the method.[19] He understood that in his system the already problematic question of the location of the commander in chief posed an even greater problem. At sea there were no hills from which a commander could survey the battlefield and dispatch orders. Once the battle began, a commander positioned in the center of his line might find himself lost in a shroud of smoke. Not that Howe could have stayed on the *Apollo*, sailing between the two lines, had an engagement actually begun. But as he saw it, time, not his signal book, had been the major impediment to his plans. But if the long summer day had been too short to bring two fleets into contact, of what use was his ability to maneuver? Sixteen years would pass before the admiral would have another opportunity to test his ideas in combat.

FOR GREAT BRITAIN, the arrival of d'Estaing's Toulon squadron in American waters not only marked the transition from a mostly local struggle to suppress a colonial rebellion into a wider and ultimately global conflict, but also presaged the strategic and operational difficulties under which Royal Navy commanders would labor until the peace of 1783. The French navy, whatever its shortcomings, was at its best during the 1778–1783 war; Great Britain's Royal Navy was beset by troubles, and not solely those related to its tactics. Quite simply, there were not enough ships to meet all the demands placed on the Royal Navy. At the strategic level, as Piers Mackesy concluded in his study of the American war, "the British fleet was never strong enough to impose a sustained blockade" as had Hawke, for example, during the Seven Years' War.[20] Operationally, the French were able to send powerful fleets and squadrons, such as d'Estaing's, to North American, Caribbean, and Indian Ocean waters. As a result, at the tactical level Royal Navy commanders rarely possessed more than numerical parity with their French, and later Spanish, foes.

Thus when the French entered the war in the spring of 1778 they held the strategic initiative. Nevertheless, they were not prepared to launch an invasion of Great Britain at that time. French planners had developed myriad schemes to invade the British Isles, but considered such a move premature until Spain entered the war with its large fleet.

When the conflict began, the British were uncertain about French intentions, especially the destination of d'Estaing's Toulon squadron. The prime minister, Frederick Lord North, and John Lord Sandwich, first lord of the admiralty, did not expect an immediate invasion, but Vice Admiral Augustus Keppel, commander of the Channel fleet, did expect one and insisted on the reinforcement of his command. Since the Royal Navy's senior leaders, including Sandwich, Howe, and Keppel, believed their service lacked sufficient force to establish a close blockade, their short-term options were limited: reinforce the Channel fleet or send a squadron to Gibraltar to prevent d'Estaing from leaving the Mediterranean. The ministry's political weakness led North and Sandwich to choose the safest course—reinforcing Keppel.[21]

The French foreign minister, the comte de Vergennes, was not an advocate of an all-out invasion and had no intention of launching an assault with even limited goals until Spain added the weight of its fleet to the scales already tipped against Britain. In the interim, Vergennes adopted a plan drawn up by the navy. The main fleet from Brest would demonstrate in the vicinity of the Channel, not to seek battle but to hold the attention of the Royal Navy in Europe, while the Toulon squadron quit the Mediterranean and crossed the Atlantic, giving France at least temporary naval superiority in American waters.[22]

In the summer, Vice Admiral Louis Guillouet, comte d'Orvilliers, sailed from Brest with thirty-two of the line under orders to avoid battle but to remain at large for at least thirty days. D'Orvilliers doubted that he could do both, but sailed nonetheless. Keppel's Channel fleet, now reinforced and thirty ships of the line strong, sailed in pursuit. The French, holding the wind advantage, avoided battle for several days but, as d'Orvilliers had foreseen, an inevitable shift of the wind finally brought the two fleets into contact on 27 July 1778 off the island of Ushant, about thirty miles west and somewhat north of Brest. The resultant battle was a confused, inconclusive, daylong encounter. The French suffered higher casualties among their crews; British ships suffered greater material damage, especially to their rigging. In the afternoon, when both commanders had opportunities to concentrate force against a portion of their opponent's fleet, first Keppel, then d'Orvilliers, and then Keppel again lost control of their forces and failed to bring on a "decisive" engagement. In London, as after the battles of Toulon and Minorca, there were recriminations: charges and countercharges followed by a pair of courts-martial—one of Keppel, the other of his recalcitrant subordinate Vice Admiral Sir Hugh Palliser.

One can attribute the lack of results at Ushant to the two navies' adherence to the "stultifying" line ahead, but the important lessons of the battle have little to do with linear formations. Like the battles at Toulon and Minorca, Ushant was the first major naval battle of the war. As Captain John Jervis wrote soon after Ushant: "Two fleets of equal force can never produce decisive events, unless they are equally determined to fight it out, or the commander-in-chief of one of them *bitches* it so as to misconduct his line." The main problem that plagued both Keppel and d'Orvilliers was not their adherence to the line but the failure of their command systems. At critical junctures during the battle, the system of control—relying on visual signals and messages passed to subordinates in frigates—proved woefully unresponsive. Haze and smoke often blocked the views of the commanders in chief. Their signals often were ignored, went unseen, or were misinterpreted.[23]

The stifling effect of a system of command reliant on visual signals was also evident at the July 1779 battle of Grenada. After d'Estaing's failure at Rhode Island, he retired to Boston and refitted his fleet before sailing in November to the West Indies, where French forces had already captured Dominica. The arrival there of his powerful French squadron placed the British on the defensive, though at first they weathered the storm. In December the British captured St. Lucia, where a well-handled British squadron of seven ships commanded by Rear Admiral Sir Samuel Barrington fended off d'Estaing's dozen of the line, while ashore the island's garrison repulsed a French counterattack.[24] Not until the spring of 1779 did the French achieve any marked successes. In June d'Estaing learned that the British fleet, now commanded by Vice Admiral Sir John Byron, had escorted a convoy northward. The French sailed from their anchorage at Martinique and landed a small force that captured St. Vincent. Emboldened by his victory, and reinforced by the arrival of a squadron from Brest, d'Estaing led his fleet and transports farther south to attack Barbados, but because of contrary winds decided to strike at Grenada instead. When Byron learned that the French were out, he raced south, but too late to intercept. Informed that the enemy had landed a force on Grenada, Byron sailed on, encumbered by his own convoy of transports, in an effort to relieve the besieged garrison of Georgetown. On the morning of 6 July he surprised the French at anchor in St. George's Bay.

Byron ordered a general chase, although his twenty ships of the line were in a somewhat ragged order and three of the liners had been detached to protect the convoy because of his shortage of frigates. Sensing that he had a chance to trap and destroy d'Estaing's sixteen ships in the harbor, he was intent on bringing on an engagement.

Unfortunately for Byron, he was operating under three critical misconceptions. Georgetown had already fallen, and the town's fort and cannon were in French, not British hands. D'Estaing commanded not sixteen but twenty-four ships of the line. Worse yet, the French fleet, though a picture of disorder in the harbor, responded with unusual and, to Byron, surprising celerity as the able and aggressive Suffren led the van out of the harbor. By the time Byron recognized that he had arrived too late, was outnumbered, and had failed to trap the French, his leading ships were in trouble. He signaled for the disordered fleet to reverse course, and ultimately to form into a line, though to continue to engage closely. There followed some desperate fighting, but by midafternoon Byron's fleet was clearly beaten.

The French had won the battle; the initiative lay with d'Estaing. As the two fleets sailed toward the northeast, Byron feared that the longer French line might double his own or that d'Estaing might detach his frigates and send them after the British convoy. From his flagship, d'Estaing surveyed the situation and at 1545 signaled for his fleet to tack and to sail back toward St. George's Bay. Three British ships of the line, heavily damaged earlier in the day, lay directly in the path of the French fleet, but, to the astonishment of many in both commands, d'Estaing's men-of-war sailed by, content to exchange a few desultory broadsides before returning to the bay without having taken as much as a prize.[25]

Grenada is of interest in part because Byron departed the line, lost the battle, and suffered neither execution nor court-martial: so much for any stultifying effect. Byron, believing he had caught an inferior and disordered fleet at anchor, promptly attacked. He failed because of inaccurate intelligence and an unusually quick French reaction. The British, despite their positional and numerical disadvantage, performed fairly well. They suffered about six hundred casualties; the French nearly a thousand. And although Byron had thrown out Howe's signal book and resurrected the old fighting instructions, the divisions and ships of the fleet cooperated better than had Keppel's at Ushant, or would Howe's at the Glorious First of June in 1794. At a critical stage of the battle of Grenada, as Byron's fleet wore (brought its stern across the direction of the wind) and reversed course as it tried to re-form, a gap opened between Barrington's van and the center. Rear Admiral Joshua Rowley, commanding the liners with the convoy, "saw Barrington's three ships unduly separated and doubtless visibly mauled. Instead, therefore, of blindly following his leader, he cut straight across to the head of the column to support the

van,—an act almost absolutely identical with that which won Nelson renown at Cape St. Vincent. In this he was followed by the *Monmouth*, 64,
[from Rear Admiral Hyde Parker's rear division] the brilliancy of whose
bearing was so conspicuous to the two fleets that it is said that French officers after the battle toasted 'the little black ship.'"[26]

One could portray d'Estaing's inability to make the most of the victory to his refusal to depart the line ahead. But the factors that constrained d'Estaing were not to be found in the realm of French tactics,
but in that of operations and strategy. French admirals sought not victory
over their opponent's fleet in a quest for control or command of the seas,
but support for a successful operation ashore. D'Estaing's problem was
not an overly strict adherence to the line, but his unwillingness to risk the
sole prize he had to show for his efforts in American waters—Grenada.[27]

WHILE BYRON escaped censure, his failure at Grenada did nothing to
hinder the march of the new orthodoxy of centralized control within the
Royal Navy. After Howe's resignation, Richard Kempenfelt became the
point man for the effort to adopt a French-style signaling system.

Kempenfelt, though still only a captain, was well suited and positioned to serve as an advocate for the new system. As Corbett noted,
Kempenfelt had a "philosophical intellect ripened by long and active service and profound thought." He had traveled in France before the war
and was thoroughly versed in the most recent French tactical concepts.
He also had the proper service and political connections. He was well
known and respected by Lord Howe and maintained a regular back-
channel correspondence with Rear Admiral Sir Charles Middleton, later
Lord Barham, then comptroller of the navy. He was also the first captain
of Great Britain's most powerful and important naval force—the Channel fleet, commanded by the aged and infirm Admiral Sir Charles Hardy.
Kempenfelt, appointed to the post in May 1779, wrote to Middleton the
following August: "There is a fund of good nature in the man [Hardy],
but not one grain of the commander-in-chief. I hear it often said the salvation of Britain depends upon this fleet. I never hear the expression but
I turn pale and sink. My God, what have your great people done by such
an appointment!"[28]

Given Hardy's deficiencies, Kempenfelt—a mere captain—shouldered
tremendous responsibility within the Channel fleet and garnered well-
deserved prestige from the admiralty. But his rise to prominence was not

solely tied to Hardy's shortcomings. Given the trend toward professional-ism and ever more centralized methods of command and control, many admirals, even competent ones, relied heavily on the assistance and judg-ment of their first captains. Sailing-age navies, unlike their army counter-parts, had not developed a general staff system. As one commentator noted: "The nature of ships, the nature of naval combat, and the nature of naval preparation for battle is such that naval *general staff* systems have not evolved anywhere."[29]

Flag officers, be they admirals or commodores—senior captains placed, or temporarily, in charge of a fleet or squadron—usually had "flag captains" to look after the flagship, thus allowing the commander in chief to focus his attention on the fleet. Small staffs, including an admi-ral's secretary and several clerks, assisted the admiral. By the middle of the eighteenth century, the British admiralty frequently assigned, or an overworked admiral might himself appoint, a "first captain" to help com-mand large fleets. In the spring of 1777, for example, Lord Howe moved Captain Roger Curtis from the *Senegal* sloop to the flagship, the *Eagle,* freeing the *Eagle's* captain, Henry Duncan, to act as "Adjutant to the Fleet and assistant to the Admiral." When the much larger Channel fleet put to sea in 1778 a flag officer, Rear Admiral John Campbell, served as Keppel's first captain.[30]

At times the "first captain" or "adjutant" also served as the "flag cap-tain." In 1780 Captain Walter Young was both the captain of Rodney's flagship and the admiral's first captain, whereas two years later Sir Charles Douglas was first captain only, while another officer actually commanded Rodney's flagship.

The duties of the first captain, also known as the captain of the fleet, were ill-defined. Not until January 1782 did a royal proclamation settle a century-old dispute about the relative seniority within a fleet of its first captain. King George III decreed that in a fleet of twenty or more ships the captain of the fleet, whatever his actual rank, would hold the effective rank of a junior flag officer, a major consideration when it came to the division of prize money. First captains reviewed the admiral's incoming and outgoing correspondence and often conducted back-channel com-munications with senior members of the admiralty, as did both Young and Douglas while serving Rodney. So situated, a senior captain or junior admiral with ambitions for advancement was likely to develop his own opinions. Since his responsibilities were not fixed, the extent of his influ-ence within a fleet depended upon a variety of circumstances, especially his relationship with the commander in chief. Not infrequently, the more senior flag officers who commanded the divisions of the fleet were jealous or mistrustful of first captains. Sir Charles Douglas, whose gunnery reforms contributed significantly to the British victory at the Saintes in the Caribbean in 1782, could well be considered the consummate first captain, but Hood distrusted Douglas, considering him "very weak, and irresolute" and "no more fit for the station he fills than I am to be an archbishop."[31]

During the American war the position of first captain continued to evolve into what could be termed that of a proto-chief of staff (minus much of the staff). But this evolution was by no means orderly. Kempenfelt, writing to Middleton in April 1780, described the position's myriad but undelineated responsibilities in terms that American vice presidents would probably find familiar: "I don't suppose that there is an office in the whole state that is considered to be of any consequence, whose duty is so vague and undetermined as that of an admiral's first captain. If I ever had a prescribed duty, it has been lost and forgot with the disuse of the office."[32]

Whatever the uncertainties, Kempenfelt certainly made the most of his tenure as first captain. While serving in the Channel fleet, he vigorously pursued his vision of reform. Kempenfelt, like Howe and other reformers in the Royal Navy, never intended to copy the tactical methods employed by the French. "Their reform," Corbett noted, "went far deeper and wider—mere methods of attack were not its characteristic." The reformers were interested in the means by which the French initiated and executed their varied evolutions.[33]

Kempenfelt believed the British navy suffered from a "deficiency of discipline for regular manoeuvring and fighting." After noting that the French strength had long been "theory" while the Royal Navy had been "superior in practice," he warned Middleton: "They are in a way to remove the difference in the last, and how will the comparison then stand between us?" For Kempenfelt, the obvious response to the qualitative improvement of the French navy was to introduce "theory" into the British. He wished to meld the seeming responsiveness of the French signaling system with more aggressive and innovative British tactics. Through his efforts he not only brought French-style sailing orders and modified numerary signaling to the Royal Navy but also introduced, or reintroduced, a series of tactical evolutions, including an instruction to break the enemy's line, to the Channel fleet during his tenure as first captain.[34]

Signaling systems lay at the core of Kempenfelt's reforms. From his correspondence it is clear that he preferred French systems, specifically that of "M. de la Bourdonnais," even regarding the use of triangular pendants instead of rectangular flags. Nevertheless, he had to make do with the resources at hand and worked to improve the existing system of signals. "I therefore followed in a great measure Lord Howe's mode," Kempenfelt wrote in March 1781, "he being a popular character. The night and fog signals we use are almost entirely his, and both extremely defective."[35]

While Kempenfelt's tactical and signaling reforms were significant and his intentions good, he remained oblivious to the dangers of overreliance on visual signaling systems. He had no interest in allowing subordinate commanders, or worse yet individual captains, any exercise of initiative. He wrote to Middleton in January 1780:

Fleets, as well as armies, require rules to direct their several motions. In the movement of a fleet to perform any evolution, the way of doing it with most regularity, facility and expedition, is to be preferred; and tactics lays down rules for this purpose, by which every ship knows what they have to do when any evolution by signal is ordered, by which the whole of the fleet act together in concert, to the same end, by the same method; *and nothing is left arbitrarily to the captains,* who, without some determined rule known to all, by taking different methods for the execution, would embarrass each other.[36]

The Channel fleet, despite its centrality in British strategy, did not fight another major battle during the American war, and neither Kempenfelt nor Howe, who took command of the fleet in May 1782, had an opportunity to test the new signaling systems in battle. For Great Britain this was no doubt fortunate, since after the dismissal of Keppel a series of mediocrities commanded the Channel fleet, including Admirals Hardy (May 1779–May 1780) and Sir Francis Geary (May 1780–September 1780), and Vice Admiral George Darby (September 1780–March 1782). Hardy, with his able first captain Kempenfelt, survived the most serious invasion scare of the war during the summer of 1779 after Spain's entry into the war. Bad weather and the half-heartedness of the French, who were more interested in the West Indies, and the Spanish, who had their eyes set on Gibraltar, did more than the Royal Navy to save England from invasion. The only notable action fought by a detachment of the Channel fleet took place in December 1781 off Ushant, where Kempenfelt, by then a rear admiral commanding a force of twelve of the line, intercepted nineteen French ships of the line escorting a large convoy with ships bound for the Caribbean and the Indian Ocean. Kempenfelt deftly avoided an engagement with the more powerful French fleet, cut out fifteen merchantmen, and dispersed the convoy.[37]

In May 1782 Howe took command of the Channel fleet and the possibility of greater reform and more decisive action beckoned. With Howe's assent and support, Kempenfelt introduced the Royal Navy's first truly numerary signal code. The Channel fleet spent an active summer, cruising and demonstrating off both the Dutch and French coasts, with Howe occasionally maneuvering against stronger fleets using Kempenfelt's signaling system. In August the fleet returned to Spithead and prepared to escort a large relief force to Gibraltar. On 29 August 1782, as crews worked to slightly heel over Kempenfelt's flagship, the *Royal George* 100, to repair a leak just below the waterline, the ship suffered a structural collapse and sank, taking down "about 900 souls," including women, children, and Rear Admiral Richard Kempenfelt.[38]

NOT ALL COMMANDERS appreciated the efforts of Howe and Kempenfelt to introduce reforms. Under the old system the British had fared very well. And, as events over the next thirty years would demonstrate, there were good reasons to be suspicious of the newfangled and centralized system of signaling and maneuver. Kempenfelt came face to face with such skepticism one day in 1780 during Admiral Geary's tenure of command of the Channel fleet. Kempenfelt was exercising the fleet, directing its evolutions with his new signals, when lookouts sighted what they incorrectly believed to be an enemy squadron. Amid the "hurry and confusion of preparing for battle," the signals "somehow or other were not managed so well as when made at more leisure. Geary at last grew impatient, and going up to Kempenfelt, and laying his hand gently on his shoulder, exclaimed with a good-natured earnestness, 'Now, my dear Kempy, do, for God's sake, do, my dear Kempy, oblige me by throwing your signals overboard, and make that which we all understand—"Bring the enemy to close action!"'"[39]

It is easy to view Geary, a man too old and infirm to command the fleet, as little more than recalcitrant. But his instinct to toss the signals overboard and to come to close action was rooted in his service with a friend and colleague who had achieved notable success with close action and was still committed to it—Edward Hawke. In September 1780, before Geary sailed, Hawke wrote to him:

My good friend, I have always wished you well, and have ever talked freely and openly to you upon every subject relative to the service. Recollect some of these passages; and for God's sake, if you should be so lucky as to get sight of the enemy, get as close to them as possible. Do not let them shuffle with you by engaging at a distance, but get within musket-shot if you can. That will be the way to gain great honour, and will be the means to make the action decisive.[40]

Hawke was right, although the question of how two fleets could best be brought to close action remained subject to debate. Hawke preferred an approach that relied on the initiative of his subordinates; Howe and Kempenfelt advocated a system in which the commander directed the movements of the fleet. Which system was the better?

The struggle for America, despite its being the most intense period of naval warfare up to that point in modern history, failed to resolve this fundamental question.[41] Rear Admiral Thomas Graves, the only Channel fleet man to command in a major battle—fought at the mouth of the Chesapeake in September 1781—lost what was perhaps the most significant engagement of the conflict. The Royal Navy's most significant victory, off the Saintes in April 1782, was won by Admiral Sir George Brydges Rodney, who rejected Howe's system in favor of tinkering with the old system of instructions and signals.

After Howe returned to England in 1778, Byron commanded the ships in American waters and fell back on the old instructions. His successor, Vice Admiral Marriot Arbuthnot, adopted a compromise form— a signal book laid out in a fashion similar to Howe's, but in which the signals were keyed to the old standard instructions, not to any of the new evolutions. Later, after Rear Admiral Thomas Graves arrived with reinforcements from the Channel fleet, Arbuthnot amended his signal book to include most of Howe's additions.[42]

The two naval historians who have looked most closely at questions of tactics and doctrine—Sir Julian Corbett and his son-in-law, Brian Tunstall—took somewhat different tacks to explain the depth and significance of the influence of the Channel fleet on the British fleet in American waters. After all, Graves's failure in the Chesapeake hardly served as a testimonial to the value of the work of Howe and Kempenfelt. In Tunstall's view, "Graves identified himself with the obscurantism of Arbuthnot's regime and made no attempt to introduce the new ideas germinating in the Channel fleet. Though he had persuaded Arbuthnot to accept a few Channel fleet items in the previous year."

Corbett, in contrast, wrote that Arbuthnot's final instructions "show a strong trace of Channel Fleet influence." Whatever the truth, when Arbuthnot returned home, Graves, unaware that he was to be superseded by Rear Admiral Robert Digby, assumed the command and continued to use Arbuthnot's signals, issued them to Rear Admiral Samuel Hood when his division joined Graves at New York in late August 1781, and fought under them at the battle in the Chesapeake.[43]

As Graves sailed south for the Chesapeake, the war in the American colonies was about to reach its climax. Britain's main southern army, commanded by Lieutenant General Lord Charles Cornwallis, following its Pyrrhic victory at Guilford Courthouse in North Carolina, had retreated into Virginia and was awaiting reinforcement or withdrawal at Yorktown, on the York peninsula. Unbeknownst to the British, Cornwallis's army had become the focal point of Franco-American strategy for the late summer campaign of 1781. The American general George Washington and the commander of the French contingent in America, Lieutenant General Jean-Baptiste-Donatien de Vimeur, comte de Rochambeau, had settled on a plan to trap and destroy the British force. The main Franco-American army would march overland from New York to Virginia. The comte de Barras's French naval squadron at Rhode Island would sail south with the siege train, while the main fleet under the command of Vice Admiral François-Joseph-Paul, comte de Grasse, carrying 3,000 troops, would sail north from the Caribbean, both for the Chesapeake. The allies would thus concentrate their land and naval forces at the decisive point, isolate Cornwallis, and force his surrender.

The plan was excellent, although akin to many of the French schemes drawn up for the invasion of England, schemes that had routinely gone awry because of the impracticability of exercising effective command and control at the strategic and operational levels of war, missteps on the part of commanders, bad weather, or British interference with the movements of any one of the cogs in the plans' machinery. As Don Higginbotham commented in his history of the American Revolution: "The cooperation between Washington, Rochambeau, de Grasse, de Barras, Lafayette, and the Virginia authorities in a difficult and complex undertaking was virtually unparalleled in the history of eighteenth-century warfare. The allies' strategy was based upon certain calculated risks such as the ability of de Barras to escape from Newport, the unwillingness of [British General Sir Henry] Clinton to strike at the greatly reduced American forces outside New York, and the hazards of de Grasse's leaving the French West Indies unprotected."[44]

It was morning on 5 September 1781 when the opposing fleets came into view. Visibility was unusually good and the ships could be made out at a great distance. At about 0800 a French frigate spotted several vessels approaching the mouth of the Chesapeake. At first de Grasse assumed they belonged to the Newport squadron, but as nineteen ships of the line crossed the horizon, he realized they were British. Graves's lookouts did not sight the French fleet until 0900. Graves, like his French counterpart, at first thought the ships anchored along the Virginia coast might belong to de Barras's squadron, but with twenty-four French ships of the line in view, he realized that de Grasse's West Indian fleet had already reached the Chesapeake.

Four hours after the first sightings, the two fleets were still too far distant to engage. The British sailed on toward the southwest, the wind blowing from the north-northeast. At noon, as the tide began to flow out of the bay, the French cut their cables and headed out to sea. Twelve miles still separated the fleets. At 1300 Graves made the signal to form the line, heading west into the Chesapeake. He maintained this course until his center division was abreast of the French van, then signaled his fleet to wear. Now heading east, the British line was parallel to and ahead of the French.

The range was still too great to engage, but Graves, with the weather gauge and running ahead of the French fleet, was in an advantageous position. If his ships turned to starboard, they would close the distance, but not at so great an angle that they would be unable to fire as they approached the enemy's line. But there was a problem—no number in the signal book corresponded perfectly with the required maneuver. Graves chose signal X—"If at any time I would have the leading ships in the line alter the course to starboard, I will hoist a flag half red, half white at the main top masthead"—despite the ambiguity of its language. Were the ships to turn simultaneously, or in succession as they reached the leading ship's turning point? In an effort to make his intentions clear, Graves had his flagship turn to starboard in concert with the leader, but the other ships missed the cue and continued on course, prepared to turn in succession. Graves repeated the signal twice more, hoping that the repetition would indicate to his subordinates that he sought a different response, but to no avail. Frustrated, Graves signaled individual ships and directed them one by one to turn to starboard. This method worked, but wasted precious time and ensured that the van division closed more rapidly with the French than did the rest of the outnumbered fleet.[45]

After an hour the two lines were still well apart. At 1546 Graves made the signal to form the line at one cable and followed that with another for close action, perhaps hoping that his subordinates would close the remaining distance on their own. When they did not, at 1611 he lowered the signal for the line ahead, afraid that it might "interfere with the signal to engage close." There was still no response from his fleet. A few minutes later the twelfth ship in the British line luffed, turning toward the wind, and began its cannonade, but at a distance well beyond effective range and in a manner that placed the ships to the rear at risk of being hit by friendly fire if they continued on course. At 1622 Graves's flagship once again ran up the signal for the line and hauled down that for close action. Five minutes later, after his ships had re-formed, the signal for the line came down yet again, and that for close action went up.[46]

Finally, at about 1630, the British van began to engage, although the center and rear divisions were still out of range. In an effort to bring his whole fleet into action, Graves attempted to lead by example and turned his flagship, the *London* 98, directly toward the French line. But one of the ships ahead of Graves luffed and fired, forcing the *London* to turn away to avoid being hit. As a result, the ships of the British center division failed to close as quickly as they might have. Also, the commander of Graves's rear division, the usually aggressive Rear Admiral Sir Samuel Hood, did not notice that the signal for the line was down until about 1730, by which time it was too late for his division to play any part in the battle. By 1815 only ten of the nineteen British ships of the line were in action against eleven of their twenty-four French counterparts. Given the contours of the developing engagement and the lateness of the day, Graves recognized that there was no point in pressing the battle. At 1823 the *London* raised the signal to form the line and lowered that for close action. By 1830 the two fleets had ceased firing and were drawing apart.[47] Lord Charles Cornwallis's British army was abandoned and left to face defeat and surrender.

Most historians fault Graves for his adherence to the line. "Perhaps," John A. Tilley speculated, "Graves's mind . . . was so infested with the sanctified doctrine of the line of battle and the Fighting Instructions that he was incapable of imagining how to fight in any other manner." For Russell F. Weigley there was no need to speculate: "The dead hand of the line ahead gripped a British fleet once more." Michael Lewis concluded: "In the whole history of sailing-warfare no rigid adherence to the line was ever more fatal than that of Thomas Graves on the afternoon of the 5th September, 1781."[48]

Graves was not a tactical genius. He might well have handled his fleet more aggressively, and more successfully. But he had just had the command thrust upon him in July when Arbuthnot returned to England. Fourteen of his nineteen ships had come north from Rodney's Caribbean fleet under Hood, who, while junior in seniority, was a year older and far more experienced than Graves, who had never commanded a fleet or even a ship in a major battle. And Graves had not had time to discuss with Hood and his captains the differences in signaling and doctrine between what had been Arbuthnot's and Rodney's squadrons.

What, then, might Graves have done? He could have ordered a general chase and thrown his fleet against the French van, or even ignored de Grasse's ships and sailed into the bay to reach Cornwallis. But he did not realize how desperate Cornwallis's situation had become, and even if he had, sailing into the bay would have achieved little. Graves had no transports. There were no facilities to water or supply the fleet in the bay. And de Grasse, who was soon to be reinforced by de Barras, might well have closed the harbor and trapped the British fleet along with Cornwallis's army. Graves's responsibilities included both the extraction of Cornwallis and, more important, the survival of his fleet, upon which depended the security of the army in New York and Canada and the island colonies in the West Indies.[49]

While it is easy to attribute Graves's failure to pursue a different course to his attachment to the line ahead, there were other factors to consider. At Grenada, Byron had ordered the general chase and thrown his fleet against a stronger French force caught at anchor—and lost. Furthermore, Graves was not of one mind with his subordinates, as Hawke and Anson had been before their general chase battles and Nelson would be at the Nile and Trafalgar.

Nor is it accurate to portray Graves as a tactical Neanderthal, desperately clinging to his primitive tools—the line ahead and the fighting instructions. As Corbett noted, whatever the imperfections of Graves's scheme of battle, his well-intentioned efforts were undermined by the poor judgment and execution of his subordinates. "Why Hood," Corbett wrote, "of all people did not show more initiative, it is difficult to understand; but he chose to keep the line as it was formed, obliquely to the enemy."[50]

The reason Hood did not "show more initiative" should be obvious: he understood that his commander was intent on controlling his fleet from the quarterdeck of the flagship. Graves's mind was not "infested" with tactical concepts built around the line and the fighting instructions. During his service with the Channel fleet, his mind had become infected by the tactical approach advanced by Howe and Kempenfelt. As the latter wrote of his system in a letter already quoted, "nothing is left arbitrarily to the captains."[51] It was not the line that held Hood in its grip; it was the need to wait for a signal from the flagship, a signal that went unseen. It was not the line that so encumbered Graves; it was the failure of his subordinates to do what he needed them to do when the line signal came down, as it did several times during the afternoon. As future battles would demonstrate, lack of initiative, along with misunderstood, misinterpreted, wholly missed signals and missed opportunities, was a hallmark of a signals-based system of command.

Nevertheless, the fundamental difficulties facing Graves in the Chesapeake had less to do with tactics than with operations and strategy. While his defeat was in no sense preordained, the chain of events that brought him to the mouth of the bay on 5 September 1781 predisposed his command to failure. The merits of French policy and strategy were equaled only by the shortcomings of those of the British. The admiralty's inability to maintain a close blockade of Brest allowed the French to send powerful squadrons and whole fleets from Europe to the New World. As a result, the allies had temporary naval superiority in American waters. Operationally, the French concentrated virtually all of their naval forces at the decisive point—in the mouth of the Chesapeake—while the British failed to concentrate their forces within the theater. Rodney, who mistakenly thought de Grasse would send no more than fifteen ships north, sent fourteen under Hood while another eleven escorted convoys or sailed for home. Two of these were the flagships in which both Arbuthnot and Rodney set out for England. Thus Graves found himself outnumbered by five ships of the line, equal to a quarter of his force. Worse yet, de Grasse had four additional ships in the James River supporting the operations of the army, and another eight on their way under de Barras. A week after the battle, the French had assembled thirty-two ships of the line in the Chesapeake, twice the number Graves commanded. He would have no second chance.[52]

IF THOMAS GRAVES symbolized the failure of the Royal Navy during the American war, Admiral Sir George Brydges Rodney epitomized its successes. Rodney was a combative, irascible man who fought and won more battles than any of his Royal Navy contemporaries.

On 1 October 1779 the admiralty appointed Rodney to command the Leeward Islands squadron. He was a gouty sixty-two-year-old who had spent a good portion of the previous forty-six years at sea. Rodney served under both Anson and Hawke and fought at Second Finisterre in October 1747. During the Seven Years' War he saw service in the Channel and, most notably, in the Caribbean. A flag officer since 1759, he commanded the Jamaica station from 1771 to 1774. He returned to England accused of mismanagement and encumbered by debt before fleeing his creditors and seeking refuge in Paris. Ironically, Rodney was able to return to London to seek a new command only because Louis-Antoine de Gontaut, duc de Biron and Maréchal de France, advanced him a substantial sum to pay off the creditors.[53]

Rodney, while perhaps prize-hungry, was a skilled, aggressive, experienced commander. And yet he was also, according to Tunstall, one of "the most inflexible and unreceptive of contemporary tacticians." Rodney was little influenced by French works, although there is some speculation that he read Morogues's treatise.[54] And while he was acquainted with Howe's and Kempenfelt's systems, he would have nothing to do with them. Walter Young, the able first captain who kept an eye on Rodney for the navy's comptroller, wrote to Middleton: "I received [Kempenfelt's] signal books and delivered them to Sir George, with whom they may continue for a length of time, and never be looked at or studied." But Rodney did give considerable thought to tactical questions. He was, like Howe, a centralizer, but one who chose to rely on the existing and familiar system of instructions and signals. Rodney's major contribution to Royal Navy tactics involved the concept of concentration: the tightening up of ships in the line, or even the grouping together of the most powerful men-of-war, and the application of their massed firepower against a portion of the enemy fleet.[55]

Rodney sailed from Spithead on 27 December with a force of twenty of the line, including his own squadron of four ships and a strong detachment from the Channel fleet, escorting two convoys, one destined for the West Indies and the other for the fortress of Gibraltar, which was besieged by the Spanish. Once clear of Brest and Rochefort, the West Indian convoy headed west, while the remainder of the fleet continued south. On 8 January off Cape Finisterre, Rodney ran across a Spanish convoy and captured the lot: a 54-gun ship, six frigates, and sixteen transports.[56]

Eight days later off Cape St. Vincent, Rodney's lookouts sighted another clutch of sails to the southeast. The ships were Spanish; a fleet sent out to intercept the relief convoy known to have sailed for Gibraltar. Unfortunately for the Spanish, their otherwise accurate intelligence reports did not reveal that a strong detachment from the Channel fleet had accompanied Rodney south. Thus, when Don Juan de Lángara y Huarte's nine of the line and two frigates discovered the British rounding Cape St. Vincent, predator became prey.

According to the account of Captain Young, Rodney, ridden with gout, fought the battle from his bed while his first captain, desperate to prevent the escape of the Spanish ships, struggled to overcome the "Admiral's ill state and his natural irresolution." Young's first reaction to the sightings was to signal for a general chase, but Rodney hesitated until the weakness of the Spanish force became evident. After Young made the signal to chase, he followed it promptly with those for close action and to engage to leeward.

The engagement proper began at about 1600 and ended after midnight, earning the appellation "The Moonlight Battle." Despite a "half gale and a heavy sea" that blew all the ships toward a dangerous lee shore, the British captains on their own initiative pursued their enemies in the dark. One Spanish ship exploded during the battle, the strong wind drove two ashore where they wrecked, and the British captured four others.[57]

While Rodney's twin victories, soon to be combined with his relief of besieged Gibraltar, were a heavy blow to the Spanish, there were few tactical lessons to be drawn from the Moonlight Battle. The action demonstrated the proficiency of the British ships and the ability of their commanders to act aggressively on their own initiative, but Rodney owed his victory principally to the fact that the Spanish in both encounters were woefully outmatched, qualitatively and quantitatively. As Young wrote to Middleton after the battle: "I am perfectly of your opinion that it is a dangerous practice to make the signal for a general chase after an enemy equal or superior to you, particularly if they are formed in line of battle, or are near each other."[58] If the answer to the Royal Navy's tactical problems had been as simple as hoisting the signal for a general chase, Byron would not have failed at Grenada.

Young portrays Rodney as a reluctant hero: a cautious and uncertain commander who had to be cajoled by his first captain to allow the fleet to chase.[59] Rodney's initial hesitation to trust in the initiative of his subordinates epitomizes his desire to retain tight control of his ships in battle, even when bedridden. Rodney would reveal this Howe-like disposition in future battles as well, including the victory at the Saintes in April 1782.

Rodney reached Gibraltar on 26 January. The arrival of his mighty fleet, accompanied by more than a score of captured warships and transports, not only improved the supply situation but also boosted the morale of the beleaguered garrison. From Gibraltar Rodney, with his own flagship, the *Sandwich* 90, and three coppered 74s, sailed to the West Indies, while the rest of the fleet and the prizes returned to England. Rodney reached Barbados on 17 March and several days later rendezvoused with the sixteen ships of the Leeward Islands station at St. Lucia.[60]

Rodney's opponent in the islands was d'Estaing's replacement, the able and energetic Luc-Urbain du Bouexic, comte de Guichen. In April de Guichen sailed from his base at Martinique with twenty-three ships of the line and 3,000 troops. His plan was to lure Rodney away from the islands and then to double back and invade either Barbados or St. Lucia.

The French sailed on 13 April, in company with a convoy bound for St. Domingue. As soon as Rodney learned that the French were out, he pursued. At about noon on 16 April British lookouts sighted de Guichen's fleet still beating against unfavorable winds leeward of Martinique. Rodney signaled for a general chase, not as a prelude to battle, but as a sensible means to close the range more quickly. But it was too late in the day for a battle. When the fleets were in close proximity, Rodney made the signal for line abreast. He managed to maintain contact throughout the night and at dawn of 17 April prepared to fight.

The engagement fought off Martinique that spring day of 1780 was the first of three clashes between Rodney and de Guichen that Raoul Castex considered perfect examples of "the classic genre in action."[61] These three encounters may well have been the most eloquent battles of maneuver of the entire age of fighting sail.

In the first engagement, that of 17 April, Rodney skillfully orchestrated the movements of his fleet, from line ahead to line abreast and back into line ahead, until he had concentrated his ships in a compact formation ranged against a portion of the French fleet. At about 0845, as the British prepared to engage from windward, de Guichen ordered his fleet to wear and reverse course. Rodney, frustrated but determined, began the whole process anew as the two fleets sailed north. By late morning he had once again concentrated his fleet against the French center and rear. He intended to exploit his windward position to bring his fleet into action against the rearmost two-thirds of the French line. De Guichen's unengaged van, strung out and downwind, would be too poorly positioned to come to the assistance of the rest of the fleet. Rodney was on the verge of "a miniature version of Trafalgar."[62]

But there remained problems of communications and execution. At 0645 Rodney had signaled the fleet his intention "to attack the enemy's rear." More than four hours later, he assumed that his subordinates would interpret his signals within that framework. At 1100 he signaled for the fleet to prepare for battle, at 1128 for the rear to close up with the center, and at 1150 for Article 21, a long instruction the heart of which was that "every ship in the squadron is to steer for the ship of the enemy, which from the disposition of the two squadrons, it must be her lot to engage." Rodney then made the signal to engage, followed by another to engage more closely.[63]

Unfortunately for the admiral, Captain Robert Carkett, commanding the leading British ship, the *Stirling Castle* 64, had forgotten Rodney's intention to focus against the rear of the French fleet. Usually fleets engaged van to van, center to center, and rear to rear. So it was that Carkett, instead of sailing down on and engaging the French ship to which he was currently abreast, raced after the leading ship of de Guichen's van. The other ships in the British line followed, including that of the commander of what was then the van division—Rear Admiral Hyde "Vinegar" Parker. As Rodney watched in disbelief, his compact fleet extended itself and his maneuvers of the morning came to naught. Young later wrote: "Had the captains attended to the signals and movements of the *Sandwich*, the day would have been a glorious one indeed."[64]

Many historians have attributed the problem to the line. Michael Lewis noted Carkett's "clinging to the Conterminous Line"; Russell F. Weigley wrote of the "fetish of the line ahead." But Rodney's signals did not necessitate any abandonment of the line. And while his plan to concentrate his strength against a portion of the enemy's fleet was a departure from established practice, Carkett's decision to chase de Guichen's van actually violated Article 12 of the additional fighting instructions then in force, which admonished captains "to keep at the same distance those ships do that are next the commander in chief, always taking from the centre."[65]

Nor can all the blame be fixed on Carkett. The other ships in the van reacted in the same fashion, as did the *Princess Royal* 90, flagship of Rear Admiral Parker. There was evident confusion in the center, right under Rodney's watchful eye. And during the final stage of the battle when the French rear wore and bore away, the British rear, commanded by Rear Admiral Rowley in the *Conqueror* 74, did the same. Chastised by Rodney after the battle, Rowley explained that he had assumed "twas your intention to make your greatest impression on their Rear." In response Rodney noted that "the painful task of thinking belongs to me," and to Rowley nothing more than "*obedience* to signals and orders."[66]

Responsibility for the failure of execution at the battle of Martinique lay with Rodney. He had failed to explain fully his intention to concentrate his fleet to his subordinates: "Rodney was not a man who took his juniors into his confidence: he planned to command the fleet as a sergeant drills a squad of men." Sir Gilbert Blane, Rodney's physician and defender, later wrote that the admiral had "either by oral or written communication acquainted each captain in his fleet" with his intention to attack the rear. But John Knox Laughton commented: "If Blane's memory was not playing him false, if Rodney really did this, we can only say that power of exposition was altogether wanting to him; for it is quite certain that not one man to whom he thus explained his intention had the faintest notion of what Rodney wanted him to do, or how he wanted him to do it."[67]

We know from the correspondence of others who served under Rodney that his intentions were frequently unclear. Young often mentioned Rodney's lack of resolution. Sir Samuel Hood, who served under Rodney later in the war, was also often at a loss to comprehend his commander in chief's intentions. "His manner of talking is, to be sure," Hood once informed Middleton, "very extravagant and extraordinary, but without much meaning."[68]

Rodney placed the responsibility for his failure at Martinique entirely on subordinates who had not "properly supported" either their commander or the British flag. He threatened to dismiss or court-martial several of his captains and criticized his flag officers in his letters to the admiralty, actions that did little to endear him to any of them. And he did not make much of an effort to explain his tactical views to his subordinates. For example, a letter written four months after the battle by Captain Sir Frederick Lewis Maitland, commander of the *Elizabeth* 74 and one of the van captains who had gone astray, demonstrated that he still did not comprehend what Rodney had intended in the battle. Rodney's style of command remained unchanged. He continued to stress strict obedience to his signals, and to ensure compliance he decided that he would fight his next battle as Howe had fought d'Estaing off Rhode Island in 1778—from a frigate. Like a shepherd, Rodney would herd his sheep into position.[69]

On 6 May a British frigate reached St. Lucia with intelligence that de Guichen, who had retired to Guadeloupe, was back out to sea. Rodney immediately took his fleet south toward Martinique, de Guichen's presumed destination. On 10 May lookouts sighted the French leeward of the island and Rodney closed for battle. Over the next ten days, the two fleets resumed their sea-borne promenade and repeated numerous and spectacular displays of maneuver. Rodney tried time and again to force an engagement, while the wily de Guichen, in keeping with French doctrine and his specific orders, avoided any encounter likely to bring on a full-fledged battle. On 15 and 19 May the fleets, or at least parts of them, engaged, but when the ballet ended neither side had lost a ship sunk or captured. The British had suffered nearly two hundred casualties and many of Rodney's men-of-war were badly shot up; the French were similarly battered and their casualties higher. Rodney was ready to go another round, but not so de Guichen, who had lost a son in one of the encounters and subsequently "broke down under the strain."[70]

The "battles" of 15 and 19 May demonstrate that the old British signaling system and fighting instructions could be made to function efficiently, at least in what was little more than a sparring match. Rodney had no reason to complain about the performance of his captains as he put his fleet through its paces in mid-May 1780. Nevertheless, although the two fleets remained in close proximity for nearly a fortnight, he had been unable to force a fight on the enemy, a well-handled fleet commanded by an admiral intent on avoiding battle. Moreover, if Rodney had managed to bring on a full-scale engagement, his rigid system of command would probably have collapsed, and quickly.

For example, one of Rodney's signal books—that of Captain John Houlton, commander of the 74-gun ship of the line *Montagu*—is held in the United States by the Historical Society of Pennsylvania, in Philadelphia. The book folds open in the center so that eighteen tabbed, hand-colored flags lie to either side. For each flag, different placement indicates a reference to a different instruction. The problems inherent in such reliance on visual systems to control the movements of a fleet are evident in the placement of the red pendant at the mizzen peak—the signal to wear in succession if the flagship discharged a single cannon, or together if the flagship discharged a pair of cannon. But how was a commander in chief to communicate his intention to wear if his flagship was engaged?

Recall that Rodney planned to control his fleet from a frigate, an announcement that had actually drawn praise from the king, who was aware of and shared Lord Howe's views on the matter. Rodney went on board the frigate *Venus* 36 on 13 May and remained until the fleet returned to St. Lucia on 22 May. He discovered that a fast sailing frigate free to race along the length of the entire line gave him certain advantages but also had distinct disadvantages. Once the shooting began, he found it far more difficult to control his fleet. Only from the quarterdeck of the flagship could a commander gain a feel for a developing battle; only from the quarterdeck of the flagship could a commander seize the moment and lead by example, as would Rodney himself at the Saintes in April 1782. Some of these difficulties are evident in a letter Captain Young addressed to Middleton:

> I have said in my letter I made signals. This was settled with the admiral after he left me, to make the signals as I saw necessary for the good of the service; which signals I was to show him by hanging them out at where they were to be made; and continued so doing until I saw him blunder, and then I wrote him that I would not be responsible for errors, as I had his flag to defend, as well as to make signals, but that I would repeat any signals he made and give him any information I could.
>
> . . . I did by no means approve of his going into the Venus . . . I have discharged my duty . . . though my situation requires great patience with so unsteady and irresolute a man. His being in the frigate was of no service, as he always kept to leeward of our line. The enemy being to windward, he could never be a judge of it; but, at last, I got him persuaded to keep between us, which he attended to the last recounter.[71]

While Sir George had fought his last engagement from a frigate, he had one more battle yet to fight, and to win. In February 1782 he returned once more to the West Indies, this time with a fleet of twelve of the line. The substantial reinforcement was meant to shift the balance of naval power, not off the North American coast, for the situation in the colonies after Cornwallis's surrender was beyond hope, but in the Caribbean, where the fleet of the Comte de Grasse was undefeated and at large. Great Britain could not afford a West Indian Yorktown in 1782.

Whatever Rodney's shortcomings as a human being and a commander, he was an optimist determined to force a battle and to win it. "*Persist and Conquer* is a Maxim that I hold good in War," he reminded his wife in a letter written a month before the Saintes.[72] Despite his declining health, he seemed immune to the worries that plagued so many other admirals. On reaching the islands he learned that the French had already made an unsuccessful attempt against Barbados and captured St. Christopher (St. Kitts). Where would they strike next? In Rodney's mind, there was no doubt—Jamaica.

De Grasse was, in fact, planning a combined Franco-Spanish invasion against the crown jewel of Great Britain's Caribbean empire. During the initial phase of the plan, de Grasse's fleet would cover the movement of two large convoys to Cap François on the north coast of St. Domingue. On 8 April the French fleet of thirty-five sail of the line left Martinique in company with the invasion flotilla and a large merchant convoy bound for France.

Rodney, well served by his frigates, knew that the French were about to sail and took his own fleet of thirty-seven liners to sea on the morning of 8 April. They raced north in pursuit and the next day overtook elements of de Grasse's fleet, slowed by ill winds and the ponderous convoys. In a skirmish between Hood's van division and the French rear, the British forced one ship, le Caton 64, from the line, heavily damaged. The following day, as the French continued northward, le Zélé 74 collided with le Jason 64, damaging the latter badly. On 11 April British lookouts spied the two stragglers and Rodney ordered a general chase. De Grasse, anxious to avoid the loss, turned about and maneuvered to cover the damaged men-of-war. Rodney called off the chase, though he still pursued. During the night le Zélé crossed paths with de Grasse's flagship, la Ville de Paris 104, and suffered extensive damage.

At dawn the next morning, 12 April 1782, only a few miles of sea separated the two fleets in the Dominica Passage—between the northern end of Dominica and the Saintes. Had de Grasse continued to work his way through the passage, he might have been able to avoid combat, although the vagaries of wind and weather were many and unpredictable.[73] But de Grasse, his fleet already outnumbered, was unwilling to abandon any of his damaged ships of the line. At 0545 he signaled for his fleet to form a line of battle on the larboard tack, running south toward Dominica. The French, holding the windward advantage, were going to risk battle to save le Zélé.

When Rodney saw the French forming their line to the south, he sensed that he might be able to force a fight if he could pass his fleet across de Grasse's path. At 0600 Rodney, unwilling to throw Hood's division against the fresh French van, signaled for Rear Admiral Francis Sam-

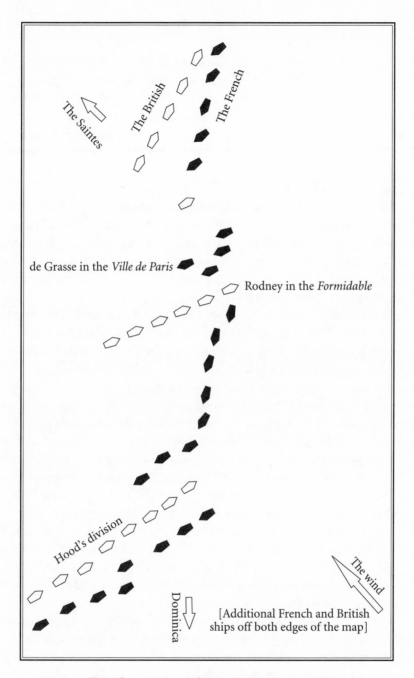

The British   The French

The Saintes

de Grasse in the *Ville de Paris*

Rodney in the *Formidable*

Hood's division

Dominica

The wind

[Additional French and British
ships off both edges of the map]

THE SAINTES, 12 APRIL 1782, CA. 1100
The proximity of Dominica (off map to the south) and the hauling wind
forced the French to alter course from the south toward the southwest and
thus set the stage for Rodney to break their line. De Grasse should not
have been surprised by the wind, which normally hauls—that is, shifts in a
clockwise fashion to follow the direction of the sun.

uel Drake's rear division to take the lead and for Hood to form the rear of the British line. Rodney's captains executed this rather difficult shift with alacrity, and Captain Taylor Penny, commanding the *Marlborough* 74, led the close-hauled line toward the northeast. At about 0730 the French van opened an ineffective fire at long range. Penny continued on course but at about 0740, realizing that he could not weather the French line, he turned toward the north and returned fire. Within ten minutes Drake's entire division was in action.

The two fleets slowly engaged on parallel but opposite tacks, the British sailing north, the French south. While an engagement between two relatively equal fleets, both arrayed in line, headed in opposite directions, was a formula for indecision, de Grasse's inability to control his fleet once the battle began was about to provide Rodney with an opportunity unique in the history of naval warfare.

De Grasse knew that his fleet could not stay on its close-hauled course to the south. The channel between the Saintes and Dominica was no more than ten miles across, less considering the shallow water surrounding the islands, and the French line was at least five miles long. The French commander also knew that it was natural for the wind to haul— to shift in a clockwise direction—during the course of a day. As the wind began to shift from the east toward the southeast, the French ships would have to point ever more to starboard, forcing them out of their line and into the guns of the British. As Morogues had warned in his study of naval tactics, such a change of wind was the "most disadvantageous that could test a fleet in line, because order is very difficult to reestablish, particularly in the face of the enemy." Thus, after forming and extending his line to the south, de Grasse planned (or at least after the battle claimed to have planned) to reverse course and sail back toward the north, on a course parallel to the British. Such a maneuver would allow the French, who held the wind gauge, to concentrate their efforts, as they had three days earlier, against the British van.[74]

While de Grasse's captains possessed a state-of-the-art signal manual and were practiced at the types of maneuvers their commander envisioned using, such evolutions, as Morogues had warned, were extremely difficult to execute in the midst of battle. At 0815 de Grasse signaled for his fleet to tack and to reverse course. By that time both the van and the center were in action, and the ships ignored the signal. Few sailing-age captains were eager to tack while under determined enemy fire. De Grasse attempted to lead by example, but *la Ville de Paris,* damaged aloft, would not maneuver properly. At 0830 de Grasse signaled again, this time directing his captains to wear together. Such maneuvers began with a signal—a discharge from one of the flagship's cannon. But with *la Ville de Paris* in action, firing at the enemy, how were de Grasse's subordinates, some of whom were more than two miles from the flagship, to know which cannon shot meant they should begin the maneuver? Not surprisingly, the French line continued on course to the south. At 0845 a frustrated de Grasse signaled for a third time, this time directing his captains to wear in succession, a maneuver that began with the rear ship. His repeating frigates duly passed the signal down the line, but the commander of the rear division ignored the command. The ships of the French rear and the British van were within "musket shot" range—under 200 yards—and the prospect of performing a 180-degree turn by swinging one's vulnerable stern across a line of enemy ships held few attractions.[75]

Shortly after 0900 the wind slackened and hauled to the south, forcing the French to alter course to starboard—directly into the guns of Rodney's ships. Absent much of a breeze, smoke from more than 2,000 cannon enveloped both fleets in a dense cloud and markedly increased the chaos of battle. Gaps opened in a confused French formation that could no longer be termed a line ahead. At about 1000 Rodney led the way through one of these gaps. A few moments later Hood led the rear division through another. The French fleet was shattered. By day's end five captured ships of the line, including de Grasse's flagship, graced Sir George's triumph.[76]

Despite the fact that Rodney's fleet had won a notable victory, two historical controversies arose soon after the battle. The first involved who made the decision to pierce the French line. The decision has been attributed to Rodney, to his first captain, Sir Charles Douglas, and to John Clerk, author of *An Essay on Naval Tactics,* which was published the same year of the battle and in Rodney's possession. But Clerk, who discussed the battle of the Saintes at some length in a later edition of his work, never claimed that his book had inspired Rodney's maneuver. As for Douglas, even Rodney's modern biographers have generally acknowledged that he was the principal advocate of the maneuver, badgering his commander in chief until he yielded, commenting: "Well, well, do as you like."[77]

What can be said with certainty is that Rodney had not planned to break the French line. While the signal books of the Channel fleet, in which Douglas had recently served, included such an instruction, there was no comparable number in Rodney's set. He directed the evolution by

example, not by signal. And to a great extent the effective dissolution of
the French line preceded Rodney's breaking maneuver. The wind,
far more than the evolutions of the British fleet, destroyed de Grasse's
battle order. Moreover, the decision to pass through the French line may
have been a mistake. "By going through to windward," John Creswell
noted, "Rodney's flagship and the ships following him allowed the already battered French ships in his neighbourhood to get a start in retreat-
ing to leeward." While breaking the line became fashionable after the
Saintes, admirals embraced it primarily as a maneuver executed from
windward to assume a leeward position to prevent an enemy's disengagement. Rodney held the leeward position on the morning of 12 April. By
breaking the French line he passed to windward and allowed the French
to retreat.[78]

As the British sailed to windward and the smoke of battle cleared,
Rodney found his fleet disengaged. He "had not yet realized that the
French ships were already slipping away to leeward through the great
gaps in his own line, and round the southern end of it." Rodney pursued,
but insisted that the ships of his fleet, many of which were badly shot
up aloft, do so in a body. During the afternoon the British ran down
four ships of the line and at 1830 took the mighty *Ville de Paris,* along
with de Grasse. Never before had the British captured an enemy commander in chief.[79]

Many of Rodney's subordinates believed that in his cautious pursuit their commander had squandered a tremendous opportunity. Hood
wrote to Lord Sandwich:

> My boat had scarcely boarded [de Grasse's flagship], but Sir George made
> the signal; and brought to, and continued to my utter astonishment to lay to
> the whole night. At this time 20 of the enemy's ships were within four
> miles of us, and some within two. In the morning not a ship of the flying
> enemy was to be seen, a misfortune that can never be sufficiently lamented.
>
> In the glorious business of yesterday, I was most exceedingly disap-
> pointed in our Commander in chief. In the first instance that he did not
> make the signal for a general chase the instant he hauled *that* down for the
> line of battle; had he done so, I am confident we should have had full
> twenty sail of the enemy's line of battle ships in possession before dark.

The day after the battle Hood raised the issue of pursuit with his commander. Rodney replied: "Come, we have done very handsomely as
it is."[80]

Hood was not alone in his frustration. Captain William Cornwallis, who commanded the *Canada* 74 in Rodney's own center division, wrote a poem to commemorate the battle, one stanza of which read:

> At night he lay to, in the victorious field,
> tho' the poor beaten French were ready to yield.
> Had a chief worthy Britain commanded our fleet,
> twenty-five good French ships had been laid at our feet.[81]

Even Rodney, according to his physician Sir Gilbert Blane, came to believe he should have won an even greater victory. "Of his victory on the 12th of April, 1782," Blane later recalled, "I know that he thought little."[82] Moreover, the views of these same critics reveal a frustration with the prevailing method of command and control in the Royal Navy. Hood, who was highly critical of both Graves and Rodney, was a major figure in this reaction. One of the younger captains much influenced by Hood, and a good friend of Cornwallis, was Horatio Nelson. In 1804, the year before Trafalgar, Nelson referred to the battle at the Saintes in a letter to Cornwallis:

> I imbibed from you certain sentiments which have greatly assisted me in my Naval career—That we could always beat a Frenchman if we fought him long enough; that the difficulty of getting at them was oftentimes more people's own fancy than from the difficulty of the undertaking; that people did not know that they could do until they tried, and that it was always to err on the right side to fight.
>
> I was then at that time of life to make the impression which has never been shaken. But, on the score of fighting, I believe, my dear friend, that you have had your full share, and in obtaining the greatest victory, if it had been followed up, that our Country ever saw.[83]

WHILE THE FINAL YEARS of the American war saw the solidification of a centralized system of command and control in Britain's Royal Navy, the French navy moved in a different direction. Suffren, who had led d'Estaing's van at Grenada, challenged the prevailing wisdom. Commanding the French squadron in the Indian Ocean between 1781 and 1783, Suffren embraced the offensive at the strategic, operational, and tactical levels of warfare.

Historians, impressed by Suffren's aggressiveness, have made him the lone Frenchman in the pantheon of great sailing-age admirals, along-side the likes of de Ruyter, Hawke, Rodney, and Nelson. This is especially true of French naval historians. Castex, for example, viewed Suffren as the successor to the aggressive Dutch admiral de Ruyter, while Lacour-Gayet concluded: "Suffren, among the grand sailors, is the perfect model." Napoleon I, during his exile on St. Helena, learned of Suffren's exploits and wondered: "Why did he not live until my time? Why could I not find someone of his kind? I should have made him my Nelson and our affairs would have taken a very different turn. Instead I spent all my time looking for such a sailor and never found one."[84]

While much of the praise for Suffren is hyperbolic, he was certainly an atypical French naval commander. Suffren was an eighth-generation French aristocrat notorious for his obesity, slovenly dress and appearance, and bullying of subordinates. "Demonic energy, frenetic impatience, un-controlled fury, contempt of caste and passion for battle," a recent biogra-pher concluded, "were the five dominant characteristics of the man who burst unexpectedly into the Bay of Bengal in January 1782, and which earned him the sobriquet from his admiring lascars of 'Admiral Satan.'"[85]

When Suffren received the Indian Ocean command in the spring of 1781, he was a veteran of thirty-eight years of naval service. He had joined the navy in 1743 at the age of fourteen and the next year fought at the battle of Toulon. At Second Finisterre in 1747 Suffren found him-self a prisoner of war after watching Hawke destroy much of the French squadron, including Suffren's own ship. During the Seven Years' War he experienced additional frustrations. In 1756 he fought with de la Galissonnière's fleet against Byng at Minorca, but, according to Castex, the failure to follow up the victory convinced Suffren that the destruc-tion of the enemy's fleet must be the goal of naval strategy. Three years later Suffren was serving in *l'Océan* 80, flagship of de la Clue's ill-fated Toulon squadron. During the action with Boscawen's fleet in Lagos Bay, the individual French ships, Suffren's among them, fought valiantly, but to no avail. The captain of the badly battered *l'Océan* drove the ship aground along the Portuguese coast, where she was later burned by the British. Suffren once again was a prisoner of war.[86]

After his release, as the French reexamined their naval policies, Suffren conducted his own reappraisal. He did not work as a member of l'Académie de Marine, the body responsible, in Castex's view, for the "pseudo-renaissance" of the French navy. Instead, he combined a reas-sessment of his own professional experiences fighting the British with the study of historical works, especially those which discussed the battles of the great Dutch admiral de Ruyter. Suffren concluded that French strategical and tactical methods had "resulted in the paralysis of the spirit of audacity, intelligent response, support under fire, and the camaraderie of combat." As Roderick Cavaliero, Suffren's most recent biographer, noted: "Suffren did not share this gallic confidence in order. He shared the conviction of men like Hawke and Boscawen that all naval action was futile unless it destroyed the enemy's ships. He chafed during the naval dress-rehearsals of the escadres d'evolution sent to sea to test the new ships and the newly trained sailors."[87]

Suffren's experiences in the first years of the American war strengthened his convictions. Unimpressed by d'Estaing's handling of the French squadron off Rhode Island and Grenada, he wrote of "idiotic maneuvers," "stupid, perfidious counsels," and lost opportunities.[88]

Early in 1781 Suffren finally gained an independent command. His responsibilities included the security of the allied Dutch colony at the Cape of Good Hope, the protection of French colonial possessions in the Indian Ocean, and support for France's ally in the subcontinent, Haidar Ali, the ruler of Mysore. Suffren sailed from Brest unfettered by French doctrine, determined to apply his own methods of naval warfare in a distant theater. Lacour-Gayet wrote that Suffren had "the spirit of initiative," the "premier quality of a commander, the most necessary, the most truly characteristic, because it is for this that he is chief." Suffren believed the best way to secure his myriad objectives was to seek out and destroy the opposing British squadron. An offensive strategy, of course, demanded an aggressive handling of the fleet at the tactical level. Thus in battle "Suffren demanded initiative from his captains," even though they were "accustomed to the rigid discipline of the line, where they waited for signals."[89]

Over the next twenty-eight months Suffren fought a half-dozen battles. In each he struggled to seize the initiative and to concentrate his entire squadron against part of the enemy's. At Porto Praya on 16 April 1781, he surprised a stronger British squadron bound for the Cape under Commodore George Johnstone. The engagement was hard-fought but inconclusive, although the damage to Johnstone's squadron delayed his sailing for two weeks and allowed the French to win the race to the Cape of Good Hope. At Sadras on 1 February 1783, Suffren fought the first of five battles against the British Indian Ocean squadron commanded by Vice Admiral Sir Edward Hughes. Suffren attacked but his captains did not support their commander and the engagement ended without either side losing a ship. The pattern was the same off Providien on 12 April 1782, Negapatam on 6 July 1782, Trincomalee on 3 September 1782, and Cuddalore on 20 June 1783.

Why such interest in these relatively inconsequential and indecisive battles? Suffren's Indian Ocean campaign has attracted attention because of its unique nature in the annals of naval warfare. First, there is the personal element: two commanders in chief dueling for naval supremacy within their theater, fighting their fleets in a series of five battles. Second, there is the atypical nature of the engagements themselves, with the French taking the offensive at both the operational and tactical levels.

But the fact remains that Suffren failed to achieve the results he sought in battle. While his strategy was sound and his tactical proclivities admirable, he was unable to fully execute his ideas. Time and again he was dissatisfied with, and often infuriated by, the lack of support from his subordinates. But why did he go unsupported? Suffren's biographer concluded that he "failed to ensure that his captains knew what was expected of them." He looked for displays of initiative from men who had only the vaguest understanding of their commander's tactical ideas, ideas that were a marked departure from French naval doctrine. Suffren expected far too much from men who not only failed to measure up to their British counterparts but also were not among the best and brightest of the French navy. "By the time that Suffren came to fight his last battle," Cavaliero wrote, "he had learnt that only time-honoured tactics would do for sailors as he commanded."[90]

Nor did Suffren, though it took as much as a year for dispatches to reach India from Paris, entirely escape the driving force behind tactical centralization within the French navy. At Trincomalee on 11 April 1783, instructions from King Louis XVI dated the previous May finally caught up with Suffren. The king, shocked by the capture of de Grasse at the Saintes, directed that henceforth any French admiral commanding more than nine vessels in battle would shift his flag to a frigate to make it easier for him to observe the maneuvers of the enemy and direct the movements of the men-of-war.[91]

Suffren had serious doubts about the directive. He understood that situated in a frigate, a commander in chief would be incapable of leading his fleet by example and would have no choice but to rely on visual signals. He obeyed, perhaps because he had recognized that his captains incapable of acting on their own initiative.[92]

In the battle fought off Cuddalore on 20 June 1783, Suffren managed the engagement from the frigate *Cléopâtre* and won what is generally considered a tactical victory. But he "was bitterly disappointed not to be in the thick of it and the *Cléopâtre* ran up and down the French line helplessly. She had no signals to make—for there was only one: to engage at pistol-shot range." Suffren declared that his effort to control the fleet from a frigate would be his "first and last attempt."[93]

Suffren's impact on naval thought was limited. Had he won a great victory over Hughes, perhaps the French navy would have reconsidered its philosophies of strategy and command. But in the absence of that victory, the French retained their "geometric preoccupation." As for the British, John Clerk included examples from Suffren's battles in *Naval Tactics*. Nelson read those sections before Trafalgar, but his penchant for aggressiveness and concentration against a portion of the enemy's fleet was by then already well established. In fact, the British had a far greater influence on Suffren's conception of naval warfare than vice versa. As Cavaliero wrote: "The most significant characteristic of Suffren's short and climactic period of command was its Englishness."[94]

Nevertheless, two important lessons about command and control can be drawn from the 1782–1783 campaign in the Indian Ocean. Suffren's inability to achieve anything approaching decisive results demonstrated that decentralization of tactical command and control, whatever its inherent advantages, demanded a significant degree of commitment and comprehension throughout the chain of command. In an age when navies were increasingly wedded to centralized systems, a commander in chief who decided to exercise a less centralized approach had to personally indoctrinate his subordinates to ensure that they understood and shared his views, be they strategic, operational, or tactical. Nor could a decentralized method work if subordinates lacked the experience and talent to recognize their commander's intentions at the point in the battle when individual captains had to act on their own initiative.

For Great Britain's Royal Navy the war for America ended without an example of an Anson or a Hawke to offset that of Howe or Rodney. Most British admirals, like their counterparts across the Channel, remained convinced of the efficacy of a signals-based approach to command, despite the shortcomings of the systems in use. In an October 1786 letter to Middleton, Captain Philip Patton admitted that "almost every action [of the] last war proved the miserable confusion and deficiency" of British signaling systems. For officers like Patton, however, the imperfections of the existing system of command called not for reliance on initiative but for the development of more sophisticated visual signaling. Patton himself turned his "whole attention" to such work and devised a manual to rival Howe's. But it was the latter's "improved" signal book of 1790 that the admirals of the navy relied upon when the second Anglo-French hundred years' conflict resumed in 1793.[95]

CHAPTER SIX

The Zenith of the Age of Fighting Sail

$\mathcal{T}$HE ANGLO-FRENCH naval struggle that began in 1793 exposed developments that had been apparent well before the outbreak of revolution in Paris in 1789. During the decade that followed the American war, the navies of Britain and France reflected the political realities of the states they served. Despite the fact that Great Britain had "lost" the American war, George III's monarchy remained secure and the empire recovered quickly. The senior administrators and commanders of the Royal Navy, disappointed by their force's performance in that war, supported reforms that strengthened the service in quantitative and qualitative terms. Britain's navy was far better prepared for war in 1793 than it had been in 1778.

At the tactical level, the spirit of reform involved continued development of a numerary signaling system. Howe and his competitors worked to devise a better and more workable scheme. Finally, in 1790, the Royal Navy's senior commanders adopted Howe's revised manual as the standard, though still unofficial, signal book.[1]

Across the Channel, the many French naval successes of the American war enhanced the navy's importance to the monarchy. "For the King as for his ministers," Simon Schama wrote, "the future of imperial France *was* the navy: the azure horizon of a great Atlantic and perhaps even oriental Empire." After 1783 Louis XVI and his ministers strengthened the navy for the inevitable next war. But their naval expansion program was uneven, handicapped by "structural weaknesses," and unsupportable in a haphazardly and maladministered state headed toward financial collapse. The effort to make France a great military power on both land and sea left the monarchy adrift in "oceans of debt" and undermined the foundations of its navy.[2]

The impetus for naval reform in France was less powerful in 1783 than it had been in 1763, after the debacles of the Seven Years' War. There was no maritime equivalent to the army reforms of Jacques-Antoine de Guibert and Jean-Baptiste de Gribeauval. French postwar tactical reforms were "retrograde," Tunstall concluded, and in 1783 the "Treaty of Versailles put a virtual stop to tactical developments in France because Pavillon's system appeared to have justified itself."[3]

What little momentum for reform existed ended abruptly in 1789. The Revolution's political and social turmoil was disastrous for the French navy. For many scholars, the anti-naval foolishness of the various French revolutionary regimes, what Joseph Martray termed "ideological stupidity," condemned the navy to defeat. But others such as William Cormack, who have examined the navy within the context of the Revolution, disagree. As for naval historians, Mahan did heap opprobrium on French naval policymakers of the Revolution and the empire, but he also admitted that their government "faithfully and necessarily reflected the social disorder" of the era. To Tunstall, the impact of the revolutionaries on the French navy was too constrained. When "the Revolutionary war began," he wrote, "the French had one great asset, a true fighting spirit, as shown by their unflinching acceptance of Howe's attack on the First of June [1794]. This spirit was frittered away as time went on, by admirals who failed to draw the conclusion—obvious enough to the soldiers—that the quadrilles and pirouettes of the eighteenth century were no longer what was required."[4]

Whatever one's favored interpretation of the effects of the Revolution, two facts remain: in 1793 the British navy was better prepared, and the French navy less prepared, for war than they had been at the start of the American war. Nor did the French have the luxury of choosing to fight a predominantly maritime war, as they had in 1778. Internally, France was torn by rebellion and civil conflict; externally, the armies of Europe's major monarchies—Prussia, Austria, Russia, and Spain—were poised to invade. French leaders did not so much turn their backs on the naval policies of Louis XVI and his ministers; rather, circumstances forced them to focus primarily upon the situation along their frontiers. By the time the situation stabilized in 1800, the French navy had suffered the loss in combat of nearly three dozen ships of the line.[5]

FOR THE FRENCH NAVY, the war against Great Britain began horribly. The Mediterranean fleet found itself torn between its patriotic duty to defend France and loyalty to a rebellious civil government in Toulon that declared for the monarchy and entered into an alliance with the traditional enemy—Britain. The fleet, deeply divided politically and weakened by mass desertion, surrendered in August 1793. In September the main French fleet, based in Brest but then anchored in Quiberon Bay, mutinied. For eight months its senior commanders, working with André Jeanbon Saint-André, a troubleshooting representative of the Convention sent from Paris, struggled to restore the fleet's loyalty and battle-readiness.[6]

The test came in the spring of 1794. In April a convoy of more than a hundred merchant ships loaded with food and naval stores sailed from the United States eastward across the Atlantic for France. In early May Howe, with twenty-six ships of the line escorting several British convoys clear of Brest, was positioned to intercept. To cover the approach of the convoy from America, the Brest fleet put to sea on 16 May under the command of Rear Admiral Louis-Thomas, comte Villaret de Joyeuse, who was accompanied on his flagship, le Montagne 120, by Jeanbon Saint-André. That the French, after the loss of Toulon and the mutiny at Quiberon, could dispatch a fleet of twenty-six sail of the line in May 1794 was "a triumph for the Revolutionary Government."[7]

On the morning of 28 May the two fleets sighted each other. There followed several days of maneuver and desultory combat as Howe sought the advantage of position and Villaret de Joyeuse led the British away from the convoy. During intermittent fighting and maneuvering on the afternoon of 29 May, elements of the British fleet actually passed through—broke, in classic form—the rear of the French line.[8] But the lateness of the day and high seas convinced Howe not to press the attack. In the early morning hours of 1 June, Howe found himself well positioned and holding the wind gauge, and after closing up his own line, made the signal to attack.

At 0716 Howe signaled for his fleet to form in order of battle on a larboard line of bearing. Nine minutes later he made signal 34: "when having the wind of the enemy, the Admiral means to pass between the ships in the line for engaging them to leeward." In his 1790 signal manual, Howe had discarded the signal for breaking the enemy's formation with one's own fleet in line, as Rodney had broken de Grasse's fleet at the Saintes. In Howe's scheme, individual British ships would turn and run down toward the enemy line and pass through the gaps that always existed in a formation, raking the enemy ships to either side. Howe's captains would then re-form their own line on the opposite, leeward side and prevent the enemy's escape.[9]

At about 0925, as the British bore down on the French, the engagement began in earnest. Howe, flying his flag in the *Queen Charlotte* 100, passed through a gap in the French line between 0930 and 1000, raked several ships, but found himself hotly engaged to both port and starboard. Meanwhile, only six British captains imitated their commander in chief. The others re-formed a line of sorts on the windward side of the French fleet.

Nevertheless, the British maneuvers confused and disrupted the French line, and Villaret de Joyeuse and his political commissar quickly lost control. (The fog of battle was so great that on his return to Brest Jeanbon Saint-André proposed that commanding admirals direct their fleets from frigates.)[10] All around the French flagship the battle degenerated into a series of single-ship actions that by their nature favored the British with their superior gunnery and seamanship. The engagement continued until shortly after 1800, by which time the bulk of the French fleet had withdrawn, leaving a half-dozen of their compatriots behind. Howe, concerned about the battered state of his own fleet, did not order a pursuit.

Strategically the battle was a French victory because the convoy reached Brest safely. While the Royal Navy's concentration on the enemy's fleet made justifiable strategic sense, the convoy ought to have attracted more attention and interest.[11] But the consequences for the French far exceeded the loss of battleships. Villaret de Joyeuse's failure to defeat Howe, given the deteriorating political situation in Paris, exacerbated the already deep divisions within the French navy. Tactically, the British won the day. The French lost seven ships of the line—one exploded, six captured—and suffered between 5,000 and 8,500 casualties. British casualties numbered about 1,200, and Howe returned to port with all of his men-of-war plus a half-dozen prizes.[12]

Howe had good reason to be proud of the day's efforts. In Tunstall's view, "Lord Howe's fleet was the best with which Britain had ever entered a war, even though by his own standards it lacked both tactical knowledge and experience." Compared with other British first battles—Toulon, Minorca, Ushant—the first of June 1794 was indeed "glorious." Howe managed his fleet well and employed original tactics that marked "something of a triumph" for what Michael Lewis termed "the new Mêlée school."[13] Howe made excellent use of the long summer daylight, wasted little time in maneuver, and before 0730 had set about not just beating the French but attempting to destroy them. In the engagement he forced, the superiority of British gunners, many now working quick-loading, larger-caliber carronades that were deadly at close range, was more pronounced than ever.

At the Glorious First of June, Howe exercised a style of command that combined the order and discipline he and Kempenfelt had sought during the American war with Hawke's preference to "get as close to [the enemy] as possible." Howe made no effort to direct his fleet as a doctrinaire centralizer. He abandoned the idea of herding his subordinates into battle from a frigate. He accepted the loss of control that came with a close fight and trusted in the initiative of his captains and flag officers, a trait that he had not displayed off Rhode Island in 1778 and that certainly was not in conformity with Kempenfelt's view that nothing should be "left arbitrarily to the captains." Despite well-founded doubts about many of his captains, Howe "left" it to them to find their way through the French line and to re-form as best they could on the other side. In preparation for that moment, for months and weeks before the battle Howe shared his ideas, especially about passing through the line, with his subordinates. Even lieutenants in the fleet understood what their commander had in mind when they met the French in battle.[14]

The victory was not perfect. Howe made no attempt to concentrate his fleet against a portion of the French line, as he might profitably have against the French center and rear. And in spite of his efforts to explain his intentions beforehand, only seven of his twenty-six captains responded to the signal to pass through the enemy line. Several captains found the gaps in the line too narrow to penetrate; others simply disobeyed the order. A few mistook the meaning of the instruction, and evidence from ship logs suggests that some missed the signal entirely. For example, Captain Thomas Mackenzie, considered by one of his lieutenants "about the stupidest man possible," commanding the *Gibraltar* 80, which was the next ahead of Howe's in line, not only missed seeing signal 34, but in the confusion of the engagement had his man-of-war fire several times into Howe's flagship. Nor did Howe pursue as aggressively as he might have. In fact, toward the end of the day, as Villaret de Joyeuse regrouped his fleet, Howe, at the behest of his first captain, Sir Roger Curtis, actually recalled two of his men-of-war that were about to capture a pair of disabled French ships, allowing the prizes to escape. "This failure to pursue was a great lapse on Howe's part," Tunstall wrote, "but, as in Rodney's case, it was due to physical and nervous exhaustion."[15]

For a variety of reasons that were often as much political or personal as they were professional, many officers voiced criticism of Howe as a commander. A disgruntled Captain Cuthbert Collingwood, whose name had not appeared in Howe's public dispatch after the battle, was extremely critical. Vice Admiral William Cornwallis, who after the Glorious First commanded the Channel fleet at sea while Howe retained nominal command ashore, was also a critic, as well as a friend of the one captain court-martialed after the victory, Anthony James Pye Molloy. John Barrow, Howe's early biographer, quotes an unnamed admiral who had fought as a young officer under Howe: "The 1st of June was the *first* general action fought in the course of the war, and led to many glorious results; had it been the *last,* not one of the French ships would have been allowed to return to port." Barrow concluded that Howe "felt this defection of so many of his captains strongly."[16]

Criticism of Howe within naval circles reached Horatio Nelson, then serving in the Mediterranean. In an oft-quoted letter to Howe, Nelson called him "the first and greatest Sea-officer the world has ever produced." But in a more revealing letter to the Reverend Dixon Hoste, whose son served with Nelson, he wrote: "Lord Howe certainly is a great officer in the management of a Fleet, but that is all." Nelson considered the Glorious First of June another Saintes. In 1794, looking ahead to a prospective clash with the French fleet in the Mediterranean, he wrote to his brother: "If we only make a Lord Howe's Victory, take a part and retire to Port, Italy is lost."[17]

WHEN WAR BEGAN IN 1793, Captain Horatio Nelson, commanding the *Agamemnon* 64, joined the Mediterranean fleet under Lord Hood. It was not to Rodney or Howe but to Hood, an able, aggressive commander though a difficult subordinate, to whom Nelson looked for inspiration.

Nelson volunteered his services to Hood for the first time in the fall of 1782 at New York. He preferred command of a ship of the line, and the prospect of battle, under Hood in the West Indies, to service on the American coast where prize money was the major consideration. Nelson, then only twenty-four but already a captain for four years, much impressed Hood. When the admiral introduced Nelson to the young son of George III, Prince William Henry, Hood told the boy that "if he wished to ask questions relative to naval tactics . . . [Nelson] would give him as much information as any officer in the fleet." Hood treated Nelson like a son, and the two men developed a lasting relationship. Hood was Nelson's patron after the war and presented his fellow viscount to the House

of Lords when Nelson took his seat on 29 October 1801. Nelson considered Hood "the greatest Sea-officer I ever knew," and "the best Officer,
taking him altogether, that England has to boast of." While his opinion of
Hood's capabilities as a commander may have been inflated, Nelson ad-
mired Hood and absorbed from him, and from his young friend William
Cornwallis, negative judgments of commanders such as Rodney and
Howe, whom Hood associated with styles of command that handcuffed
the fleets they commanded.[18]

In early November 1794 Vice Admiral William Hotham replaced
Hood in command of the Mediterranean fleet. Hotham's tenure was disappointing. He conducted a distant blockade of Toulon that "was never
very close or effective." On several occasions he had the opportunity to
bring the French to battle. On 3 March 1795 fifteen ships of the line
carrying 5,000 troops left Toulon as part of an invasion flotilla destined
for Corsica. On 13 March Hotham, commanding fourteen of the line,
intercepted the small armada in the Gulf of Genoa. Hotham began well,
ordering a general chase.[19] The French, eager to avoid a fight, fled, but
two of their ships—le Ça Ira 80 and la Victoire 80—ran afoul of one another and the former lost her fore and main topmasts. Several British
men-of-war, including Nelson's Agamemnon, converged on the crippled
ship. When the French commander doubled back to aid le Ça Ira, Hotham re-formed his line and the day ended. During the night the French
attempted to disengage. Le Censeur 74 took le Ça Ira in tow, but in the
confusion the powerful Sans Culotte 120 lost contact with the rest of
the fleet.

At dawn on 14 March, about twenty miles from the Italian coast near
Genoa, the British renewed the attack, focusing their efforts on le Censeur
and le Ça Ira. Once again the main French fleet came to the assistance of
their comrades. The fighting during the morning was at times vicious.
But the weakened French fleet, encumbered with the troop transports,
ultimately withdrew, abandoning le Censeur and le Ça Ira to their fate.
The British captured both, Nelson's Agamemnon taking the latter.

After securing his prize, Nelson went on board Hotham's flagship and
suggested immediate pursuit. Hotham's rejoinder—"We must be con-
tented, we have done very well"—sounded much like the response
Rodney had given Hood after the Saintes. Not surprisingly, Nelson reacted much as Hood had. "Sure I am," Nelson wrote, "had I commanded
our Fleet . . . that either the whole French Fleet would have graced my
triumph, or I should have been in a confounded scrape."[20]

On 13 July, off Hyères, Hotham again caught the French at sea. The British had twenty-three of the line; the French only seventeen. When it became clear that the French had no intention of fighting, Hotham signaled for a general chase. Throughout the morning and well into the afternoon, the British slowly gained ground, and the leading British ships went into action against the French rear. At about 1300 a French 74-gun ship struck, but the leading British ships passed it by and pressed on in chase until 1442, when a wind shift gave the advantage to the French. Hotham recalled his ships and ended the engagement, "to the general astonishment" of many in the fleet. The sole prize, the stricken 74, blew up before it was boarded. Nelson later wrote: "Hotham has no head for enterprise, perfectly satisfied that each month passes without any losses on our side." Even the admiral's nephew, likewise named William Hotham, was critical of his handling of the fleet.[21]

In December 1795 Admiral Sir John Jervis arrived from England to take charge in the Mediterranean. Jervis labored diligently to improve the fighting trim of a force that had suffered under Hotham's lax command. Nelson, who had hoped Hood would return, nevertheless believed Jervis to be "a man of business" and was positively disposed toward him. The two men met in January 1796 and immediately developed a personal and professional rapport. Nelson was soon writing home that he had "never beheld" a fleet "equal to Sir John Jervis's."[22]

But despite Jervis's best efforts, the British position in the Mediterranean continued to deteriorate as the French recaptured Corsica and an army under General Napoleon Bonaparte overran northern Italy. In November Spain switched sides and declared war against Great Britain. By early December Jervis had brought his hard-pressed fleet back to Gibraltar, as he redirected his immediate strategic focus from the Italian to the Iberian peninsula.[23]

In mid-February 1797 Jervis had his fleet of fifteen sail of the line at sea off Cape St. Vincent—the southwestern tip of Portugal—hoping to intercept what he knew to be a larger Spanish fleet that had left Cartagena and passed through the Strait of Gibraltar on 5 February. At 0230 on the morning of St. Valentine's Day, Sir John learned from the captain of a Portuguese frigate, an expatriate named Donald Campbell, that the Spanish were about five leagues to windward. At about 0630 Jervis's frigates sighted the Spanish, still invisible from the flagship in the early morning fog.[24]

At about 0830, as the British fleet sailed close-hauled in two columns on a starboard tack toward the southeast, the Spanish began to emerge from the fog.[25] Sir Robert Calder (the captain of the fleet) and Captain Ben Hallowell, a supernumerary who would command the *Swiftsure* 74 under Nelson at the Nile, joined Jervis on the quarterdeck of his flagship, the *Victory* 100. Calder kept count as the enemy ships came into view. From eight the number of ships of the line rose to a score, then twenty-five. Each time Calder reported an increase, Jervis calmly replied, "Very well, sir." When Calder announced, "There are twenty-seven sail of the line, Sir John," Jervis responded: "Enough, sir, no more of that; the die is cast, and if there are fifty sail I will go through them." "That's right, Sir John," Hallowell exclaimed. "That's right, by God we shall give them a damned good licking."[26]

The Spanish ships were under the command of Vice Admiral Don José de Córdoba, whose abilities as a commander were as suspect as the discipline of his fleet and the doctrine under which it intended to fight. His ships were undermanned and the officers and men poorly trained. Don José commanded only because his predecessor had refused to take such an unprepared force to sea. His fleet was ultimately expected to sail to Brest to join the French in an invasion of Britain, but its immediate task was to rendezvous with four mercury-laden merchant ships and escort them safely to Cadiz.[27]

Don José's fleet was arrayed in three disordered "columns" that were little more than clusters of ships sailing more or less parallel on a starboard tack toward the east-southeast. When he sighted the British, de Córdoba made the signal to form a line on a larboard tack. Confusion ensued among the Spanish ships. John Wilkie, master of the *Prince George* 98, the flagship of Rear Admiral William Parker's van division, described the Spanish maneuver as "so Ill, that on viewing them with a Seaman's eye, it was sufficient to inspire us with a Confidence of success in spite of the superiority of their numbers." The Spanish remained in three packs, now heading toward the northwest, with a gap between their center and rear.[28]

Jervis, who knew nothing of the mercury convoy, saw the gap and decided to exploit it in an effort to inflict as much damage as possible on what was obviously the main Spanish fleet. Between 0920 and 0950 he signaled for his five leading ships, joined by a sixth—the *Orion*—commanded by Captain Sir James Saumarez, to chase. At 1057 Jervis made the signal for the fleet to form a line ahead and astern of the *Victory* "as most convenient" on course toward the south-southwest.[29]

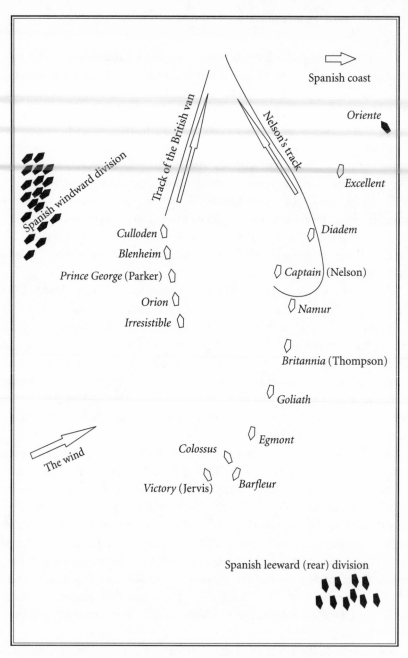

THE BATTLE OF CAPE ST. VINCENT,
14 FEBRUARY 1797, CA. 1250

As Jervis signaled to tack, smoke may have prevented the commanders along his line toward the rear from seeing his signals. Nelson, in the *Captain,* out of line to the northwest, did see the signals, but instead of tacking he ordered his ship to wear. Nelson realized that the ships in the British rear were well placed to reinforce Parker's van division and fend off the likely assault of the Spanish ships to windward.

At 1126 Sir John made signal 40, indicating that he intended "to pass through the enemy's line." This was the same signal as Howe's number 34 made on 1 June 1794, renumbered because of revisions to the signal book. But Jervis's interpretation of the signal favored the traditional, and controllable, lance-like method of breaking the enemy's line. Captain Thomas Troubridge's *Culloden* 74 led the way, nearly colliding with a much larger Spanish three-decker. The two ships passed so closely that the British could see the Spanish crews working their guns, from which they were quickly driven by a double-shotted broadside delivered at pistol-shot range.[30]

Jervis had broken the Spanish line, but he still had to find some way to exploit his position against a force more than twice the size of his own fleet. He held his course until noon, keeping a close watch on the Spanish rear, now cut off from the rest of the fleet, as it first turned away toward the southeast, then doubled back and headed toward the British line. At 1208 he signaled for his fleet to tack in succession. Troubridge led the van, tacking smartly, and at Jervis's direction stood on a course toward the north-northwest.

As the van finished tacking, Jervis's position began to seem somewhat parlous. The Spanish rear squadron, which had come about, began a half-hearted effort to break through his center division. To windward, nineteen Spanish ships, including the world's largest, the four-decked, 136-gun, first-rate *Santísima Trinidad,* prepared to run down with the wind toward the five ships of the British van. Worse yet, the wind had backed two points, forcing the British center and rear ever more toward the southwest, and away from the van. As David Steel noted in his book on naval tactics published the year of the battle, such a change was "the most disadvantageous change of wind that can happen to a fleet in line of battle." He cautioned: "The order is oftentimes but with difficulty reformed, particularly if the enemy be in sight."[31]

Jervis made his way to the *Victory's* poop deck to survey the situation to his rear. As he scanned the scene, a shot from one of the Spanish ships to leeward took off the head of a marine standing next to him. Covered with blood and brains, Sir John assured those who rushed to his side that he was uninjured, requesting only an orange to douche his mouth. Calmly, he resumed his observations. Given the shift in the wind, the center and rear divisions had to alter course, and as soon as possible, before they were forced out of line and farther away from the van. The Spanish attack from leeward appeared to have spent itself, and the ships were again heading southeast. The ships of Jervis's own center could now safely tack. They would sail close-hauled and gain a position to windward of the main Spanish fleet. Jervis would thus have not only broken the enemy's line but also doubled the major portion of it. But could the five ships of the van hold off nineteen enemy vessels until Jervis completed his maneuver? Uncertain, Jervis decided to reinforce Rear Admiral Parker with the ships closest at hand—those of the rear division commanded by Vice Admiral Charles Thompson in the *Britannia* 80. Given the relative positions of the British van and rear, the most efficient method to initiate the necessary maneuver was to direct Thompson's ships to wear and to take up positions ahead of Parker's line. But no such signal flew from the *Victory*.

For nearly two centuries, Jervis's failure to make the "correct" signal has dimmed the luster of the victory for which he earned his earldom.[32] Even the best of naval historians have failed to consider the strictures of the signal book, the unique nature of the battle, and the shortcomings of the Royal Navy's centralized system of command. There were only two signals in the entire manual—numbers 86 and 100—that Jervis could make to direct the rear of his fleet to wear, and given the situation shortly before 1300, neither was appropriate.

Signal 86 read: "to come to the wind together on the larboard tack, 1 gun." But with the *Victory* and several of the ships to Jervis's rear in action against the Spanish to leeward, most notably the liner *Oriente,* which ran down the length of the British line in an effort to find a way through, the firing of a single cannon would be lost in the cacophony of battle. Signal 86 was for use by the fleet while maneuvering before or after, but not during, an engagement.

Signal 100 read: "to veer, sternmost and leewardmost ship first, in succession and come to the wind on the other tack." This was the signal meant for use in battle, but Jervis, who had just come from the poop deck, had not been able to see the last ship in his line—Captain Cuthbert Collingwood's *Excellent,* then about three miles to the rear. Because of the action against the Spanish to leeward, a pall of smoke hung over the central part of the British fleet. Jervis reasoned wisely that if he could not see the *Excellent,* Collingwood could not see the *Victory.* Such visibility problems were by no means unusual in battle. Under normal conditions the British frigates, deployed on the unengaged flank, would have "repeated" the signal, passing it down the line. But with Spanish ships to both port and starboard, the British frigates had sought safety in the rear.

With the frigates unavailable, Jervis could have made signal 100 and hoped that it would eventually make its way to Collingwood, who could then begin the maneuver. But Sir John, an experienced commander, knew it could take from ten to fifteen minutes to pass the signal along a line of seven ships stretching back for three miles, and that only if none of the captains failed, or was unable, to send it on its way.

Thus Jervis, handcuffed by the signal book, had few options. The most promising was to begin a maneuver with the leading ship of the rear division—Thompson's *Britannia*—which he could clearly see four ships to his rear. At 1250 he made signal 80—"to tack in succession"—for the *Britannia,* and a minute later sent aloft signal 41, general to the fleet, for each ship "to take suitable station and engage as arrive up in succession." Jervis expected Thompson to tack and lead his division to reinforce Parker's, the ships of the two merging into a line as best they could.[33]

The response to Jervis's pair of signals demonstrates the problems of reliance on visual systems to direct the movements of a fleet during a battle. Thompson did not respond and instead followed along in line behind the center division. A damaged jib boom and a fire may account for Thompson's failure to react; if so, he was remiss in not signaling the other ships in his division to tack. It is not clear from the extant documents that Thompson even saw the signal. Whatever the facts, the ships of his division, including, despite accounts to the contrary, Collingwood's *Excellent,* followed their leader.[34]

Only one ship to Jervis's rear did respond to the signal—the *Captain* 74, commanded by Horatio Nelson. Nelson was flying a commodore's broad pennant and was not part of Thompson's command. Nor was the *Captain* in its proper station in line. Positioned to windward of Jervis's line, Nelson was closer to the action about to develop between the Spanish and Sir John's van, and was also clear of the smoke that hung over the rear of the British line.

Nelson saw Jervis's signal to "tack in succession," but instead ordered his ship to wear. As he later explained: "Observing . . . that the main body of the enemy were pushing to join their friends to leeward, by passing in the rear of our squadron, I thought unless by some prompt and extraordinary measure, the main body could be diverted from this course, until Sir John (at that time in action in the *Victory*) could see their plan, his well arranged designs on the enemy would be frustrated. I therefore ordered the *Captain* to wear."[35] Nelson knew the signal book, and its limitations, as well as anyone in the fleet. He recognized in Jervis's signal evidence of a "well arranged design" and, in an extraordinary display of initiative, acted accordingly. Nelson sailed between the rearmost ships in the British line—the *Diadem* and the *Excellent*—and joined Parker's van division in its battle with the Spanish. While several of Nelson's fellow captains witnessed his maneuver, not one followed his example.

As Jervis led his center to windward, desperate fighting developed between Parker's division, supported by Nelson's *Captain,* and the bulk of the Spanish fleet. The British, heavily outnumbered, were hard pressed to hold their own. Virtually unsupported, Nelson and Troubridge in their 74s fought off the *Santísima Trinidad* and two three-deckers. Jervis again attempted to direct his rear to assist Parker. At 1319 he made signal 85, general to his fleet: "to come to the wind in succession on the larboard tack after leading ship. Imply veering on the starboard tack." Since only Thompson's ships remained on a larboard tack, the meaning of the signal should have been obvious: wear, and sail on a larboard tack to the assistance of the van. But again the fleet failed to respond as Jervis expected. The *Diadem* 74 wore and joined the van, but the *Britannia,* the *Namur* 74, and the *Excellent* tacked and merged into the line ahead and astern of the *Victory.*

Jervis's plan to double the Spanish had come undone. Seven British ships could not forever hold off more than twice their number of Spanish *navíos.* At 1405 Sir John made the signal for close action general to the fleet, and ten minutes later he made the signal for Collingwood's *Excellent,* then just ahead of the *Victory* in line, to pass through the enemy fleet.

Collingwood responded promptly and, at pistol-shot range or less, blasted his way through. The *Excellent* passed "so close alongside" one Spaniard, Collingwood wrote, that "a man might jump from one ship to the other." After forcing the *San Salvador del Mundo* 112 to strike, Collingwood continued on and engaged the *San Nicolas* 84 and the *San Josef* 112, both busily hammering away at Nelson's *Captain.* The *Excellent* loosed its broadside at such close range that shot "passed through both ships."[36]

Collingwood's arrival could not have been more timely. The *Captain* was a near-wreck, its fore topmast gone, the wheel shot away, and the rigging in tatters. But as Nelson watched his friend "Col" fire into the *San Nicolas* and the *San Josef,* the two Spanish *navíos* ran afoul of each other. Nelson saw his opportunity. He ordered Captain Ralph Miller to luff and called for boarders. The *Captain* was soon alongside the *San Nicolas.* Captain Edward Berry, a supernumerary who had until his recent promotion been one of Nelson's lieutenants, led the first boarders and seized control of the poop deck. Nelson followed a soldier through a quartergallery window and fought his way to the quarterdeck in time to see one of Berry's men hauling down the Spanish flag. As the banner of imperial Spain reached the deck, the *San Josef* opened fire on what was now a British man-of-war. Nelson immediately called across to Miller for reinforcements and minutes later led the *Captain*'s boarding party across "Nelson's Patent Bridge for Boarding First-Rates," quickly securing his second prize.[37]

By the time the battle ended at about 1600, the British had captured four Spanish ships of the line—a 74, an 84, and two of 112 guns. Captain Saumarez actually forced the mighty *Santísima Trinidad* to strike, but the world's largest warship escaped when the *Orion* sailed on to assist hard-pressed comrades.[38]

While Jervis captured only four of the twenty-seven enemy ships and failed to intercept the mercury convoy, his victory was noteworthy, given the disparity of force, and proved timely in both a strategic and a political sense. In Geoffrey Marcus's view: "The battle of St. Vincent possibly saved England. It certainly saved the Government." The battle also demonstrated the resiliency of the British, and the sorry state of the Spanish navy. "The veil that covered its rottenness was stripped away," Mahan wrote of the Spanish navy, "and at the same time were revealed to [Britain], which feared it had no naval chiefs, the striking and brilliant figures of Jervis and Nelson." From the admiralty, Lord Spencer wrote to Jervis of the people's "exultation and applause." In reward, the government raised Sir John to the peerage as the Earl of St. Vincent. Nelson, who had been promoted to rear admiral on 20 February before news of the battle reached England, gained the Order of the Bath and became a popular hero.[39]

FOR NELSON the St. Valentine's Day 1797 battle reinforced an already strong belief that the centralization inherent in reliance on visual signals handicapped the fleet in action. From the quarterdeck of the *Captain* Nelson had watched Jervis, whom he considered an excellent commander in chief, lose control of his fleet because of the limitations of the signal book. Nelson had not been the only commander in the rear who recognized what needed to be done; he had simply been the only one willing to take the professional risk to react. Why? The traditional answer has been: because of too strict doctrinal adherence to the line. And this was true to some extent. But the root of the problem was that in a centralized system captains expected directions, and in their absence waited for them.

When Nelson commanded his own squadron he rejected the notion that a commander could control his fleet in combat. In his view personal initiative, and not management, was the key to success in battle. As he wrote to Lord Spencer in 1799 after the Nile: "The circumstances of this war so often vary, that an Officer has almost every moment to consider—What would my superiors direct, did they know what is passing under my nose?"[40]

At the Nile Nelson earned for himself great glory, a peerage, the affections of Emma Hamilton, and a reputation among historians as the best battle commander in naval history. But why was Nelson able not only to reject the signaling catholicon of the day but also to entrust his professional fate to his subordinates? The answer may rest with his religiousness and its inverse—his rejection of the rationalism of the day. Nelson, simply put, was not a very rational or enlightened fellow by late-eighteenth-century standards. C. S. Forester discovered in his analysis of Nelson's letters that "he seems to have remained quite untouched by any of the fashionable fads of irreligion." Forester concluded: "Throughout the correspondence there runs a strong religious sentiment, of whose sincerity we can have no doubt."[41]

As the son, brother, and grandson of Anglican priests, Nelson was no stranger to religion. He also had a personal religious experience when, aged seventeen, he was returning from the Indies in the *Dolphin* frigate, weakened by fever and "reduced to a mere skeleton." He later recalled:

> I felt impressed with the idea that I should never rise in my profession. My mind was staggered with a view of the difficulties I had to surmount, and the little interest I possessed. I could discover no means of reaching the object of my ambitions. After a long and gloomy reverie, in which I almost wished myself overboard, a sudden glow of patriotism was kindled within me, and presented my king and country as my patron. My mind exulted in the idea. "Well, then" I exclaimed, "I will be a hero, and, confiding in Providence, I will brave every danger."

There then appeared in Nelson's "mind's eye," according to his earliest biographers, ". . . a radiant orb . . . which urged him on to renown." A more recent biographer, Christopher Hibbert, described Nelson's epiphany as "a sudden transformation of feeling such as that which overwhelmed St. Paul on the road to Damascus."[42]

What role could religious faith play in the formulation of naval tactics? Perhaps none. But if one perceives the key to Nelson's facility for command, not in tactics, but in a willingness to trust to the initiative of his subordinates, then his receptivity toward a fundamental belief structure in the spiritual realm may help to explain his approach to command and control in the material. After all, if Nelson truly believed he was destined to succeed, whether that expectation was rooted in faith in God or in himself, he must have believed his subordinates would succeed as well.

Nelson throughout his life—and not just until the end of the first chapter of his biography—remained the son of the rector of Burnham Thorpe in an age in which men sought to bring order from chaos and to replace beliefs with understanding. He rejected the received dictates and sought instead interaction—communion, not with the Almighty, but with his own subordinates. In 1798, before the Nile campaign, Nelson wrote to the Society for Promoting Christian Knowledge requesting Bibles and prayer books for his crews. George Charles Smith, who at age nineteen fought under Nelson at the battle of Copenhagen in April 1801 and founded the London Mariner's Church, noted years later: "We gloried . . . that we followed in the wake of Nelson, as the only Jesus Christ or Saviour we acknowledge in the fleet." Nelson's famous letter to Lady Hamilton is replete with religious overtones and imagery. His meeting with his subordinates in his flagship before Trafalgar, as he describes it, has more in common with Christ's Last Supper with his apostles than with a council of war. "When I came to explain to them the 'Nelson Touch,' it was like an electric shock. Some shed tears, all approved—'It was new—it was singular—it was simple!' And from Admirals downward, it was repeated—'It must succeed, if ever they will allow us to get at them! You are, my Lord, surrounded by friends whom you inspire with confidence.' Some may be Judas's, but the majority are certainly much pleased with my commanding them."[43]

While others sought to bring order to the chaos of battle, Nelson sought to bring chaos to the order of battle. In his quest for victory, he was willing not only to forgo the linearity of his fleet and of his decision-making but also to embrace chaos, even the bedlam of a night action. Where others saw "pell-mell" or "promiscuous battle," Nelson perceived a disparate form of harmony. In battle he hoped to "surprise and confound" his enemies. "They won't know what I am about," he told a friend before Trafalgar; "it will bring forward a pell-mell battle, and that is what I want."[44]

NELSON WAS NOT the only commander in the Royal Navy willing to accept the risks of a pell-mell engagement. On 11 October 1797, off Camperdown, along the Dutch coast just south of the entrance to the Texel, Admiral Adam Duncan achieved one of the most complete victories in the age of fighting sail. Duncan, who had been born in Scotland in 1731, was an imposing presence, for at six feet four inches he towered over his contemporaries. His eldest brother died in the service of the East India Company; his second brother joined the British army and was immortalized by James Fenimore Cooper in *The Last of the Mohicans;* Adam, who joined the navy at the age of fifteen, was often referred to as "the finest and handsomest man in the service." He was a captain by his thirtieth birthday and in August 1762 took part in the final assault against Havana, where along with his captain's share of the prize money he contracted a fever that often kept him ashore and slowed his rise in his profession. Twenty-six years later, at the age of fifty-six, he finally reached flag rank. He became a full admiral in 1795, and that same year Lord Spencer offered him command of the scratch fleet assembling in the North Sea to watch the Dutch.[45]

In January 1795 the French completed their conquest of the Netherlands, soon renamed the Batavian Republic. The imperatives of French power on the continent outweighed the demands of a maritime empire, and Dutch allegiance to France left Holland's colonies and merchant marine at the mercy of the British, who took full advantage of the situation, blockading the Dutch coast and seizing their ships and colonies.[46]

For the next two years Admiral Duncan's fleet kept close watch on the Texel. Blockading duty was boring, and difficult, especially when the great mutinies of 1797 left Duncan with little more than a ship or two on station off the Dutch coast. Events appeared to be coming to a head in the summer of 1797 when the Dutch prepared their navy and a fleet of transports to take part in a French plan to invade Ireland. Duncan hoped the Dutch would sail before his ships and men had to spend another winter blockading the coast. In a letter to Lord Spencer at the admiralty, he observed that it would be "madness" for the Dutch "to risk battle" at present; if they were patient the weather would "do the business for them."[47] But the Dutch did not sail; foul winds forced the cancellation of the invasion.

In the fall the French-dominated Batavian government ordered its "Grand Fleet" to sea, hoping to catch Britain's worn ships at a disadvantage. The Dutch commander, Admiral Jan Willem de Winter, knew the strains under which the blockaders labored, but he also recognized the shortcomings of his own fleet. In numbers of ships the two commands were evenly matched. Dutch tactical doctrine was well developed, blending the aggressiveness of de Ruyter with a French-style system of signals and formations. But the Dutch had not fought a major naval battle since 1704. Nor did their ships of the line mount the carronades that lined the upper decks of Duncan's men-of-war, carronades that would wreak havoc in the close action traditionally favored by the Hollanders. But orders were orders and de Winter sailed from the Texel on 7 October with sixteen sail of the line prepared to risk battle, though only if conditions heavily favored his fleet.[48]

Shortly before de Winter sailed, the British, whose ships had been out for nineteen weeks and whose crews were showing signs of scurvy, returned to Yarmouth for provisions and repairs. Duncan left a small squadron commanded by Captain Henry Trollope—his own *Russell* 74, the *Adamant* 50, and the frigate *Beaulieu*—to keep watch on the Dutch. On the night of 8 October, because of the malfeasance of a lieutenant on watch who was "in an unfit state to keep the deck," Captain William Hotham's *Adamant* found itself in uncomfortably close proximity to the Dutch. Hotham quickly extracted himself from his predicament and alerted Trollope, who dispatched a small, fast ship to Yarmouth to warn Duncan.[49]

The lugger bearing Trollope's report reached Yarmouth on the morning of 9 October. At about 1100, with the wind from the northeast, Duncan weighed with eleven of the line. Three additional ships joined him later that or the next day. Word that the British were out reached de Winter on 10 October when he queried the master of a fishing vessel. He decided at once to return to the safety of the Texel. De Winter's preferred strategy, he later confessed to Duncan, was to remain in port to keep the British fleet "in a constant state of suspense" until they were worn down by the rigors of a winter blockade, and then in the spring "to bring a fleet to sea superior to ours."[50]

In the early morning of 11 October 1797 Duncan's fleet was sailing in two disorganized divisions on a course west by south. Vice Admiral

Richard Onslow, flying his flag in the *Monarch* 74, commanded the van; Duncan, flying his in the *Venerable* 74, the main body. Shortly before sunrise Duncan turned to a new course—northeast by north—intent on keeping his fleet between the enemy and the Texel.

At about 0700 British lookouts sighted three ships of war six or seven miles distant to the south-southwest. The lookouts initially thought the three were Dutch, but one of the liners made the private signal for a British man-of-war. The ships were Captain Trollope's and soon made the signals that indicated the presence of an enemy fleet of sixteen ships of the line. Duncan bore up to allow his detached squadron to rejoin and at 0900 made the signal to prepare for battle.

At 0933 Duncan signaled for the fleet to form the line on a starboard tack. With the wind from the northwest by north, the British were running with the wind on their quarter on a course between south-southeast and south, while the Dutch were close hauled, or nearly so, heading toward the northeast. Given the relative position of the two fleets, intercepting de Winter should have been an easy task had Duncan had a specific mode of attack in mind.[51]

The British continued to run toward the south until 1012, when Duncan made the signal to chase. Duncan was not using a chase to close the range more quickly as a prelude to his planned attack, as had Byng, Anson, and Hawke. At this stage of the battle he intended to engage directly from the "chase." Six minutes later he signaled his fleet to "take stations and engage as you come up."

About a half-hour later he changed his mind. Between 1104 and 1123, shortly after lookouts first sighted the Dutch coast, Duncan belatedly attempted to get his fleet into line, signaling his captains to shorten sail and "to take station," the ships astern the *Venerable* being directed to keep in the "Admiral's wake." By 1125 Duncan had recognized the futility of his effort. He made signal 36, for "each ship independently to steer for and engage her opponent in the enemy's line." Then at 1129 the *Venerable* flew the signal for the fleet to "bear up and sail large." With the wind from the northwest by north, to "sail large" would put the British ships on an interception course sailing northeast. Duncan's intention was not to bring on a general engagement along the entire line, but to concentrate his efforts against part of the Dutch fleet. At 1136 he signaled for his van to attack the enemy rear, and at 1137 for his own division to engage the Dutch center.

Ten minutes later he changed his mind again. The officer responsible

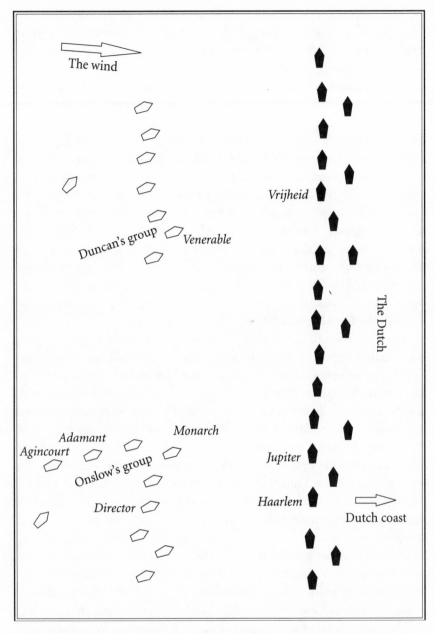

THE BATTLE OF CAMPERDOWN, II OCTOBER 1797, CA. 1230
The proximity of the coast to the east and the direction of the wind placed the
Dutch at a disadvantage. Camperdown is often compared to Trafalgar, and a comparison of the two diagrams makes the similarities evident. The principal difference was that Duncan's maneuver was rooted more in impatience and a desire to
engage than in a well-thought-out plan of attack discussed beforehand with his
subordinates.

for signals in the *Venerable*—Lieutenant William Renton—recalled that "the Dutch ships were drawing fast in shore, and the Admiral was impatient to get down." At 1147 Duncan made signal 34—Lord Howe's signal for individual ships to pass through the enemy line and to engage from leeward. Duncan, now intent on attacking the entire Dutch line, stood the *Venerable* on an interception course with de Winter's flagship, the *Vrijheid* 74. At 1205 the *Venerable* hoisted the signal for close action.[52]

Poor visibility and Duncan's changes of mind caused confusion in the British fleet.[53] Captain John Williamson, commanding the *Agincourt* 74, hesitantly wandered about the scene of battle without ever engaging to purpose. William Hotham was also unable to divine Duncan's intentions, until the admiral made signal 34 to break the line, "which he did," Hotham later wrote, "with intrepidity and address which reflects the very highest honour on his character." All of Duncan's captains understood the purport of number 34, and, as Renton later told the court-martial that tried Williamson: "It was in the power of every ship to pick out her opponent . . . and it was in the power of every ship to have passed through the Dutch line, who were by no means close."[54]

Vice Admiral Onslow, whose van division now constituted Duncan's rear, led the attack on the rear of de Winter's line. At about 1230 the Dutch opened on Onslow's flagship, the *Monarch,* but Onslow directed his gunners to reserve their first, and most carefully loaded, broadside. At about 1250 the *Monarch* passed through the Dutch line, raking the *Jupiter* 74 to port and the *Haarlem* 68 to starboard. A few minutes later Duncan led the windward division into action, raking several Dutch ships as the *Venerable* broke the line. At least five other British liners made their way through, raking the Dutch to effect, and took up positions to leeward. The engagement soon became close, confused, and hot. The *Venerable* found itself between the fires of two Dutch 74s, one of them de Winter's flagship.

Duncan had not lost control of his fleet; he had relinquished it. After signaling madly during the morning, he made no signals between 1220 and 1505 as the battle raged.[55] He trusted to the initiative and good sense of his captains and the fighting qualities of the British seamen.

The movements of the 74-gun *Director,* commanded by Captain William "Bounty" Bligh, who wrote the most detailed account of the battle, demonstrate that Duncan's faith in his officers and men was not misplaced. As the *Director* broke the line two ships astern Onslow's *Monarch,* "the Dutch gave way, and the ships became mixed, so that it required sometimes great caution to prevent firing into one another." After passing through the line, Bligh kept moving, silencing the guns of one Dutch ship before moving on to engage another. When he sensed that the Dutch rear was finished, he noticed "that some force was wanted in the van, as we saw five ships unengaged and apparently not hurt." He shifted his way along what remained of the Dutch line until he was in action with the *Vrijheid,* exchanging passing broadsides at a range of twenty yards until the *Director* reached a deadly raking position, just ahead and almost touching de Winter's flagship. A few moments later, the Dutch admiral was the only Hollander still standing on the quarterdeck. At about 1515 the *Vrijheid* struck.[56]

The battle was over and Duncan, raised to the peerage as Baron Duncan of Lundie and Viscount Duncan of Camperdown, had won a great victory. The British captured two frigates and nine of the sixteen Dutch ships of the line, including the flagship and the commander in chief. The human losses were heavy on both sides, principally because the Dutch, like the British, fired into the hull and not the rigging. British casualties totaled 228 killed and 812 wounded, while the Dutch lost 540 killed, 620 wounded, and another 3,775 as prisoners in the prizes.[57]

In form, Duncan's attack at Camperdown bore a surface resemblance to Nelson's at Trafalgar. The fleets of both admirals cut through their opponent's line in two divisions and captured or destroyed just over half of the enemy ships engaged. Once the engagement proper began, both men relied not on signals but on the initiative of their captains. Both battles demonstrated the tactical superiority of individual British ships and their crews. As a song popular in England during the winter of 1797–1798 pronounced:

> St. Vincent drubbed the Dons, Earl Howe he drubbed Monsieur,
> And gallant Duncan now has soundly drubbed Mynheer;
> The Spanish, French and Dutch, tho' all united be,
> Fear not, Britannia, My Tars can beat all three.[58]

There were obvious differences between Camperdown and Trafalgar. The command styles of the two admirals differed markedly. Nelson planned to attack in two divisions and explained his intentions and expectations to his captains beforehand. Duncan decided on his mode of attack in the midst of a situation confused, in part, by his own maneuvers and signaling. Duncan's official report of the battle offers no hint of premeditation: "As we approached near I made the Signal for the squadron to shorten sail [at 1102], in order to connect them; soon after I saw land between Camperdown and Egmont, about nine Miles to Leeward of the enemy, and finding there was no Time to be lost in making the Attack, I made the Signal to bear up, break the Enemy's Line, and engage them to Leeward, each Ship her Opponent, by which I got between them and the Land, whither they were fast approaching."[59]

Despite the use of Howe's signal to break the line, Duncan's decision to throw his fleet without forethought into a wild mêlée against an enemy line was hardly standard tactical practice. Not surprisingly, some of his contemporaries questioned the wisdom of his decision. When Captain Hotham returned to England after the battle, he was "interrogated confidentially upon this subject by one high in office." Hotham considered Duncan "a man of no extensive general knowledge nor had he much professional knowledge or experience." But Hotham believed there was no time "for tactique or manoeuvre" on 11 October. The lateness of the season and the "proximity of the coast," he explained, made "haste imperatively necessary." Perhaps St. Vincent reflected the views of those who harbored a suspicion that Duncan had been more lucky than smart. "Lord Duncan's action was fought pell-mell (without plan or system)," St. Vincent recalled years later; "he was a gallant officer (but had no idea of tactics, and being puzzled with them;) and attacked, without attention to form or order, trusting that the brave example he set would achieve his object, which it did completely."[60]

Duncan's victory, considered together with Jervis's at Cape St. Vincent and Nelson's at the Nile, demonstrated that in a close action the British held a definite advantage. During the wars of the French Revolution and Empire the "Monsieurs," "Dons," and "Mynheers" were no match for the Royal Navy's tars.

But what were the implications for a centralized system of command and control if a British fleet that had just recovered from a mutiny, commanded by a "puzzled" admiral with "no idea of tactics," could overwhelm an equal number of Dutch ships and win such a complete victory? There can be no doubt that the improved visual signaling systems were a tremendous advance that allowed admirals to maneuver their fleets into position for battle. But were attempts to manage the subsequent engagement from the flagship workable, or counterproductive?

The string of victories won between 1793 and 1798 by commanders using the manual of signals in battle convinced the admiralty to place its official imprimatur on the signal book. Further revision began in 1798 under the direction of Captain James Gambier, a noted Howe man. The new "official" signal book, in two volumes, issued on 13 May 1799, included day, night, and fog signals and instructions, a variety of scenarios for breaking the line, and, for the first time, a comprehensive list of the Royal Navy's ships with individualized identification signal numbers.[61] But two years passed before the navy had the opportunity to test the new signal book in battle.

THE ROYAL NAVY'S next major engagement—the attack on the Danish fleet at Copenhagen in April 1801—illustrated not the superiority of the new signal book but the benefits of a system that permitted initiative. After Nelson's victory at the Nile in 1798, he remained in the Mediterranean for more than two years, conducting a desultory campaign to forestall a French conquest of the entire Italian peninsula and enjoying the company of his mistress, Emma Hamilton, the wife of the British minister to the Neapolitan court, Sir William Hamilton. In early November 1800 Nelson, accompanied by the Hamiltons, finally returned to England via Naples, Vienna, Prague, Dresden, and Hamburg. In England he encountered everywhere both official and unofficial outpourings of public admiration and affection.[62]

That winter a crisis simmering in the Baltic came to a boil. In 1798 several Baltic states had begun to consider armed neutrality—refusing by force to allow their merchant ships to be searched by British men-of-war. In December 1800, at the instigation of Tsar Paul I of Russia, Russia, Sweden, Denmark, and Prussia formed the second Armed Neutrality League and embargoed British trade.[63]

The ministry of William Pitt (the Younger), determined to react forcefully to the challenge, decided to strike at Denmark—the weakest, most exposed, and also most strategically placed member of the league. If the British could defeat the Danes before the ice melted and freed the Russian and Swedish fleets, the league might come undone. The admiralty gave command of the fleet to Admiral Sir Hyde Parker, seconded by Vice Admiral Lord Nelson and Rear Admiral Thomas Graves. The fleet included eighteen of the line, several "bombs" (vessels armed with mortars that could shell Copenhagen), and transports carrying a small contingent of British troops commanded by Lieutenant Colonel William Stewart.

Parker had spent the previous several years in Jamaica, where he had amassed a fortune collecting his share of the prize money earned by the ships of his Leeward Islands command, considered by Lord Spencer "the most lucrative station in the service." Parker had consistently antagonized the Americans, whose small navy was then engaged in a cooperative but undeclared naval war against the French in the West Indies, and undermined the British government's policy toward strife-torn St. Domingue (Haiti), behavior that may have hastened his recall.[64] Nevertheless, he was held in high esteem within the Royal Navy. He had earned honors as a captain during the American war and served under Hotham in the Mediterranean, where, perhaps only in comparison, Sir Hyde appeared aggressive. Whatever his failings as a diplomat while at Jamaica, he had managed his squadron well. Lord St. Vincent himself recommended Parker's appointment to the Baltic fleet, although he had never commanded such a large force in battle.

Sir Hyde was as distracted as he was untested. When he returned to England, Parker, then sixty-one years of age, married the eighteen-year-old daughter of Sir Richard Onslow, who had commanded Duncan's van at Camperdown. With a fortune in one arm and a young wife on the other, Parker's desire to take a winter cruise to the Baltic was somewhat restrained. As Nelson wrote to his friend Thomas Troubridge, "consider how nice it must be laying abed with a young wife, compared to a damned raw cold wind." Captain Hotham also considered Parker's "attention divided" that winter. The campaign about to begin would reveal Parker as one of those men who "have their characters brought before their brother Officers and who, from the estimation in which they are held in subordinate situations, did not quite fulfill the hopes of what they would be in Chief Commands."[65]

Foul weather and Parker's lack of drive delayed the fleet's sailing. The British were off the Naze (Cape Lindesnes, the southernmost tip of Norway) on 18 March and did not reach the entrance to the Sound—the narrow passage between the Danish island of Sjaelland and Sweden—until the twenty-first. There British diplomats informed Sir Hyde that the Danes were prepared to fight, and the fleet's pilots warned him of the difficulty of a contested passage.

Despite the admiralty's orders to attack, Sir Hyde proposed to remain off the Sound, waiting either for new instructions to arrive from London or for the enemy to attack. Nelson's prodding, however, convinced him to risk an assault, if not against the Danes, then against the Russians. It was already spring, and Nelson knew that in a few weeks the ice would melt and the Russian and Swedish fleets would be able to join their allies.[66]

After more than a week of dallying, on 30 March the British began an easy passage through the Sound and on 1 April sailed past Copenhagen. Rather than attack the Danish fleet, moored in the narrow channel between Copenhagen and the Middle Ground Shoal, from the north as the Danes expected, Nelson proposed to attack from the south. Conveniently for the British, the northerly wind, which had blown their ships through the Sound, shifted on cue and blew from the south the next day.

Nelson's plan, the most detailed he ever worked out, called for his squadron to attack up the channel from the south with twelve of the line, several frigates, and the bombs, while Parker demonstrated with the rest of the fleet to the north. The Danish force included two forts armed with sixty-eight 24- and 36-pounders, twenty moored warships of varying strength, armed hulks, floating batteries, and several shore batteries. Nelson's ships would work their way up the narrow channel, from which the navigation buoys had been removed, and moor with stern anchors and springs opposite the Danes, as had the British at the Nile, from the rear forward.

At 0930 Nelson's squadron weighed, and thirty-five minutes later the engagement began. The first ships into the channel dropped their stern anchors as planned and opened on their allotted Danes at point-blank range. As Nelson's flagship, the *Elephant* 74, worked its way toward the channel, he made good use of the signal book, trying to hurry laggard vessels and warning others of suspected shoal water. Two British ships nevertheless ran aground on the Middle Shoal. Nelson signaled, trying to make adjustments to his own line, but ultimately had to trust to the common sense of his captains. From 1118, shortly after the *Elephant* anchored and opened fire, until 1430, he made no signals. From the starboard side of the quarterdeck he watched as his following ships forced their way up the channel. The fighting soon became general and hot. Rear Admiral Graves later wrote his brother: "*I am told* the battle of the Nile was nothing to this."[67]

As Nelson's ships fought their bloody fight, Sir Hyde Parker watched the engagement from the quarterdeck of his flagship, the *London* 98. After three hours of battle, the Danish fire appeared undiminished. He could see that three of Nelson's liners were aground and several ships were flying distress signals. From Parker's perspective, the chaotic scene reeked of disaster. At 1300 the *London* made what Dudley Pope aptly termed the "most controversial signal in the history of sea warfare"—signal 39, "to discontinue the engagement."[68]

But a battle that appeared confused and ominous to Parker was just the sort of engagement Nelson sought. Four days earlier he had confided to Troubridge that the situation off the Danish coast was one "where the spur of the moment must call forth the clearest decision and the most active conduct." "On occasions," he continued, "we must sometimes have a regular confusion, and that apparent confusion must be the most regular method which could be pursued on the occasion." As he had at the Nile, Nelson sought a confusing, pell-mell engagement. Unlike Parker, who kept his subordinates in the dark until the last minute, Nelson discussed his plans beforehand with his captains. They understood his intentions and did not disappoint. When the grounding of three ships left the British line too short to extend the length of the Danish formation, Captain Edward Riou, commanding Nelson's frigates, filled the gap with his own *Amazon* 36 and four other undergunned ships.[69]

About the same time that Parker, fearing a debacle, made the signal to disengage, Nelson sensed that the southern end of the Danish line, the section that had been under British pressure for the longest time, was about to give way. In fact, within an hour of Parker's signal the southern and central sections of the Danes' defenses collapsed. Nelson could also see that while several of his ships were aground or disabled, they were nonetheless in action.[70]

At about 1300 Nelson, his keen eye surveying the battle, was pacing the quarterdeck of the *Elephant* when a shot struck the mainmast, sending splinters flying past him and Colonel Stewart. "It is warm work, and this day may be the last to any of us at any moment," Nelson remarked to the colonel, "but mark you, I would not be elsewhere for thousands." As Nelson resumed his pacing, the flagship's signal lieutenant approached and pointed out that Sir Hyde's flagship flew number 39. It was the duty of all the fleet's flag officers to acknowledge Parker and to repeat the signal to their subordinates.

The lieutenant asked if he should repeat the signal. "No, acknowledge it," Nelson replied. The lieutenant turned and headed for the poop deck, but Nelson called after him: "Is number 16 still hoisted?" Number 16 was the signal to engage closely. Told that it was, Nelson ordered: "Mind you, keep it so."

Stewart noticed Nelson's agitation, "which was always known by his moving the stump of his right arm." Nelson asked him: "Do you know what's shown on board the Commander-in-Chief, number 39?" Stewart, of course, knew nothing of signals, so an agitated Nelson answered his own query: "Why, to leave off action. Leave off action! Now damn me if I do!"

Nelson grabbed a glass and turned to his flag captain, Thomas Foley, who had led the way into Aboukir Bay. "You know, Foley," he said, "I have only one eye—and I have a right to be blind sometimes." Placing the glass to his blind eye, he exclaimed: "I really do not see the signal!" Satisfied, he told anyone within earshot: "Damn the signal. Keep mine for close battle flying. That's the way I answer such signals! Nail mine to the mast!"[71]

Nelson's steadfast example and outright disobedience ensured that most of his captains remained in place, and in the fight. Graves, who as a flag officer was duty bound to repeat the signal, waited fifteen minutes and then flew number 39 from the starboard maintopsail yardarm of his flagship, the *Defiance* 74, the northernmost of Nelson's liners. From that point the signal was visible to Parker but invisible to the other ships of the line to Graves's rear, including Nelson's *Elephant*. Graves had no intention of withdrawing and, like Nelson, kept the signal for close action flying from the main. But his acknowledgment was visible from the *Amazon,* directly ahead of the *Defiance* in line. While Riou saw both Parker and Graves flying the signal to disengage, he could not see the *Elephant*. As he considered his response, two of his frigates ahead in line cut their cables and "stood off." At 1315 Riou did the same. "What will Nelson think of us," he remarked. Three minutes later, as his frigate showed its stern to the Danes, a shot nearly cut Riou in half.[72]

Had Nelson's squadron heeded Parker's signal, disaster would certainly have followed. As dangerous as Nelson's position in the channel was that afternoon, extracting his ships under Danish fire would have been even more perilous. As Graves wrote after the battle: "Sir Hyde made the signal to discontinue the action before we had been at it two hours, supposing that our ships would all be destroyed. But our little Hero gloriously said, 'I will not move till we are crowned with victory, or that the Commander-in-Chief sends an officer to order me away.' And he was right, for if we had discontinued the action before the enemy struck, we should all have been aground and have been destroyed." In fact, after the battle Nelson's ships had trouble getting themselves out of the channel. Several, including the *Elephant,* ran aground.[73]

At about 1330 the Danish fire slackened, especially from the ships at the southern end of their line. About thirty minutes later Nelson sensed from the steadily decreasing cannonading that the Danes were finished and that a continuation of the battle would be little more than "a massacre." What he could not see through the smoke of battle was that more than three-quarters of the Danish platforms were out of action. At 1400 Nelson sent a flag of truce ashore; the Danes accepted. The battle was over.[74]

The battle of Copenhagen was a sanguinary affair. The victorious British suffered 944 casualties, including 256 killed; the Danes lost 1,035 men, of whom 370 were killed. As for the impact of the engagement, the assassination of Tsar Paul of Russia almost immediately overshadowed Nelson's triumph and led to the collapse of the league. Nevertheless, the victory in the Baltic, combined with a successful campaign in the Mediterranean to expel the French from Egypt, while too late to save the Pitt ministry, strengthened the hand of the British as they negotiated a peace with the new strongman in France—Napoleon Bonaparte.

By the time their diplomats signed the preliminary articles in London on 1 October 1801, both France and Great Britain were exhausted. Napoleon needed time to consolidate his regime. The British, who also needed time to recover their strength, were willing to accept, as Piers Mackesy termed it, "peace without victory."[75]

THE BATTLES of Copenhagen, Camperdown, the Nile, Cape St. Vincent, and, to an extent, the Glorious First of June demonstrated both British tactical superiority and also the need for a more flexible system that would make good use of that superiority by permitting subordinates to operate on their own initiative once an engagement began. At Copenhagen, for example, had Nelson allowed the commander in chief to manage the battle from the *London,* the consequences for the British fleet would have been disastrous. The lords of the admiralty recognized this fact. When they learned the details of the battle they recalled an astonished Parker and left Nelson in command of the fleet.[76] Even so, during the Anglo-French truce that lasted from the spring of 1801 until the winter of 1803–1804, the trend toward further centralization continued.

In England the major advance in signaling was the visual telegraph system published by Sir Home Popham in 1803. Popham, using the existing set of signal flags, devised a system that permitted more detailed and two-way communication between ships. He viewed his revolutionary system not as a substitute for, but as a supplement to, the signal book. Nelson would use Popham's code to send his famous "England expects" signal at Trafalgar.[77]

French and Spanish naval officers, given the battering they had undergone during the past war, were somewhat more inclined toward tactical reforms. In France Audibert Ramatuelle published his *Cours élémentaire de tactique navale* in 1802. Ramatuelle's work was far more practical than Morogues's, but retained the orientation toward linear combat and signal-based centralized control. The author, who dedicated his work to the new first consul, Napoleon Bonaparte, hoped that it would herald advances in the art of war at sea comparable to those taking place in the art of war ashore. Not surprisingly, he stressed the importance of support for the operation rather than efforts to engage and destroy the enemy's fleet.[78]

In Madrid the Spanish navy in 1804 produced what Tunstall termed "one of the most sophisticated tactical and signaling treatises which has ever been published": *Tratado de Señales de Día y Noche, e Hipótesis de Ataques y Defensas.* Unlike Ramatuelle's work, the *Tratado's* orientation was offensive. It listed numerous possible developments in a naval battle and the appropriate responses. The volume included an efficient signaling system and translated extracts from Howe's 1790 signal books and instructions.[79]

All three fleets were able to test their new doctrines when war resumed in 1803 in one of history's greatest and most fateful naval campaigns. Bonaparte, now Emperor Napoleon I, was determined to crush the British and for two years struggled to bring together the forces and conditions necessary to achieve that end. The effort culminated in one of the greatest battles of the age of sail—Trafalgar.[80] The fact that Napoleon abandoned his invasion plan well before the October battle is often overlooked in the numerous accounts that attribute England's salvation to Nelson. It was not Trafalgar that saved England; it was the Royal Navy's blockade and harassment campaign carried out for over two years. Trafalgar was the crowning achievement of that campaign, which, combined with British diplomacy on the Continent to form a new coalition against France, had already successfully prevented an invasion. Both the campaign considered as a whole and the two major battles that contributed to it—Calder's action off Finisterre in July 1805 and Nelson's off Cape Trafalgar in October—demonstrate the strengths and weaknesses of centralized command systems at the strategic, operational, and tactical levels.

When war resumed between Great Britain and France in May 1803, Napoleon's mind immediately turned to the idea of an invasion across the Channel. He had good reason to wish to destroy Great Britain. His chief continental opponents—Austria, Prussia, Russia, and Spain—came and went, but Britain always remained, with its omnipresent ships off the coast and its ubiquitous diplomats offering subsidies to stoke the fires of new anti-French coalitions. In the mind of Europe's latest caesar, England was a modern-day Carthage, and France the new Rome. In May 1803 there appeared in the *Moniteur* an anonymous editorial, written by the emperor, which concluded:

> Europe watches;
> France arms;
> History writes;
> Rome destroyed Carthage!

Preparations for an invasion, funded in part with the money gained from the sale of Louisiana to the United States, began in 1803, although Napoleon had yet to formulate a detailed military plan. The scale of the effort was impressive. The emperor wished to transport across the Channel a huge army including more than 100,000 troops and 7,000 horses in the first wave.[81]

With Spain after December 1804 an ally in the war against Britain, Napoleon had a vast armada. His plan, developed with the advice of Rear Admiral Denis Decrès, the French minister of the navy and colonies, went through myriad iterations between 1803 and 1805. All involved the coordinated movement of numerous fleets and squadrons—from Brest, Rochefort, Ferrol, Cadiz, and Toulon—to bring about a massive naval concentration in the Channel to cover the invasion.

The plan, as it had evolved by early March 1805, called for Vice Admiral Honoré-Joseph Ganteaume's Brest fleet to escape the British blockade, sail south to free a Spanish squadron trapped at Ferrol, and then proceed across the Atlantic to the West Indies. There Ganteaume would join Rear Admiral de Burgues Missiessy, who had sailed from Rochefort in January. Simultaneously, Vice Admiral Pierre-Charles-Silvestre de Villeneuve's fleet would evade the British ships keeping watch on Toulon, feint toward the east, sail west, lift the blockade of the Spanish fleet at Cadiz, and proceed to Martinique, the planned rendezvous point. Under de Villeneuve's command, this fleet of more than forty sail of the line would then recross the Atlantic.

Napoleon expected the British, always concerned for the safety of their West Indian colonies, to pursue, only to discover that their quarry had doubled back toward European waters. De Villeneuve's combined Franco-Spanish armada would then sail up the English Channel, disperse the small British squadrons watching the invasion ports, and cover the transport of the army for the invasion of England.[82]

Like the earlier invasion projects of Philip II, Louis XIV, and Louis XVI, Napoleon's was devised by a general, not an admiral. No doubt the plan looked good to the emperor on his map, but the scheme was far too involved. There would be, including the invasion flotilla itself, six separate forces sailing about the Mediterranean and Atlantic basins with only rudimentary means of communication to coordinate their movements. What if one of the major French squadrons failed to escape the blockade? What if the Spanish were not ready to sail? What if the weather proved too rough for an invasion? Or what if the British failed to react as expected? The plan ignored many of the realities of war that Clausewitz termed "friction." While Napoleon may have been the most successful general in history, he had only a rudimentary understanding of naval and nautical matters, a fact evident in his handling of a 20 July 1805 naval review at Boulogne. When the naval commander, who could see a storm approaching, attempted to cancel the event, Napoleon insisted that it continue. Not long after the crowded transports took to the Channel, the sky darkened and high waves swamped the boats. Between two hundred and four hundred men lost their lives.[83]

As Napoleon planned, the British did not sit by idly. Pitt, who returned to power as prime minister in May 1804, oversaw a crash program of naval expansion and preparation. The admiralty worked to build up the strength of its blockading squadrons watching the French and, after December 1804, Spanish squadrons. The Royal Navy's smaller ships conducted aggressive raiding operations to harass the French and slow their preparations for invasion. All the while British diplomats on the continent struggled to accelerate the formation of a new, third coalition against France.

In early March Napoleon set his plan—in its sixth version—in motion, ordering both the Brest and Toulon fleets to sail as soon as possible. On 26 March Ganteaume prepared to leave Brest with twenty-one of the line, hoping for a foul wind that would blow Admiral William Cornwallis back to Torbay. Ganteaume's move, though long expected, caught the British unprepared. Cornwallis was in England, and only fifteen of the line remained on station off Brest. Ganteaume sensed his moment but, rather than act on his own, sent a telegraph dispatch to Paris describing the circumstances and seeking permission to attack. Napoleon refused, explaining that there was nothing to be gained by a purely "naval victory." "You have but one objective," he reminded the admiral, "that of fulfilling your mission. Sail without fighting." The moment passed. The favorable wind shifted and blew fair from the west. One by one the British ships returned to their station. Ganteaume would not escape, with or without a fight.[84]

As the Toulon fleet sailed on 30 March with eleven of the line, fortune nevertheless seemed to shine on the emperor's plans. De Villeneuve not only escaped Toulon but also eluded Vice Admiral Nelson, who practiced a not-too-close close blockade in the hope that his prey would venture out and risk battle. As Nelson searched for a French fleet sailing east, De Villeneuve sailed west, and on 7 April he reached Cartagena, where a small Spanish squadron had yet to receive its orders to sail. Two days later, as the French approached Cadiz, Vice Admiral Sir John Orde, commanding the small British blockading squadron, withdrew and sailed north to join Cornwallis off Ushant. On the afternoon of 9 April Admiral Don Federico Carlos Gravina and five Spanish ships of the line sortied from Cadiz and joined de Villeneuve. That very night the combined fleet sailed westward for Martinique.[85]

De Villeneuve's escape left Nelson in a quandary comparable to that he had faced in 1798 before the Nile. Where were the French? To the east? Or to the west? Not until 18 April did he learn that they had sailed west and passed the Gut. He raced after them in hard pursuit and on 8 May received intelligence that the French and Spanish fleets had sailed from Cadiz for the West Indies. Nelson immediately sailed for Portugal and put into Lagos Bay where he hastily provisioned his ships for a transatlantic crossing. He sailed on 12 May and neared Barbados on 3 June when he learned that de Villeneuve's fleet was indeed in the islands.

The allied fleet had reached Martinique without incident on 14 May, but only to discover that Missiessy's Rochefort squadron had already sailed for home. De Villeneuve waited nervously and impatiently for Ganteaume, eager to keep moving and eager to turn over responsibility for the operation to the commander of the Brest fleet.

But on 30 May a frigate arrived from France bearing new instructions—Napoleon's latest "final" plan. The emperor now looked to de Villeneuve to bring the invasion project to fruition. If Ganteaume failed to reach the West Indies within thirty-five days, de Villeneuve was to sail first to Ferrol to free the Spanish squadron there, then to Brest to drive off Cornwallis, and finally to rendezvous with Ganteaume off Ushant between 9 and 19 July. Napoleon expected the armada to reach Boulogne on 29 July.[86] In the interim de Villeneuve was to make the best use of his temporary naval superiority in the islands to reinforce Martinique and Guadeloupe and to conquer St. Vincent, Antigua, Grenada, and, if possible, Barbados—and all before sailing for Europe no later than 22 June. The emperor also assured his admiral that there was no need to worry about Nelson, whose fleet was roaming about the eastern Mediterranean.

It took until 5 June to load the troops and outfit the fleet for amphibious operations. On 7 June, as the allies rounded Antigua, they intercepted a British convoy and captured all fifteen ships. When the interrogation of prisoners revealed that Nelson was already in the islands with a dozen or so sail of the line, de Villeneuve recognized that to continue as planned involved great risk. He assumed, incorrectly though not without reason, that Nelson had been joined by Rear Admiral Sir Alexander Inglis Cochrane's squadron of six of the line, which had pursued Missiessy to the islands in January but now remained in the Caribbean. The allied fleet totaled twenty sail of the line. De Villeneuve had no desire to risk a battle with, at best, a marginal quantitative advantage, and he assumed, correctly, that the emperor shared that view. During the reign of Napoleon I there was to be no departure from the traditional French focus on "the operation" at the expense of a given battle. De Villeneuve returned to Martinique, where he unloaded his troops, and on 1 June sailed for Ferrol.

Off Antigua on 12 June a disappointed Nelson learned that the allied fleet had evaded him once again. Unsure of de Villeneuve's next stop, Nelson chose Cadiz, set a course for Cape Spartel, and detached Commander George Edmund Byron Bettesworth's sloop Curieux 18 to England with dispatches and intelligence. His fleet sighted the cape on 18 July and two days later reached Gibraltar, where "he set foot ashore . . . for the first time in almost two years."[87]

En route across the Atlantic, Bettesworth spied the allied fleet sailing farther north than expected and carried that news, along with Nelson's dispatches, to Plymouth, where he anchored on 7 July. Bettesworth raced to London and arrived at the admiralty at about 2300 on the eighth, to be told that Lord Barham, the first lord, had retired and no one would wake him. Bettesworth finally met with a "furious" first lord the next morning. Barham, still in his nightclothes, immediately penned an unofficial letter to Cornwallis, alerting him to the approach of the allied fleet and directing him to reinforce Vice Admiral Sir Robert Calder's fleet off Ferrol with the Rochefort squadron and have Calder cruise thirty to forty leagues west of Cape Finisterre.[88]

The twenty-second day of July 1805 dawned foggy, as Calder led his fleet of fifteen of the line on a southwesterly course about thirty-nine leagues northwest of Cape Finisterre. At about 1100 lookouts from one of Calder's liners, the *Defiance* 74, sighted the allied fleet ahead. The Franco-Spanish fleet of twenty of the line was sailing toward the east-southeast in three columns, the wind light from the west-northwest.[89]

The sun failed to burn off the morning fog, and throughout the afternoon Calder struggled to direct the maneuvers of his fleet from his flagship, the *Prince of Wales* 98. Only with difficulty was he able to keep his force in something approaching a line positioned between the enemy and Ferrol. Sporadic cannonading began late in the day, and the engagement became general about 1800. Amid the confusion caused by the fog combined with the smoke of battle, the bulk of Calder's line engaged the Spanish *navíos* of de Villeneuve's van division, which was supported by, at best, three ships from the French center. At about 2000 two Spanish ships struck, and twenty-five minutes later Calder made the signal to discontinue the action.

For two days the fleets remained in proximity, making repairs and guarding their prizes and cripples. Calder had opportunities to renew the battle but, aware that twenty allied liners were now unblockaded at Rochefort and Ferrol, withdrew, satisfied with his effort. The British, although outnumbered by a third, had won the day. Calder's casualties totaled about 200 killed and wounded; de Villeneuve lost two ships and suffered almost 500 casualties, not including the 1,200 men captured in the prizes.

Sir Robert's decimation of the allied fleet pleased few in Britain. While he may have had a good day by eighteenth-century standards, the capture of two ships paled compared with the crushing victories at Copenhagen, the Nile, and Camperdown. Worse yet, in an England gripped by an invasion scare, Calder's failure to demolish de Villeneuve's fleet prompted widespread dissatisfaction with what became known as an "action" rather than a battle. Public criticism and rumor-mongering ultimately led Sir Robert to demand a court-martial to clear his reputation, but the result was not what he expected. The court cleared him of charges of cowardice but reprimanded him for not renewing the engagement.

Calder was certainly no Nelson; but, then, as St. Vincent observed, there was "but one Nelson." Had Sir Horatio commanded the fleet on 22 July, there can be little doubt that he would have been far more aggressive than Calder. For Calder, an admiral attempting to control his fleet with visual signals, the fog was an impediment. But Nelson, the victor of the battle fought in the dark in Aboukir Bay, might well have considered the fog advantageous to an outnumbered fleet commanded by aggressive captains.

Calder was an able commander, but one who was intent on directing the movements of his fleet no matter the situation. It was the cautious Calder, Sir John Jervis's captain of the fleet on St. Valentine's Day 1797, who had criticized Nelson's departure from the line. As the naval historian John Knox Laughton concluded: "Calder was a good, commonplace officer, and was tried according to a standard of which he had no conception."[90]

AFTER THE "ACTION" off Cape Finisterre, de Villeneuve retired to Vigo Bay, where he provisioned and relieved himself of two cripples. The Spanish contingent then sailed for Ferrol, while the French went to Corunna. There de Villeneuve received further instructions from his emperor. The combined fleet was now to sail south to release the Spanish squadron blockaded at Cadiz, sail back north into the Bay of Biscay to rendezvous with the Rochefort squadron, now commanded by Commodore Zacharie Allemand, then set a course to Ushant, drive the British blockading squadron from Brest, join Ganteaume, and proceed into the Channel. A few days later, in yet another set of instructions from Paris, Napoleon directed de Villeneuve to forget Cadiz, sail directly for the bay, join Allemand who was already out, and thence make direct for Brest.

By this point in the campaign de Villeneuve had exhausted both his patience and his reservoir of mental stamina. The admiral wrote to the minister of marine, his old friend Decrès, and referred openly to "the sailors in Paris" who were "blind, reprehensible, and stupid." "I cannot conceal my belief that we have no chance of winning," he added, and in a revealing admission wrote: "I cannot pull out of this deep depression into which I have fallen."[91]

De Villeneuve, convinced that the invasion plan was doomed to failure, chose to ignore Napoleon's latest directive and to obey, to an extent, his penultimate instructions. The French sailed from Corunna, drove off Calder, who promptly retired to Ushant, rejoined the Spanish at Ferrol, and set a course into the Bay of Biscay. There de Villeneuve sailed about for a few days making a half-hearted and unsuccessful attempt to locate Allemand. Considering the emperor's instructions now moot, de Villeneuve turned and headed south. The allied fleet arrived off Cadiz on 20 August, brushed aside the small British blockading force, and entered the port that evening, after which Vice Admiral Collingwood, although he commanded only three ships of the line, dutifully resumed his watch on Cadiz. When he looked into the port the next morning he found the allied armada "thick as a wood." De Villeneuve had brought about a massive concentration of thirty-five ships of the line, but he had also left the emperor "standing on the cliffs of Boulogne with an army of 165,000 men."[92]

For Napoleon, the opportunity to invade England had passed. His imperial pretensions, combined with the work of British diplomats and the lure of British subsidies, had secured a new anti-French coalition. Austria and Russia were already mobilizing. Napoleon had no choice: on 29 August 1805 the invasion army at Boulogne broke camp and began its march east toward the Rhine, Ulm, and Austerlitz.

As DE VILLENEUVE debated his course of action at Corunna, off Brest Admiral Cornwallis found himself in command of thirty-six of the line. Calder, coming north from Ferrol, rejoined the fleet on 14 August, and most of Nelson's ships, though not their commander who returned to Portsmouth, arrived the next day. A cautious admiral charged with responsibility for the security of the Channel and the blockade of Ganteaume's twenty-one ships at Brest might well have kept his force concentrated off Ushant, but not "Billy Blue" Cornwallis. On his own initiative, on 16 August he detached Calder with twenty of the line back to Ferrol.[93]

Napoleon considered Cornwallis's decision the height of stupidity.[94] Now both the admiral's weakened fleet and Calder's detachment were outnumbered by the forces of Ganteaume and de Villeneuve. But Cornwallis, determined to bring the Franco-Spanish armada to battle, believed that Ganteaume was as likely to escape Brest as de Villeneuve was to become aggressive. And even if the allies did force an engagement, had not an outnumbered Calder more than held his own off Cape Finisterre?

Events confirmed the soundness of Cornwallis's judgment. Ganteaume could not get out of Brest, and de Villeneuve, after his brief sortie into the Bay of Biscay, sailed south. Cornwallis, kept abreast these allied moves by alert frigates, deduced that de Villeneuve was bound for the Mediterranean and sent new instructions to Calder to sail to Cadiz to join Collingwood. So it was that Cornwallis, acting on his own, set in motion the concentration of naval force that would ultimately enable his good friend Nelson to fight and to win the battle off Cape Trafalgar.

When reports that de Villeneuve had sailed to Cadiz instead of Brest reached Paris, an outraged Napoleon vented his frustration on the "miserable coward."[95] On 16 September the emperor dispatched new orders to Cadiz for the fleet to return to the Mediterranean, and the next day he directed that Admiral François-Etienne, comte de Rosily-Mesros, relieve de Villeneuve. But not until 20 September did Decrès write the painful letter informing his old captain that he had been replaced.

De Villeneuve received Napoleon's instructions on 28 September and promptly, and uncharacteristically, began preparations to sail, no doubt relieved that the emperor had abandoned plans for an invasion of England. The allied fleet totaled thirty-three of the line—nineteen French and fourteen Spanish. The latter, although their movements were not dictated by Napoleon's orders, had no desire to be left behind and hoped to return to the Mediterranean and join the squadron still at Cartagena. Had the Spanish refused to sail, de Villeneuve could hardly have considered escape. Vice Admiral Collingwood, reinforced by Calder on 30 August, now commanded a force of twenty-six of the line off Cadiz.[96]

As de Villeneuve's fleet completed its preparations, enthusiasm for action began to evaporate among many of the senior French and Spanish commanders. Rumors swept Cadiz that Nelson had arrived with reinforcements from England and now commanded the stronger fleet. At a contentious council of war on 8 October, de Villeneuve, supported by many though not all of his admirals, decided to ignore the emperor's orders and remain in port.[97]

Nelson was indeed in command, having joined Collingwood on 28 September with three ships of the line, including the *Victory* 100. But the British force was still inferior to that of the allies, at least in numbers of ships and guns.[98] Nelson commanded only twenty-seven of the line after he permitted Calder to sail home to face his court-martial in the three-decked *Prince of Wales* instead of a frigate—a notable show of compassion if not wisdom—and after Rear Admiral Thomas Louis sailed to Gibraltar with another six ships to take on fresh water. Nelson, as always eager for a fight, kept his frigates inshore but his fleet over the horizon, hoping to lure the enemy out of port and into an engagement.

But de Villeneuve had no intention of leaving Cadiz—until 18 October, when he received reports that Rosily was in Madrid bearing instructions to relieve him of command. Stung by the reports, he issued immediate orders for the fleet to prepare to sail, which it did the next day. Captain Sir Henry Blackwood, commanding the *Euryalus* frigate, sighted the Franco-Spanish armada as it worked its way out of the port and passed the appropriate signal back to the fleet. "At this moment the Enemy are coming out," he wrote to his wife, "and as if determined to have a fair fight."[99]

FOR TWO YEARS, ever since he had resumed his watch off Toulon in 1803, Horatio Nelson had prepared for the battle he was about to fight. He sought not just victory but the veritable destruction of de Villeneuve's fleet. For Nelson, the responsibility of a commander in chief was "first to bring an enemy's fleet to battle on the most advantageous terms." As for favorable "terms," he explained: "I mean that of laying his ships close on board the enemy, as expeditiously as possible, and secondly, to continue them there without separating until the business is decided." While the forms a prospective battle might take varied, Nelson focused on the aspects of engagements that were most likely to remain constant. Time was one obvious consideration. Shortly before sailing to join the fleet off Cadiz, he had told Captain Richard Keats: "No day can be long enough to arrange a couple of fleets and fight a decisive battle according to the old system." To save time, Nelson decreed that his order of sailing would double as the order of battle. He had no intention of wasting any part of the day maneuvering for position.[100]

Nelson planned to divide his fleet into three groups—windward and leeward divisions supported by an advanced squadron—but lack of ships forced him to revert to a two-division formation. He chose to lead the windward division, and his old friend Cuthbert Collingwood the leeward. "We can, my dear Coll, have no little jealousies," he wrote to his second in command on 9 October. "We have only one great object in view, that of annihilating our Enemies, and getting a glorious Peace for our Country."[101]

Nelson would exercise an extremely decentralized form of command and control, as he had at the Nile and Copenhagen. In a tactical memo-

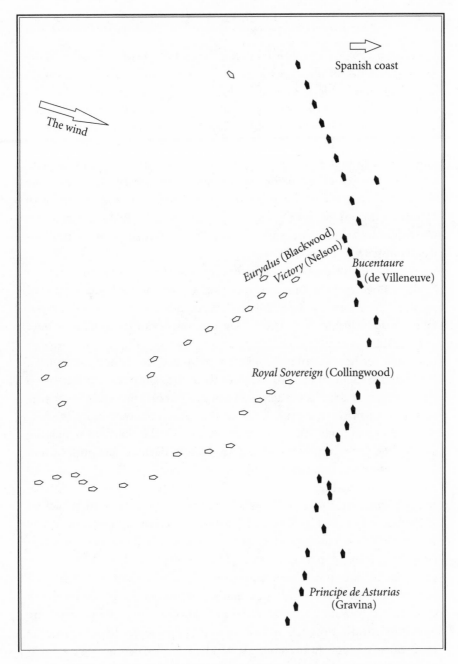

The wind

Spanish coast

Euryalus (Blackwood)
Victory (Nelson)

Bucentaure
(de Villeneuve)

Royal Sovereign (Collingwood)

Principe de Asturias
(Gravina)

THE BATTLE OF TRAFALGAR, 21 OCTOBER 1805, CA. 1100
Nelson's plan was to concentrate his attack in two divisions (his own windward and
Collingwood's leeward column) on the rear two-thirds of the allied fleet. The ships of
the allied van division would not easily be able to turn back to help their engaged
comrades. As events turned out, they did not even try.

randum of 1803 he had written that he was "fully assured that the admirals and captains of the fleet I have the honour to command will, knowing my precise object, that of a close and decisive battle, supply any deficiency in my not making signals." Collingwood would bear the heaviest responsibility; he would, "after my intentions are made known to him, have the entire direction of his line; to make the attack upon the enemy, and to follow up the blow until they are captured or destroyed." On the morning of the battle Nelson also entrusted Blackwood of the *Euryalus,* an experienced captain ten years his senior, with a degree of "latitude seldom or ever [possessed] again, that of making any use I pleased of his name" to ensure that the "sternmost ships" were into action as quickly as possible.[102]

Nelson's intention was to concentrate his effort against the Franco-Spanish fleet's center and rear, to bring on a pell-mell mêlée, and to paralyze de Villeneuve's centralized command structure by a direct assault on his flagship. The British lee division—Collingwood's—would cut through the allied line "about the twelfth ship from the rear (or wherever he can fetch)." Nelson would lead the windward division through the enemy line "two, three, or four ships ahead of their centre, so far as to ensure getting at their commander in chief on whom every effort must be made to capture." Before the allied van could react, the battle would be decided. To ensure that the two British divisions struck the enemy line at the appropriate location, Nelson decided that both he and Collingwood would lead their respective formations. The decision may have cost him his life.

De Villeneuve, the lone French flag officer who had escaped Nelson at the battle of the Nile, expected (or perhaps feared) an unconventional attack. He warned his subordinates that Nelson would not attack in a traditional line ahead, but in divisions. He expected the British to attempt to break his line, and to concentrate their attack against the allied rear. But his perspicacity was matched neither by resolution nor by an ability to devise a counter to Nelson's tactics. Though prepared to fight, he hoped to avoid action, and instead of sailing out boldly to join battle he set a course of flight to the south. When he saw the British bearing down on the allied rear, he realized he could not avoid an engagement and reversed course, wearing his fleet. The resultant disorder, rather than any prearranged tactical design, left the allied fleet in an irregular, concave, crescent formation that, quite by chance, proved more difficult for the British to defeat. The maneuver also left de Villeneuve's twelve-ship squadron of observation, commanded by Admiral Gravina, in the rear of the fleet and somewhat to windward of the rest of the line, well placed to counter Collingwood's thrust or to reinforce the center of the allied formation. The Spanish admiral, however, confused to find himself trailing rather than leading, ignored de Villeneuve's signals to keep the wind and fell into the wake of the allied rear.[103]

De Villeneuve had advised his subordinates that in a pell-mell engagement he would probably be unable to control his fleet with signals. He appealed to their sense of honor, exhorting them to support one another and not to wait for signals from the flagship. This was sound advice, almost Nelsonian in its tenor, but little more than a vain attempt to shape doctrine by afterthought, pronounced as it was on the eve of battle to captains schooled entirely in a highly centralized system which allowed subordinates little, if any, initiative.

NELSON'S AND DE VILLENEUVE'S fleets sighted each other at about 0600 on 21 October. The allies were sailing on a starboard tack in an ill-formed line toward the south-southwest, about a dozen miles to windward of Cape Trafalgar, the wind then blowing from the northwest. The two British divisions were on a course north by east about twelve miles farther west. At 0700 Nelson made the signal to prepare for battle and to steer east under full sail. By 0800 only nine miles separated the two fleets.

De Villeneuve could see the British divisions bearing down on his center and rear. Whatever his professional shortcomings, he was experienced enough to recognize that he could not avoid a fight. At about 1000 he ordered his fleet to wear and to come to a course toward the northeast and Cadiz.[104] The maneuver only exacerbated the disorder in the fleet. With the wind light, the allied ships could not make more than a half-knot and struggled vainly to form a proper line.

The British, with the wind on their quarter, were forging ahead at about three knots and steadily closing the distance. Nelson, on the *Victory* 100, led his division in an irregular line, steering, after the Spanish course change, somewhat toward the northeast, possibly feinting toward the allied van or perhaps simply searching the crowd of enemy men-of-war for de Villeneuve's flagship. Collingwood, flying his flag from the *Royal Sovereign* 100, led his ships in line abreast, intent on reaching the allied line as quickly as possible and breaking through in a fashion similar to Howe's maneuver at the Glorious First of June.

At about 1130 the ships toward the rear of the allied fleet opened fire on Collingwood's division. Nelson had by that time begun his own final run toward the enemy and telegraphed, using Home Popham's code, his intent "to push or go through the end of the enemy's line to prevent them from getting to Cadiz."[105] At about 1140 the *Royal Sovereign* fired as it passed between two allied ships. Minutes later the head of Nelson's column came under fire. At 1156 Nelson telegraphed his famous signal— "England expects that every man will do his duty"—and followed it with another to prepare to anchor after the battle, a wise precaution as events would demonstrate. At about 1204, as the *Victory* opened fire, Nelson made the superfluous but characteristic signal to engage the enemy more closely. The *Victory* crashed into, rather than through, the allied line at about 1220. From that point in the battle until he fell wounded on the quarterdeck, Nelson made no signals.

Considering the scale of the engagement, the British made relatively quick work of the allied armada. At 1345 de Villeneuve's flagship, the *Bucentaure* 80, struck. The log of Nelson's flagship recorded: "Partial firing continued until 4.30, when a victory having been reported to the Right Honourable Lord Viscount Nelson, K. B., and Commander-in-Chief, he then died of his wound."[106] The British had captured or destroyed eighteen of the thirty-three allied ships of the line, although all but four prizes were lost in the gale that blew up after the battle.

The engagement off Cape Trafalgar on 21 October 1805 marked the end of a dramatic ten-month campaign played out on the oceans of the new and old worlds. Lord Nelson, the most famous naval commander in history, fought the most famous naval battle in history and won one of the most complete naval victories in history. But was it a decisive victory? Nelson certainly achieved the "annihilating" victory he sought, but that triumph did not earn Great Britain a "glorious peace": the war against Napoleon continued for another nine years. Nevertheless, French naval power would not seriously challenge Great Britain again in the war.

Despite the wealth of literature on Trafalgar, many topics remain subjects of dispute. What exactly was Nelson planning during his approach toward the allied line? Had Collingwood obeyed Nelson's signal to anchor after the battle, would the British have saved more of their dearly won prizes? Were some of the French and Spanish commanders negligent, or worse, in failing to support de Villeneuve after the mêlée began? One aspect of the battle that has long been evident is that Nelson's approach to command and control—his "touch"—was central to his victory. The signal book was not the key to Nelson's success. Once the *Victory* engaged, he stopped signaling and relinquished control, as he had at the Nile and Copenhagen. Nelson's faith in his subordinates, combined with his ability to convey to them beforehand his conception of how an engagement was likely to unfold, made him a master of the art of command. The tactical defects of the French and Spanish navies were many, and as evident as the tactical superiority of the British, but it was Nelson's brilliance as a commander that allowed him to fully exploit his advantages.

Nelson's ultimate personal sacrifice on the quarterdeck of the *Victory* demonstrated perfectly the virtues of a decentralized system of command: at a critical point in the fighting, one of the most charismatic commanders in naval history fell mortally wounded, and his death had no impact on the outcome of the battle. Once Nelson set the *Victory* on its final course for the allied line, his physical presence was superfluous. His spirit walked with every admiral and captain who paced a British quarterdeck that first "Trafalgar day."

WHILE TRAFALGAR was the last notable "major" fleet engagement of the age of fighting sail, the battle did not mark the end of the long naval struggle against Napoleon and his empire. After October 1805 the war continued for nine difficult years of blockade and *guerre de course*. For a study of command and control, the end of the age of fighting sail came not at Trafalgar but twenty-two years later—on 20 October 1827— when a French-British-Russian armada monitoring the Greek rebellion against Ottoman rule attacked a Turkish-Egyptian fleet anchored in the small harbor of Navarino on the western coast of the Peloponnese.[107]

Vice Admiral Sir Edward Codrington, the British commander in chief of the allied fleet at Navarino, was a veteran of Trafalgar, where he had commanded the *Orion* 74, and, not surprisingly, a devotee of Nelson. "Lord Nelson is arrived!" he wrote to his wife in 1805 after the new commander joined the fleet off Cadiz. "A sort of general joy has been the consequence." Codrington noted the "superiority of Lord Nelson in all these social arrangements which bind his captains to their admiral," in stark contrast to the cold, hard style of micromanagement practiced by Collingwood.[108]

When Codrington assumed the Mediterranean command in February

1827, he inherited a complex diplomatic Balkan conundrum. The British public felt great sympathy for the Christian Greeks, who were rebelling against the harsh rule of the Muslim Ottoman Turks. But complications related to the "Eastern Question" made full recognition and support for the rebels impossible. The British government sought accommodation—an armistice—fearing that a Greek victory might prompt the collapse of the Ottoman Empire and open the door for further Russian encroachment into the Balkans and the Near East.

In his new command, Codrington displayed initiative at the strategic and operational levels and modeled his tactical approach after Nelson's. The British government, still operating in the pre-telegraph era, had necessarily granted its Mediterranean fleet commanders great leeway in their instructions. Codrington, alarmed by reports that the Turks planned to reinforce their army and to depopulate—by what would later come to be known as "ethnic cleansing"—the Morea, decided that the Turkish-Egyptian fleet, then at Navarino, needed to be rendered ineffective. Since he considered a winter blockade too taxing, he led his fleet into the bay, intending to force the Muslim fleet to surrender or risk destruction. The Turks and Egyptians chose to fight, and a full-scale battle ensued. The allied fleet consisted of twenty-seven men-of-war, including eleven of the line; the Turkish-Egyptian fleet numbered sixty-five mostly smaller ships, many armed transports, and only three of the line.

The battle was fought in the Nelson style. The day before the attack Codrington gathered his senior commanders in his flagship and outlined his plan. He ended the meeting by quoting Lord Nelson to the effect that "no captain can do very wrong who places his ship alongside that of an enemy."[109] The battle, though hard fought, was hardly close run. Only fifteen Muslim ships remained afloat at the end of the day. But if the Ottomans suffered a tactical defeat, they gained a strategic diplomatic victory, and Codrington, while a hero to the Greeks, became an expendable scapegoat to a British foreign office that repudiated and apologized for his actions in order to prevent a broader conflict. The victory at Navarino gained Codrington not fame but recall and brought a long and distinguished career to a frustrating end.

Codrington's somewhat superficial embrace of Nelson's method was by no means universal within the Royal Navy. Nelson's victories did not prompt a turn away from centralized command and control systems; paradoxically, the very extent of his triumph over the French and Spanish fleets fostered a return to the centralized orthodoxy. After Trafalgar, the

British did not have to fight another major fleet action for more than two decades.[110] Nelson's crushing victory had eliminated much of the momentum and the pressing need for continued experimentation and reform. As a result, the British remained as enamored as ever of signaling and of centralized methods of command.

As Sir Julian Corbett noted, the Royal Navy failed "to grasp the whole of Nelson's tactical principles." Few of Nelson's contemporaries understood the secret of his achievements. Those officers who considered Nelson's tactics the key to victory attempted to institutionalize his success by including a Trafalgar maneuver—"Cut the enemy's line in the order of sailing in two columns"—in a later edition of the signal book, as if the "Nelson touch" could be reduced to a mere signal. Others, focusing on his aggressiveness and penchant for close battle, embraced a prompt, headlong attack, but failed to appreciate the extent to which the admiral's charismatic leadership and personal doctrine were central to his method.[111]

Thus, as the age of fighting sail came to a close, not only linear formations and tactics but also, and more important, the signal book continued to dominate European naval thought. Formalism and centralization of command reigned supreme for the next century, despite the technological changes wrought by the industrial revolution.

CHAPTER SEVEN

The Age of Steam through the Great War

$\mathscr{T}$HE END OF THE PERIOD of the sailing men-of-war was not suddenly apparent," noted the maritime historian Howard I. Chapelle, "nor was it marked by a dramatic flourish." During the three decades after the wars of the French Revolution and Empire, the refinement of the sailing warship continued, reaching its apogee in the late 1840s. Except for their rounded sterns, the new ships looked much like their predecessors, although they were larger, more strongly built, and more heavily armed. But as designers, shipwrights, and carpenters crafted ships that were veritable works of art, the products of the technicians of the industrial revolution slowly penetrated the "wooden world." Even as Lord Nelson stood watch off Toulon and Cadiz, steam-powered boats plied some of the major rivers of England and America, while men such as Robert Fulton envisioned steam-powered men-of-war. During the War of 1812 the Americans began construction on the *Demologos,* a steam-powered, 2,475-ton, 30-gun, 156-foot frigate designed by Fulton with the vulnerable paddle wheel placed for safety in the middle of the ship's catamaran-like hull. The war ended before the *Demologos,* rechristened the *Fulton* after the designer's death, saw action. In the late 1820s steam-powered dispatch boats entered the British naval service. In the 1830s the French and the Greeks were the first to use steam-driven warships in combat, often armed with the new explosive-shell guns designed by Major Henri-Joseph Paixhans. In the 1840s the Royal Navy employed gunboats powered by steam, such as the infamous 600-ton *Nemesis,* armed with a pair of 32-pounder pivot guns, to deadly effect in Asian waters.[1]

Also during the 1840s, the adoption by the world's major navies of the Swedish inventor John Ericsson's screw propeller accelerated the shift to steam. "The sailing warship might have survived longer had she been required to compete only with side-paddle steamers," Chapelle concluded, "but the appearance of the screw propeller made the auxiliary steamer practical and hastened the end of the sailing ship."[2] By the late 1840s and early 1850s even the largest warships—frigates and ships of the line—relied on steam power as an auxiliary, and in combat the principal, source of propulsion.

The impact of the industrial revolution on navies was by no means limited to propulsion. Warships were, after all, nothing but platforms for weapons, principally cannon, designed to destroy an enemy's ships or to batter masonry or earthen forts into submission. After the defeat of Napoleon I there began an unending and ultimately unwinnable race between gun and armor, a race that could be run only because of the availability of the steam engine to power more heavily armed ships. In the 1820s advanced industrial and metallurgical techniques allowed the casting of much larger, though still muzzle-loading, guns, their killing power enhanced by a more scientific approach to sighting.[3] Simultaneously the French developed the "Paixhans" explosive-shell gun that threatened to turn wooden ships into combustible piles of splinters. Although the successes of the Paixhans gun in the Greek war for independence, the Crimean War, and the French intervention in Mexico were exaggerated by many contemporaries, midcentury advances in firepower prompted navies to "clad" their wooden ships with plates of iron. The French launched their first armored steam warship—the 13-knot la Gloire—in 1859. The British countered in 1861 with the Warrior, an iron-hulled, 400-foot man-of-war capable of 14 knots mounting thirty-eight 68-pounder naval guns.

During the American Civil War, the navies of the North and the South reflected the revolutionary changes overtaking naval establishments. The Federal navy continued to employ numerous wooden sailing men-of-war outfitted with auxiliary steam power. The infamous Confederate raiders, such as the Alabama, likewise relied on their sails for cruising and used steam as a combat auxiliary. The principal armament of these raiders and the ships that hunted them was massive, centrally mounted, rifled pivot guns capable of firing to port or starboard. For coastal defense the South clad many of its wooden ships, such as the Virginia, with iron and dispensed with sails. The North countered with its own ironclads as well as several classes of iron-constructed and -armored "monitors" mounting heavy muzzle-loading cannon in powered turrets.

This contest between the gun and armor placed a premium on penetration rather than explosive power. To defeat armor, navies adopted ever larger rifled cannon capable of hurling shot, increasingly designed to pierce armor plate, with greater range, accuracy, and penetrating ability. Rifling, in turn, led to longer barrels, which promoted a shift to breech-loading mechanisms in the 1860s.

As a result of these changes, during the decade after the American Civil War the "modern" warship began to emerge. In 1872 the Italians launched the *Duilio,* with armored decks and turrets set in echelon. The following year the British commissioned the *Devastation,* the man-of-war that established the "pattern for the future development of the battleship so decisively that even the revolutionary and famous *Dreadnought* of 1906 was only a final extension of the principles which she embodied."[4] By the end of the century, the lines of the "modern" battleship were clearly recognizable: steel construction, compartmentalization, steam power, substantial armoring, and heavy breech-loading rifled main guns supported by lighter but more quickly firing weapons.

As engagement ranges increased, sighting the arched fire of myriad naval guns became next to impossible. The chaotic patterns of splashes made the correction of individually sighted guns impractical. The solution involved controlled salvo firing by batteries of uniform type[5] and led to the introduction of the first all-big-gun battleships, the most famous of which was the Royal Navy's *Dreadnought,* launched in February 1906. The 17,900-ton ship mounted ten 12-inch guns in her main battery and was the first man-of-war powered by steam turbines. Thereafter battleships became larger, faster, and more heavily armed, but the *Dreadnought* pattern remained unchanged for another forty years.

The fruits of the industrial age wrought a revolution in ship types and tactics. At first glance, the fleet seemed little more than a modern equivalent of its sailing-age predecessor. Steel dreadnoughts replaced the wooden ship of the line in the line of battle while the protected and armored cruisers assumed the frigate's role as commerce raider and scout. But new types of light, fast, deadly smaller ships milled about the battleline, waiting for opportunities to disrupt the enemy's formation.

Central to this revolution was the "automotive" torpedo. In the mid-nineteenth century the term "torpedo" actually referred to what in the twenty-first century would be classified as a mine—a stationary, and thus defensive, explosive device detonated by contact or remote control. The potentially devastating effect of a sub-surface torpedo exploding near or against the hull of a ship led navies to search for a means to deliver the torpedo offensively to the target. During the American Civil War both the Federal and Confederate navies experimented with a variety of small hand- or steam-powered mobile platforms—most notably the Confederate submarine *Hunley*—armed with torpedoes mounted at the end of a spar, but with mixed success. In the late 1860s the Englishman Robert Whitehead refined an Austrian design and manufactured the first self-propelled or "automotive torpedo."

Until the development of effective internal combustion engines later in the century, the preferred means of delivering the new automotive torpedo was with small, steam-powered, fast surface craft, duly termed "torpedo boats." The ability of these diminutive boats to "hole" and sink a ship of the line, a capability smaller sailing-age warships had never possessed, added a new dimension to naval tactics. To screen the battleline from these dangerous interlopers, navies developed "torpedo-boat destroyers," which became the modern destroyers, and subsequently "light" cruisers, whose job it became to counter the destroyers, which, armed with their own torpedoes, eventually supplanted the torpedo boats.

By the beginning of the Great War in 1914, navies had assumed their new pattern. Warships were now steel constructed and steam driven. Dreadnoughts mounted long-ranged, rifled breechloaders, while new classes of smaller warships screened and scouted for the fleet. The impact of these technological developments in the realms of naval strategy, operations, and tactics was marked.

The industrial revolution also dramatically changed strategic geography. Steam power shortened cruising radii: gone were the days of the six-month cruise under sail. Navies now needed more overseas bases, particularly coaling stations, a factor that had a regressive impact on strategy and planning and accelerated the centuries-old trend toward European imperial hegemony. Because the new ships were more expensive, fleets became somewhat smaller. The industrial revolution also spawned two new non-European centers of naval power—the United States and Japan. The rise of the American and Japanese navies prompted Great Britain to seek a turn-of-the-century strategic rapprochement with the United States and in 1902 a formal alliance with Japan.

The shortened logistical tether of steam navies also imposed substantial operational difficulties. It was now difficult, if not impossible, to conduct a close blockade comparable to the British effort off Brest during the wars of the French Revolution and Empire.

At the tactical level, new technologies offered solutions to old problems. Mounting heavy guns in turrets and later barbettes solved the previously intractable problem inherent in the design of the sailing-age
man-of-war—the fact that its axes of movement and fire lay at right angles. The new dreadnoughts could cover their vulnerable bows and
sterns and apply a substantial portion of their fighting power forward and
aft, although commanders still preferred to arrange their fleets in a line
ahead to maximize firepower. Steam power eased the problem of maneuvering a fleet arranged in a linear formation. Naval commanders no
longer had to rely on the wind for propulsion, or to struggle to gain the
wind gauge (though wind direction retained some importance in battle
in that it was best to have the wind blowing the smoke away from your
range finders). Wider arcs of fire permitted the application at the fleet
level of what had formerly been a ship-to-ship maneuver—raking. In the
steam age "crossing the enemy's T" became a favored tactic, permitting a
concentration of firepower against the head of an enemy column in a
manner impossible during the age of sail because of the limited traverse
of deck guns mounted on wooden trucks.

But the advent of advanced industrial technologies at sea introduced
several new tactical problems and exacerbated existing ones. Steam freed
the fleet from the vagaries of the wind, but it also propelled warships
through the water at greater speeds. Proper station keeping became more
difficult. The combination of increased speed, which permitted more
rapid closure between opposing fleets, and new breech-loading guns,
with ranges measured in miles rather than yards, dramatically shrank the
decisionmaking windows of naval commanders. An enemy force within
visible range now posed an immediate, rather than a potential, threat.
Twentieth-century commanders would rarely have the opportunity, as
had Nelson at Trafalgar, to pipe their crews to breakfast before opening
an engagement. While sea battles remained two-dimensional (until the
development of effective submarines and aircraft) and a fleet's main
units were still arrayed in a line ahead, the presence of agile and deadly
torpedo boats and destroyers made early-twentieth-century naval encounters complex affairs. Every man-of-war, not solely those arrayed in
the formal line of battle, now possessed the capability to sink the most
powerful dreadnought.

If the new technology increased the demands on naval commanders,
that same technology offered few compensating advances in the area of
command and control. This was especially true at the tactical level of
warfare. At the strategic and operational levels, the telegraph revolution-

ized, albeit slowly, the contours of naval command and control. For the first time in history the submarine telegraph offered admiralties, and the governments they served, the prospect of commanding and controlling fleets and squadrons operating on distant stations.

But the impact of the telegraph on naval warfare was limited, perhaps more psychological than physical. "Before [the submarine cable] was laid," recalled Rear Admiral Casper F. Goodrich, who had commanded the United States Asiatic Squadron, "one really was somebody out there, but afterwards one simply became a damned errand boy at the end of a telegraph wire."[6] In fact, the officers of the U.S. Navy, along with those of the other major navies, were slow, and often reluctant, to exploit the new technology. Cost was a factor, and all but the most pressing messages traveled by mail. Reliability and security were additional problems. A global telegraph network with redundant cables did not exist until the eve of the Great War, by which time wireless telegraphy was already offering a more workable, though by no means secure, alternative. Moreover, since Great Britain controlled most of the network of submarine cables that did exist, access to the telegraph lines in time of crisis was problematic for most nations.

The relative paucity of naval wars during the century after Waterloo gave admiralties few opportunities to test the viability of the telegraph network. At the strategic level the existence of telegraph cables allowed quick communication between admiralties and naval bases, most often along land lines. During the American Civil War the navy department in Washington used the telegraph lines to communicate with naval yards at New York, Philadelphia, Boston, and elsewhere. A notable strategic use of the submarine telegraph came in 1898 on the eve of the Spanish-Cuban-American War. On 25 February Theodore Roosevelt, then assistant secretary of the navy, used British submarine telegraph lines to warn the commander of the Asiatic squadron at Hong Kong, Commodore George Dewey, to prepare his command for battle. On 24 April the navy department directed Dewey to steam from Hong Kong to the Philippine Islands to seek out the Spanish fleet. In a lopsided engagement on 1 May, Dewey destroyed the Spanish squadron in Manila Bay. Not surprisingly, the Spanish authorities refused to allow Dewey to use their telegraph facilities to report his triumph, and his need for supplies and reinforcements, to Washington. Dewey cut the cable and sent his messages in a fast cutter to Hong Kong for transmission along the British-controlled network.[7]

While the telegraph proved useful at the strategic level of warfare, it was less so at the operational level. Once fleets sailed from port, their commanders were beyond the immediate reach of the cable.

The first use of the telegraph in naval operations came during the Crimean War, as Great Britain, France, and Sardinia supported the Ottoman Empire in its conflict with Russia. The British and French quickly laid a telegraph line within the theater of war. In May 1855, in "one of the earliest messages that passed over the newly-laid cable to the seat of war," Emperor Napoleon III in Paris ordered the cancellation of a planned assault against the port of Azov at the head of the Gulf of Taganrog.[8] This technologically based micromanagement was without doubt a first in the history of warfare. This intrusion from afar also caused the outraged resignation of the French commander in chief.

A more noteworthy and naval operational use of the telegraph occurred during the American Civil War. On 11 June 1864 the Federal steam sloop of war *Kearsarge,* commanded by Captain John Ancrum Winslow, was repairing damaged copper plates at Flushing, in the Netherlands, when the Confederate cruiser *Alabama* arrived at Cherbourg, France. The next day the American minister in France, W. L. Dayton, sent a telegram to Flushing alerting Winslow to the presence of the *Alabama.* Winslow, who assumed that he would have to blockade Cherbourg, sent a telegram to Tangier directing Commander George H. Preble to steam north with the *St. Louis.* Winslow arrived off Cherbourg on 14 June and began his watch. He did not have long to wait. At dawn on Sunday, 19 June, Captain Raphael Semmes brought the *Alabama* out of the harbor, not to escape, but to accept battle. In a ninety-minute engagement the two evenly matched American steam sloops fought in full view of the French until Winslow's *Kearsarge* finally sent the *Alabama* to the bottom.[9]

If the cable telegraph had transformed naval command and control at the strategic level, and the wireless telegraph had done the same at the operational level, what of the tactical level, where the revolution in naval warfare was marked, rapid, and constant? The tools of the naval warrior—ships, guns, engines, and armoring—underwent a dramatic transformation during the nineteenth century. But no technological advance in the area of command and control, comparable to the telegraph, occurred concurrently at the tactical level of warfare.

Amid the confusion of rapid technological change, naval commanders still struggled to develop appropriate methods to control their fleets in combat. The infrequent and mostly short wars of the era offered only occasional opportunities to test new weapons, tactics, and doctrine. Thus lessons drawn from wartime experience were few, and were often inconclusive or contradictory. Conversely, peace gave naval officers time to think about their profession, and to write. The near-century between Navarino and the Great War was a golden age in naval literature, especially at the tactical level. This new generation of naval writers tended to eschew rigidly centralized, flag-reliant systems of command and control. Mid- and late-nineteenth-century naval commanders turned, or more accurately re-turned, to less centralized approaches based on doctrine, more often than not personal doctrine. And once again, after innumerable experiments with box, round, spherical, oblique, and other formations, commanders settled on the line ahead as the standard fighting formation.

The Crimean War and the American Civil War, which did not involve fleet or even squadron engagements, had little impact on tactical and doctrinal development. The American Civil War certainly demonstrated the importance of steam power, the screw propeller, iron armor, and the new ordnance, but European navies had already embraced these technologies. This is not to say that American naval officers failed to develop their own tactics and doctrine. They did just that, although for the most part these developments involved the use of ships against fortifications ashore.

Rear Admiral David Glasgow Farragut's handling of the Union fleet at the battle of Mobile Bay, Alabama, on 5 August 1864 demonstrated a novel use of tactics adapted to the newly available technologies, well-thought-out doctrine, and a decentralized approach to command and control. Farragut had to run his fleet through a narrow channel past Confederate Fort Morgan, which guarded Mobile Bay. As had Nelson, Farragut discussed his plans beforehand with his subordinates, a task eased by the fact that he knew, or thought that he knew, the strength and position of the Confederate defenses. Farragut had no wish to place his fate in the hands of his signalmen. In fact, he wished to lead his column into Mobile Bay, and only reluctantly yielded that honor to Commander James Alden, captain of the *Brooklyn*. Alden knew the harbor well, and his ship was fitted with bow-mounted chase guns and an anti-torpedo device.[10]

Farragut's decision not to lead his line almost cost him the battle. As the Federal ships steamed past Fort Morgan, the *Tecumseh,* one of the monitors screening the head of the line, struck a torpedo (mine) and sank in minutes. Alden was uncertain if he was out of the channel or if the Confederate minefield extended farther east than expected. What was he to do? As the Federal fleet was already well into the channel, it was impossible to turn back; any attempt to do so, given the extremely limited visibility, would have resulted in a disastrous "pileup" under the guns of Fort Morgan. Nor was there time to request direction from Farragut. Despite the fact that the admiral's initial plan had gone awry, Alden should have continued on course. Instead, he slowed the *Brooklyn* and signaled news of the loss of the *Tecumseh* back to the flagship, the *Hartford.* Farragut, who was literally lashed to the port rigging of the mainmast so that he could see above the smoke, directed that the signal be made to order Alden to proceed. But Alden, fearful and uncertain, perhaps unable to see the signal, instead reversed his engines. Farragut saw disaster in the offing: the other ships in line, including the *Hartford,* were bearing down on the *Brooklyn* in the smoke. At Farragut's direction, the flagship and her ironclad consort, the *Metacomet,* turned hard to port to avoid collision. As Farragut steamed past the *Brooklyn,* Alden warned that a line of mines barred the way into the harbor. "Damn the torpedoes!" Farragut exclaimed. Then he yelled down to the deck: "Four bells, Captain Drayton, go ahead."[11]

As Americans fought their civil war, Europeans struggled to develop a new system of tactics and doctrine for their steam-powered and increasingly armored ships. While midcentury tactical manuals retained the old line ahead, they also embraced various line-abreast formations akin to those employed in the age of galleys, such as the wedge or inverted V. Now freed from the wind, naval officers devised often elaborate maneuvers that allowed them to alter course while either maintaining or changing formation. As early as the 1860s tacticians recognized that greater arcs of fire and longer ranges made crossing an opponent's T an effective maneuver.[12]

The first test of the new tactics for steam-powered and armored ships came off the Adriatic island of Lissa on 20 July 1866 during the Austro-Italian War. The battle, the largest naval encounter since Navarino, was a confused affair. If rapid technological change had thrown naval tactics and doctrine into a general confusion, the situation among the Italians was chaotic. In 1861 the newly unified Italian state established a navy— cobbled together from the remnants of three old, but by no means distinguished, marine services—those of Sardinia, Naples, and Tuscany. Italian crews came from "different cultures" and shared "no common doctrine."[13] The navy adopted, but had little time to absorb, a translation of a leading French doctrinal manual only months before Lissa. The absence of any agreed-upon doctrine or set of tactics placed an enormous burden on the commander of a fleet.

Sixty-year-old Admiral Count Carlo Pellion di Persano was no Farragut and no Nelson. On the contrary, the Italian admiral was a pusillanimous man who ranks as one of the worst commanders in naval history.[14] The government had, quite literally, to order Persano to leave his base at Ancona. Once at sea, he decided that the island of Lissa, then controlled by Austria, would make an excellent forward base for a blockade of the Austrian coast, which at the time extended southeastward along the Adriatic. Persano sailed south with twenty-eight ships, but without a clearly developed plan of action, and reached the island on 17 July without any troops to land. He waited several days before cutting the telegraph cable that linked the island to the mainland. The Italian bombardment was somewhat effective, but the Austrian guns severely damaged two of the Italian ships. On 20 July Persano prepared to land his invasion force—2,200 troops who had arrived in two frigates the previous day. But shortly after dawn, as the Italians readied themselves for the landing, one of Persano's scouts appeared on the horizon making the signal for "suspicious" ships to the northwest. Persano correctly deduced that the Austrian fleet had arrived, alerted because of his delay in cutting the telegraph cable, and signaled for his fleet to prepare for battle.

Although Persano's force outnumbered the Austrians in every quantitative category—ironclads, wooden ships, guns, weight of metal, overall tonnage, and number of men—the Italians were in trouble. "The Austrian warships had inferior guns," the historian Lawrence Sondhaus wrote, but "the Italians the incompetent gunners." Persano, who had been in command of the fleet for months, had spent little time training and drilling his crews. He had not held tactical discussions with his subordinates that might have led to a scheme to make the best use of their eleven wooden ships, which were instead relegated to the role of passive observers. One of Persano's subordinates later wrote: "I was unable to form any idea of what the commander in chief meant to do."[15]

Persano's fleet was steaming toward the southwest in line-abreast formation when the Austrians came into view, arrayed in a somewhat similar formation, heading on a southeasterly course. Persano made the

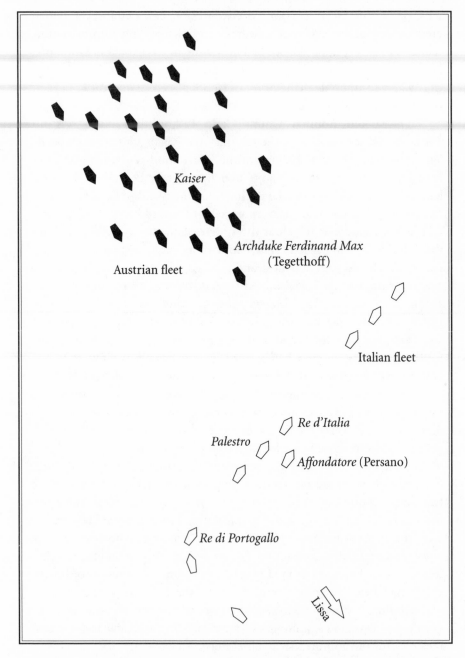

Kaiser

Archduke Ferdinand Max
(Tegetthoff)

Austrian fleet

Italian fleet

Re d'Italia

Palestro

Affondatore (Persano)

Re di Portogallo

Lissa

THE BATTLE OF LISSA, 20 JULY 1866

Persano tried to cut off the approach of the entire Austrian fleet with only his
ironclads. Tegetthoff's ships, painted black, steamed at full speed (about ten knots) toward the ill-formed Italian line of gray-painted men-of-war. The Austrians easily overwhelmed the Italians, not because the latter were outnumbered, but because they were
confused and poorly led.

signal for his ironclads to re-form into line ahead on a course toward the northeast, which would carry them directly across the path of the Austrian fleet.

Thirty-nine-year-old Rear Admiral Baron Wilhelm von Tegetthoff commanded the fleet bearing down on the Italians. Tegetthoff was an aggressive man who knew that he was outnumbered and outgunned but intended nonetheless to bring on a mêlée at close range. Unlike Persano, he had discussed his plans with his captains, and his fleet had sailed from its base at Pola in battle formation. Tegetthoff had arrayed his ships into three wedges—the first his seven outgunned ironclads, the second his wooden steamships, and the third his lighter and smaller ships. As the Austrians neared the Italian line, Tegetthoff made only two signals: "Ironclads, charge the enemy and sink him," followed by "ram everything gray!"[16]

Tegetthoff's decisiveness was matched by Persano's indecision. With the Austrian wedge closing the range, Persano decided at the last moment to switch his flag from the *Re d'Italia* to the new British-built *Affondatore* (in English, the *Sinker*), a powerful ship that carried two turreted 300-pounder muzzleloaders and sported a 26-foot-long ram. As the Italian flagship, the fourth vessel in line, slowed to allow the transfer, the three ships ahead continued on course, while those behind the *Re d'Italia* reduced speed. As a result, a wide gap yawned in the Italian line. Worse yet, Persano's captains had no idea that their admiral had changed ships and looked to the *Re d'Italia,* from which his flag still flew, for signals that never came. Meanwhile their commander, to his horror, discovered that *Affondatore* did not carry a complete set of signal flags.

Why Persano decided to make this last-minute transfer is unclear. His move may have reflected current tactical thinking regarding the proper station for the commanding admiral. By the 1860s many naval officers had begun to doubt that visual signaling systems were flexible enough, even if functioning properly, to allow effective control of a fleet in battle. The higher speeds of steam-powered ships placed a premium on rapid and responsive decisionmaking.

There were three, not entirely exclusive, alternatives to relying on signals. Commanders could allow their subordinates more autonomy, as had Nelson. They could lead the line, as had Nelson and Collingwood at Trafalgar. Or they could operate from a lighter, faster ship not part of the formal battle line, akin to Howe's and Rodney's experiments during the American war.[17] At Lissa, Tegetthoff led the Austrian fleet himself, placing his flagship, the *Archduke Ferdinand Max,* at the point of the leading wedge, and once the battle began he trusted, for the most part, to the initiative of his captains. Persano initially planned to direct his fleet via signals from the center of his line, as had been the norm in the age of sail. His decision to transfer to the *Affondatore* may have been an attempt to employ Howe's method. Alternatively, he may have been motivated by simple fear, a view supported by the fact that during the battle the *Affondatore,* with its mighty ram, thrice balked when presented with opportunities to ram Austrian ships. Whatever Persano's reasoning, his decision to leave the flagship was ill considered and proved disastrous for the Italian fleet.

At about 1050 the Austrians broke the Italian line, steaming through the gap created by Admiral Persano. There followed one of the more chaotic battles in naval history. Smoke produced by the big guns and more than a score of steam-powered men-of-war soon cast a black pall over the Adriatic arena, reducing visibility to, at best, two hundred yards.[18] Persano steamed about in the *Affondatore,* signaling madly, but to no avail since all eyes not blinded by the smoke were on the *Re d'Italia.*

The battle continued for nearly thirty minutes without either fleet gaining a clear advantage. Despite the surfeit of shot and shell expended, few ships were hit, and those hit were not seriously damaged. But the tide of battle began to turn as the Austrians focused their attack against the rear of the Italian line. The old *Kaiser,* a 92-gun wooden ship of the line, rammed the *Re di Portogallo,* not damaging the Italian ironclad but shocking its crew. Austrian guns set the armored gunboat *Palestro* on fire. Then Tegetthoff's flagship, the ironclad *Archduke Ferdinand Max,* rammed the American-built *Re d'Italia,* punching a huge hole in the side that caused an immediate list and in minutes sent the Italian flagship to the bottom. Soon the *Palestro* exploded and sank. The battle of Lissa was over. Persano withdrew, and Tegetthoff, his fleet slower and still weaker than the surviving Italian force, chose not to pursue. The Austrians had 38 men killed and another 138 wounded. The Italians lost two ships and suffered nearly 800 casualties, including more than 600 dead.

The battle of Lissa has become inextricably linked with the ram bow. The Austrian success, especially the sinking of the *Re d'Italia,* ensured that ramming became an accepted, and in some quarters the principal, tactic in naval warfare, a fact that influenced the design of battleships for the rest of the century. According to William McElwee: "The ram had been obsolete for centuries and should never have been reincorporated into naval design. Lissa demonstrated over and over again that no ship which had not already been partially disabled need have any difficulty in dodging out of the way of a ram." To McElwee, the willingness of "the senior officers of every great navy" to embrace the ram was prima facie evidence that they all "lived in a cloud-cuckoo land."[19]

As is true of the historical debate over the adoption and retention of the line ahead, historians have been too quick to portray mid-nineteenth-century naval officers as fools. To be sure, the ram did not represent the future of naval warfare. But how were naval officers in the 1860s to know that? Well before Lissa new propulsive technologies had led many naval officers to draw parallels between steam-powered warships and galleys—and galleys rammed. The midcentury superiority of iron armor over the gun did little to lessen the attraction of ramming. Nor did the limited experience gained in the American Civil War and the Austro-Italian War. Moreover, at Lissa, while the combatants discovered that it was extremely difficult to ram their opponents under actual battle conditions, they had an even more difficult time sinking ships with gunfire. Following McElwee's logic, naval officers should have abandoned their ineffective rams *and* thrown overboard their even less effective guns.[20]

Lost amid the debate over ramming is the more important question of command and control. At Lissa Tegetthoff demonstrated the continued viability and effectiveness of the decentralized approach. After the battle he wrote: "The whole thing was chaos, a mêlée in the fullest sense of the word . . . It is a miracle that we did not lose a ship."[21] Persano, in contrast, attempted to control his fleet in battle.

After 1866, naval officers interested in tactics garnered few lessons from either the Russo-Turkish War of 1877–1878 or the Chilean-Peruvian Pacific War of 1877–1881. Armor dominated the gun. Ramming seemed to be a workable, if hard to execute, form of attack. There could be no doubt of the lethality of the ram bow. Accidental peacetime rammings, more generally known as collisions, cost the British two battleships and the Germans one. In the Mediterranean in 1893, Vice Admiral Sir George Tryon, cruising off the Syrian coast on a clear, calm day, signaled his fleet, then arrayed in two columns about 1,200 yards apart, to execute a 180-degree turn. Both the commander of the starboard column, Rear Admiral Albert Hastings Markham in the *Camperdown,* and the flagship *Victoria*'s captain, Maurice Bourke, judged the distance between the columns to be too narrow for the maneuver. But Tryon insisted, chastising the reluctant Markham by signal: "What are you waiting for?" Two minutes later the *Camperdown* rammed the starboard side of the *Victoria*. Tryon went down along with 358 of his officers and men.[22]

The irony of the tragedy was that Tryon was the era's noted advocate of "independent steaming" and "command initiative"—a British admiral in the tradition of Vernon, Anson, Hawke, and Nelson. Tryon believed that in the turmoil of technological change the British had lost sight of the realities of battle and had too strongly embraced a "thoroughly dangerous cult" of reliance on visual signals. In response he developed sets of what he termed "Action Principles" that had at their core the old concepts of initiative by subordinates and decentralization.[23]

Tryon believed, as had Nelson, that in battle a commander could not expect to rely on visual signals to control the fleet. Damage, smoke, and the pace of the modern naval battle would make signaling impractical. With ships moving at speeds above 10 knots, delays of up to four minutes in response to visual signals were likely. He argued that "decentralization was essential in a fleet. An Admiral must make his general plans clear to all his Captains and must trust chiefly to their loyalty and initiative in carrying out those plans during the course of an action." Tryon favored simple doctrine, simple signals, hard and frequent training, and maneuver by divisions following the guide of the flagship. He attempted to develop a system that would "leave the fleet in the hands of its chief, plastic, and free to move in any direction without delay." After Tryon's death and the loss of the *Victoria,* a "counter-reformation" occurred within the Royal Navy: proponents of visual signaling were dominant in the decades before the Great War. The sinking of the *Victoria* was also evidence that ramming was an effective tactic.[24]

The fact that the gun had begun to take the measure of armor did not become clear until the Sino-Japanese War of 1894–1895. At the mouth of the Yalu River on 17 September 1894, the Japanese fought and won a long-range battle during which guns, especially rapid-fire guns, proved their importance. The Korean peninsula was the focal point of that war, which pitted a rapidly modernizing Japan intent on imperial expansion against the moribund Qing Dynasty. The commander of the Chinese Beiyang Fleet, Admiral Ding Ruchang, had hoped to duplicate the Austrian victory at Lissa. Ding deployed his twelve ships in a wedge and, like Tegetthoff, adopted a decentralized approach to command. Instead of planning to direct the movements of his fleet once the battle began, he instructed his captains to "follow the motions of the Admiral." With regard to doctrine, Ding's intentions were simple: to keep the bows of his ships facing toward the Japanese. The two most powerful Chinese ships, the 7,500-ton, German-built battleships *Ting Yuen* and *Chen Yuen,* each mounted four 12-inch Krupp guns in barbettes placed obliquely so that all four could fire simultaneously forward or aft, but not broadside.[25]

The battle did not unfold as Ding planned. His ships opened the engagement at a range of 5,000–6,000 yards, but the Chinese gunners scored few hits. Ding discovered that when the *Ting Yuen* fired all four guns in a salvo the concussion shook and strained the superstructure. In fact, about twenty minutes into the engagement Ding fell to the deck unconscious, his leg crushed when the flying bridge he stood on collapsed. As one historian wrote: "Thereafter, the cohesion of the Chinese fleet disappeared."[26]

As the Japanese line led to port across the tip of the Chinese wedge, Ding's ships turned to starboard to keep "bows on." But as they did so the wedge formation disintegrated. The ships that had been on the trailing edge of the wedge were now leading the flagship, making it impossible for them to "follow the motions of the Admiral." Then the "Flying Squadron" of the Japanese Combined Fleet turned and retraced its previous course, while the main body circled around the right flank of the Chinese ships. Ding's fleet was now caught "between two fires." In the confusion, two Chinese captains fled the battle (they were subsequently beheaded). Another ran aground. When the fighting ended, the Chinese had lost five ships and well over 1,000 men.

The lessons of the battle of the Yalu were many, though by no means self-evident to contemporaries. It was the first engagement fought at long range—between 2,000 and 3,000 yards—heralding the arrival of a new age in naval warfare. While the shells fired from naval guns all too often failed to penetrate armor, they shredded the unarmored parts of a ship. The problem for naval gunners was that very few of the shells they fired ever found a target. Admiral Ding's approach to command and control failed, chiefly because his doctrine was inadequately developed and his subordinates lacked the expertise, and in at least two cases the courage, to make it work.

Nor was the Japanese victory a triumph for centralization. The Japanese commander, Admiral Yuko Ito, coordinated the movements of his two squadrons, which began the battle in a line but subsequently separated and at times were miles apart, not by signal, but through prearranged doctrine, much as Admiral Heihachiro Togo, himself a victor at the battle of the Yalu, would a decade later in the Russo-Japanese War. The Japanese relied on speed and firepower while always seeking the vulnerable ends of the enemy formation. The problems of command and control so evident at the Yalu, combined with the defeat of a fleet deployed in a wedge, inexorably led naval commanders, after decades of experimentation with other formations, to what the naval writer Wayne P. Hughes has termed the "reemergence of the fighting column." As the turn-of-the-century Russian tactician Vice Admiral Stepan Osipovich Makarov wrote: "We can not see how an admiral will be able to control a battle if his squadron be formed in any other way than in a column. Change of formations may be indicated by signals, but before fighting begins. Signals are also possible during battle, but only those that are not too complex."[27]

Many uncertainties remained in the realm of naval tactics and doctrine. Even the discerning Makarov was committed to the ram. Tegetthoff's wedge had defeated Persano's line; Ito's line had destroyed Ding's wedge. Makarov concluded: "We should put more trust *in our common sense than in military precedents, which are completely insufficient.*"[28]

The Spanish-American War of 1898 reinforced the lessons, such as they were, of the Yalu. The war began over American dissatisfaction with Spanish policy in Cuba, but the conflict soon spread to the Pacific. At the battles of Manila Bay (1 May 1898) and Santiago de Cuba (3 July 1898) the U.S. Navy won easy victories. At Manila a squadron commanded by Commodore George Dewey destroyed seven Spanish ships, killing 200 men; the only American casualty was one man who collapsed and died from heat prostration. At Santiago de Cuba Rear Admiral William T. Sampson's squadron destroyed six Spanish men-of-war and killed more than 300 Spanish sailors, again for the loss of a single American life.

The two battles demonstrated the woeful inaccuracy of naval gunfire. Although Dewey's and Sampson's ships engaged the Spanish at close range compared to the ranges at the Yalu, the Americans scored few hits and the Spanish even fewer. Such poor gunnery prompted reexaminations of training methods and techniques for range-finding and sighting. The search for new methods, conducted simultaneously by all the major navies, led early in the next century to advanced fire-control systems that, in turn, helped lead the way toward the all-big-gun battleships epitomized by the *Dreadnought*.

Whatever the shortcomings of their gunners, both Dewey and Sampson displayed a penchant for decentralized command and control.

Dewey, who had served with Farragut in the 1860s, discussed his plans with his captains the day before the battle, and then led his line into Manila Bay. Sampson likewise met with his captains as they conducted their watch off Santiago de Cuba. He issued several tactical memoranda, the most important of which enjoined his subordinates to "close and engage as soon as possible" in an effort to destroy the Spanish when they attempted to break out of what the American ground campaign in southeastern Cuba was quickly turning into a trap. The ensuing engagement took the form of a classic "chase" battle, reminiscent of the Royal Navy's eighteenth-century triumphs off Capes Passaro and Finisterre.

The senior officers of the Imperial Japanese Navy found few lessons to be learned from the Spanish-American conflict. They chose instead to draw lessons from their own war with China. The line ahead, dependence on gunnery rather than ramming, and reliance on doctrine and initiative were central to their plans for battle.[29] They had opportunities to test those plans after Imperial rivalries with the Russians, who had supplanted the Chinese as the major power in Korea and Manchuria, erupted in a surprise Japanese strike against the Russian fleet at Port Arthur (now Lushun), the major ice-free Manchurian port on the Liaodong Peninsula, on 8 February 1904.

The Russo-Japanese War of 1904–1905 was the first major naval conflict in which the telegraph figured prominently. The Russians and the Japanese used land and submarine cables as well as new "wireless" telegraph systems. The Japanese laid submarine telegraph cables to link their network in the home islands with a new network in the Korean peninsula and Manchuria. Via the telegraph, Admiral Heihachiro Togo, the commander of the Combined Fleet, could communicate directly with the naval staff in Tokyo as well as with his subordinates commanding squadrons and flotillas operating from forward bases along the Korean peninsula and the Manchurian coast. For example, in June 1904 the commander of the Japanese ships watching the main Russian base, Port Arthur, sent messages by land lines warning Togo that a Russian force under Rear Admiral Vilgelm Vitgeft was leaving the port; Togo received the news in time to meet Vitgeft's sortie. The operational utility of the telegraph to Togo was not lessened by Vitgeft's decision to return to port as soon as the main Japanese force came over the horizon. Not until August 1904 in the battle of the Yellow Sea did Togo catch up with and defeat Vitgeft's squadron.[30]

With the Japanese navy firmly in control of the sea, and the army tightening its grip on the besieged garrison of Port Arthur, the Russians' hopes rested on their Baltic Fleet. The tsar's naval staff had drawn from its prewar plans, assessments, and war games two conclusions regarding a war with Japan: control of the sea would be likely to determine the outcome; and the Japanese would initially possess naval superiority over the Russian forces in the Pacific. The solution was to dispatch a powerful contingent from the Baltic Fleet to reinforce the Port Arthur squadron, and preparations for just such a detachment had begun in the spring of 1904. Months passed, however, before Vice Admiral Zinovi Petrovich Rozhdestvensky's Second Pacific Squadron was ready to embark on the difficult and dangerous voyage, made more so by that time by the defeat of the squadron he was supposed to reinforce in the battle of the Yellow Sea.

Both conventional and wireless telegraphy played central roles in what turned out to be the death ride of Rozhdestvensky's fleet. Telegraph cables buzzed with messages to St. Petersburg or Tokyo reporting the progress of the Russians on their epic voyage. Once Rozhdestvensky reached the Pacific, the wireless sets on Togo's ships, as well as those in the Russian fleet, became important. Telegraph communications between the Far East and St. Petersburg kept the tsar and his naval staff informed about events in the Pacific. The naval staff was able to forward the latest information to Rozhdestvensky as his fleet stopped at various ports along the African and Asian coasts to replenish supplies of coal or food and water. In January 1905 Rozhdestvensky learned by telegraph of the fall of Port Arthur, a catastrophe for his fleet, which would now have to steam for Vladivostok—a port that could be reached only through narrow straits patrolled by the Japanese.

The final stage of the campaign began when the Russian fleet anchored in Canranh Bay along the coast of French Indochina in April 1905. Reports of Rozhdestvensky's arrival quickly reached Tokyo. Japanese diplomats protested what they deemed unneutral French behavior while Admiral Togo prepared his fleet for battle and alerted his scouting squadrons watching the straits through which the Russians would have to pass to reach Vladivostok. By this point in the war, both sides had equipped some of their ships with wireless telegraph transmitters and receivers. The Russians' sets would prove to be woefully inadequate, though apparently not useless.[31]

As Rozhdestvensky steamed north, he intercepted the wireless communications transmitted by the Japanese. From these messages he deduced that seven Japanese scouts were guarding the Tsushima Straits between the Korean Peninsula and Japan. This intelligence, though accurate, was of limited use. Rozhdestvensky assumed, correctly, that the other passages were just as well guarded. He chose to transit the eastern passage of the Tsushima Straits, hoping to catch the Japanese off guard but prepared to fight his way through if necessary. As the Russians entered the straits, the Japanese scouts spotted them and alerted Togo by wireless.[32] With the benefit of the scouts' detailed and generally accurate reports of position, course, and speed, Togo maneuvered his ships into a favorable position to intercept. This operational use of wireless telegraph transmissions marked the advent of a new era in naval warfare. Navies had invaded the ether.

ON THE MORNING of 27 May 1905, as the Japanese and Russian fleets closed in the Tsushima Straits, the Japanese commander in chief took several actions that demonstrated that the fruits of the industrial revolution had yet to trickle down to the tactical level of warfare. Togo directed all his ships to disconnect their wireless sets, hoisted his battle flag, and then, a century after Trafalgar, made a rather Nelsonian signal: "The existence of our Imperial country rests on this one action, and every man of you must do his utmost."[33]

Togo's decision to turn off his wireless sets was not a Luddite reaction to advanced technology; he understood that wireless telegraphy, whatever its strategic and operational virtues, was not the solution to the tactical problems of command and control. The new sets were too fragile, too unwieldy, and too vulnerable to breakdown or jamming. While naval battles had changed markedly since Trafalgar, the tools of command and control at the tactical level remained virtually unaltered. To be sure, navies had developed more advanced and functional systems of visual signaling, but admirals were still communicating with colored flags.

Togo, perhaps more than any other naval commander since Nelson, embraced the decentralized approach to command and control. He understood, as had Nelson, that he could not manage his battles by flag hoist. Instead he prepared for every admiral and captain in the fleet sets of "battle plans" far more detailed than anything Nelson had ever distributed to his subordinates. Togo planned to fight with his fleet arrayed in line ahead formation, although the individual divisions, their columns led by flag officers, would maneuver independently, working together to bring about a powerful concentration of force against a portion of the enemy fleet. In the midst of battle Japanese division commanders were expected to exercise a great deal of initiative. "The Officer Commanding each part of the fleet," Togo decreed, "will decide the tactics and the use of the armament and torpedoes of the part under his command."[34]

The battle, which began shortly before 1400, ended the next morning, although by dusk the outcome had been decided by the loss of four of the eight Russian battleships. During the night Togo attempted to finish off the Russians, launching his destroyer and torpedo boat flotillas in an attack. The attack, dependent on the initiative of his flotilla commanders and captains, failed miserably. Of the eighty-seven torpedoes fired, only four found targets.[35] Nevertheless, the Russian position was hopeless and the next morning most of the surviving ships surrendered.

Tsushima was a classic battle of annihilation. Rozhdestvensky lost twenty-nine of his thirty-eight men-of-war, including all eight battleships, and nearly 5,000 sailors. The Japanese lost not a ship and only 117 men. Togo's triumph was more complete than Nelson's victories at the Nile and Trafalgar, and far more decisive. Tsushima all but ensured eventual Russian defeat in the Far East and assured Japan of a dominant position in northeastern Asia. Within three months the Russo-Japanese War was over.

GIVEN THE REMARKABLE advances in technology, the experience of naval warfare during the century that followed Trafalgar was too limited to draw many clear lessons, although a few realities or trends were apparent. The tempo of naval battles under steam was much faster than that of the age of sail. The end of reliance on the wind for mobility, the marked increase in the speed of ships, and the ever lengthening ranges of the big guns placed a premium on rapid decisionmaking. Naval warfare remained two-dimensional and dominated by the now-steam-driven and armored ships of the line, but torpedo boats and destroyers, which had no place in the line, had become important elements of the fleet. "Combined arms" had finally come to naval warfare.[36] In the battles of the Russo-Japanese War, the largest of this period, the elements of Togo's fleet maneuvered and fought in independent squadrons or divisions, each governed by its own doctrine. Toward the end of the day at Tsushima, Togo even allowed his two main battle squadrons to separate and operate independently. But despite these advances, at the end of the first decade of the twentieth century admirals were still dependent on centuries-old means of command and control: doctrine and visual signals. As a result, many commanders, and most of the successful ones, adopted decentralized approaches to command and control. Farragut, Tegetthoff, Ito, Dewey, Sampson, and Togo relied heavily on doctrine communicated to their subordinates before battle, personally led their usually linear formations, and trusted to their subordinates' initiative once an engagement began.

Perhaps the work of Adrien Baudry, a French naval lieutenant and tactical analyst, epitomizes the mood of the era before the First World War. In *The Naval Battle*, the English-language edition of which was published in 1914, Baudry wrote of the need for prompt responses by commanders to rapidly changing situations in battle, noting that "communication between chief and subordinates takes time, wastes time, loses time." His solution was to ensure "that every one should know, *foreknow*, the chief's plans. Orders and signals should merely be to confirm, perhaps to complete, but at most only to modify, the idea embodied in the Memorandum, the idea that every one has turned over and over in his mind until it has become his very own to carry out." He added:

> "Memorandum." The word is Nelson's. But Suffren, Tegetthoff, Togo, too, did not act otherwise than Nelson acted. All of them communicated their intentions in advance to their captains. It was an encouragement for the captains to know that their leaders had intentions. Not one of those leaders went into battle with the pre-conceived idea of fighting by signal. And outside regulations and doctrines, outside individual actions and group fights, outside the cannonade and the catastrophe, their thoughts in each case hovered over the field of battle.[37]

Nevertheless, the natural human tendency to assert control persisted, and was reinforced by the application of new technology at the strategic and operational levels of war. To many naval officers, the prospect of comparable advances in tactics overshadowed the innumerable present shortcomings of the wireless. Transmission ranges were short and dependent on atmospheric and weather conditions. The sets were bulky, unreliable, and subject to jamming and interception. In an illustrative Rudyard Kipling short story entitled "Wireless," published in 1908, a man operating his own set eavesdrops on two Royal Navy men-of-war struggling to communicate by radio. "Can make nothing of your signals," one ship transmits. "Signals unintelligible," the other replies. The man tells an acquaintance: "That's one of 'em complaining now . . . It's quite pathetic. Have you ever seen a spiritualistic séance? It reminds me of that some-times—odds and ends of messages coming out of nowhere—a word here and there—no good at all." But with each passing year, as the sets became smaller, more reliable, and longer ranged, their potential for tactical use grew. In 1914 Rear Admiral Bradley Fiske of the U.S. Navy felt confident enough to write that the wireless radio would "give the commander-in-chief a means which Nelson did not have, of giving commands, and these commands must be obeyed." The improved wireless thus offset the de-monstrable virtues of a decentralized approach to command and control and ensured the continuance of the debate between the centralizers and decentralizers.[38]

Fiske's prediction regarding the future of radio was, in the purely tech-nical sense, by no means overoptimistic. The war that began in August 1914 spurred further advances in wireless communications that revolu-tionized the technical means of command and control at the tactical level much as land and submarine cables and the first primitive wireless sets had done earlier at the strategic and the operational levels.

Debate over the causes of the First World War—alliance systems, the Anglo-German naval race, German hegemonic tendencies, the inevitable product of capitalist competition—persists. The immediate cause was the assassination of the Austro-Hungarian Archduke Franz Ferdinand by a Serbian assassin in the Bosnian city of Sarajevo. Serbia's refusal to bow to Austria's subsequent demands led the latter to declare war. There followed a chain reaction of declarations that pitted the Central Powers (Austria-Hungary and Germany) against the Allied and Associated Powers (Serbia, Russia, France, and, after the German invasion of Bel-gium, Great Britain). In November 1914 the Ottoman Empire joined the Central Powers, followed in 1915 by Bulgaria. Italy (1915), Romania (1916), and the United States (1917) entered the war against the Central Powers.

On 5 August 1914 Great Britain committed one of its first acts as a belligerent: the cable ship *Teleconia* located, dredged up, and cut the sub-marine lines that connected Germany with much of the rest of the world.[39] In Berlin, this predictable British act brought more annoyance than difficulty, for the Germans were in the forefront of the develop-ment of wireless telegraphy and possessed the necessary high-powered transmitters to communicate with distant stations—even ships and sub-marines.

Germany's possession of a fairly well developed system of wireless communications was a blessing, but it was also an Achilles' heel, and would become a curse. Because wireless transmissions could be intercepted, virtually all the major powers routinely encoded important messages. By late 1914 British codebreakers, working in what became known as "Room 40," were already reading some of the German codes. Reliance on wireless combined with British codebreaking efforts played a major role in shaping the course of the First World War.

The best-known use of Room 40 involved the infamous "Zimmermann Telegram." On 17 January 1917 British naval codebreakers intercepted and decoded a partial message from the German foreign minister, Alfred Zimmermann, to his ambassador in Washington. In the dispatch Zimmermann warned that Germany was about to resume unrestricted submarine warfare, an action that the Germans knew might well lead to American intervention. Zimmermann instructed his ambassador to feel out the Mexicans regarding an alliance and possible military cooperation against the United States. On 1 March, the British, who by then had acquired and decoded a copy of the complete transmission, passed the information to the Americans. The message, which included a German promise to help Mexico regain territory it had once controlled in the southwestern United States, helped to convince a somewhat reluctant President Woodrow Wilson, and a large segment of the American population, that America should enter the war.[40]

Many less celebrated contributions of Room 40 were equally important. This was especially true regarding the naval war, for the Germans relied heavily on wireless communications at sea. German submarines, the dreaded U-boats, carried excellent radios for their day, capable of sending and receiving signals while operating as far as three hundred miles from headquarters. British submarine radios, in contrast, could transmit little more than fifty to sixty miles. So armed, the German U-boatmen proved to be not only effective, but also, in the words of the historian Patrick Beesly, "unduly garrulous" raiders of Allied commerce.[41]

Wireless was central to the success of the German unrestricted submarine campaign that began in February 1917. The centralized control exercised by the German submarine command was not as extensive as it would be during the 1939–1945 war. In the latter conflict the Germans would use radio to bring about the tactical concentration of U-boats in "wolfpacks" to overwhelm the defenses of escorted convoys. During the First World War they sought only operational concentrations. Advanced radio technology permitted U-boats to relay to the high command information about the intensity of merchant traffic and the strength of Allied patrols. The Germans were thus able to deploy the boats to those areas where the prospects for success were the most promising.

Room 40 intercepted and decoded many of these reports, but Allied navies lacked the technological means to exploit the intelligence fully at the all-important tactical level. Great War antisubmarine escorts were armed, at best, with primitive hydrophones and depth charges. Until the development of sonar, radar, and improved weapons in the 1930s and 1940s, escorts posed a minimal, though not inconsequential, threat to the U-boats. Nevertheless, Room 40's codebreaking efforts bore substantial operational fruit. Just as the radio allowed the Germans to concentrate their submarine effort, radio interception allowed the British to avoid those concentrations. The intelligence gleaned from decoding enabled the British to identify areas where the Germans were concentrating their U-boats. Once the Allies adopted the convoy system, in which warships accompanied merchant vessels, in the late spring of 1917, the admiralty was able to use this intelligence, and its own improved wireless network, to reroute convoys. Each convoy included at least one wireless-equipped vessel, the commodore's flagship. When rerouting proved impossible or impractical, the admiralty could dispatch antisubmarine vessels to rendezvous with convoys that had to pass through shipping lanes where large numbers of German submarines were known to be patrolling. Additionally, decoded messages revealed the routes German submarines took from the North Sea into the Atlantic, enabling the Allies to patrol these routes heavily and, in many cases, to mine them.

The U-boat campaign of 1917 and 1918 marked a major change in naval command and control. Wireless telegraphy allowed the Germans, for the first time in history, to profitably coordinate—to centralize—a *guerre de course*. Ironically, this coordination was offset to a fair degree, not by any denial of initiative to individual U-boat commanders, but by a new factor in the command and control equation: the vulnerability to interception and decoding of centralized systems reliant on electronic signaling. The very process of communicating had become dangerous in a way that sending up a signal flag had never been.

As a result, the wireless was a proverbial two-edged sword, and not solely for submarines. The German High Seas Fleet nearly met disaster off Jutland Bank on 31 May and 1 June 1916 principally because of its strategic and operational reliance on radio. But those same wireless sets twice helped the German dreadnoughts to escape destruction at the hands of a quantitatively superior fleet.

In 1916 the High Seas Fleet held a strong advantage in wireless technology. German surface ships carried continuous-wave wireless sets capable of reliable signaling on multiple wavelengths, a necessity for effective tactical use by a large fleet in action. Not until the end of that year did the British Grand Fleet begin to receive similar equipment. At the time of the battle of Jutland, British warships relied on spark transmitters, fine for operational communication between the elements of the fleet, but susceptible to jamming and poorly suited for tactical application.[42]

The Germans possessed excellent equipment but were reckless in its use. Their codes were simple and changed infrequently. Their approach to communications security was remarkably cavalier. Even in port their ships relied on radio for routine communications. As Beesly wrote, the Germans "contributed to their own insecurity by excessive and quite unnecessary use of wireless. They fell into this trap partly because of the very excellence of their transmitters, which were not only better than those of the British but better than the Germans themselves realized."[43]

In the spring of 1916 the recently appointed commander in chief of the German High Seas Fleet, Vice Admiral Reinhard Scheer, decided to adopt a more aggressive posture in the North Sea in an effort to whittle down the British superiority in dreadnoughts. As the Germans set their plans in motion they relied on wireless, and the British codebreakers in Room 40 quickly deduced that something was afoot. In mid-May the movements of U-boats within the North Sea, far from the routes followed by merchant ships, pointed toward a possible fleet operation. On the morning of 30 May the British intercepted and decoded a message from Scheer to the ships of the High Seas Fleet directing them to assemble that evening in the outer roads of the Jade estuary. A few minutes later the U-boat wireless station at Bruges, Belgium, sent a warning to all submarines that the fleet would be at sea on 31 May and 1 June.[44]

On the afternoon of 30 May the decoding of the German messages was still incomplete and the British did not know the details of Scheer's plans. Nevertheless, the intelligence was sufficient to convince the admiralty to preempt any German move in the North Sea. At 1320 the admiralty sent telegrams along secure land lines from London to Scapa Flow, Scotland, warning Admiral Sir John Rushworth Jellicoe, commander in chief of the Grand Fleet, that the German fleet would probably sortie the next day. At 1728 the admiralty directed Jellicoe to raise steam, and at

1755, now in possession of somewhat more detailed information, wired: "Germans intend some operation commencing to-morrow and leave via eastern route and Horns Reef L[ight] V[essel]. Operation appears to extend over 31st May and 1st June. You should concentrate to the eastward of Long Forties ready for eventualities." At 1930 Jellicoe directed his 2d Battle Squadron at Cromarty to "leave as soon as ready" and to rendezvous with the main fleet the next day. At 1937 he sent similar orders to the commander of his battlecruiser squadron, Vice Admiral David Beatty, at Rosyth. Beatty was to reach his assigned position, south of the main fleet, at 1400 on 31 May. If he had failed to contact the Germans, he was to turn and steam north to join the rest of the fleet. Once concentrated, the entire Grand Fleet would "steer for Horn Reef."[45]

The admiralty's decision to order Jellicoe to sail was fortuitous. Scheer had deployed nearly a dozen and a half U-boats off the three British bases. By sailing at night, Jellicoe not only avoided the attacks that Scheer had hoped would weaken the British fleet, but also put to sea unobserved by the German submarines, who were thus unable to warn Scheer by wireless that the enemy had sailed. At 2200 Jellicoe, who fully recognized the dangers inherent in reliance on wireless, signaled his fleet: "Cease W/T communication except on sighting the enemy or replying to the admiral."[46]

Scheer, whose fleet was still in the Jade, did not know that his plan had already come undone. His concept for the operation had depended heavily on telegraph and wireless communication. The High Seas Fleet was to steam north along the Danish west coast into the Skagerrak, as far as the Naze. Scheer assumed that the Danes or the Norwegians would report the fleet's presence, by cable or wireless, to London, prompting a British response. When the Grand Fleet steamed out of its three main bases, U-boats placed in ambush would torpedo several of Jellicoe's dreadnoughts and then advise Scheer, by wireless, that the British had sortied. Scheer would then maneuver, guided by additional wireless reconnaissance reports from zeppelins, into position to concentrate the entire High Seas Fleet against part of Jellicoe's larger force. By the time Vice Admiral Franz von Hipper's Scouting Force finally got under way at 0100 on 31 May, however, the British had already been at sea for three hours. Bad weather had also grounded the zeppelins.

If wireless gave the British the strategic advantage, it also shaped the operational procedures adopted by both fleets. The advent of steam had exacerbated a problem that had plagued commanders in the days of sail:

the question of the proper use of sailing and battle orders. The line ahead, long the preferred fighting order, was an unnecessarily unwieldy formation for a fleet not in contact with the enemy. Most commanders employed distinct sailing orders that divided fleets into separate divisions so arranged that they could deploy into a line of battle if an enemy force appeared on the horizon. But as the range of naval cannon increased, the distance at which an enemy fleet could be seen was frequently the range at which it could be engaged. A fleet attempting to deploy from columns of division into the line ahead while under fire would be at a distinct disadvantage during the perhaps all-important first minutes of an engagement.

One solution to this problem, and the one adopted by the smaller German fleet, was to steam in battle formation. The solution adopted by the British, which was also used by the Germans, was to deploy scouting forces far enough ahead to locate the enemy and allow the main body time to deploy. For the Grand Fleet the deployment took between twenty and twenty-five minutes. With two fleets armed with big guns capable of hurling armor-piercing shells more than ten miles, closing on each other at a combined speed of over forty knots, scouting forces—at Jutland the respective battlecruiser squadrons of Hipper and Beatty—had to be at least thirty miles ahead of the main body, well beyond visible range. Thus the very formations employed by the two fleets at Jutland depended on wireless communication.

Wireless, however, offered no solution to Jellicoe's tactical dilemmas. Assuming all went well and he intercepted the High Seas Fleet, he faced a conundrum. If he met his operational goals—concentrating his fleet *before* encountering the Germans—he would, by definition, have frustrated Scheer's aim to engage part of the Grand Fleet with the whole of the High Seas Fleet. In that event, there was a good chance that Scheer would withdraw rather than risk a battle at unfavorable odds. Thus, at the tactical level, Jellicoe faced the same problem that had dogged sailing-age commanders for more than a century: how to force a battle on an enemy intent on withdrawal with a fleet deployed in an effective but unwieldy line ahead.

On the eve of Jutland, British naval commanders had yet to reach a consensus regarding tactics, doctrine, or a philosophy of command and control. This was especially true at the highest levels of the Grand Fleet. Filson Young, a journalist cum naval reserve officer who served on Beatty's staff during the first years of the war, observed that "[Jellicoe] and Beatty represented diametrically opposite schools of naval thought." Jellicoe was cautious and, although he often mouthed the vocabulary of a decentralizer, remained at heart committed to centralized control; Beatty, the senior British commander who most resembled Tryon, was the more aggressive of the two men and a classic decentralizer. Beatty, Young noted, "worked diligently to eliminate the elaborate signaling of orders—it is not so long ago since the signal 'On boots' was made, as an 'evolution,' from the flagship to the whole Fleet—and put independent and co-ordinated responsibility in its place; in a word, to restore and stimulate initiative which Admiralty policy had steadily discouraged; and, most revolutionary of all, to insist upon leave being given and taken on every opportunity, instead of being doled out, like a dangerous drug, in homaeopathic doses."[47]

In February 1915 Beatty revised the Battle-Cruiser Fleet Orders—the published doctrine issued to all captains of his command. Citing the lessons of the previous "Great War," the Anglo-French struggle of 1793–1815, he wrote: "Cruiser captains and battle-cruiser Captains, to be successful, must possess, in a marked degree, initiative, resource, determination, and fearlessness of responsibility." Beatty, whose experience and study of history convinced him that it would be too difficult to direct a large fleet action from the flagship, advised his subordinates: "The Admiral will therefore rely on Captains to use all the information at their disposal so as to grasp the situation quickly and anticipate his wishes, using their own discretion as to how to act in unforeseen circumstances and carrying through every operation with resolution and energy." "Ships must never suppose," he stressed, "that the absence of a signal implies that any given action is not sanctioned by Flagship; on the contrary it usually denotes that the Admiral relies on each ship to take whatever action may be necessary without waiting to be told."[48]

Beatty, after assuming command of the Grand Fleet in early 1918, became a somewhat more cautious admiral than he had been when he flew his flag from a battlecruiser, but he did not change his fundamental philosophy of command. He revised, and symbolically renamed, Jellicoe's Grand Fleet Battle Orders as Grand Fleet Battle Instructions. In the new, somewhat abbreviated document, Beatty wrote of what he termed "the decentralization of command": "When action is joined, the Flag Officers commanding battle squadrons and divisions of the battlefleet have full discretionary power to manoeuvre their squadrons or divisions independently whilst conforming generally to the movements of the Commander-in-Chief."[49]

Beatty's approach to command had more in common with those of Tirpitz, Scheer, and Hipper than with that of Jellicoe. In the 1890s, as the Germans began to build up their navy, they experimented with myriad formations, tactics, and methods of command. Ultimately they adopted the line ahead as their principal battle formation, a squadron-division organization, and a flexible, somewhat Nelsonian approach to tactics and command and control.[50] Admiral Alfred von Tirpitz, the central figure in the expansion of the German navy, wrote in his memoirs:

> The natural tendency of the Commander-in-Chief to lead the whole fleet as a tactical unit only meets the case in certain situations. On the other hand, it is frequently only a certain independence on the part of the squadron commanders that can produce the best results from the fleet. The larger the fleet, the more difficult it is to handle when concentrated. Its manoeuvrings become clumsier, and the Commander-in-Chief is easily prevented by smoke, rain, and particularly the smoke from gunfire, from reviewing the position of the various units. This is the most important reason why we decided upon the squadron as the tactical unit, and thus gave the squadron commanders and the equivalent leaders of flotillas the right to act "According to circumstances."

In Tirpitz's view, German tactics were more advanced than those of the Royal Navy; the British were "behindhand in tactics" because they had relied on their quantitative superiority for a century after Trafalgar. The Germans, conversely, knowing they could not match the British in numbers, had sought to construct the better ships and to develop the superior tactics so evident at the battle of Jutland.[51]

There was an element of truth in Tirpitz's observation that the British were "behindhand in tactics," but other factors also influenced Jellicoe's handling of his fleet at Jutland. He did not share a belief in the tactical superiority of Royal Navy ships and crews with his predecessors such as Anson, Hawke, Howe, St. Vincent, and Nelson. The overall strategic situation he faced in the spring of 1916 also did little to inspire anything other than caution. And then there was "wireless."

The German navy pioneered the wireless and was among the first to attempt to use it to control ships tactically. But the effort was premature and ultimately led to the expenditure "of a great deal of money" and "endless trouble with the technical difficulties."[52] This wireless fiasco may have been a blessing for the Germans, for it forced them to rely more on flexible tactics and traditional methods of command and control. When the radio industry produced more advanced types of wireless, the German navy introduced them to the fleet as supplements to, and not replacements for, existing approaches to command and control.

Because the British lagged in the development of effective naval wireless sets, they were spared the frustrations of the Germans and, as a result, continued to view radio as a potential catholicon for the problems of command and control. The advent of the wireless, in the view of the historian Arthur Marder, "strengthened one-man control, leaving even less scope for initiative by subordinates." Andrew Gordon, in his superb study of command at Jutland, considered the spread of wireless throughout the British fleet an "insidious influence." The Royal Navy was replete with officers prone to extreme centralization. "They were already signals junkies," Gordon noted, "and their dependency expanded to match the range of the new technology." Wireless "did more to change the conditions of fighting than any other single thing," Filson Young concluded in an observation that probably reflected David Beatty's thinking; "it meant the abolition of independent action and the consummation of highly organized and concerted action."[53]

Admiral Sir George Callahan, who commanded the main British fleet on the eve of the Great War, resisted this trend toward centralization. His prewar instructions, which amounted to little more than two or three pages of material, stated: "In carrying out the intentions of the Admiral, Commanders of Squadrons, divisions or subdivisions should be given wide discretion as to the conduct of the ships under their immediate control." Callahan intended to control only the division of the fleet in which he steamed: "The control of other portions or of squadrons must be delegated to their commanders, subject to the general instructions given below or to others which I issue."[54]

Jellicoe, who replaced Callahan in August 1914, brought a somewhat confused tactical philosophy to the fleet. He drew up lengthy Grand Fleet Battle Orders—about seventy pages of them. In those issued the week before Jutland, Jellicoe observed that amid the confusion of battle he might not be able to control the entire fleet: "It therefore becomes necessary to decentralize command to the fullest extent possible, and the Vice-Admirals commanding squadrons have discretionary power to manoeuvre their squadrons independently whilst conforming generally to the movements of the Commander-in-Chief and complying with his known intentions." But such pronouncements were, in Gordon's view, mere "platitudes," not the true observations of a decentralizer. Jellicoe contradicted them in the very next section: "In all cases the ruling principle is that the 'Dreadnought' fleet as a whole keeps together, attempted attacks by a division or squadron on portion of the enemy line being avoided as liable to lead to isolation of the ships which attempt the movement, and, so long as the fleets are engaged on approximately similar courses, the squadrons should form one line of battle." Jellicoe fully recognized, and admitted, the problems inherent in attempting to manage a fleet in battle using visual signals, but he *"hoped* that difficulties in signalling will be largely overcome by the use of wireless telegraphy."[55]

If Jellicoe's approach to command was rather traditional, what of his tactics? During the age of sail, the Royal Navy's more successful admirals, centralizers and decentralizers alike, had aggressively sought engagements at close range, where the qualitative superiority of individual British ships and crews came to the fore. Jellicoe, lacking a similar faith in his instrument, adopted a series of defensive tactics related to his most important decision—to engage the Germans at long, and not close, range.[56]

For some historians, Jellicoe's decision to avoid a close fight was a mistake that all but nullified his superiority in numbers. But a close battle at Jutland could have favored the Germans, who now possessed the better ships and crews. In a close fight, both sides would have scored more hits, but, as the battle demonstrated, the well-built German men-of-war had to be battered into submission, while British vessels had a disturbing tendency to suffer catastrophic hits and explode. Beatty certainly had a change of heart after the battle. In February 1915, during the action off Dogger Bank, he had, in grand Nelsonian fashion, signaled his ships to "keep nearer to the enemy" and to "keep closer," signals that according to Filson Young "could not more simply have expressed his conception of war." But when Beatty took command of the Grand Fleet in 1918, instead of pressing for close action he decreed that the fleet would engage no "nearer than 16,000 yards."[57]

Vice Admiral Sir Doveton Sturdee, commander of the Grand Fleet's 4th Battle Squadron and victor of the December 1914 engagement off the Falkland Islands, was Jellicoe's most vocal contemporary critic within the fleet. Sturdee's reading of history convinced him, in Marder's words, "that while the single line ahead was a good defensive order, no battle in British history had ever been won in that order, and that divisional tactics would be more effective." Sturdee doubted the wisdom of several other aspects of Jellicoe's tactical doctrine, for example the decision that the fleet would turn away from, and not toward, the enemy ships to counter a torpedo attack, a maneuver that Sturdee believed would lead to disengagement. The "arch-heretic" Sturdee voiced his concerns in 1915 and 1916 in a number of letters, and finally in a paper in which he laid out his own tactical principles and suggested a meeting of flag officers to discuss tactical questions. Jellicoe refused to call such a meeting, rejected Sturdee's advice, and countered that his actions introduced "controversy" into the fleet and undermined confidence. Sturdee later wrote: "I was ordered by the C.-in-C. never to discuss or try dividing the Fleet for the purpose of overpowering the enemy, and thus bringing a superiority of fire on part of the enemy's Fleet, so ceased having Tactical Games on board my flagship until there was change in the Command."[58]

Given the overall strategic situation, Jellicoe's caution and desire to maintain control may have been entirely appropriate. He knew he was the "only man who could lose the war in an afternoon." The advantages to be gained for the alliance should Jellicoe crush the German fleet were few and relatively insignificant, whereas the price of defeat would be disastrous. To be sure, Jellicoe was no Nelson, but neither were his captains Troubridges, Berrys, Hardys, Foleys, or Collingwoods; nor were Scheer and Hipper Villeneuves, or de Grasses; nor the High Seas Fleet the equivalent of the French and Spanish navies that the British had so often savaged during the age of sail. Jellicoe confronted what few Royal Navy commanders had faced since the Anglo-Dutch Wars: a qualitatively superior fleet. Wayne P. Hughes summed up the situation succinctly: "There was no tactical initiative open to Jellicoe that would have been consistent with the offensive spirit of Nelson. It is difficult to imagine one even in theory, given the weapon characteristics of 1916."[59] Jellicoe's superiority rested on numbers—more ships and more guns— and to reap the fullest advantage of that quantitative superiority, he had to keep his fleet concentrated. To do otherwise risked defeat and total disaster for the Allies.

If Jellicoe believed, and perhaps rightly, that he lacked the tactical means to force a decisive engagement, the wireless might have provided an operational solution to his dilemma. The admiralty might have made better use of the intelligence gained from intercepted German transmissions by directing the concentration of the Grand Fleet farther to the southeast, rather than to the east of Horn Reef. Jellicoe himself might have chosen for his rendezvous a location from which he could have steamed into a position between Scheer and his base before, rather than during, the battle. In February 1915, before the battlecruiser action off Dogger Bank, the admiralty had similarly failed to take full advantage of the intelligence gained by Room 40 and had directed Beatty to an inter-ception position northwest of the Germans. Beatty subsequently failed in his attempt to interpose his squadron between the Germans and their base, and they escaped. Beatty blamed the admiralty for not directing him to a position farther to the south and east. Just who, if anyone, Beatty faulted after Jutland is unclear, but it is noteworthy that in his January 1918 Grand Fleet Battle Instructions he informed his subordinates that if the Germans again sortied, he would "endeavour to place the fleet be-tween the enemy and his base."[60]

While neither the admiralty nor Jellicoe made the best operational use of the signals intelligence available to them, British interception of German wireless traffic nevertheless made likely a major fleet encounter on 31 May 1916. Late that morning, as Jellicoe's ships steamed across the North Sea, Rear Admiral Thomas Jackson, director of operations on the admiralty staff, visited Room 40 and asked if the British DF (radio direction finding) stations had located "DK," the call sign for the flag-ship of the High Seas Fleet. Jackson received a prompt answer—Wilhelmshaven—and returned to his office where he drafted the fol-lowing telegram for Jellicoe: "No definite news enemy. They made preparations for sailing early this morning Wednesday. It was thought the fleet had sailed but direction signal placed flagship Jade at 11.10 G.M.T. Apparently they have been unable to carry out air reconnaissance which has delayed them."[61]

The Germans, of course, were at sea, and the personnel of Room 40 knew it. Jackson had grossly misunderstood what he had been told. DF did place "DK" in the Jade, but only because the Germans routinely transferred the call sign to the wireless transmitting station at Wilhelmshaven whenever Scheer put to sea. This was no secret to the personnel of Room 40, although it was to Jackson, who thought little of the efforts of his codebreakers. No one in Room 40 knew of Jackson's message to Jellicoe.

Jellicoe received the misleading report at 1248. Battle suddenly seemed less imminent. Since he might need to stay at sea an extra day to engage the tardy Germans, he slowed the progress of the fleet to save fuel. As a result, he fell about an hour behind schedule, and was an additional fif-teen nautical miles from Beatty when the engagement began. Moreover, when Beatty did finally make contact with the High Seas Fleet a few hours later, Jellicoe entered the battle without much confidence in the accuracy of Room 40's intelligence.

The battle of Jutland began at about 1420 when the British light cruiser *Galatea* hoisted the "enemy in sight" signal and simultaneously sent a wireless received by both Jellicoe and Beatty: "Urgent. Two cruisers, probably hostile, in sight bearing E.S.E., course unknown." The sighted ships, actually a pair of destroyers, belonged to Hipper's battlecruiser Scouting Force. Beatty, who had been preparing to turn to the north to head for his rendezvous with Jellicoe, redeployed his destroyers and, at 1432, signaled for the fleet to turn toward the southeast to get between the Germans and their base. Beatty, although radio silence had already been broken, made the signal by flag only, and it went unseen by the new oil-fired, fast battleships of Rear Admiral Sir Hugh Evan-Thomas's 5th Battle Squadron, which had been attached to Beatty's command shortly before the start of the campaign. Evan-Thomas, who by 1432 had already begun his turn to the north, continued on that course, although he had heard the *Galatea's* "urgent" report of contact and could see Beatty's other ships steaming toward the southeast. Perhaps no example so well illustrates the problems inherent in an overly centralized system of command and control that strips initiative from subordinate commanders. As a result, Beatty's four most powerful ships were too far to the northwest to give him immediate support.[62]

As Hipper's and Beatty's ships dueled, eventually conducting what became known as "the run to the south," the German scouting vessels used their wireless sets to keep Scheer well informed. Scheer raced north to support his battlecruisers. After receiving additional wireless reports at about 1345 indicating that Hipper, steaming on a southeasterly course, was being chased by fast, heavy ships, Scheer altered course to the northwest. With the German fleet already deployed in line ahead, he intended to trap Beatty's ships between the guns of the two German lines.[63]

Beatty conducted an aggressive pursuit and kept closing the range with Hipper, despite the loss of two battlecruisers—the *Indefatigable* and the *Queen Mary*—to catastrophic hits and explosions, until shortly before 1600. At 1554 the light cruiser *Southampton,* the flagship of Commodore William Edmund Goodenough's 2d Light Cruiser Squadron, sighted the German fleet. Goodenough signaled a report of the contact by searchlight and wireless.[64] Beatty reacted promptly, sending up the signal for the entire fleet to alter course to the northwest—toward Jellicoe. But the 5th Battle Squadron again missed the visual signal and also failed to receive the *Southampton's* wireless report, probably because of German jamming efforts. Evan-Thomas, whose ships had only just caught up with the rest

of the fleet and joined the engagement, saw Beatty's battlecruisers heading north but held on toward the south until he received a direct flag signal from Beatty as he sped past in his flagship, the battlecruiser *Lion*.

Thus began "the run to the north," with the British leading the German battlecruisers, and the rest of the High Seas Fleet, toward the Grand
Fleet. Jellicoe was not kept as well informed as Scheer had been during
the run to the south. Between 1559, when Jellicoe received a wireless report from Beatty that he had engaged the enemy, until the *Southampton*'s
1638 report, no information from the "scouting" forces reached
Jellicoe.[65] At 1645 he received a garbled wireless message from Beatty
that placed the Germans to the southwest but provided no details on
their course. Over the next hour he received little additional information
and remained uncertain what was happening to the south and, most important, from which direction and in what formation Scheer's ships were
approaching.

At about 1800 lookouts on Jellicoe's flagship, the *Iron Duke*, could see
Beatty's *Lion* to the south, straddled by shell splashes. This sudden appearance of the battlecruisers, obviously hard pressed, surprised Jellicoe, who
had calculated that Beatty was ten to fifteen minutes farther to the south.
With the two fleets now closing at over a half-mile per minute, and with
the Grand Fleet still deployed in its six division columns of four ships
each with five miles between columns, Jellicoe had to determine when,
and in what direction, to deploy into his battle line. At 1801 he signaled
Beatty by wireless: "Where is Enemy's Battlefleet?" Five minutes passed
before Beatty, who had temporarily lost sight of the main German fleet,
responded: "Enemy battle cruisers bearing S.E." But what of Scheer's
battlefleet? At 1810 Jellicoe repeated his query and there followed another interminable pause before Beatty replied: "Have sighted Enemy's
Battlefleet nearing S.S.W."[66]

Jellicoe sensed that he had only minutes to make a critical decision. He
had yet to sight the head of Scheer's line. All he knew was that the German fleet lay somewhere to the south-southwest, and within range of
Beatty. But how far to the south-southwest, and on what course? Jellicoe
examined the compass for less than a half-minute and told his fleet signal
officer: "Hoist equal-speed pendant SE." The signal directed the Grand
Fleet initially to deploy to port, roughly on a heading to the northeast,
but the first ship in the portmost column, after completing the evolution,
would then turn toward the southeast.[67]

Scheer, steaming north in pursuit of Beatty, was heading into a trap.

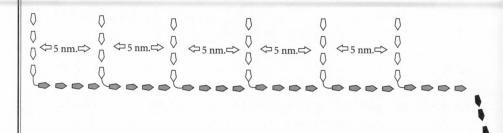

Initial position (in divisional columns)

Second position (in battle line)

Third position (only lead division shown)

THE BATTLE OF JUTLAND, 31 MAY 1916, CA. 1811:
JELLICOE'S MANEUVER

The British fleet was too large to steam in battle order as the German fleet did.
Instead, the British steamed in divisional columns far enough apart to allow them
to transition rapidly into a line. Once the leading ship of the column leading the
turn completed its 90-degree turn, it could, depending on the signal, alter course.
The ships following it would proceed to the leading ship's point of turn, and then
similarly alter course. At Jutland the port division led the columns into line heading northeast and, when the six columns had completed their turns, led the line to
the southeast.

Jellicoe was deploying in a great arc directly in the path of the High Seas
Fleet. The German T was crossed. Scheer, well aware of the tactical situation, ordered his destroyers to conduct a torpedo attack while the High
Seas Fleet executed a *Gefechtskehrtwendung,* a "battle about-turn" or "battle turn-away"—a 16-point, 180-degree turn to the right, beginning
with the rear ship in the line.[68]

The *Gefechtskehrtwendung* was a dangerous maneuver. The possibilities
of delay if the rear ships missed the signal, or of collisions given the limited visibility, were real. For historians of the battle the Germans' ability
to execute the maneuver is an indication of their tactical superiority over
the British. No doubt they were ahead in tactics, for during the evolution
the initiative shown by one of the German captains played a crucial role.

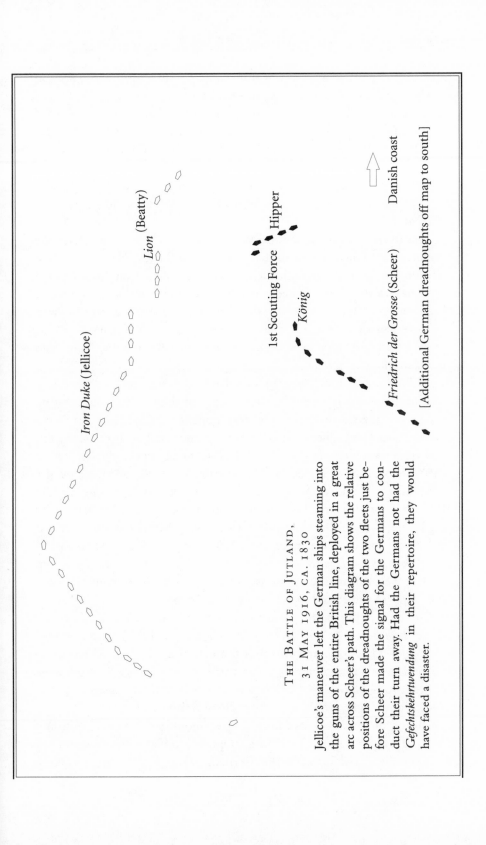

THE BATTLE OF JUTLAND,
31 MAY 1916, CA. 1830

Jellicoe's maneuver left the German ships steaming into the guns of the entire British line, deployed in a great arc across Scheer's path. This diagram shows the relative positions of the dreadnoughts of the two fleets just before Scheer made the signal for the Germans to conduct their turn away. Had the Germans not had the *Gefechtskehrtwendung* in their repertoire, they would have faced a disaster.

Iron Duke (Jellicoe)

Lion (Beatty)

1st Scouting Force   Hipper

König

Friedrich der Grosse (Scheer)   Danish coast

[Additional German dreadnoughts off map to south]

But tactical proficiency was not sufficient to ensure a prompt execution of the signal. Scheer's sixteen ships formed a line between six and seven miles long. Visibility was poor, and getting worse. More than a hundred coal-burning ships were spewing smoke into the air. Reliance on visual signals to direct such a complex evolution while steaming at high speed under fire would have been foolhardy had the Germans not possessed reliable continuous-wave wireless sets. Throughout the battle, Scheer signaled his subordinates by both visual means—flags and lights—and wireless.[69]

The movements of individual ships in Scheer's line demonstrate the importance of the wireless to the execution of the *Gefechtskehrtwendung*. The dreadnought *König,* which led the German line, seven ships ahead of the *Friedrich der Grosse,* Scheer's flagship, failed to respond to the signal because its wireless antenna was damaged and it was too distant to make out the flag signal.[70] Conversely, Captain Johannes Redlich's *Westfalen,* positioned eight ships to Scheer's rear, received the wireless signal and initiated the maneuver.

Redlich decided to begin the *Gefechtskehrtwendung* on his own initiative, since his was not actually the last ship in the German line. During the race to the north, the six pre-dreadnoughts of the High Seas Fleet's 2d Squadron had fallen behind the more modern German battleships and a gap of about a mile and a half had opened between the last ship of the 1st Squadron, Redlich's *Westfalen,* and the first of the 2d Squadron, the *Deutschland.* With the range between the two fleets closing rapidly, Redlich knew that time had become critical: there was no point in waiting for the ships of the 2d Squadron to conduct their turnabouts, nor was there any appreciable danger of collision given the gap between the *Westfalen* and the *Deutschland.* Redlich, instead of waiting for the last ship in the 2d Squadron, the *Hannover,* to begin its reversal of course, turned the *Westfalen* about, and the rest of the fleet followed.

Twice more during the evening Scheer ordered his fleet to execute a *Gefechtskehrtwendung,* once in an effort to get around the rear of the British line, and later to extract his fleet from another disadvantageous tactical position. Without wireless, and without other displays of initiative rather than blind obedience to orders, these subsequent maneuvers, conducted in twilight, would have been all but impossible.

During the night the two fleets groped about in the dark, each trying to avoid a night action. The British attempted to maintain a position between Scheer and his base; the Germans twisted and turned seeking a way to safety through the British fleet. As usual, the Germans were talkative, and Room 40 intercepted and decoded several messages. In one Scheer called for zeppelin reconnaissance in the morning over the Horns Reef Channel. In another of 2155 the codebreakers learned that the High Seas Fleet was headed for port. At 2241 the admiralty sent a synopsis of these messages to Jellicoe: "German battlefleet ordered home at 9:14 P.M. battle cruisers in rear, Speed 16 knots. Course SSE3E."[71]

Given the German course, Jellicoe might have deduced that Scheer was heading for the Horns Reef Channel. But Jellicoe had doubts—both about Scheer's likely route and, having been told earlier that the Germans were still in the Jade, about the value of the intelligence emanating from Room 40. Jellicoe instead moved his fleet farther to the west, well out of position to intercept the Germans. Historians can only wonder, as did Jellicoe when he learned of the admiralty's failure to use the available intelligence, what might have happened had Scheer's call for zeppelin reconnaissance been passed to Jellicoe. Lord Mountbatten later concluded that the admiralty's error prevented Jellicoe from winning a second "Glorious 1st of June."[72]

Jutland, the only great naval battle of the First World War and the only large-scale clash of dreadnoughts in history, was a disappointingly inconclusive engagement. The Germans declared, and achieved, a tactical victory, but the British bested the Germans operationally and could also claim the more important strategic victory: nothing changed at sea after Jutland; the British blockade of Germany did not falter. But among naval officers, historians, and analysts the battle sparked often contentious debate about Jellicoe's and Beatty's leadership, about engagement ranges, divisional tactics, formations, scouting, and communications, and about the roles of destroyers, submarines, and aerial reconnaissance. The "fog of war" was particularly thick at Jutland; the dichotomy between centralizers and decentralizers was sharply defined; and new methods of command and control were employed at all levels of warfare.

Jellicoe faced a "fog of war" so dense that he might as well have been blindfolded. He was a tactical commander struggling to fight a twentieth-century battle with eighteenth-century means of command and control. In March 1934 Jellicoe attended a conference on the battle prepared with German as well as British records. After listening to the presentation, he said that this was the first time he had ever had a clear picture of the battle. According to Lord Mountbatten, he "picked up a duster and laid it in a circle around the models representing the four leading German Battleships. He said that at no time did he ever see more than three or four of the twenty-two German Battleships . . . or get any true picture of where they all were or what they were doing."[73]

The battle of Jutland demonstrated that wireless telegraphy had changed the face of naval warfare. Strategically and operationally, heavy and careless reliance on wireless led Scheer toward destruction when in the early evening of 31 May he discovered the Grand Fleet arrayed in all its glory. But those same wireless sets enabled the Germans to execute their turnabout and escape the British trap. Remarkably, while navies were just beginning to employ effective wireless sets at sea, they were already intercepting and decoding messages, employing radio direction finding, jamming enemy transmissions, and at times operating under radio silence. By the spring of 1916 naval warfare had entered the electromagnetic spectrum in the forms of what would become known as signals intelligence (sigint), traffic analysis, electronic warfare, and emissions control (emcon).

The British failure to make the best use of the intelligence gained from intercepted German messages was an important lesson to be learned from the battle. Admiralties and naval commanders had always had to coordinate intelligence with their strategic and operational plans. But Jutland was the first battle in which a commander had access to nearly immediate intelligence, albeit in limited form, of potential tactical importance.

The campaign confirmed that despite the advance of technology, the old debate between centralizers and decentralizers had not been resolved. The Germans successfully harnessed a new technology to a flexible and decentralized system of command. Under Jellicoe's direction, the British, still lacking effective wireless sets for tactical ship-to-ship communication, relied on visual signals and a highly centralized approach, although commanders such as Beatty and Sturdee advocated a more Nelsonian system.

CHAPTER EIGHT

From 1918 through the Second World War

$\mathcal{T}$HE NAVAL BATTLES of the Great War, though few in number, offered hints of tremendous changes to come. By 1918 naval warfare had become a three-dimensional exercise, with aircraft operating above the ocean's surface and submersibles below it. Advocates for aviation and submarines appeared in all of the world's militaries, but these visionaries were often as premature in their expectations as their opponents were troglodytic in their assumptions about the continued centrality of the battleship.

Questions about naval command and control remained subject to debate. The war had demonstrated that the fruits of the industrial revolution were at last reshaping what could now properly be termed the "technology" of naval command and control. Wireless telegraphy had played a major role in naval strategy, operations, and at times even tactics. But even as new technologies offered the prospect of better control, concurrent technological advances placed additional strains on commanders in chief. The pressures of command at sea in the twentieth century were far greater than they had ever been during the age of sail. Fleets moved more quickly, covered more ocean, included a far more complex mix of forces with varying strengths and weaknesses, and could strike at distances unimaginable a century earlier. While the technology of command had advanced, that progress had been more than offset by the narrowing of a commander's decisionmaking window. It remained unknown whether, in the face of these formidable challenges, the technology of command could ultimately provide a solution to the problems of control.

During the war the dichotomy between the centralizers and the decentralizers had been as powerful as ever, epitomized within the British Grand Fleet by the different approaches taken by Jellicoe and Beatty. The pair of inconclusive engagements in the North Sea—Beatty's Dogger Bank action of 1915 and Jellicoe's fleet action at Jutland the following year—hardly offered sufficient evidence to support either man's philosophy of command.

Among the world's navies studying the 1914–1918 conflict, pondering the future of naval warfare, and attempting to formulate a coherent doctrine and an appropriate approach to command and control was the U.S. Navy. Because Americans, and their navy, had been in the forefront of wireless development, they had early on recognized its potential as a new element in the command and control equation.[1]

The most vocal proponent of a decentralized approach to command and control was Lieutenant Commander Dudley W. Knox, then serving on the staff of the Naval War College in Newport, Rhode Island. Knox, whose memory is kept alive at The Dudley W. Knox Center for Naval History, located at the Navy Yard in Washington, D.C., published several articles on command and doctrinal issues that influenced the generation of American naval officers who fought and won the Second World War.

The first of these seminal articles appeared in the U.S. Naval Institute *Proceedings* in March 1913. Knox, combining a professional knowledge of the navy with a sure grasp of history, concluded that the "modern" naval battle would be "a kaleidoscopic drama" in which "initiative and decision" would be "almost constantly demanded of commanders, from the highest to the lowest." He warned that neither "signals, radio-messages, nor instructions, written or verbal, can suffice, either singly or in combination, to produce the unity of effort—the concert of action—demanded by modern conditions in a large fleet." The means to achieve such unity, he proposed, was a system that relied on the issuance of general instructions to be executed by well-trained and well-indoctrinated subordinates able and prepared to act upon their own initiative. Such an approach, he noted, had been the secret to the success of commanders such as Horatio Nelson, afloat, or the great Prussian commander Helmuth von Moltke, ashore. Knox criticized the navy's current reliance on "highly centralized authority" that made it necessary "to issue lengthy orders covering a great number of details." He believed that such a system prevented the development of independent action by junior officers, who, years later, would be incapable of exercising initiative. He called for the creation of a unified, understood, and ongoing system of naval doctrine and an official promulgation that the "'initiative of the subordinate' shall govern the relations between seniors and juniors."[2]

In early 1914 Knox used as the "motto" for his second essay a quotation from the British military historian G. F. R. Henderson: "Intelligent co-operation is of infinitely more value than mechanical obedience." This essay was more historical in its details: Knox examined Nelson's battles and noted the famous admiral's trust in the initiative of his subordinates. But Knox also stressed that the "initiative to a degree necessary for the united automatic action of a large number of units, cannot be safely allowed until the unit commanders are educated, trained, and indoctrinated."[3]

On the eve of the Great War Knox published his third article, in which he pointed to the battles of Lissa and Tsushima to buttress his argument for the adoption of a system of command that relied on doctrine and initiative and not signals to achieve unity of action. He wrote: "Signals are a poor means for conducting a fleet during action and far inferior to that co-ordination produced by a plan combined with the united intelligent effort of subordinates."[4]

In his fourth essay, published in 1915, Knox detailed the preeminence of human factors in warfare. "Good leadership or command, as distinguished from administrative management," he wrote, "is then obviously a cardinal requisite to successful military operations." But, he lamented:

> For some unaccountable reason the American Navy . . . [has] never seriously endeavored to indoctrinate [its] officers, and thus to furnish a basis for harmonious decisions during hostilities. It is all the more striking that the navy has failed in this respect, because of the supreme importance of the time factor afloat. With us "time is everything," even more than with Nelson, whose conspicuous successes were largely due to a high degree of mutual understanding that existed among his subordinate commanders; and Nelson's indoctrination, more than anything else, made such understanding possible.[5]

While it is unclear whether Knox shaped, or simply reflected, what would soon become the prevailing mood in the U.S. Navy, his influence is without doubt. His second and fourth articles won the Naval Institute's prize essay contest, and during the interwar years students at the Naval War College read those two works in a collection of readings assembled for the college by Captain Harold J. "Betty" Stark, a future chief of naval operations (CNO).[6]

At least one prominent student's work reflected Knox's views. In a paper of May 1933, William F. Halsey argued that in battle the "more ably commanded and better trained fleet" would prevail. Halsey's approach to command mirrored that of Knox. "The commander-in-chief must convey his intentions to his subordinates through a plan or plans," Halsey wrote. "These plans assign tasks to the subordinates. Discretion is left to the subordinate in executing these tasks. The controlling thought of the subordinate must be, will my action support the plan." Halsey stressed the need for indoctrination and frequent conferences with subordinates to ensure that they understood their commander's intentions. He concluded:

> In this day of easy and fast communications, the temptation of a commander to interfere with a subordinate acting independently, is very great. From the information available, it is very easy to size up the situation in a distant theatre. It is also easy to size up this situation entirely wrong. The man on the spot may have information, not available to the commander, that gives an entirely different picture. The subordinate must be trusted, or if not trusted removed. The commander should furnish the subordinate with all available information, and leave the execution of the mission to the man on the spot. To interfere may be to invite disaster. By the same token, the man on the spot must act and act now, and never commit the unpardonable offense of asking instructions.[7]

Dudley W. Knox, through his writing, helped to turn the tide against the centralizers in the U.S. Navy. The service's 1924 manual of "war instructions" included a foreword that might well have been written by Knox:

> Commanders of all ranks must carefully bear in mind that in war it is impossible for them to exercise over their commands the same personal control that finds place in peace time exercises. Delegation of command is a necessity, and commanders must, therefore, take every opportunity of training their subordinates in accepting responsibility for departure from, or variations in, the mode of carrying out orders or directions originally given, impressing on them at the same time that such departures or variations must always be justified by the circumstances of the case. It is imperative that all officers should be taught to think, and, subject to general instructions and accepted principles, to act for themselves.
>
> The commander in chief, O.T.C. [officer in tactical command], the senior officer present, or other competent authority on the spot, may, in their discretion, change the disposition of forces, the character of operations, or

movements of any standard procedure to meet the conditions which obtain at the time.

Changes in the disposition of forces or of procedures, however, are to be in general accord with the plans of the commander in chief, or other superior authority, and are to further the mission of the forces acting.[8]

The 1924 war instructions also reflected what might be termed David Beatty's lessons learned from the battle of Jutland, calling for U.S. Navy forces to conduct a "vigorous offensive" and to attempt, conditions permitting, to destroy the enemy fleet. A commander of a large force was free to deploy part of his force as a detached wing in an effort to bring on a battle and to achieve a concentration against part of an enemy line. The aggressive and post-Jutland character of the instructions is evident in the paragraph on the "torpedo menace": when attacked by an enemy American ships were to turn toward the threat, and not away from it as had Jellicoe, in conformity with his own doctrine, at Jutland.[9]

With regard to operational and tactical communications in battle, the Americans learned many lessons from the British. The 1924 instructions emphasized the "desirability of reducing radio communication . . . even to the point of absolute radio silence."[10] Senior American commanders knew, thanks to their wartime cooperation with the Royal Navy, that the Germans' profligate use of wireless had given away their intentions and, on occasion, their positions. To ensure unity of action in the absence of wireless transmissions, an American battlefleet would be deployed in a series of concentric rings, not simply to achieve what could be viewed as defense in-depth but, more important, so that information could be passed by visual signals—flags or lamps—from ship to ship. Thus the fleet could maintain radio silence while also giving the commander in chief better information about the size, location, and relative bearing of an approaching enemy force than Jellicoe had received at Jutland.

This desire to maintain radio silence placed a premium on training and doctrine, as did the call for the employment of a detached wing and possible freedom of action by division commanders. Paragraph 3003 stated: "Initiative on the part of squadron or division commanders may be called for and is expected when necessary to make use of an opportunity for gaining a tactical advantage, or to avoid a tactical disadvantage." While subordinate commanders were permitted a fair degree of freedom of action, they were expected to remain "loyal" to their commander in chief's overall battle plan.[11]

The fact that the U.S. Navy was, perhaps, adequately prepared to refight the battle of Jutland ultimately was of little importance, for the dreadnought era was rapidly drawing to a close. When war began again in 1939, aircraft (including the ships, aircraft carriers, from which they operated) and submarines dominated the naval battlefield.

Often acrimonious interwar debates raged in Washington, London, Berlin, Tokyo, Rome, Paris, and other capitals over naval budgets, force structures, doctrine, and tactics. Advocates of the big-gun battleship dominated all the major navies and were slow, in some cases painfully slow, to recognize the new directions already discernible in naval warfare. Such recalcitrance impeded the development of new weapons platforms along with appropriate tactics and doctrine. Nevertheless, many of the proponents of the new weapons offered exaggerated, or at least premature, claims. Despite the protestations and showmanship of Brigadier General William "Billy" Mitchell, the American advocate of air power, in 1921 land-based aircraft did not yet pose a dire threat to warships.

The history of submarine development provides an excellent example of the issues at stake in attitudes toward new technology. The world's major navies treated the submarine as a stepchild during the decades between the world wars. Had Adolf Hitler embarked in the mid-1930s on a massive submarine-building program, the battle of the Atlantic in the early years of the Second World War might have taken a different course. In retrospect, Hitler's unwillingness to support such a program has been considered foolish. But his decision must be viewed within the context of the national policy he shaped for his Third Reich. He planned to fight a war that would be primarily waged, and won, on the continent in a series of short, relatively bloodless (for the Germans) campaigns. Why would he pour scarce resources into the construction of a weapons system—the U-boat—that would be useful only in a long war of attrition?

The Japanese, likewise, have been criticized for failing to prepare for a submarine *guerre de course* in the Pacific. Had they done so, they would have fared better in the lengthy war of attrition that began in December 1941. But their strategy envisioned a short war and they built up their submarine arm with that kind of struggle in mind. In the first year of the war Japanese submarines operating in a fleet-support role sank or damaged several American aircraft carriers and a battleship.[12]

The U.S. Navy was also slow to develop the submarine, but, as in the German and Japanese cases, this slowness was perfectly consistent with national policy. The Americans had forsworn the use of submersibles to raid commerce, a type of attack employed by the "ruthless" Germans and condemned by the United States in 1917.

Interwar navies were similarly slow to pursue the development of the aircraft carrier. The Royal Navy, which had pioneered the carrier in the Great War, failed to capitalize on its lead after 1918. But the British, or more generally speaking the Allies, had a very limited need for big carriers in the European theater during the Second World War. Moreover, the development of aircraft carriers lagged, to no small degree, because of the ineffectiveness of carrier-based aircraft relative to their land-based counterparts. The carrier did not emerge as a fully developed weapons system until the very eve of the Second World War. Neither the Japanese nor the American navy deployed powerful, well-armed, capable, modern, monoplane carrier-based fighters until 1940—the Mitsubishi A6M2 Zeke (the infamous Zero) and the Grumman F4F-3 Wildcat, respectively.

However slow they were to embrace the submarine and the aircraft carrier, the world's navies were well aware of the evolution and steadily growing importance of these platforms. Interwar navies struggled to find ways to incorporate these novel weapons systems into comprehensive schemes of doctrine and tactics. As had been the case in the nineteenth century, rapid technological change in peacetime made such doctrinal and tactical developments a guessing game.

The U.S. Navy's 1934 war instructions, the first set issued since 1924, reflected the changing nature of naval warfare. To be sure, dreadnoughts arrayed in a battle line were the core of the fleet's fighting power. Given the relative numbers of battleships and carriers in the service, as well as the limited range and striking power of the fleet's air arm, this was by no means inappropriate. But the U.S. Navy envisioned for its carriers far more than a mere scouting role. In the event of a fleet action, the squadrons flying from the carriers were assigned what have since become recognizable missions—scouting, striking, combat air patrol. Fighters were expected to destroy enemy aircraft operating in the vicinity of the fleet, to provide an airborne screen to prevent an enemy from either scouting or conducting aerial attacks, and to escort bombing and torpedo squadrons during their strikes. The latter were assigned the tasks of hitting the enemy's battle line, detached forces, or carriers.[13]

Despite the continued improvement of shipborne and airborne radios, the U.S. Navy had not yet succumbed to the temptation to use radio to centralize command and control of the fleet. Wireless communications, now termed radio, were to be "kept to the minimum limit consistent with the needs of the situation," while complete "radio silence" was to be "imposed when required." The 1934 instructions also retained the 1924 edition's foreword with its call for initiative. The fifth section of the fifth chapter included the following paragraph:

> A subordinate commander may find himself faced with an unexpected situation that has not been foreseen or covered in his orders from higher authority and which necessitates action on his part before he can communicate with his superior and receive instructions . . . Such situations will probably be emergencies. The subordinate must grasp the full importance of the situation and decide whether or not he can carry out the assigned task. If he decides his task can and must be executed, he may have to make a different plan for its accomplishment. If he decides to assume a new task for himself, it is essential that the task selected be one which will further the general plan of his superior.[14]

But despite the tone of the official instructions, as the 1930s drew to a close and war clouds gathered in Europe and Asia, the human tendency to maintain control, a task made easier by advances in radio, began to threaten the tradition and practice of initiative within the U.S. Navy. To counter this trend, on 21 January 1941 Admiral Ernest J. King, then commander in chief of the U.S. Fleet, circulated a navy-wide memorandum regarding the "exercise of command." King wrote: "I have been concerned for many years over the increasing tendency—now grown almost to 'standard practice'—of flag officers and other group commanders to issue orders and instructions in which their subordinates are told 'how' as well as 'what' to do to such an extent and in such detail that the 'custom of the service' has virtually become the antithesis of that essential element of command—'*the initiative of the subordinate.*'"[15]

King's reference to "the initiative of the subordinate" marks a direct link between Knox, who first used the phrase in his 1913 essay, and King, who would serve as the U.S. Navy's CNO during the Second World War. King, as a young navy lieutenant, first worked with Knox in 1911 on the staff of the commander in chief of the Atlantic Fleet. King, Knox, and Harry E. Yarnell (then a lieutenant commander) shared an interest in military history and read and discussed works on the theory and practice of war. Subsequently, Lieutenant Commander King served as editor of the *Proceedings* in 1913 and 1914, when the journal published three of

Knox's important essays. Nearly three decades later, on the eve of war, King made Knox's phrase the watchword for the service.[16]

THE SECOND WORLD WAR was the largest and most destructive conflict in the history of humankind, a war fought on land, in the air, and at sea. Ground and air forces dominated the conflict in the European theater, but the Allied navies played a crucial role. Without victory in the battle of the Atlantic, there never would have been a second front in Europe. Had the Allies failed at sea, the impact along the Russian front would have been enormous. The consequences of a German victory, a negotiated draw, or even a Soviet triumph in which the Red Army "liberated" all of continental Europe are incalculable. The campaigns in North Africa, the Middle East, and South and Southeast Asia likewise depended heavily on naval forces. And the campaign in the Pacific theater was largely a naval struggle.

Because of the global nature of the conflict, communications, specifically wireless radio transmissions, were central to the effective prosecution of the war. In the Pacific, American submarines often operated more than a thousand miles from their bases. The Japanese May–June 1942 effort in the central Pacific to force a decisive battle stretched for more than 1,500 nautical miles, from the Aleutians in the north to Midway and the Hawaiian Islands in the south. Without radio, the control and coordination of myriad forces deployed in far-flung theaters would have been difficult if not impossible.

The advances in communications ability were not without costs. The coming of age of the radio strengthened the hand of the centralizers in the world's navies and presented them with a new tool with which to exercise the at-times-stifling control they sought. "My commander in chief may make me an admiral," it has been said, "but only communications can put me in command."[17] And yet many commanders discovered that the tactical use of the wireless was not always an adequate solution to the problems of control in a fast-paced battle shrouded by the fog of war. Moreover, as in the First World War, reliance on radio for communications and control proved to be an Achilles' heel, for such transmissions were subject to interception, decoding, and decryption.

Given the grand scale of the Second World War at sea, a full discussion of the issues of naval command and control between 1939 and 1945 is beyond the scope of this book. For that reason, the sections that follow

focus on selected campaigns or operations that well illustrate the state of
the art in communications capability, the continuing tussle between centralizers and decentralizers, and the strengths and weaknesses of both approaches to command and control at sea. In the Pacific theater the U.S.
Navy relied heavily, as King had proclaimed, on the initiative of subordinates at all levels of the tactical chain of command. This reliance paid
handsome dividends in many campaigns and battles, for example in the
cruiser-destroyer actions fought in the southwest Pacific in 1943, but almost cost the Americans dearly in October 1944 during the opening
stage of the liberation of the Philippines—at the battle of Leyte Gulf.
Conversely, the battle of the Atlantic, the longest campaign of the war in
the European theater, exemplified the operational and tactical capabilities
of the new communications technology, but also demonstrated, once
again, the susceptibility of such systems to codebreaking. In the Mediterranean theater, Admiral Andrew Browne Cunningham demonstrated
that the spirit of Nelson survived in the Royal Navy.

THE STRUGGLE the U.S. Navy waged in the Pacific theater between
December 1941 and September 1945 was not just the greatest sea war in
history but also one of the few naval conflicts fought by a service consciously committed to a decentralized approach to command and control. That is not to say that every American commander in a chain of
command that stretched from Washington to the far reaches of the western Pacific was a dedicated decentralizer, or that the U.S. Navy's approach to command and control was uniformly successful. American
naval officers strove to find a balance between the sensible use of available communications and the counterproductive overreliance on them.
Moreover, at Leyte Gulf the navy's decentralized system led to a near debacle.

    The high stakes involved in the Pacific war, and the pressures on
the American naval commanders following the debacle at Pearl Harbor,
meant that the temptation to centralize was always present. Even the
most ardent proponents of decentralization were prone to attempt to influence the actions of their subordinates. For example, Admirals King
and Halsey, whose convictions about initiative were quoted above, were
known to interfere with their subordinates' work.

    In early 1942 King, in his capacity as CNO, commander in chief of the
U.S. Fleet, and the U.S. Navy's representative on the U.S. Joint Chiefs of

Staff and the Allied Combined Chiefs of Staff, was the senior American officer in the naval service. King's commitment to decentralization, while pronounced, was often more theoretical than real. In fact, he drew up his 1941 navy-wide memoranda regarding "the initiative of the subordinate" after he realized that he himself had become an excessive centralizer, refusing to trust his subordinates to carry out assigned and well-understood duties. Throughout the war he was willing to offer advice and direction to his principal subordinates, especially Admiral Chester W. Nimitz—the wartime commander in chief of the Pacific Ocean areas (CINCPOA) and commander in chief of the Pacific Fleet (CINCPAC). It was King, for example, who insisted on the "Doolittle Raid" on Japan of April 1942 over Nimitz's objections. At various times during the first year of the war, King communicated directly with American forces operating in the southwest Pacific.[18]

Early in the war Nimitz, too, was unable to resist the temptation to reach over the shoulders of his subordinates. In January 1942 Nimitz directed the task force commanded by Rear Admiral Halsey on the U.S.S. *Enterprise* to raid the Japanese-controlled Marshall Islands in the central Pacific. Nimitz, possessing limited intelligence about the Japanese defenses, wisely issued Halsey general orders. Halsey's staff did the detailed planning and adjusted those plans as the operation unfolded, maintaining all the while strict radio silence. Nimitz, under increasing pressure from King in Washington to undertake active and aggressive operations, waited impatiently at Pearl Harbor for reports of the raids, and when no word came sent a message directing Halsey to "exploit the situation," "expand" his operations, and "extend" his strikes against given islands for more than a single day. As E. B. Potter, a biographer of both Halsey and Nimitz, wrote: "Now Admiral Nimitz, who had never piloted a plane, commanded a carrier, or fought an engagement, was telling Admiral Halsey, the navy's senior carrier commander, how to fight his battle."[19]

Halsey diplomatically ignored these messages from his superior. "It is perhaps fortunate that Halsey was operating under radio silence," Potter commented, "or else he might have replied in more or less official language with a resounding 'shut up!' for the messages from CinCPac seem to have exasperated him. Having commanded carriers since 1935, he felt he could handle his assignment without any coaching from Nimitz." During a raid in March 1942 against Wake and Marcus Islands, Halsey again maintained strict radio silence. What little information reached Nimitz came from intercepted Japanese communications. Potter concluded that Halsey's silence "appears to have been his counterpart to the Civil War general's cutting of the telegraph lines to forestall interference from Washington."[20]

Unlike King, Nimitz learned from the early raids. "Nimitz got the point," Potter wrote. "Thenceforth he made it his firm practice, once a commander had departed on a mission with an approved operation plan, not to send out any directive or advice as to how that mission should be carried out."[21] This hands-off, decentralized approach served Nimitz well during the course of the war. Those commanders who were successful, such as Halsey, gained promotion and greater responsibility; those who failed, such as Robert L. Ghormley, were removed from command.

Despite King's memoranda, reliance on the "initiative of the subordinate" did not extend uniformly throughout the chain of command in the Pacific theater. Some commanders were unable or unwilling to delegate responsibility. Given the quick tempo of naval warfare, such commanders often operated at an extreme disadvantage. The fortunate ones, like Nimitz, had opportunities to adjust; the unfortunate did not.

One of the fortunate was Captain Arleigh A. Burke, who took command of Destroyer Division 43 in early 1943 and within six months became famous as "31-knot Burke." Burke later would serve as chief of staff to Marc A. Mitscher, commander of the navy's "Fast Carriers"; would play a prominent role in shaping the navy's forces, structure, and strategy after the war; and would serve an unprecedented three terms as CNO during the Eisenhower and Kennedy administrations. He epitomized the tactical commander committed to decentralized command and control. His command of "the Little Beavers" in the southwest Pacific harks back to Nelson and his Band of Brothers.

Nearly a century and a half separated the careers of Burke and Nelson. During that time naval warfare underwent a vast transformation. The ships of the Second World War were larger, faster, and more heavily armed than those of Nelson's day. The radio had replaced the signal flag as the state of communicative art. Battle tactics had evolved as well, the optics- and radar-expanded horizon of the gun and torpedo being measured in thousands rather than tens of yards. But while the technology of warfare at sea changed dramatically, ships remained tools in the hands of men, and Burke and Nelson faced the same problem—command. Both adopted a style of leadership that sought not greater centralization of authority and dependence on communications, but decentralization and reliance on doctrine: not formal, official doctrine, be it the Royal Navy's fighting instructions or the U.S. Navy's *Sound Military Decision* of 1942, but the informal, personal doctrine formulated by commanders in time of war.[22]

When Burke made his name, distance, smoke from guns or funnels, and nightfall no longer interfered with the exercise of command. Wireless communications, instantaneous and infinitely more flexible than flag signals, significantly increased the ability to centralize command functions. During the early years of the Second World War the men commanding American surface forces believed that ship-to-ship radio, combined with the new radar sets that could provide a clear picture in day or night of both friendly and enemy forces, would allow them to direct their ships in battle. However, in the night battles fought in the Solomon Islands in 1942 and 1943, the Americans were outsmarted and outfought by the Japanese. New technology was no match for superior Japanese training and doctrine. The fog of war was thick during the chaos of the night actions and all too many American ships sank to the floor of what became known as Iron Bottom Sound.

What many American naval officers had not recognized was that the technological advances that produced radar and radio telephony, advances that would have answered the problems of command and control in 1805, had also produced long-range guns and torpedoes. The entire framework within which commanders made their decisions had changed, and markedly so. In the age of sail, it was not uncommon for the crew to be piped to dinner when the enemy fleet was sighted, for the approach to battle could take hours. At Trafalgar, for example, the fleets came into action about six hours after the initial sightings. By comparison, in Burke's first action, fought in the Kula Gulf in March 1943, he hesitated only ninety seconds after the first radar contact before ordering a torpedo attack. That brief hesitation proved to be long enough to guarantee failure, though not defeat.

Burke recognized that there was "no time in battle to give orders." Like Nelson, he concluded that in action "damage to the flagship may prevent the order from being given or the task force commander might be so involved . . . that he cannot determine the most opportune time for . . . attack, or facilities in the flagship may be reduced." The difference between a poor officer and a good one, Burke informed one junior officer, was "about ten seconds."[23]

Both Burke and Nelson discovered that centralization bred confusion, hesitation, and inactivity among subordinates. Nelson had seen the mo-

ment for action pass for Sir John Jervis at Cape St. Vincent; Burke felt it
slip away in Kula Gulf. Time, as Burke put it, was "the only commodity
which you can never regain." And both men believed it preferable not to
waste a moment. Nelson insisted on engaging his enemy as quickly as
possible and made the order of sailing double as his order of battle, for
otherwise "the opportunity would probably be lost of bringing the enemy to battle."[24] Appropriately, Halsey termed the battle of Cape St.
George, Burke's last fight in command of his "Little Beavers," "the Trafalgar of the Pacific."[25] The comparison is warranted in that Burke's ships
likewise sailed in the formation in which they intended to engage the
enemy. On contact Burke believed it best to launch a "wholehearted attack [at] the first opportunity." History taught, he noted, that "luck usually rides with the bold." Although he could not foresee the exact form
an engagement might take, his battle doctrine was tried and tested: "The
idea was to keep the enemy on two horns of a dilemma so that no matter
which way he went, no matter what he did, somebody would be able to
hit him."[26]

Burke recognized in himself the natural desire of commanders to centralize, "to hold a check rein." The alternative, relying on the initiative of
subordinates, given the "disastrous consequences" of error, "required
more than is usually meant by confidence. It required faith." Nevertheless, Burke considered the latter the preferable course: "[Commanders]
all know that subordinates have neither the knowledge nor the information that is available in the flagship, yet, past actions in this war and in
other wars indicated that successful action result[ed] from the exercise of
initiative by well indoctrinated subordinates. If that were true the problem resolved itself into teaching the subordinate how to react and act in
situations similar to the [way] the task force commander would in the
same situation."[27]

To the end of his life, Burke's views on initiative remained unchanged.
"Some naval officers . . . like to have their fingers in all commands, to
make sure it is . . . done their way, to direct everything. That will work
. . . as long as communications and the man are good enough to make it
work. But it does not work as well as if he does not have to say anything
and people automatically do what they think is best and fits in with what
other people think is best too."[28]

For Burke, victory resulted from the application of "simple doctrine,"
applied "under very adverse conditions." When in port he held daily
conferences with his subordinates, his "Little Beavers." During these

meetings he and his commanders exchanged information and ideas and established doctrine—the guidelines for the next operation. Burke also met regularly with his superiors to make sure they understood what he would be doing in battle. He stressed the importance of knowing "beforehand what you are going to do under various circumstances." He commented on the battle of Empress Augusta Bay: "There were no orders during that torpedo attack. The entire attack was on doctrine. Very fortunately in the explanation of doctrine, an example was used which was very similar to what actually happened that night."[29]

The comparison of the ideas and methods of Nelson and Burke reveals that these two successful commanders drew very similar lessons from their early combat experiences. They shunned centralization and came to believe that delegation of authority—decentralization of command—offered the best hope of enhancing fighting power and achieving victory. They did so during periods when much-heralded communications technology seemed to offer the prospect of ever greater centralized control.

THE EXPERIENCE gained in the first two years of the war by American naval commanders such as Nimitz, Halsey, and Burke demonstrated two things: first, the need for new doctrine incorporating the lessons of the aerial, surface, and subsurface battles and the capabilities of the many new weapons systems reaching the fleet; and second, the importance of a decentralized system of command and control. In the summer of 1943, as the U.S. Navy prepared to begin its war-winning drive across the central Pacific, the service was brimming with new doctrinal ideas, but in the wartime environment these concepts were only slowly finding their way into print. Nevertheless, Knox's principle of "the initiative of the subordinate" remained the centerpiece of American naval doctrine.

Perhaps the best-known wartime U.S. Navy doctrinal manual was *PAC-10: Current Tactical Orders and Doctrine, U.S. Pacific Fleet,* published in June 1943. Before the myriad sections on cruising and fighting instructions, directions for the operations of submarine and amphibious forces, as well as for offensive air action, the foreword stated clearly: "PAC-10 is not intended and shall not be construed as depriving any officer exercising tactical command of initiative in issuing special instructions to his command . . . The ultimate aim is to obtain essential uniformity without unacceptable sacrifice of flexibility." Officers in tactical command were to seize the initiative and to conduct "attacks of opportunity" when they encountered a favorable opportunity, the exploitation of which would not jeopardize the mission; when the opportunity was "probably not apparent" to the senior commander; and when "lack of time or communication restrictions prohibit informing the officer in Tactical Command and awaiting his instructions."[30]

This adherence to the principle of the "initiative of the subordinate" was not limited to the Pacific Fleet. The navy-wide *War Instructions, United States Navy,* issued in November 1944 was even more forceful regarding decentralization. The instructions, published as they were in the midst of a world war, are surprisingly theoretical, beginning with a chapter on "the human element in Naval Strength" that might well have been written by an academic historian or theoretician, or perhaps even by Dudley Knox. The successful commander, according to the *War Instructions,* possessed "responsible courage," "decision of character," "sound judgment," and "initiative, the ability to understand and take advantage of new situations." Section 213 directly addressed the exercise of initiative: "A subordinate commander may find himself confronted with a situation which has not been foreseen or had not been covered in his orders from higher authority and which necessitates action on his part before he can communicate with his superior and receive instructions. The subordinate then decides whether his assigned task will properly meet the new situation and thereby further the general plan of his superior. If not, he selects a new task which will do so."[31]

The navy published the new war instructions only a few weeks after it won the largest naval battle in world history, that fought in and around Leyte Gulf between 23 and 26 October 1944. If the successes of the American navy in the Pacific highlighted the virtues of a decentralized system of command and control, the battle of Leyte Gulf revealed the dangers of such a system, even one staffed by such astute and experienced men as Nimitz and Halsey.

For both the United States and Japan, the battle for the Philippine archipelago was the critical encounter of the Pacific war. For the Americans, the conquest of the Philippines would be as much a political victory as a military triumph. Taiwan (Formosa) might have been a more useful military objective, but the liberation of the Philippines, an American possession seized by the Japanese in early 1942, and the "return" of General Douglas MacArthur to the islands, would be a powerful symbol of American strength and resolve. For the Japanese, an American victory would isolate Japan from the resources to the south, especially the oil necessary to keep the economy running and the Imperial Japanese Navy at sea. If the Americans retook the Philippines, Japan was doomed.

The American plan for the Philippines called for the cooperative operations of two major Allied commands: that of General MacArthur, supreme commander of Allied forces in the Southwest Pacific area; and that of Admiral Nimitz. MacArthur's command was responsible for the main landing operation on Leyte, in the central Philippines. MacArthur's army units would be transported and supported by the U.S. Seventh Fleet, commanded by Vice Admiral Thomas C. Kinkaid. The Seventh Fleet controlled a variety of amphibious and support ships including more than a score of small escort or "jeep" carriers, as well as older battleships that were too slow to keep up with the fast carriers concentrated in Halsey's Third Fleet. Halsey, who answered to Nimitz in Hawaii, bore two main, and potentially conflicting, responsibilities. His operational orders directed him to "cover and support the forces of the southwest Pacific in order to assist in the seizure and occupation of objectives in the central Philippines," but also said: "In case opportunity for destruction of major portion of the enemy fleet offer or can be created, such destruction becomes the primary task."[32]

Nimitz's orders to Halsey were neither vague nor contradictory; they were simply general, and drafted in that fashion by planners working months before the operation began, at a time when the situation could not be entirely foreseen. But the orders, combined with Nimitz's decentralized style of command, allowed Halsey unusual, but to CINCPAC necessary, leeway. Indeed, if the opportunity to strike a destructive blow against the Japanese fleet arose, Halsey was more than likely to seize it. Like most senior American naval commanders, he eagerly sought a Pacific Trafalgar—a climactic and decisive battle with the main Japanese fleet. Moreover, "Bull" Halsey was a frustrated flat-top admiral: despite his seniority as an aviator, he had missed the major carrier battles fought in the Coral Sea, off Midway, and most recently in the Philippine Sea. In the last-named engagement, Admiral Raymond A. Spruance's failure to destroy the Japanese carriers was already a subject of debate within the navy, and yet another factor likely to encourage Halsey to take greater risks in an effort to complete the job of the destruction of Japan's carrier force. Add to this his conviction, born of wartime experience, that carriers, not battleships, were the preeminent ships of the new era, and the stage was set for what would soon become known as "Bull's Run."

The Japanese plan, to defend the Philippines while simultaneously striking a powerful blow at U.S. naval and amphibious forces, was well thought out, though desperate in nature. The Japanese were prepared to use every weapon in their arsenal: nothing, not their carriers, nor their super-battleships *Yamato* and *Musashi* with their 18.1-inch guns, nor the lives of the pilots who would fly as kamikazes against the American fleet, would be held back in this last-ditch attempt to stop the American advance. Through their planning, the Japanese, in part by design and in part by good fortune, gained several advantages. They achieved a fair degree of surprise. While the Americans, thanks to their codebreakers, knew that the Japanese were planning a major counterattack, many details were missing because the Japanese, unlike the Germans in the Atlantic, maintained operational radio silence. The Japanese attack also struck the Americans, in part at least, at the weakest point of any military structure: the hinge between two commands. The Japanese planners also succeeded, like masters of the martial arts, in pulling the Americans off balance, thus allowing the weaker Japanese fleet to throw its more powerful opponent to the mat.

On 17 October, when the first American forces landed on Leyte, the Japanese quickly finalized their plan. The naval element of the plan involved three major forces. Vice Admiral Jisaburo Ozawa's Northern Force of several carriers and screening vessels would steam south from the Inland Sea toward a position east of Luzon. Ozawa's carriers, virtually denuded of aircraft, were expected to lure the carriers of the Third Fleet away from Leyte Gulf. Meanwhile, Vice Admiral Kiyohido Shima's Southern Force would steam from the Ryukus, pass west of Taiwan and Luzon, slip through the Sulu Sea, rendezvous with several battleships sailing from Singapore under Vice Admiral Shoji Nishimura, and then prepare to enter the gulf from the south, through the Surigao Strait. And Vice Admiral Takeo Kurita's powerful First Striking, or Center, Force would steam from Lingaa Roads, near Singapore, pass through the Palawan Passage, and race toward Leyte, entering the gulf through the northern San Bernadino Strait.

The mid-October landing on Leyte marked an acceleration of the American plans for the liberation of the Philippines, the result of initiative shown by Halsey, who had relieved Spruance and taken command of Third Fleet on 26 August 1944.[33] Halsey learned from Vice Admiral Marc A. Mitscher, commander of the Third Fleet's Fast Carrier force, Task Force (TF) 38, that Japanese air strength in the southern part of the archipelago was weaker than anticipated. Rather than staying in the south as planned to cover the amphibious operations in the Palaus, Halsey, on his own initiative, shifted the Third Fleet farther north, believing that Kinkaid's Seventh Fleet was strong enough to ensure the safety of the landings. On 12–13 September planes from TF 38 raided airfields in the central Philippines, destroying more than 200 Japanese aircraft in the air and on the ground for the loss of eight American planes. Halsey and his staff, now convinced of the weakness of the Japanese defenses throughout the archipelago, recommended that the invasion take place as soon as possible. Nimitz and MacArthur agreed and forwarded Halsey's recommendations up the chain of command. At Quebec, where the Combined Chiefs of Staff were conveniently meeting, Halsey's suggestions were accepted and the date for invasion was moved from 20 December to 17 October.[34]

In mid-October TF 38 aircraft began the invasion preliminaries by striking at the Japanese defenses on Luzon. Once again the Americans found the air defenses weaker than expected. When the landings on Leyte began on 17 October, the Third Fleet was in a covering position to the east of Luzon. Halsey was eager for battle, waiting for reports from his reconnaissance aircraft or submarines that would reveal the position of the Japanese fleet.

The first sighting reports reached Halsey on 23 October. The American submarine *Darter* spotted elements of Kurita's First Striking Force. That day and the next the *Darter*, joined by the *Dace*, stalked the Japanese, sinking two heavy cruisers and damaging a third. On the 24th Halsey's search planes located Kurita's ships in the Subuyan Sea, and shortly thereafter sighted the Southern Force in the Sulu Sea. Mitscher's carriers launched strikes at both Japanese forces, while simultaneously fending off kamikaze and conventional attacks by aircraft flying from airfields on Luzon. The Japanese mortally wounded the light carrier *Princeton*. The American attacks, which focused primarily on Kurita's more powerful group, damaged a heavy cruiser and sank the super-battleship *Musashi*.

By midafternoon reports from reconnaissance aircraft indicated that Kurita, evidently stung by the effective loss of four heavy cruisers and the mighty *Musashi*, had reversed course. Halsey considered the change of course temporary, and believed that the Japanese might yet come about and try to pass through the archipelago under cover of darkness. As a contingency, at 1512 Halsey issued what he labeled a "Battle Plan": if circumstances required, he would form TF 34, to include four battleships,

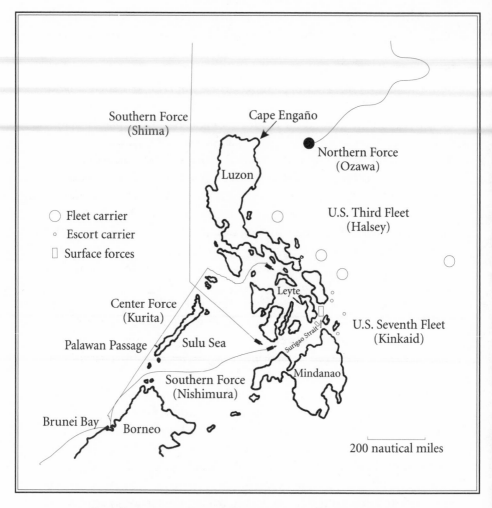

Southern Force
(Shima)

Cape Engaño

Northern Force
(Ozawa)

Luzon

○ Fleet carrier
○ Escort carrier
▢ Surface forces

U.S. Third Fleet
(Halsey)

Center Force
(Kurita)

Leyte

U.S. Seventh Fleet
(Kinkaid)

Palawan Passage

Sulu Sea

Surigao Strait

Southern Force
(Nishimura)

Mindanao

Brunei Bay

Borneo

200 nautical miles

THE BATTLE OF LEYTE GULF, 23–25 OCTOBER 1944
Leyte Gulf was one of the largest and most wide-ranging naval battles in history.
The Japanese came close to victory for two reasons. First, they presented Halsey
with a dilemma and he made the wrong choice. Second, they struck the Ameri-
cans at a weak point, namely the junction between two commands: the Third and
Seventh Fleets.

two heavy cruisers, three light cruisers, and fourteen destroyers, under
the command of Vice Admiral Willis A. Lee. Both King and Nimitz,
listed as information addressees, received copies of this message. So did
Kinkaid, whose radio operators were surreptitiously listening in on the
Third Fleet's radio frequencies because MacArthur, insistent on a proper

respect for the chain of command, refused to allow Halsey and Kinkaid to communicate directly.[35]

Halsey believed he had weathered the crisis. American fighters flying combat air patrols had beaten off the air attacks from Luzon. While the *Princeton* had been lost, the Fast Carriers remained intact and their air wings combat-ready. Kurita had turned about, and if he again struck east Halsey was prepared to meet him with TF 34. To the south, the Seventh Fleet's old battleships were strong enough to prevent the Southern Force from passing through the Surigao Strait. But where, Halsey and his staff wondered, were Ozawa's carriers? The Japanese had obviously mounted a major effort, and a major naval undertaking had to involve aircraft carriers.

Shortly after 1700 Halsey's scouts spotted Ozawa's Northern Force about 180 miles east of Cape Engaño. Halsey suddenly found himself facing a difficult decision. As he saw it, he could guard San Bernadino Strait against a possible sortie by Kurita. Halsey "rejected" this course because it would have left his fleet sitting passively between two approaching enemy forces. Moreover, so placed, the longer-ranged Japanese carrier aircraft could outrange the American ships. Alternatively, Halsey could detach TF 34 and send it south to guard the San Bernadino Strait, while he shifted the carriers north to meet Ozawa. He "rejected" this option, too, as a "half-measure" that might leave TF 34 vulnerable to air attack and would also strip the Fast Carriers of the antiaircraft protection provided by the battleships. He instead chose to leave the strait unprotected and to steam north to meet Ozawa with the whole of the Third Fleet. He reasoned that a move north "preserved my fleet's integrity, it left the initiative with me, and it promised the greatest possibility of surprise. Even if the Central Force meanwhile penetrated San Bernadino and headed for Leyte Gulf, it could only . . . hit and run." Halsey later wrote: "My decision to strike the Northern Force was a hard one to make, but given the same circumstances and the same information as I had then, I would make it again." The decision made, he pointed to a position on the chart and told his chief of staff, Rear Admiral Robert B. "Mick" Carney: "Here's where we're going. Mick, start them north."[36]

As the Third Fleet cruised north at 16 knots, night reconnaissance aircraft located Kurita's Striking Force again heading east toward the San Bernadino Strait. But Halsey was already committed, psychologically if not physically, to a run toward the Japanese carriers. At 2024 he conveyed this information in a message sent directly to Kinkaid, with Nimitz and King as addressees. He added: "Am proceeding north with three groups to attack enemy carrier force at dawn." Halsey's message was intended to warn Kinkaid that the Third Fleet was not guarding the strait, but to both Kinkaid and Nimitz the mention of "three groups" implied that TF 34 had been formed and left behind while Halsey steamed north with the three carrier task forces that made up TF 38.[37]

As Halsey headed north, the Japanese Striking and Southern Forces steamed toward Leyte Gulf. Because of Kurita's reversal of course after the American air attacks, the Striking Force was well behind schedule. But during the evening of 24 October the Southern Force tried unsuccessfully to force its way through Surigao Strait. In the last major surface action fought by the U.S. Navy, Rear Admiral Jesse B. Oldendorf won one of the most complete victories in American naval history, sinking two battleships and two cruisers as well as several other ships.

Where was Kurita? Reports from the reconnaissance aircraft placed him steaming east, but Halsey and the senior members of his staff remained convinced of the wisdom of heading north. Halsey, exhausted, retired for the night. But not everyone shared Halsey's confidence. Commodore Arleigh Burke, now serving as Marc Mitscher's chief of staff, worried that the Japanese, after their defeat in the battle of the Philippine Sea, surely knew that Ozawa's four carriers were far too weak to defeat the sixteen heavy and light carriers of TF 38. If so, why were the Japanese flat-tops coming south? Burke concluded that they were decoys meant to draw Halsey north, away from Leyte Gulf. He woke Mitscher, who listened to his theory and replied: "I think you're right, but I don't know you're right." Mitscher, who assumed that Halsey possessed the same information available to Burke, refused to intervene. Rear Admiral Lee, the would-be commander of TF 34, reached a conclusion similar to Burke's and took his concerns to Halsey's staff, but to no avail. Carney and other members of the Third Fleet staff had already considered and rejected the idea that the Japanese carriers were decoys, suggested earlier that evening by several of Halsey's intelligence officers who had access to intercepted transmissions. Carney refused to wake the sleeping Halsey.[38]

In Hawaii Nimitz, too, was worried. Like Kinkaid, he initially assumed that Halsey had formed TF 34. But had he made any provision for air cover? Nimitz wanted more information, but recalling his earlier experiences with Halsey, was reluctant to interfere. He waited impatiently, monitoring the radio traffic from both the Seventh and Third Fleets. The glowing reports from Oldendorf about the victory in Surigao Strait lessened the tension. But why were there no reports from Lee? As the uncertainty gnawed at Nimitz, he received a copy of a message from Kinkaid to Halsey asking if TF 34 was guarding the strait. Gradually the suspicion began to grow in Hawaii that there was no TF 34.[39]

Nimitz, after reviewing the message traffic, sought assurances from his assistant chief of staff, Captain Bernard Austin, that all the relevant messages were in the file. Austin replied in the affirmative and asked the admiral if he was looking for something specific. Nimitz said there seemed to be no clear indication that TF 34 had been formed and was guarding San Bernadino Strait, a fact that left him "very concerned." "Well, Admiral," Austin replied, "that is an unclear point in dispatches, and several other people are wondering the same thing." Nimitz dismissed Austin, but later buzzed him twice more, again asking about the message traffic. Finally, the captain suggested that Nimitz query Halsey directly. Nimitz, in his biographer's words, "thought for a moment and then gave Austin the expected answer—he did not want to send any dispatch that would directly or indirectly influence the responsible tactical commander in the tactical use of his forces."[40]

As Nimitz marked time in Hawaii, Kurita led the Striking Force through San Bernadino Strait and into Leyte Gulf. The Japanese, elated at their uneventful passage, were nonetheless surprised to have found the strait undefended. Had the Americans laid some sort of ambush? When the lookouts first sighted ships to the south—the Seventh Fleet's escort carriers and destroyers of Rear Admiral Clifton A. F. Sprague's TF (Taffy) 3—the Japanese, who had never seen an American carrier close up, assumed that the Jeep carriers belonged to Halsey's fleet. Kurita sped south to engage, and there began a furious, confused, and for Sprague's small ships desperate and heroic fight that pitted destroyers with their 5-inch guns and torpedoes against the 18.1-inch guns of the mammoth *Yamato*.[41]

Sprague's calls for help were heard not only on Kinkaid's flagship but also on Halsey's. They reached CINCPAC in Hawaii as well. An aide handed Nimitz a copy of a dispatch from Kinkaid to Halsey requesting support from Lee's TF 34. Halsey responded by promising to send one of his three carrier task forces back south to strike at Kurita, but said nothing of Lee's battleships. So where, exactly, was Task Force 34? At Captain Austin's suggestion, Nimitz decided it was time to ask Halsey for some clarification.

To make decryption more difficult, U.S. Navy coded messages included meaningless padding at the beginning and the end. Thus the actual query sent by Nimitz to Halsey, with King and Kinkaid as information addressees, was: "Turkey trots to water GG Where is RPT where is Task Force thirty-four RR the world wonders."[42] The parts of the message appearing before and after the double consonants were padding and ought to have been dropped by anyone decoding the message.

But a crisis atmosphere was building in the *New Jersey,* Halsey's flagship, an atmosphere that lent itself to error. At about 1000 Halsey received a disturbing message from Kinkaid: "My situation is critical. Fast battleships and support by air strikes may be able to keep enemy from destroying CVEs and entering Leyte."[43] As Halsey digested the import of Kinkaid's dispatch, the signalmen in his flagship's radio room decoded Nimitz's query about TF 34. But in the confusion, a signalman, perhaps reflecting the second thoughts that must have been gripping Halsey and his staff at the time, passed the message from the radio room to the commanding admiral without removing the padded phrase "the world wonders."

Halsey, who apparently overlooked the fact that the end of the message following the double consonants was padding, broke down. The combination of the strains and fatigue of battle, the sarcastic tone of the message, and the humiliation of knowing that King and Kinkaid were addressees, was more than Halsey could take. He threw his cap to the deck "and broke into sobs." Mick Carney rushed to his admiral's side, shouting: "Stop it! What the hell's the matter with you? Pull yourself together!" Halsey sent the fast battleships of TF 34, covered by one of his three carrier groups, south to support Sprague, while the rest of Mitscher's TF 38 continued north to finish off Ozawa's Northern Force.[44]

"Bull's Run" was over; now began the race to the south, a race Halsey was destined to lose. Admiral Kurita, who had probably never expected to reach Leyte Gulf, was psychologically ill-prepared to take advantage of the opportunity presented to him. Amid the confusion of the battle, and in the face of desperate counterattacks by Sprague's little ships and aircraft, Kurita withdrew without doing much damage, and well before Halsey's reinforcements reached the scene.

The near-debacle at Leyte Gulf was less an example of the pitfalls of divided command than it was of the pitfalls of a decentralized system of command and control. Nimitz, despite his concerns about what was happening in the Philippines, was philosophically opposed to interfering with the ongoing operations of a subordinate. Halsey's actions demonstrate the dangers inherent in an initiative-based system. Subordinates exercising initiative are free to make not only correct but also incorrect decisions. During the carrier raids of early 1942 and the bitter fighting in the Solomons later that year and in 1943, Nimitz had trusted time and again in Halsey's judgment, and had never been disappointed. Between August and October 1944, during the lead-up to the invasion, Halsey, operating on his own initiative, had performed well. In fact, had it not been for Halsey's willingness to depart from the letter of his instructions, there would not have even been a landing on Leyte until December 1944. But on 24 October Halsey chose wrong. Fortunately, Kurita, also exercising his own initiative, did the same and withdrew prematurely from Leyte Gulf.

WHILE THE AMERICANS were preparing for their war in the Pacific, anxious about reliance on radio and determined to allow subordinate commanders a fair degree of initiative within a decentralized system of command and control, Germany was waging the major naval campaign of the war in the European theater—the battle of the Atlantic—with a highly centralized system. The Germans were well aware of the advantages the British had gained during the Great War from their ability to intercept and decode wireless transmissions, from radio traffic analysis, and from direction finding. Nevertheless, the German navy, the Kriegsmarine, remained committed to even more centralized naval command and control heavily dependent on the use of radio.

The driving force behind German submarine operations was Karl Dönitz, a First World War submarine commander who lost his boat in an attack on a British convoy late in 1918.[45] Dönitz's experience convinced him that U-boats operating alone against escorted convoys were at a distinct disadvantage. Interwar developments in submarine-detection technology, namely sonar (or what the British called ASDIC), worsened the odds against the U-boat. Dönitz, who commanded the German submarine force in the years before the Second World War, concluded that the way to counter escorted convoys was to mass a group of U-boats in the vicinity of the enemy force and to attack on the surface at night, thus rendering the escorts' sonar useless. The Germans termed this new concept *Rudeltaktik*—pack tactics. Thus was born the concept that became known in Anglo-American circles as the "wolfpack."

Dönitz's scheme was simple. He would employ a large number of U-boats in a scouting line across the maritime approaches to Great Britain. When a U-boat located a convoy, it would radio the relevant information—size, strength of escort, course, and speed—back to the controlling headquarters, Befehlshaber der U-boote (BdU). BdU would then direct the other boats in the scouting line and any additional boats nearby to an intercept position. The pack would concentrate at that point and begin its attack on the convoy. The night surface attack from all points of the compass would confuse and overwhelm the escorts and allow the U-boats to destroy their prey—the merchant ships that kept Great Britain supplied.

Central to the *Rudeltaktik* concept was wireless telegraphy. According to the historian of British intelligence F. H. Hinsley, the "U-boat Command developed a signals network which, for complexity, flexibility, and efficiency, was probably unequaled in the history of military communications." Radio allowed the U-boats to transmit the necessary information back to BdU, just as it permitted Dönitz to bring about the concentration of his submarines in a pack.[46]

Dönitz knew that reliance on radio posed dangers to his planned operations as well as to individual U-boats, since transmissions were subject to traffic analysis, direction finding, and interception and decoding. But he also believed that his operational method avoided these dangers. Since the few signals the U-boats would send back to BdU would generally follow a standard form, the information could be condensed into a shorthand, allowing very abbreviated transmissions that would frustrate British direction finding and traffic analysis. The Germans also developed powerful short-wave radios for their U-boats, the transmissions of which were less susceptible to direction finding than the older long-wave sets. Moreover, Germany possessed a mechanical means—known as Enigma—not just to encode, but to encrypt messages, thus protecting them from British codebreakers.

There are good reasons to question the wisdom of Dönitz's plans for the submarine campaign in the Atlantic. His tonnage-based strategy—*tonnageschlact*—called for the sinking of Allied merchant ships faster than new ones could be built. But the approach only made sense in the context of a protracted war of attrition, just the type of conflict that Hitler sensibly, though unsuccessfully, sought to avoid. Likewise, Dönitz's oft-accepted claim that he could have defeated Great Britain had his prewar recommendations been followed and had the Germans possessed 300 oceangoing boats early in the war ignores several questions. Why would

Hitler, who hoped to avoid a conflict with Britain, have poured so many resources into strategy that would surely have provoked British hostility? And if Hitler had agreed to such a drastic reallocation of materials and manpower, building more U-boats and thus fewer aircraft and tanks, how might the course of the war on land or in the air have been different? And how might British or American defense policies have changed if Hitler had embarked on such an ambitious submarine-building program? What is known is that Dönitz's determination, in the face of massive losses, to keep sending his boats to sea, led to the loss, by the end of the war, of nearly 70 percent of his U-boats.

It can be stated with certainty that Dönitz's assumptions about the security of his radio links were misplaced. The "enormous burden of wireless traffic" necessary to direct operations in the Atlantic proved heavier than foreseen; the Allies developed advanced direction-finding gear, including sets small enough to be employed on the escorts themselves; and the British managed to read the encrypted messages flowing from the Enigma machines.[47]

Locating Allied convoys in the North Atlantic also proved far more difficult than Dönitz had anticipated. This was only partly due to the rerouting of convoys based on intelligence gained from reading German coded messages. Dönitz had not fully appreciated the dangers of Allied antisubmarine aircraft patrols, or the corresponding virtues of using German land-based aircraft to search for convoys. Long-range Allied patrol aircraft, armed with depth bombs and by the middle of the war outfitted with radar and searchlights, posed a grave danger to U-boats and forced Dönitz to deploy his patrol lines farther than expected from the approaches to British ports. The farther west he deployed his U-boats, the longer the arcs they had to search for convoys. The need to reposition U-boats along these lines, often on the basis of intelligence gleaned by German codebreakers and direction finders, "resulted in heavy radio traffic" that provided the British "with a continuous flow of standardized and predictable messages—the necessary grist for the codebreakers' mills." Longer patrol lines also required more boats and thereby delayed the shift to true "pack attacks."[48]

This extensive radio traffic also proved susceptible to direction finding, both operationally and tactically. Even before the war, unbeknownst to the Germans, French, British, and American scientists had been developing high-frequency direction-finding (HF/DF) apparatus capable of determining the bearing of short-wave signals. In the first years of the war

the Allies used this new technology operationally to steer convoys clear
of concentrations of U-boats. By the time the battle of the Atlantic
reached its climax in late 1942 and early 1943, compact HF/DF sets were
deployed on individual escort ships. Well-trained Allied crewmen operating HF/DF sets were able to establish the bearing of a given U-boat's
radio transmission and also its likely range from the convoy, on the basis
of differences between the ground and sky waves that emanated from
short-wave radios. Radio direction finding thus became not just an operational but also a tactical asset, since escorts, or aircraft when available,
could be sent out along the bearing to either catch the U-boat on the
surface or force it to submerge, after which its slow speed and limited
search horizon rendered it far less dangerous. The German naval historian Jürgen Rohwer, a specialist on the U-boat war, concluded that the
Allied shipborne HF/DF rather than the breaking of the German codes
was *the* critical factor in turning the tide of the battle of the Atlantic. He
wrote: "If we analyze the great convoy battles between June 1942 and
May 1943—including both those operations which the Germans regarded as successful and those which ended either as minor successes or
failures—the remarkable fact is that the outcome of the operation always
depended on the efficient use of HF/DF."[49]

The strategic and operational impact of Allied codebreaking also played
a critical role in ensuring Allied victory in the Atlantic. The history of
efforts to break the German codes during the Second World War—"the
Ultra secret"—is well known. The Kriegsmarine's codes were among the
last to be routinely read, but by 1941 British codebreakers were beginning to penetrate the German navy's main code. Although the definitive
impact of codebreaking is impossible to establish, Hinsley, the author of
the official and most authoritative account of Ultra and its significance,
wrote of the battle of the Atlantic: "The very fact that the struggle was so
prolonged and so finely balanced suggests that the ability to read [Ger-
man] communications must have been an asset of crucial importance to
the Allies." Codebreaking allowed the Allies to reroute shipping, reinforce threatened convoys, disrupt U-boat patrols, sink important German
assets such as the U-tankers needed to replenish the fuel and supplies of
the U-boats at sea, and gain remarkable insight into the workings of the
U-boat command structure.[50]

In retrospect it is clear that, at the tactical, operational, and strategic
levels of warfare, the Germans' reliance on radio proved their undoing in
the Atlantic. A highly centralized command structure failed, not because
it denied subordinate commanders latitude in their operations, but be-

cause the network of communications itself, thanks to insecure codes, was open to the enemy.

Would the German navy have fared better with a less centralized system of command and control, perhaps akin to that employed by the Americans in their submarine campaign in the Pacific? Had BdU used such a system, deploying individual U-boats to hunt singly while maintaining radio silence, the operations of the submarine force would undoubtedly have suffered a substantial loss of efficiency. But at the same time, had their radio silence deprived the British of the wealth of intelligence they gleaned from the transmission of data demanded by BdU— names of U-boat commanders, location of boats, fuel capacity, number of torpedoes, course, speed, current orders, Dönitz's plans and intentions and even state of mind—the effectiveness of Allied operations would have suffered as well. As for the net loss or gain, no definitive answer can be given.

It should be noted that not everyone within the Kriegsmarine high command, or even the U-boat arm, supported Dönitz's plans for group attacks. One prewar naval staff study presciently argued "that the wireless traffic necessary would forfeit surprise and aid detection of the boats by the enemy." Dönitz's eve-of-war maneuvers in the Atlantic revealed many shortcomings of his concept of operations, and fed the doubts of those who opposed him. Moreover, after the war began, the Germans achieved some of their greatest successes early on, when their naval codes were not yet compromised and before they began operating in groups or wolfpacks. Before late 1941 most U-boats hunted alone, as they had in the Great War, and as American submarines did in the Pacific. Not until the first quarter of 1943 were the majority of the Allied ships sunk by U-boats vessels that had been sailing in convoy. In the first twenty-eight months of war, nine hundred Allied convoys crossed the Atlantic, but Dönitz's U-boats achieved major victories, that is, sinking six or more confirmed ships, on only nineteen occasions. According to the historian Clay Blair, "although occasionally successful, group or 'wolf pack' tactics were on the whole a failure." While it is impossible to prove, Dönitz's heavily centralized system of command and control may well have decreased the fighting power of his submarine force.[51]

AS THE COMMONWEALTH, American, and German navies waged a somewhat unconventional struggle in the Atlantic, Great Britain's Royal Navy engaged in a far more traditional naval war in the Mediterranean.

The Middle Sea was as confined as the Pacific was open and vast—bound on all sides by landmasses, including the Iberian, Italian, Greek, and Anatolian peninsulas, and punctuated with islands, some large and some small. Land-based air power posed a constant threat to naval forces, both surface and subsurface.

The major navies engaged in the Mediterranean during the critical years of the war, 1940–1942, were Great Britain's Royal Navy and Fascist Italy's Regia Marina Italiana (RMI). German participation in the campaign took the form of light vessels, submarines, and, primarily, Luftwaffe aircraft. By 1943, when American naval forces arrived in significant numbers, the critical North African phase of the struggle had drawn toward a conclusion.

The Italian navy reflected the realities of Fascist Italy, ruled, though perhaps not fully governed, by its dictator-leader Benito Mussolini—Il Duce. The Italians had many excellent ships manned by capable and thoughtful officers of all ranks and courageous sailors.[52] But the modern Italian navy's sole major battle had been Lissa in 1866, an ignominious defeat at the hands of the Austrian navy, avenged and offset only in part by Lieutenant Commander Luigi Rizzo's motor torpedo boat attack that sank the Austro-Hungarian battleship *Szent Istvan* in June 1918.

When Mussolini led his country into war in June 1940 his navy was woefully unprepared. The Italians had based their naval programs on two major misconceptions: that there would be no war until 1942 and that the RMI's enemy would be France. As a result, they had sought naval parity with the French, not the British. For that reason, as well as deficiencies in the industrial base and shortage of resources, they had not built an aircraft carrier. Other important shortcomings included a lack of working radar and sonar systems, light armor (the trade-off for speed), the absence of strategic and doctrinal clarity (*guerre d'escadre,* against an enemy's fleet, versus *guerre de course,* against the enemy's commerce; the offensive versus the defensive), inadequate training and doctrine (especially for night fighting), limited ability of the shipbuilding industry to construct new vessels and repair damaged ones, the absence of a naval air arm, shortage of fuel for their ships, and poor coordination with the air force—the Regia Aeronautica Italiana (RAI).

The command structure of the RMI was a further weakness. At the top of the naval hierarchy was Supermarina, a land-based headquarters in Rome that attempted to command and at times control operations both ashore and afloat. Marc'Antonio Bragadin, who served on the

Supermarina staff during the war, concluded: "Supermarina, . . . like every other man-created thing, turned out to have some defects. The principal one, perhaps, was its tendency to centralize the functions of command more than was actually necessary. A second serious defect was that shore-based commanders as well as unit commanders at sea, always feeling the invisible presence of the Supermarina at their backs, sometimes preferred to wait for orders or to request them from Supermarina, even though they could have acted or should have acted on their own initiative."[53] In the late 1930s several high-ranking naval officers criticized the proclivity of Supermarina to micromanage. Admiral Arturo Riccardi, chief of the Italian naval staff, slept with a biography of Lord Nelson at his bedside. Angelo Iachino, who would command Italy's battlefleet at Cape Matapan in March 1941, preferred the approach to command he observed in the British and American navies, one that placed responsibility on "the man on the spot." Conversely, Bragadin admitted that at times Supermarina, in an attempt to avoid micromanagement, "committed more sins of omission than of commission."[54]

The admiralty in London made no comparable effort to control British naval forces in the Mediterranean or elsewhere. On the eve of the Second World War the admiralty had made clear that it held the power to "alter" fleet dispositions, but also that it recognized that such "control" had to "cease as soon as possible." Nevertheless, a misunderstanding developed shortly after Italy entered the war in late June 1940, when the British prime minister, Winston Churchill, sought assurances from the admiralty that Admiral Sir Andrew Browne Cunningham ("ABC"), then the Royal Navy's commander in chief in the Mediterranean, whose position in the eastern Mediterranean was tenuous, would remain on the defensive. "Nothing was further from our thoughts at the time," Cunningham noted in his memoirs, "than to act on the defensive." He deplored the negative impact that messages such as the prime minister's had on local commanders, classifying them not as "encouragement," but as "merely an annoyance." "Moreover," he concluded, "they implied that something was lacking in the direction and leadership, they did positive harm. If such messages were really necessary, if Commanders in chief on the spot who knew all the risks and chances were not prepared to get at the enemy on every possible occasion, the recipients ought not to have been in the position they held."[55]

Cunningham epitomized the Nelson approach. He pursued the offensive whenever possible and prudent. To the extent that he sought any degree of control over operations, he did so afloat, in his flagship accompanying the battlefleet. No one ashore in Alexandria, and certainly no one at the admiralty, attempted anything approaching detailed control over ongoing operations in the Mediterranean as did Supermarina on occasion from Rome. When a commando landing on the island of Kastelorizo, the easternmost of the Dodecanese Islands, went terribly awry in March 1941 when the commander of the operation "cracked," Cunningham, back in Alexandria, did not intervene. He later wrote to the admiralty: "I should have stepped in myself and straightened things out." During the Battle of Sirte in March 1942, when a British force commanded by Philip Vian, escorting a convoy to Malta, was set upon by a more powerful Italian air and surface force, Cunningham monitored the battle from his operations room in Alexandria but refrained from interfering. He wrote in his memoirs: "Never have I felt so keenly the mortifying bitterness of sitting behind the scenes with a heavy load of responsibility while others were in action with a vastly superior force of the enemy." Only after the worst of the attacks had ended did Cunningham, to "take some of the responsibility off Vian," suggest the option of dispersing the convoy and letting its ships make their own way to Malta while the battle squadron withdrew toward Alexandria. Vian had "anticipated" Cunningham and done just that.[56]

One of the senior officers who had a major influence on Cunningham was Admiral Sir William W. Fisher, who commanded the Mediterranean fleet in the late 1930s. Fisher embraced the night attack, despite its confusion and risks, and expected his subordinates to demonstrate the "proper initiative whenever the chance came." ABC assigned to Fisher a "high place" among those British admirals who "maintained and cherished" the "fighting efficiency" of the Royal Navy between the world wars. Cunningham noted: "I, personally, owe more to him than I can ever hope to express, and in my two years of close contact with him as Commander-in-Chief in the Mediterranean I recognized him as an outstanding leader and a great man."[57]

When Cunningham himself assumed the command in the Mediterranean, he consciously followed many of Fisher's examples, as well as those of Hawke and Nelson. When two destroyers collided during high-speed night maneuvers, Cunningham rejected disciplinary action lest it "stifle the initiative" of his subordinates. His tactical instructions were written out in longhand before their circulation through the fleet. He expected his subordinate commanders "to disregard instructions, when in contact with the enemy, provided the senior officer was convinced that the Commander-in-Chief was unaware of the contact." When Cunningham read one draft instruction that called for halting pursuit of a retiring enemy fleet at the 200-fathom line, he wrote in Hawke-like fashion in the margin: "Damn the 200-fathom line! Where the enemy battlefleet can go, we can follow." To a subordinate he wrote: "The time for central direction is in previous exact and detailed training, so that every commander will know, should he be in doubt, exactly how the Commander-in-Chief is thinking. Nelson's instructions—drafted eleven days before Trafalgar—'in case signals cannot be seen, or clearly understood, no captain can do very wrong if he places his ship alongside that of an enemy' is a nice case in point of a simple direction covering all eventualities."[58]

IN EARLY 1941 the war was not going well for Mussolini's Italy. The June 1940 Italian offensive along the Alpine front of the already tottering Third French Republic had proven abortive and embarrassing. The September 1940 drive into Egypt and the October 1940 offensive from Albania into Greece had stalled. On the night of 11–12 November 1940 the British struck the main Italian naval base at Taranto. A surprise night strike by torpedo bombers launched from the aircraft carrier *Illustrious* badly damaged three battleships, one of which would never again be operational. In early December the British counterattacked along the Egyptian front, and the Greeks along the Albanian front. The outnumbered forces routed Mussolini's "legions." As the new year dawned, the Italian position in East Africa stood on the verge of collapse. Then on 5 February a Gibraltar-based British squadron bombarded Genoa.

On 13 February, the day after General Erwin Rommel, the newly designated leader of Hitler's Deutsche Afrika Korps (DAK), arrived in Libya, the commanders in chief of the German and Italian navies—Admirals Erich Raeder and Arturo Riccardi—met at Merano, a resort town northwest of Bolzano in the Alto Adige, to work out the details of Axis naval cooperation in the Mediterranean. For the Italians, Merano was a major conference concerning the future of the campaign in the Middle Sea and, ultimately, the very course of the war itself. The same was not true for the Germans, a reality evident in Raeder's failure to even mention the meeting in his memoirs.[59]

The Germans, who were about to begin transferring the three divisions of the DAK to Libya, sought to convince the Italians to use their surface forces more aggressively, especially in the Aegean, where British convoys from Alexandria regularly carried supplies to Greece. The Italians were willing to consider such operations, but sought in return a variety of commitments from the Germans, most notably for fuel oil, stocks of which were running low. What Riccardi did not know was that Hitler had already decided to shift his focus of operations eastward—to strike the Soviet Union in a massive surprise blow in June. The Mediterranean was about to become a secondary theater. In preparation for the eastern offensive the Germans were stockpiling their limited petroleum resources. As a result little more than promises was forthcoming at Merano and Admiral Riccardi remained reluctant to risk his fleet, and his single operational battleship, in waters beyond friendly air cover.

On 18 February Hitler made the decision to invade Greece with the German forces that had been moving into the Balkans. In early March the British, well aware of the German movements, began to transfer more than 60,000 men to Greece in convoys code-named Luster. These transfers forced the discontinuation of the British offensive in Libya and exacerbated the strains on an already stretched British naval force in the Mediterranean.

The arrival of British forces in Greece prompted the Germans to increase their pressure on the Italians to send ships into the Aegean. Riccardi initially resisted pressure from Mussolini, the Italian high command, and his own fleet commander, Iachino. But on 18 March Rear Admiral Eberhard Weichold, the German liaison officer to Supermarina, informed the Italians that a Luftwaffe strike had sunk two of Cunningham's three battleships. Riccardi, promised support from both the RAI and the Luftwaffe, finally relented, and planning began for an offensive sweep into the Aegean.[60]

The Italians based their plan on surprise and concentration. Their battlefleet—the battleship *Vittorio Veneto,* six heavy cruisers, two light cruisers, and thirteen destroyers—would operate in three groups. Iachino would initially lead his ships south toward Cyrenaica, Libya, but as the fleet passed the latitude of Crete it would turn east and begin its sweep. Iachino would possess greater strength than the British naval elements expected to be at large in the Aegean or its approaches. The Italian fleet would then retire to the west, rendezvous southwest of Navarino Bay, and return to port. The sweep would begin on 24 March.

The plan went awry before the operation even began. Because the Germans had never operated with the Italian fleet in the Mediterranean, the plan called for the Luftwaffe's Fliegerkorps X to exercise with the Italians as they passed through the Strait of Messina. But the Germans were not ready, even when the ships left their ports two days late on 26 March. Moreover, British codebreakers warned Cunningham about the sortie, and the secrecy of the operation was lost before the Italians sailed. The RMI relied on secure ground lines for its communications before the sweep, but the Luftwaffe depended on wireless—the infamous German Enigma machines, the signals of which were being read by the British.[61]

Cunningham planned his own surprise, much as had Jellicoe in May 1916 when he learned of Scheer's sweep. ABC did his best to foil the Italian threat to the convoys by altering schedules to avoid the sortie, and he also shaped his response in a fashion that, he hoped, would not alert the Italians to his plans. He kept his main force in Alexandria harbor, which was being reconnoitered daily, as long as possible. To maintain the ruse he went ashore for a day of golf on a course frequented by the Japanese consul, and ostentatiously carried a large bag to suggest that he would be spending the night.[62] But at 1900 on 27 March Cunningham's main force, which included the battleships *Warspite, Barham, Valiant,* the carrier *Formidable,* four light cruisers, and twenty-one destroyers, began its own sortie.

The Italians had steamed south on the morning of 27 March under clear skies. The British, informed about the Italian movements, dispatched no aircraft toward Crete for fear of forewarning the Italians of the approaching danger. Nor did any Luftwaffe aircraft provide the promised cover for the Italian battlefleet. Not until 1220 did the cruiser *Trieste,* leading the easternmost of the three Italian battle groups, spot a British Sunderland flying boat that had been dispatched by Cunningham to provide cover for the Ultra secret.[63]

By late afternoon Iachino knew that he had been spotted and that Cunningham probably knew of his sortie. Despite the absence of Luftwaffe cooperation, Iachino decided to press ahead. The British had sighted only his leading cruiser group, not the main body with the *Vittorio Veneto.* Intelligence also indicated that Cunningham's main force, which Iachino believed contained only a single battleship, was still in Alexandria. Iachino knew that the British advanced force operating from Greece consisted of only four light cruisers and supporting destroyers, which could pose little threat to the much stronger Italian fleet. To cancel the operation because of the appearance of a lone Sunderland flying

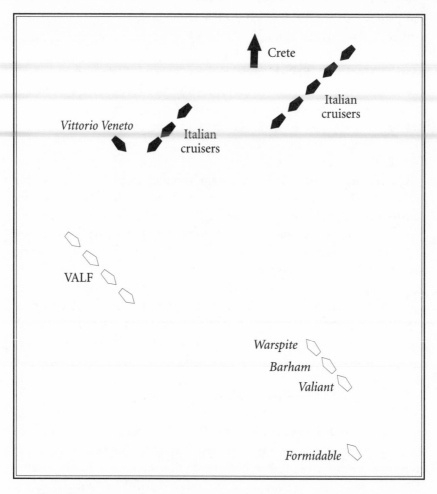

THE BATTLE OF CAPE MATAPAN, 28 MARCH 1941, CA. 0700
Pridham-Whippell (VALF), after nearly steaming into the Italians, turned away
and attempted to lead the enemy into the guns of Cunningham's battleships.
About two hours later the Italians would change course and try to lead VALF toward the *Vittorio Veneto.*

boat would be unnecessary, and also would appear somewhat ridiculous.
As Bragadin later noted: "It must be remembered that this occasion was
not born of a real tactical opportunity. Rather it was the result of a plan of
considerations that were predominantly political."[64]

What Iachino did not know was that the German report of the sinking of two British battleships was erroneous. The Germans informed

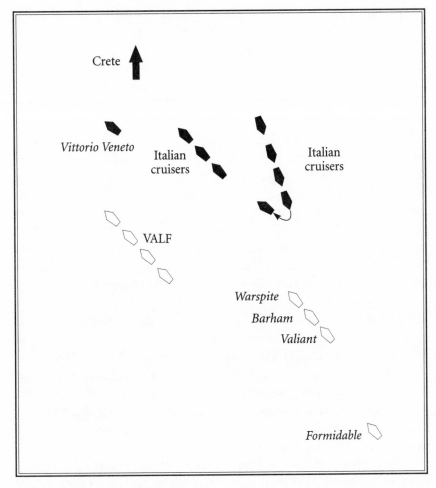

THE BATTLE OF CAPE MATAPAN, 28 MARCH 1941, CA. 1130
Attacks by British carrier aircraft forced Iachino to break off his pursuit of VALF
and led him to make his decision to retire. Subsequent air attacks damaged the
Vittorio Veneto and later the heavy cruiser *Pola*. These attacks convinced
Cunningham to risk the night action that ultimately cost the Italians an entire
heavy cruiser division.

Supermarina of the mistake, but the corrected report failed to reach
Iachino—a failure that remains a point of some controversy.[65] Nevertheless, Supermarina did order a change in plan—Iachino would cut short
his sweep toward the east and concentrate his three groups off the western end of Crete, south of the island of Gavdo.

On the morning of 28 March both battlefleets were south of Crete. The Italians were steaming southeast in three groups, with two cruiser groups leading and the lone battleship bringing up the rear. On an almost parallel course with the leading Italian cruiser group was Vice Admiral H. D. Pridham-Whippell's "Light Force" (VALF), with four light cruisers. Pridham-Whippell, flying his flag in the *Orion,* was steaming toward his planned rendezvous with Cunningham.

At 0633 an Italian floatplane spotted VALF. Pridham-Whippell, noting the type of aircraft, assumed, correctly, that Italian surface ships were in the area. Shortly afterward a plane from the carrier *Formidable* spotted four cruisers at a position somewhat northeast of VALF. Pridham-Whippell was unsure if these were his own or Italian men-of-war.[66] But the ships were Italian and they were closing on VALF. Iachino had directed Vice Admiral Luigi Sansonetti's 3rd Cruiser Division—the heavy cruisers *Trieste, Trento,* and *Bolzano,* and supporting destroyers—to engage the British. The other two Italian groups closed in support.

Pridham-Whippell realized his mistake when his lookouts sighted Italian heavy cruisers. Since the Italian 8-inch guns outranged the 6-inch guns of the British light cruisers, VALF wisely chose to bear away from the Italians, who pursued. The British raced south and then worked eastward in an effort to lead the Italians toward Cunningham's main force, which lay about seventy miles to the southeast. Neither side scored a hit during the long-range gunnery duel. Shortly after 0900 the frustrated Italians, unable to close the range on the nimble light cruisers, broke off the action and turned back toward the west.

Like Hipper in pursuit of Beatty in the "run to the north," Pridham-Whippell followed, and as he did so Iachino maneuvered to trap VALF between the Italian heavy cruisers and the *Vittorio Veneto.* At 1058 British lookouts sighted the Italian dreadnought on the horizon. Pridham-Whippell immediately turned to the south as his destroyers laid a smokescreen to shield the cruisers. The battleship scored a few near misses, but no hits. Iachino sought to press his advantage, but at 1115 British carrier planes attacked the Italian fleet. They scored no hits, but the need to evade their torpedoes brought an end to the pursuit. Iachino, alarmed at the appearance of British carrier aircraft, and troubled by the failure of either the Italian or the German air force to provide cover, considered further pursuit pointless. He ordered his fleet to retire.[67]

But the battle had not yet ended. Cunningham knew that his battleships lacked the speed to overhaul the quicker Italians, but he still had his carrier. At 1230 he directed the *Formidable* to launch its second air strike of the day. Hours passed without a firm fix on the retiring Italians. Then, shortly before 1530, a reconnaissance aircraft spotted them. Fortuitously, land-based Blenheims flying from Crete found the Italians at the same time and launched a simultaneous though by no means coordinated strike. None of the Blenheims' bombs found their marks, but the torpedo bombers reported three hits on the *Vittorio Veneto*. In fact, only a single torpedo struck the stern of the battleship, slowing her. Even damaged, the *Vittorio Veneto* was faster than the British battleships.[68]

Iachino, with his last operational battleship now damaged, requested air cover for his force as it withdrew. Supermarina passed on the request to Fliegerkorps X, but the Germans considered it too late in the day to undertake operations over water. Nevertheless, Iachino considered the threat to his force minimal, assuming that darkness would provide cover from further air attack and that Cunningham's main surface force had not left Alexandria before the morning of 28 March. Even a report from Supermarina that placed a British force seventy-five miles to the east failed to alarm the Italian commander. The two air strikes indicated that there was a British carrier nearby, but Iachino believed that the largest surface force in the vicinity was VALF's light cruisers.[69]

At 1800 Iachino learned from his on-board codebreakers that the British had launched another air attack. He tightened up his formation to maximize antiaircraft coverage. The British planes appeared at 1823, but they hovered about the Italian fleet until the onset of darkness. At 1920 the planes finally began their attacks. Amid the confusion, only one torpedo found a target. The heavy cruiser *Pola* was left dead in the water. Iachino, still convinced that only British light forces were nearby, detached his 1st Cruiser Division to cover the *Pola* and take her under tow. The remainder of his force withdrew toward the northwest.

Reports of "probable hits" by the *Formidable's* aircraft gave Cunningham hope that he could still engage the Italians.[70] But he also knew that by the morning his force would be exposed to air attack. He had either to run the risk of a night engagement or to break off his pursuit and return to Alexandria. He chose the former option, knowing that he would possess two major advantages in any night battle. First, the British ships had radar, and the Italians did not. Second, the Mediterranean fleet had trained for more than a decade for night action, and the Italians had not. Cunningham also held a third advantage, although he did not know it. While he was aware of the presence of the Italian main force, including the *Vittorio Veneto,* Iachino was unaware that three British dreadnoughts were approaching.

At 2111 radar on one of the VALF ships indicated a lone static target, the *Pola,* to the southwest. Pridham-Whippell continued his pursuit of the Italian main force while Cunningham, with his battleships, closed on the reported position. At 2210 the *Valiant's* radar detected a large contact about six miles off the port bow. As the British closed, radar indicated two additional large vessels, probably cruisers. Cunningham brought his battleships into line ahead using a relatively secure short-range wireless signal, and at 2228 the destroyer *Greyhound,* in an oft-practiced proce-dure, illuminated one of the targets with a searchlight. The *Warspite* opened fire with its 15-inch guns and the engagement began. Cunningham later wrote: "The enemy were seen to be two cruisers of the *Zara* class on an opposite course; they were apparently completely taken by surprise and their turrets were fore and aft. *Warspite's* first 15-inch broadside hit the rear cruiser with devastating effect, five of six shells hitting. Both cruisers were thereafter repeatedly hit, set severely on fire and put out of action."[71]

Ten minutes after the firing began, Cunningham sensed that it was time to finish off the crippled cruisers with a destroyer attack. He wisely decided to draw his battleships away to the north, to clear the area and to preclude the possibility of mistaken identity in the confusion. But Pridham-Whippell interpreted Cunningham's signal—for "unengaged" ships to steam north—to apply to VALF and broke off the pursuit of the main Italian force.

And so the battle of Cape Matapan came to an end. The Italians suf-fered their heaviest losses for a single engagement: three heavy cruisers and two destroyers sunk and the *Vittorio Veneto* damaged. About 3,000 Italian sailors perished. The British lost a handful of torpedo planes. Cunningham oversaw the rescue of hundreds of Italian sailors, and when forced from the scene the next morning by the Luftwaffe, radioed the position of the survivors to the Italian navy. At one point during the rescue operation a British signal reported: "Prisoners when asked why they had failed to fire at us replied that they thought if they did we would fire back."[72]

Cape Matapan was not a great naval victory, comparable to Trafalgar or the Nile. The Italian fleet was not crippled, nor did the battle se-cure British command of the Aegean, let alone the Mediterranean. But Matapan was a lopsided triumph that removed three powerful heavy cruisers from the Italian order of battle. In the short term, the victory lessened greatly the likelihood of Italian interference with British convoys in the Aegean. A British defeat at Cape Matapan would most assuredly have made the subsequent British evacuation of Greece and Crete far more problematic. Cunningham's success also gained the British government some badly needed capital, in both the political and morale arenas, capital that would be needed to offset the coming Dunkirk-like debacle in the Balkans.

While it would be a mistake to overplay the importance of Matapan, it would also be a mistake to attribute Cunningham's victory to British aplomb and sheer good fortune. A cursory examination of the battle could lend itself to an image of two fleets stumbling around semi-blindly in the dark. But that is the nature of naval warfare, and night actions are among the most confusing of engagements at sea. It was for this reason that the British trained regularly to fight in the dark, and that ABC chose to press his position on the night of 28 March 1941.

The Royal Navy's victory can in part be attributed to its superiority in command, control, and communications. The admiralty in London allowed Cunningham a free hand to run his operation. Thanks to codebreaking, he achieved the advantage of surprise that the Italians had expected to enjoy. The British possessed effective radar sets and operators who knew how to interpret the reflections they saw. Cunningham's well-trained force employed effective night doctrine. But the British did make mistakes: Pridham-Whippell failed to overtake the damaged *Vittorio Veneto* and misinterpreted Cunningham's signal to "unengaged" forces.

By comparison, Axis forces made innumerable errors of commission and omission. Germany's overreliance on Enigma undermined the entire operation and cost Iachino the element of surprise. Neither the German nor Italian air force played any effective role in the battle, whereas a handful of aircraft from the carrier *Formidable* plagued the Italians throughout the day and set in motion the events that led to the loss of three heavy cruisers. But the Italians lacked more than aerial cooperation or an aircraft carrier of their own. During the interwar years they had failed to develop radar or night doctrine and tactics. As a result, Iachino's ships were at the mercy of Cunningham's torpedo bombers until nightfall, then at the mercy of his radar-equipped ships crewed by officers and men trained for night action.

Thus, among the admirals in the Royal Navy in the twentieth century, it was Andrew Browne Cunningham who could best claim Nelson's mantle. As Michael Simpson, editor of ABC's papers, concluded: "[Cunningham] exhibited many of the characteristics and espoused many of the objects associated with Nelson. The instilling of his captains of a simple, well-understood doctrine and a corresponding expertise in carrying it out, together with the latitude to exercise one's judgement, was a policy he shared with Nelson . . . Like Nelson, he took risks but only if the object justified them . . . he was Nelson's heir . . . he had the Nelson touch."[73]

DURING the Second World War the technology of naval command and control came of age. Wireless communications became a critically important tool in the shaping of naval strategy, operations, and tactics. But the radio was not a panacea for the problems, new and old, facing commanders at sea. Moreover, this tool, however useful, could be, and often was, turned against the user. Reliable radio communications allowed navies to conduct theater-wide operations with a degree of assurance absent in the era when Philip II, Louis XIV, or Napoleon I attempted to invade the British Isles. Without radio, Dönitz could not have waged his campaign in the North Atlantic, nor could the Americans have concentrated their vast resources off the Marianas in June 1944. But reliance on radio posed dangers, as had been the case during the Great War, and as was evident before Cape Matapan. Successful Allied codebreaking in both the European and Pacific theaters helped to ensure the defeat of the Axis powers. In fact, the course of the two world wars suggests that since 1914 codebreaking has been more the rule than the exception. Given the historical record, no military service ought to operate on the assumption that its codes are secure.

Even when codes were believed to be secure, commanders of most Second World War navies understood the dangers of radio communications. Fleets generally observed radio silence during operations, both to frustrate the codebreakers and to prevent radio traffic analysis. The huge fleets of the war often operated much as had their predecessors in the days of sail—communicating by visual signals. In such instances, as both the Japanese and American navies demonstrated in the Pacific, well-developed and well-understood doctrine was indispensable to the effective functioning of naval forces at all levels.

The Imperial Japanese Navy's avoidance of excessive radio traffic limited the impact of American codebreaking in the Pacific. Thanks to the codebreakers, the American high command usually knew the Japanese strategic objectives and the resources assigned to achieve them. As a result, Admiral Nimitz was able to counter Japan's thrusts into the Coral Sea in May and against Midway in June 1942. But because the Japanese relied less on radio than on doctrine and initiative once an operation began, American codebreaking did not ensure success at the operational or tactical level. While the Americans frustrated their enemy in the Coral Sea in the spring of 1942, the Japanese nevertheless achieved a tactical success, trading the small carrier *Shoho* for the much larger American carrier *Lexington*. At Midway, Nimitz positioned his three carriers to ambush the approaching enemy. But because the Japanese navy operated under strict radio silence, it was not the work of the codebreakers but a string of fortuitous (for the Americans) circumstances that secured the U.S. victory at Midway. The history of the Pacific war is replete with instances in which the Japanese, despite their enemies' reading of their codes, surprised the Americans. Leyte Gulf is but one example.

At the tactical level, the advent of radiotelephony—ship-to-ship communication—in the 1930s appeared to some commanders to be the answer to the problems of command and control. But during the Second World War Arleigh Burke and other American surface warriors discovered what the Japanese had long understood, and what Dudley Knox had warned of in 1913—that radio was no substitute for leadership, training, or doctrine.

CHAPTER NINE

The Cold War and Beyond

*D*URING THE COLD WAR no major fleets contested by force the
control of the sea. For more than forty years, the Soviet and American navies stalked each other on, above, and under the surface of the
world's seas in preparation for a conflict that never came. Myriad questions concerning policy, strategy, ship design, technology, doctrine, tactics, and command and control were still largely unresolved. The U.S.
Navy was able to test itself to a degree in "limited" wars in the Korean peninsula, Indochina, and the Persian Gulf. Not so the Soviet navy,
the capabilities of which will forever be the subject of debate and speculation.

There exists a parallel between the final halves of the nineteenth and
twentieth centuries with regard to naval warfare. Both periods witnessed
extraordinary technological advances during times of relative peace, broken by only a handful of wars or crises, not one of which generated a naval battle comparable to Trafalgar, Jutland, or Leyte Gulf. While there
were examples aplenty of the use of naval air power against targets ashore,
analysts had only a handful of encounters at sea from which to draw lessons or a sense of the interplay of new weapons systems. While the capabilities of a new system could be tested in peacetime, the interaction of
these systems in war remained largely conjectural.

This was, and is, especially true in the area of command and control.
New technologies, including space-based communications systems, provide naval commanders with capabilities undreamed of in Nelson's day.
These systems are routinely tested, but they have never been put to the
ultimate trial of a full-scale naval conflict. So most of what can be said of

the postwar period is conjectural, although certain patterns of development are evident.

ON 2 SEPTEMBER 1945, on the deck of the battleship U.S.S. *Missouri,* representatives of the Imperial Japanese government signed the instrument of surrender ending the Second World War in the Pacific. The signing of the capitulation afloat, rather than ashore, symbolized the nature of the Pacific war. Four years of bloody fighting carried the American navy across an immense oceanic expanse—from Pearl Harbor to Tokyo Bay. In the course of the conflict, the largest maritime war in history, the U.S. Navy destroyed the fleet of its principal enemy—Japan. The American effort, indeed the Allied effort, was, as the strategic commentator Stefan T. Possony termed it in 1945, a "vindication of sea power."[1]

Those who during the interwar years had predicted the demise of navies were, in almost every instance, proven incorrect. Despite early setbacks in the battle of the Atlantic, surface forces eventually mastered the submarine threat and kept open the sea lines of communication between the Old and New Worlds. In the Pacific, air power, far from replacing naval power, increased its utility and reach.[2]

For the U.S. Navy, the war's outcome had an additional meaning. For more than a century and a half the navy had lived in the shadow of a larger, more experienced, tradition-rich Royal Navy. Alfred Thayer Mahan, a philosopher of sea power as well as an American naval officer, had looked to the history of Great Britain's navy to illustrate his principles. Decades after Mahan had written, the U.S. Navy had yet to test itself in battle with a first-class enemy. Americans had yet to win their Trafalgar. But during the Second World War the U.S. Navy grew to overshadow not only the Royal Navy but also the combined forces of the rest of the world. Coral Sea, Midway, the Philippine Sea, and Leyte Gulf marked the coming of age of the American service. The U.S. Navy, which had begun as a minuscule challenge to Britain's naval supremacy in 1775, had become by 1945 an immense, battle-hardened, confident force ready to don the mantle so long worn by the Royal Navy.

The American victory was also a vindication of a decentralized approach to naval command and control. Over the preceding three centuries many naval officers had relied on decentralized command—the names Vernon, Anson, Hawke, Suffren, and Nelson come immediately to mind—but since the end of the Anglo-Dutch Wars no navy had officially embraced such a philosophy. The U.S. Navy was the first to do so, following a debate sparked by Dudley Knox in 1913, with the war instructions of the 1920s and 1930s, then with Ernie King's 1941 memoranda on the "initiative of the subordinate," and later with the war instructions of 1944 and their focus on leadership and the human factor in warfare.

The very scale of the U.S. Navy's triumph, however, contained within itself the seeds of future problems. The navy had fulfilled its Mahanian purpose, but would there be at the end of the next war any pursuable Mahanian goals? And lacking a clearly defined role, how would the navy weather postwar challenges from those who believed they had found, at last, a panacea for air power in the atomic bomb, or from those who sought to centralize the administration and function of the American armed forces?

At various points during the Cold War, several factors pressured the U.S. Navy to shift away from—if never to fully abandon—its traditions, including the "initiative of the subordinate," toward a more centralized system of command and control. Increasing insistence on "jointness" (collaboration with other branches of the military), the development of enhanced communications technologies, the advent of atomic weapons, and competition with the extremely centralized and seemingly more "scientific" Soviet military model—all these influences moved the U.S. Navy away from decentralization.

Two major elements drove the American military toward greater jointness after 1945. The immediate cause was the evident failure of the services to cooperate effectively before and during the Second World War. From the confusion that reigned in Hawaii in the weeks before the Japanese attack on 7 December 1941 to the near-disaster at Leyte Gulf, proponents of unification found myriad examples to justify their calls for the reform of the American military. The second contributing cause was a widely held conviction in U.S. society in the 1940s (one still embraced by many Americans more than sixty years later) that larger, centralized organizations are more efficient than smaller, decentralized ones. During the first postwar decades the United States moved inexorably toward "big government," "big business," and "big labor unions." This trend fostered a belief that the unification of the armed forces—the creation of one "big" military—combined with the establishment of a hierarchical structure to ensure that a single commander was in charge in a given theater, would produce greater efficiency across the board, from peacetime procurement of weapons to wartime combat operations.

This push for jointness caused, and continues to cause, problems for the world's major navies. Whatever the wisdom of the concept in principle, unification ignores a basic historical fact: that navies *began* as joint endeavors—extensions of armies from land onto the sea. Navies evolved their somewhat peculiar approaches and traditions because the army officers who first commanded a king's ships discovered that what worked well ashore did not necessarily work afloat. The guns and carriages the artillery corps employed were not suitable for shipboard use. The long pikes the infantry carried were too unwieldy to use 'tween decks. The boots needed for long marches were ill suited to climbing the rigging.

The work of twentieth-century unifiers to achieve jointness often met with failure and, on occasion, led to a measurable decline in "fighting power." In human terms, the attempt to centrally control military operations contributed to disaster for the United States in Indochina. In fiscal terms, some of the worst boondoggles of the Cold War era involved applying the principle of jointness to the procurement process, for example, the development of the Tactical Fighter Experimental (TFX) for both air force and navy use in the 1960s, or the Joint Tactical Information and Distribution System (JTIDS) in the 1970s and 1980s. One analyst noted: "The TFX case is a succinct reminder of the limits of commonality in weapons procurement and an object lesson well worth remembering in appreciating the problems of joint command and control."[3]

Nevertheless, unification as a governing philosophical concept made sense. The evolution of modern warfare had ended the era when navies operated independently on the high seas. States had to find ways to make their military services coordinate their efforts. In the United States unification became the law of the land, and the navy had little choice but to cooperate, however grudgingly. Civilian authorities of both political parties were committed to unification and jointness. The army, and after 1947 the now-independent U.S. Air Force, dominated most of the newly established joint commands and staffs. Naval officers resisted these changes, to the point of "revolt" in the late 1940s, but little by little naval officers drifted toward, if not into, line. The navy found itself having to alter its approaches to strategy, operations, tactics, command, communications, and even methods of procurement to accommodate the new mantra of "jointness," often interpreted by those in the navy as being forced to do things the army or air force way.[4]

With regard to command and control, the traditions and experiences of the American army and air force during the Second World War were ones of centralization, not decentralization.[5] The respective approaches taken by the army, air force, and navy were understandable, as the applicability of any single approach to all three services proved problematic. The army and the air force employed, for good reason, more rigid planning processes, operational concepts, and command structures than did the navy. Army and air force planning and doctrine focused on territorial objectives. The rivers that the army had to cross did not move; the cities that the air force had to bomb did not change location. When ground forces moved, they were confined to relatively few axes of advance. Thus U.S. Army and Air Force staffs could develop rather detailed plans for operations against fixed targets defended by relatively static forces. Naval wartime planning involved strikes again mobile targets of uncertain size that might appear, or strike themselves, from any direction. So naval planning tended to be more flexible and to leave greater discretion to subordinate commanders.

The command and control systems developed by the respective services to support operations reflected these divergent approaches. For example, when war came to the Korean peninsula in 1950, navy and air force aircraft radios were incompatible, a situation that could be interpreted as evidence of incompetence or pigheadedness. But both services equipped their aircraft with radios appropriate to their needs. U.S. Air Force planes, sent to their targets as part of a grand plan, had little need to communicate with one another, or with forces on the ground, and used only four VHF channels. The U.S. Navy and Marine Corps fighter planes, which were expected to communicate with ground controllers and other friendly aircraft, had ten.

During most of the Cold War era the push for jointness and more centralized control often proved to be incompatible with the U.S. Navy's more flexible system of command. The strains were often marked, most notably during the Indochina war, and perhaps never will be completely resolved.

AFTER THE DROPPING of the second atomic bomb on Nagasaki in August 1945, President Harry S Truman recognized that nuclear weapons were something other than more powerful super bombs. From that time on, any proposed use of nuclear weapons required some degree of presidential approval.[6] That requirement fostered, and to a great degree necessitated, the development of a structure of command and control centralized enough to prevent, to the greatest extent possible, unauthorized use of nuclear weapons, but also sufficiently flexible to ensure their use in appropriate circumstances. The concepts of "the initiative of the subordinate" and thermonuclear war were incompatible. But as nuclear warheads became more compact and ever more platforms—strategic bombers, strike aircraft flying from carriers, ballistic missile submarines, the army's atomic cannon—became potential delivery systems, the network of executive control spread throughout the military chain of command.

The "almost personal" control Truman held over atomic weapons did not last. As more nuclear weapons became available, and after the Soviets exploded their own bomb, the need for quick reaction to a possible atomic attack forced the civilian executive to yield back to the military some degree of control. As the nuclear arms race intensified, strategic theorists and planners viewed potential "decapitation" of the nation not only as a dire wartime possibility but also as a peacetime threat to stability. Successive American administrations sought greater redundancy and decentralization in the structure of command and control for nuclear weapons. In general, American presidents found themselves forced to "pre-delegate" authority for releasing nuclear weapons either to the system itself, in the form of a predetermined, near-automatic response to an attack, or to various subordinate commanders operating under extremely circumscribed criteria. But, ironically, as the command and control of nuclear weapons became less centralized, the structure established for their control became the vehicle for the increasing centralization of conventional—that is, nonnuclear—operations.[7]

Initially, this decision to closely control nuclear forces had little direct impact on the navy, since the air force and its long-range bombers held a virtual monopoly on delivery systems. The U.S. Navy's first post–Second World War instructions, USF 1, issued in 1947 by Ernest J. King's successor as chief of naval operations, Chester W. Nimitz, had a new and different tone, reflecting the concepts of jointness and unity of command that were beginning to permeate the language of American military officers. The content of the new instructions, however, preserved the spirit of decentralization and initiative. Paragraph 212 noted: "The commander controls and coordinates the execution of his plan . . . [but] he must decentralize responsibility and delegate authority to his subordinate com-

manders by assigning them tasks, which together accomplish the plan . . .
The subordinate commander has full authority to modify his part in the
plan and to initiate new action as, in his opinion, is necessary in order to
accomplish the objective of the command as a whole." Commanders
were expected to communicate with their subordinates to facilitate this
process: "Responsible [subordinate] commanders should understand fully
the basic reasons behind the details of their planned participation in the
operations . . . When such basic reasons are understood fully, the commander is then more ready to act intelligently when there is reason to
depart from the plans of his superior."[8]

But despite the lip service paid to decentralization and initiative, as
atomic warheads became smaller, and as the navy acquired platforms capable of delivering them, naval forces were inevitably drawn into a more
centralized command network. In the early 1950s the navy began to operate nuclear-capable attack aircraft from its forward-deployed carriers;
in the late 1950s and early 1960s the development of ballistic missile
submarines (SSBNs) further enhanced the service's nuclear capabilities;
and in the 1980s the operational deployment of cruise missiles—Toma-
hawks—in battleships, cruisers, destroyers, and attack submarines gave
the U.S. Navy an almost service-wide capacity for atomic strikes. For obvious reasons, the trend was toward more centralization.

A related factor driving the navy toward greater centralization was the
possibility of accidental nuclear war. Given the tensions of the Cold War,
policymakers realized that any spark—something as simple as a clash between two fighter aircraft—might lead to a thermonuclear conflagration.
To minimize the likelihood of such an incident, U.S. forces operating in
the vicinity of the Soviet Union or other potentially hostile countries,
and those forces were often naval, were brought under stricter control by
the national command authority. The commanders of these forces, as
well as their subordinates, were constrained in their use of initiative by
restrictive rules of engagement. These rules, combined with an ever
more intrusive system of communications, lessened the probability of accidental war, but they also eroded the ability of naval commanders to exercise initiative. The stakes were simply too high, whatever the talents
and character of a particular officer.

DURING THE COLD WAR advances in communications technology
both allowed and to an extent drove greater centralization in command

and control. Cold War competition and the development of communications satellites led to ever more capable and sophisticated systems. Naval communications technology became more powerful and flexible and exploited broader bands of the electromagnetic spectrum. Extra-low frequency radio transmissions permitted the national command authority to transmit one-way "emergency action messages" containing nuclear firing orders to SSBNs running submerged, while extra-high frequency transmissions linked surface platforms to satellites and the satellites to one another. The new systems carried not just voice or coded transmissions but data collected from platforms in space, in the air, or on the surface. To Norman Friedman, a prominent naval analyst, "the most striking development in naval technology since 1945 has been the progressive displacement of weapons by sensors and command/control devices."[9]

The attractions of these systems to naval officers were many. Enhanced communications capabilities appeared to offer solutions to both longstanding and new problems facing naval commanders. As two prominent naval analysts wrote in the mid-1980s: "The 'fog of battle' has from ancient times been a formidable hazard to the conduct of war, but the marvels of electronics now on the horizon may do much to minimize this obstacle."[10] Voice and data links also offered commanders a means to tie together the various components of the dispersed modern fleet. In the postwar era the greater range and speed of platforms and weapons and the threat of nuclear attack made tactical concentration unthinkable. Dispersion of platforms plus concentration of firepower became the order of the day. Battlefleets of aircraft carriers, surface ships, and submarines, often operating in conjunction with land-based aircraft and in communication with space-based satellites, spread over thousands of square miles of ocean. Powerful and dependable communication "links" now became a central element of the command and control of the fleet.

The ever increasing speed of platforms and weapons placed a premium on early warning and quick reaction. One solution to this threat was to rely on automated, computer-driven systems to both detect and respond to threats. In a fashion, such reliance was the ultimate form of doctrine, being not just an automatic but an automated response. In the 1960s the U.S. Navy began to deploy the Navy Tactical Data System (NTDS), which used computers to track threats detected by a ship's sensors. Collected data could be shared between ships and fed directly into the firing-control subsystems. Subsequent systems, such as the Advanced Combat Direction System (ACDS) and Aegis of the late 1970s and

1980s, were more capable and more automated. Work continues on various programs intended to exploit the capability of the computer to manage and distribute data and to link that capability to improved artificial intelligence capable of more than a canned, predetermined response. One project involves developing a battle-management system for a carrier battle group that would serve almost as a subsidiary staff.[11]

Despite these advances, even peacetime exercises were sufficient to demonstrate to most naval commanders that the new technologies did not provide solutions to problems of command and control. Virtually all of the systems, such as NTDS, relied to some extent on human input. Duplication and error remained problems. In July 1988 the cruiser *Vincennes,* outfitted with the navy's much-vaunted Aegis system, mistakenly downed an Iranian civilian airliner, not because of faults in the system but because of errors committed by the men who managed it. Electronic sensors were also subject to deception. During the initial allied attack against Baghdad on 16 January 1991, U.S. Navy aircraft launched drones that emitted the electronic and radar signatures of attacking aircraft. The approaching drones prompted the Iraqis to turn on their own radar and missile systems, which were then targeted for destruction by allied attack aircraft armed with high-speed anti-radiation missiles that homed in on and destroyed sites using active radar to search the sky.[12]

Systems dependent on communications were also vulnerable to electromagnetic interference caused by a nuclear attack or by more conventional means. The allies used jamming aircraft, such as the navy's EA-6B Prowler, with great success during the Persian Gulf War. There was also the problem of emissions, which had dogged navies since the adoption of the wireless. Modern ships steaming about with active sensors, sending volumes of data and voice communications through the ether, were subject to detection, and their transmissions to interception and decryption. During the Cold War naval forces generally operated under various degrees of emissions control. Commanders, denied access to the sensory and communications abilities built into the platforms, found themselves forced either to risk concentrating their ships within visual range or to rely on doctrine and initiative.

Thus the availability of advanced communications systems undermined but never completely destroyed the navy's tradition of reliance on "the initiative of the subordinate." The adoption of such systems allowed the higher echelons of command to severely limit the scope of initiative and, in many instances, to micromanage ongoing operations. With each passing decade, as the ability to communicate improved, the tendency to interfere grew stronger. In May 1986 a *Christian Science Monitor* report on the expanded use of satellite communications noted that "direct conversation between a president and a Marine patrol in the Middle East" had become possible.[13] The reporter might well have asked: Why would a president need, or want, to communicate directly with that patrol?

THROUGHOUT the Cold War American naval officers and civilian analysts kept a close watch on military developments in the Soviet Union. While the increasing strength of the Soviet navy was obvious, the fundamental underpinnings of national military policy in Moscow and the basics of Soviet naval thought were less so. Westerners endlessly debated the nature of Soviet naval policy, the roles and missions of the service, and the reasons for its force structure. Did the subordinate position of the Soviet navy within the military reflect the thinking of narrow-minded Russian continentalists, or had the Soviets simply achieved the degree of civilian control and jointness that so many in the West desired? To some in the West, Soviet approaches were simply inferior—products of a bankrupt communist state. To others the Soviet models were neither better nor worse than those embraced by the West, but alternative approaches perfectly suited to the needs of a very different state. And some Western analysts saw in the Soviet approach a superior use of the study of history plus the scientific method, a dangerous combination that ought not to be ignored.

Western analysts also disagreed about the Soviet approach to command and control. There was little debate about the nature of the Soviet navy's command structure—it was highly centralized and heavily reliant on communications. But was this a reflection of the Soviet state, or of the application of the lessons of history and scientific principles? On paper, the Soviets recognized the need for a wide spectrum of approaches to command and control to fit a variety of situations. Milan Vego wrote in his study of Soviet naval tactics: "Force control in the Soviet Navy has two aspects: control during preparation for a battle or an operation, and control during combat. Force control may be conducted by centralized, decentralized, or combined methods." But in practice, Vego noted, "the Soviets believe that centralization is a critical factor in the organization of force control. All subordinate forces and assets striving toward a common goal are controlled by a single control organ. Only in this way can cooperation be organized effectively, the Soviets think. Centralized force control ensures both economy of forces and concentration of main efforts at the right time and place."[14]

Several prominent Western military thinkers saw much to admire in the Soviet system. Norman Polmar, one of the foremost American naval analysts, wrote: "The characteristics of the Soviet C³ structure—centralized, large, survivable and secure—contribute to the potential for a highly effective wartime system." Roger Beaumont, a prominent student of command and control, noted that Westerners misconstrued the fundamental nature of the Soviet system. Unlike Western militaries, the Russians made excellent use of psychological studies and of science in general. The Soviets built their command and control infrastructure on a broad foundation: "the arts, public information, propaganda, and, indeed, all forms of influence and persuasion, including the application of various psychological techniques." Beaumont wrote: "What would emerge when the proverbial chips were down might therefore constitute, in quantity and quality, a weapon in itself in terms of its impact on adversaries."[15]

Other analysts were far less admiring. Vego concluded: "The Soviets' methods of force control are a source of serious weakness in the employment of their naval forces and aviation. While the Soviets seem to stress the value of decentralized command and control, centralization in fact pervades all level of force control . . . Little initiative is left to subordinate tactical commanders." Vego added that the "Soviet system of command and control of operational-tactical- and tactical-sized forces would probably be the greatest source of weakness in wartime." Norman Friedman likewise identified the inflexibility of a "Soviet Navy . . . designed for centralized control."[16]

OF COURSE, the American and Russian navies never tested their respective approaches to command and control in direct combat. The Cold War came to an abrupt end in the years 1989–1991 with the political, economic, and social collapse of the Soviet Union. State-driven centralization proved to be a nineteenth-century relic of the industrial revolution, a form of government unable to cope with the fast-paced technological revolution of the late twentieth century. One can doubt that the Soviet approach to command and control would have fared any better in a conventional (nonnuclear) conflict.[17]

Although the U.S. Navy's operational concepts, tactics, and doctrine were never tested in a "classic" naval war in the Cold War era, those decades were times of hard peace and twilight war, with the navy on a near-constant wartime footing, operating on the edges of the Soviet empire, facing intermittent proxy wars. But these conflicts were "naval" only in the sense that the ships, aircraft, and personnel of the U.S. Navy–Marine Corps team participated. While the Democratic People's Republic of Korea (North Korea) and the Socialist Republic of Vietnam (at the time referred to in the West as North Vietnam) possessed naval forces, they did not deploy fleets or squadrons capable of challenging American command of the sea. The U.S. Navy's only "naval" conflict in this period was the "Tanker War" against Iran (1987–1988).

Nevertheless, in the wars fought in the Korean peninsula (1950–1953), Indochina (1964–1975), and the Persian Gulf (1990–1991), the U.S. Navy played an important if subsidiary role, relying primarily on its carriers to support land and air operations ashore. During each of these conflicts, the navy often found its decentralized approach to command and control challenged and undermined: first by a unified command structure dominated by other services, and second by civilian authorities enforcing restrictive rules of engagement and using, or more accurately abusing, a national command structure designed to control nuclear weapons to micromanage military operations in the field.

The Korean War was the first American conflict fought under the new unified command structure. Because of the Soviets' possession of atomic weapons and concerns about an expansion of the war beyond Asia, the Truman administration sensibly kept the war limited in scope. While tensions developed between the military and the nation's political leadership, especially during the latter years of the war, which were marked by stalemate and attrition, the U.S. Navy's biggest challenge in the area of command and control involved differences between services in concepts of operations, tactics, equipment, and doctrine.

If Korea was the first test of unification or jointness, the American military failed the test. This was especially true in the air, where the approaches of the U.S. Navy–Marine Corps team collided with the practices of the U.S. Air Force. In July 1950 the United States established a joint operations center in the Far East to manage the war.[18] But interservice cooperation was not immediately forthcoming. The air force planning structure was geared toward what James A. Field Jr. aptly termed "macro-flexibility": it was excellent at shifting the focus of operational emphasis within a theater, but it was poor at ensuring coordination or communication at the target. In other words, the air force focused on the strategic and operational dimensions of the air war, and paid less attention to the immediate tactical interface between air and ground forces—what is usually termed close air support.

To permit these rapid shifts in an air campaign, the U.S. Air Force command and control structure relied heavily on communications. Conversely, U.S. Navy and Marine Corps aviation focused on, and excelled at, close air support. The navy did not rely on a massive network of communications but instead "on doctrine supplemented by brief orders, and on delegation of control to those on the spot." Nor was an approach that had worked well in a conflict run by the air force and fought in Western Europe, rich in land telephone and telegraph lines, well suited to a joint conflict waged in a communications-starved theater such as the Korean peninsula. With few land lines ashore, and none linking the shore to the navy's carriers, "Air Force verbosity" often overtaxed the wireless networks. Field noted "an extreme example . . . the grandfather of all radio messages, received by Task Force 77 in November 1950, which took 8,000 encrypted groups to set forth the air plan for one day, and which required over 30 man-hours for processing."[19]

For the American military, the Korean War failed to resolve the problems of unified command and joint command and control. A study of joint air operations concluded: "Korea marked a step backward in the effective command and control of joint operations."[20] Recriminations flew fast and furious, but, as Field observed, "both services, in a sense, were right in this matter, and both wrong." The air force and the navy did have very different, often conflicting views of command and control, but those views were rooted, and properly so, in each service's experiences. The question ought not to have been whose approach was correct, but rather how wise it was to assume the existence of a single best approach to a given problem.

The American experience in Indochina only exacerbated the problems left unresolved in Korea. Worse yet, the expansion of a global network of military communications, established to ensure the control of nuclear weapons, allowed civilian authorities in Washington to exercise an unprecedented degree of control over the most minute tactical details.

As in Korea, the main clashes over command and control involved air operations. According to the same study of joint air operations, "During the early years of the U.S. military involvement in Vietnam command

and control of tactical air operations was unsatisfactory and would have led to disaster if U.S. forces had faced a capable opponent."[21] Once again the air force and the navy were often at odds over the application of air power. But in Indochina, in contrast to the situation in Korea, civilian interference in operations and tactics posed the biggest threat to effective command and control.

The micromanagement of the air war in Vietnam predated the passage by the U.S. Congress of the Tonkin Gulf Resolution on 7 August 1964. In June 1964 Secretary of Defense Robert S. McNamara began questioning the armament of individual aircraft, the number of missiles carried, and ordnance expended in the execution of assigned missions over Laos. When, on 5 August 1964, President Lyndon B. Johnson announced to the nation and the world, including the North Vietnamese, that retaliatory strikes for the Gulf of Tonkin attacks were "being given as I speak to you tonight," naval aircraft from the carriers *Ticonderoga* and *Constellation* were actually two and four hours respectively from their targets. The navy's carriers, already fully engaged in air operations over Laos, had been unable to comply with short-fused operational orders timed to coincide with the television habits of American viewers rather than with military necessity. As early as February 1965 Admiral Thomas Moorer lamented the military's loss of "flexibility to select weapons, aircraft, and the timing of strikes based on their knowledge of the target, enemy defenses, and environmental conditions." But McNamara was unconcerned about any loss of military effectiveness. In his mind, "our primary objective, of course, was to communicate our political resolve."[22]

As the war progressed, civilian control only strengthened. The historian Mark Clodfelter noted: "Despite air leaders' pleas for heavier bombing, Johnson and his principal civilian advisers tightly controlled the target selection process."[23] At the president's Tuesday luncheons, he and his principal civilian advisers—McNamara, Dean Rusk, William Bundy, and press secretary Bill Moyers—selected the targets and restricted areas for the week. Only months later did Johnson deign to invite the chairman of the Joint Chiefs of Staff. The luncheon group allocated targets in packages that specified numbers of sorties and desired damage rates.

This exercise of centralization run amok proved both ineffective and incredibly stupid. Targets already destroyed were bombed again to expend allocated sorties, while those undamaged in a no-sortie package went unbombed. Washington issued extremely rigid rules of engagement and established numerous buffer areas and prohibited or restricted zones where the military could not operate, or could not do so effectively.[24] American airmen watched helplessly as the communists constructed surface-to-air missile (SAM) batteries, declared off-limits by an administration unwilling to risk killing the Russian or Chinese advisers assumed to be working at the sites. American pilots were able, or in some cases directed, to strike only when the SAMs were operational and prepared to shoot them down.

The reaction within the American military to the Indochina experience was by no means monolithic. The movement toward greater jointness continued unabated. But the war also sparked a renaissance of thinking in the American military that began to bear fruit in the late 1970s and early 1980s. The services rethought their approaches to the art of war. The army, for example, developed its "airland battle" doctrine; the navy its "maritime strategy"; the marines "maneuver warfare"; and the air force a renewed concept of an "air campaign" that exploited technological developments, especially precision-guided munitions. Along with this flowering of military thought, shaped to a great extent by the bitter experience of civilian interference during the Vietnam war, came a new appreciation of the concept of decentralization. The navy began to reflect on its traditions of the initiative of the subordinate. The army chose to look abroad and discovered that same principle in the German concept of mission tactics—*Auftragtaktiks*.[25]

DESPITE the oft-stated determination of American political and military leaders never to fight another war in what might be called "Vietnam style," when a new twilight conflict began in the Persian Gulf in 1987 the desire to closely control the military response proved too difficult to resist, even for the hawkish administration of President Ronald W. Reagan. The United States fought the American-Iranian Tanker War, as the 1987–1988 conflict became known, under extremely restrictive rules of engagement, with operations and at times even tactics dictated from Washington.

In 1980 Saddam Hussein's Iraq invaded neighboring Iran, which had been weakened by the revolution epitomized by the rise of the Ayatollah Ruhollah Khomeini. After initial Iraqi successes, the war bogged down into a long struggle of attrition that had more in common with the First than the Second World War. Both Iraq and Iran sought to isolate their opponent from outside support. The Iraqis struck at Iranian ports along the Persian Gulf. But the Iranians had no comparable targets to strike, since Iraq shipped most of its oil via pipelines. Instead, the Iranians struck in the Persian Gulf at oil tankers owned by Arab states that supported Iraq, most notably Kuwait. When the Kuwaitis sought help, the United States responded in 1987 by reflagging Kuwaiti tankers with the American flag and sending additional naval forces to the area.

Centralized communications-based control shaped the Tanker War. The Reagan administration, fearful that the conflict might escalate, chose to rely on a show, rather than a use, of force by American naval units in the Gulf and its approaches to deter Iranian attacks. The administration permitted no direct strikes against Iranian territory, nor even operations on the Iranian side of the Persian Gulf. Instead of using naval air power against the handful of Iranian ships capable of laying mines, the U.S. Navy conducted a costly, difficult, and at times ineffective campaign of measures against mines. When the policy of deterrence failed, and Iran continued to mine and to attack shipping, the Reagan administration countered these attacks in a Vietnam-like fashion—with controlled, tit-for-tat responses.

Not until the U.S. Navy frigate *Samuel B. Roberts* struck an Iranian-laid mine on 14 April 1988 did the administration consider more than "proportionate" action. The on-scene commander, Rear Admiral Anthony Less, commander of the Joint Task Force Middle East (JTFME), argued for a more forceful response to this direct attack on a U.S. warship, and gained the full support of the chairman of the Joint Chiefs of Staff, Admiral William Crowe. The retaliation approved by the administration, dubbed Operation Praying Mantis, was nonetheless limited in scope, involving only strikes against Iranian forces in the Gulf. JTFME ships and aircraft would "take out" a pair of gas/oil separation platforms (GOSPs), and, thanks to Admiral Crowe's persistence, could also target an Iranian warship as compensation for the damage inflicted on the *Samuel B. Roberts*. If Less's forces could not locate an Iranian naval vessel, they would instead destroy a third GOSP.[26]

Less and his staff picked their targets carefully. The Sassan and Sirri GOSPs in the central and southern Persian Gulf were manned by Iranian forces and used to coordinate attacks on shipping. Both GOSPs were armed with ZSU-23mm automatic guns and had garrisons with rocket-propelled grenades and small arms. Sirri was also an active platform producing about 180,000 barrels of oil per day. For a naval target, attention focused on the *Sabalan,* one of Iran's four British-built 1,350-ton Vosper

Mark 5-class frigates (also known as *Saam*-class frigates). The *Sabalan* had earned a reputation in the Gulf during 1987 and 1988 for concentrating fire on the crew quarters of the tankers and other merchant vessels she attacked.

On 18 April 1988 the U.S. Navy fought its first surface engagement since the battle of Surigao Strait in October 1944. Operation Praying Mantis did not unfold as expected. The Americans destroyed the first two GOSPs, but the Iranian navy failed to respond. During the morning of 18 April, as Surface Action Groups (SAGs) Bravo and Charlie attacked the GOSPs, SAG Delta cruised into the Strait of Hormuz hoping to encounter the *Sabalan*. But the Iranian frigate remained in Bandar Abbas, moored between a pair of civilian tankers that provided protection against American sea- or air-launched Harpoon anti-ship missiles. Strike aircraft from the American carrier *Enterprise*'s surface combat air patrol (SUCAP) group were unable to get a clear target confirmation on the *Sabalan* and could not engage the frigate without risking an inadvertent hit on the adjacent ships.

The Iranian failure to respond promptly and as expected (or hoped) by JTFME had many causes. The Iranian command structure was far less coherent than the American, involving regular military forces—the navy and air force—and the Islamic Revolutionary Guards. A coordinated response necessitated centralized direction from Tehran, but on the morning of 18 April 1988 the focus of the Iranian government was elsewhere. About three hours before Less initiated Operation Praying Mantis, the Iraqi army began its "Blessed Ramadan" offensive against Iranian forces deployed in the Faw Peninsula. For the Iranians, the naval events in the Persian Gulf that same morning were little more than a distraction.

It was late morning before Tehran began to react. At about 1100 Iranian small boats sped into the southern Gulf, striking at oil facilities and commercial vessels. At 1146 Iranian speedboats attacked the American-flagged supply ship *Willie Tide* with rocket-propelled grenades. A few minutes later other Iranian boats shot up the *Scan Bay,* a Panamanian-flagged ship with fifteen Americans on board, and the British-flagged tanker *York Marine.* The SAG Delta frigate *Jack Williams* directed A-6E Intruder strike aircraft that were already airborne into attack positions. At the direction of Rear Admiral Less, two Intruders engaged the Iranians, dropping a string of Rockeye cluster bombs on the leading Swedish-built Boghammer cigarette boat. The surviving boats sped off and ran themselves aground on Abu Musa Island.

At 1130 Iran's French-built Combattante II fast-attack craft (FAC) *Joshan,* armed with a 76mm gun and an American-made Harpoon anti-ship missile, sortied from Bushire. After leaving port, the FAC headed southeast and began to close on SAG Charlie. The *Joshan's* sortie, along with the activity of the small boats, presented Less with a dilemma. Intelligence reports indicated that the larger Iranian frigates were preparing to steam out of Bandar Abbas.[27] Under the operational plan approved by the Reagan administration, JTFME was allowed to strike only a single Iranian ship. The 275-ton *Joshan* was not the chosen target, and sinking her might well end the day with the much larger *Sabalan* still intact. But the *Joshan* carried a functioning Harpoon, in fact, as the Americans knew, the only functioning Harpoon in the entire Iranian naval arsenal. The small FAC represented if not the only, certainly the most serious, threat to American naval forces in the Gulf on 18 April.

Had Less possessed the authority to act on his own initiative, his decision would have been simple. Intelligence provided information that kept him informed about the comings and goings of the Iranian military assets deployed against him. Less commanded an overwhelmingly superior force, well able to destroy the *Joshan, Sabalan, Sahand,* and any other Iranian ship afloat or in harbor that day. But the restrictions imposed by Washington gave him little room for initiative. Eager to sink one of the larger frigates, he chose not to attack the approaching *Joshan:* a decision that needlessly placed American naval personnel at risk. He ordered the *Enterprise* to launch elements of her war-at-sea strike group, in preparation for striking the *Sabalan* and the *Sahand* when they finally sortied, and directed the commander of SAG Charlie to warn off the FAC.

As the *Joshan* continued to close on SAG Charlie, the Americans issued four separate warnings to turn away, but the Iranians ignored them all. After several tense minutes, when the *Joshan* had closed to within thirteen nautical miles, Less granted SAG Charlie permission to engage. Captain J. F. Chandler, the *Wainwright's* commanding officer, directed his counterpart on the *Joshan:* "Stop your engines and abandon ship; I intend to sink you."

The commanding officer of the *Joshan* disregarded the demand for surrender and fired his lone Harpoon at the *Wainwright.* Less faced the "most tense moment" of his command in the Persian Gulf as the American-made anti-ship missile sped toward the cruiser.[28] But the Harpoon passed harmlessly down the starboard side of the *Wainwright,* either because of a malfunction or because the missile had been fired at such close range that it passed its target before reaching the programmed activation point for its homing radar.

SAG Charlie now unleashed its wrath against the small Iranian FAC. In the next few minutes the *Wainwright* and the *Simpson* fired five SM-1 Standard missiles in surface-to-surface mode at the *Joshan*. The *Bagley* followed with a Harpoon. All the SM-1s found their marks, leaving the *Joshan* a burning, sinking hulk over which the *Bagley*'s Harpoon passed harmlessly. SAG Charlie then finished off the Iranian ship with gunfire.

Having easily countered the small boats and destroyed or damaged the regular air and naval craft sent against SAG Charlie, JTFME now prepared for the third round of Iranian responses of the day. As expected, at 1459 one of the frigates finally steamed out of Bandar Abbas toward SAG Delta. Since the Iranians had demonstrated hostile intent in the attack on the *Wainwright,* Less now possessed greater freedom of action and prepared to strike at the frigates as they sortied. The *Enterprise*'s war-at-sea strike group was nearby, operating with the frigate *Joseph Strauss* near the Strait of Hormuz. The strike leader observed what he believed to be a *Saam*-class frigate, possibly the *Sabalan,* near Larak Island, proceeding on a southwesterly course at twenty-five knots. She was, in fact, the *Sahand,* sister to the *Sabalan*.

Three American aircraft—two A-6E Intruders and one F-14A Tomcat—approached and circled the frigate. The two Intruders were equipped with forward-looking infrared sensors, and the Tomcat carried an on-board television system. The Americans were convinced that the vessel was an Iranian man-of-war, but under the rules of engagement needed a visual identification before they could attack. To comply with the requirement, one of the Intruders had to conduct a low-level approach in an effort to "VID" (visually identify) the frigate. As the American aircraft approached, the Iranians replied with antiaircraft fire and launched heat-seeking SAMs. The Intruder released flares to confuse the missiles and broke hard to avoid fire. Having VID-ed the frigate, the Americans attacked. The Intruders launched two Harpoons, four Skippers, and several laser-guided bombs (LGBs); the *Joseph Strauss* fired a third Harpoon. Two of the Harpoons, three of the Skippers, one Walleye LGB, and several 1,000-pound bombs struck the *Sahand,* leaving the frigate dead in the water with decks ablaze. On the *Joseph Strauss,* crewmen felt the shock waves as the *Sahand*'s magazines caught fire and exploded. By early evening the *Sahand* had disappeared beneath the surface of the Persian Gulf.

As SAG Delta and the supporting aircraft demolished the *Sahand*, the *Sabalan* ventured out of Bandar Abbas. The SUCAP Intruders that had earlier attacked the Boghammers had refueled and were still airborne. Less directed them to an intercept position south of Larak Island. Again, to get the required VID, one of the Intruders had to risk flying low over the Iranian frigate; it drew fire and three SAMs, all of which missed. The leading Intruder dropped a 500-pound Mk-82 LGB, which struck the *Sabalan* amidships and exploded, breaking the back of the ship. As a second strike group raced toward the stricken frigate, Less, having already sunk his one frigate—the *Sahand*—requested permission from central command headquarters in Tampa, Florida, to finish off the *Sabalan*. This request went all the way up the chain of command to Washington, where Secretary of Defense Frank Carlucci and Chairman Crowe decided against further strikes. As the American forces watched, Iranian tugs took the *Sabalan*, dead in the water with stern down, in tow to Bandar Abbas.[29]

For the U.S. Navy, Operation Praying Mantis was a marked success. The early morning retaliatory strikes provoked the Iranians into the direct naval confrontation they had sought to avoid. The surface and air engagements cost the Iranians about half of their operational navy. Praying Mantis also demonstrated America's new striking power in surface warfare. Nevertheless, few new lessons were learned regarding command and control. U.S. communications worked well, although the delayed Iranian reaction and the absence of jamming or electronic countermeasures hardly amounted to a severe test of the system.

In Praying Mantis, and the entire Tanker War, global communications once again offered political leaders the means to micromanage operations, and even tactical encounters. The availability of advanced communications ensured that Admiral Less operated with his superiors, both in Tampa and in Washington, looking over his shoulder. The restrictions they imposed allowed the Iranians to fire their sole remaining Harpoon at the *Wainwright*, and forced American naval aviators to brave Iranian SAMs to get visual identification before releasing any ordnance. No one familiar with the abilities and character of Admiral Less can doubt that, had he been able to act on his own initiative on 18 April 1988, either surface-to-surface missiles fired by the ships of SAG Charlie or airborne strike aircraft would have destroyed the *Joshan* long before she was within missile range of the *Wainwright*. The fact that the pilot of an American attack aircraft had to check back up the entire chain of command for permission to finish off a ship that had entered the Gulf with obvious hostile intent recalls some of the worst examples from the Vietnam war. Against a more formidable foe, Praying Mantis would have been far from the nearly bloodless (for the Americans) operation that it was.

DESPITE GULF ARAB and indirect American support for Iraq during the long and costly war with Iran, Iraq's relations with its neighbors and with the United States deteriorated after 1988, and in August 1990 Saddam Hussein overran Kuwait. There followed a five-month-long period (Operation Desert Shield) during which the United States pieced together an international coalition to isolate Iraq, while simultaneously building up a powerful military force in the Arabian peninsula. On 17 January 1991, after Saddam refused to withdraw from Kuwait, the allies began Operation Desert Storm and unleashed a massive air campaign, striking targets not just in Kuwait but also in Iraq itself. On 24 February the U.S.-led United Nations coalition initiated a ground campaign that in one hundred hours liberated Kuwait and struck a heavy, though not crushing, blow against the Iraqi military.

While Desert Storm was another success for the American military, it was a frustrating experience for the U.S. Navy, principally because of command-related disagreements. Many of the problems regarding joint doctrine and operations that had plagued the service since the Korean War remained unresolved.

At the strategic level, the Gulf War was the first since 1950 in which the U.S. military and the U.S. Navy were able to operate without substantial civilian interference. President George Bush purposefully avoided intervening in the planning and operations of his military leaders. Bush was content to set the policy, establish the direction, assign the resources, and then allow his subordinates to execute policy largely as they saw fit. His service in the Second World War no doubt contributed to the trust and confidence he displayed in his generals and admirals. But perhaps of greater importance was the extent to which Iraq was isolated internationally. The prospects of "escalation," nuclear or conventional, were limited. Not even the Soviet Union supported the Iraqi dictator.

Operationally and tactically, the commander of the non-Arab allied forces in the Arabian peninsula, General H. Norman Schwarzkopf Jr., likewise did not interfere in the detailed planning or operations of his subordinate air, land, and sea commanders. Schwarzkopf provided the overall direction, but generally allowed his subordinates to execute their plans without undue interference.

Even without civilian or military micromanagement during the Gulf War, the U.S. Navy struggled with an operational and tactical command system that was highly centralized and rooted principally in the joint air campaign. Forty years after the Korean War, the navy still lacked the technical capacity to receive the massive air planning documents generated by the staff of the joint forces air component commander. Copies of the daily planning directive, distributed electronically between commands ashore, had to be flown out to the navy's carriers. As had been the case a half-century earlier, the navy and air force still went about their work, and for perfectly justifiable reasons, in very different fashions. As Colonel Brian E. Wages, the U.S. Air Force liaison officer assigned to the staff of the naval component commander, concluded: "Air Force-Navy interoperability was adversely impacted by fundamental differences in basic Service concepts of operations, procedures, and equipages."[30]

The air campaign reflected a high degree of air force–driven centralized planning and control. Nevertheless, the campaign worked, and worked well, destroying the Iraqi infrastructure and ensuring Saddam's defeat. But was the success attributable to the centralized planning process? The coalition employed overwhelming force against a weak, static, and unimaginative defense. Would the same approach have worked against a more formidable opponent, for example the Soviet Union? The air force chief of staff, General Merrill McPeak, admitted: "We don't really know whether the command structure was tough enough, durable enough, to really survive really difficult combat conditions." And Colonel Wages noted: "Military operations in the Gulf War were conducted under extremely advantageous circumstances: chiefly, ample time to prepare a comprehensive air campaign, and virtually unlimited resources with which to conduct it. It would be imprudent to expect to find the deck stacked so beneficially again."[31]

Analysts and historians continue to digest the lessons of the Gulf and subsequent wars, and will no doubt continue the debate in the future. With regard to naval command and control, the lessons are ambiguous. At the strategic and operational levels, the Gulf War clearly demonstrated the advantages of decentralization and reliance on initiative, while in the operational planning for the air campaign, as well as in its tactical execution, centralization remained the rule of the day.

The nature of the "global war on terror" is likely to further enhance centralization, since opponents such as al-Qaeda, the Taliban, and even the armed forces of Saddam Hussein's Iraq have lacked the technology to disrupt American communication networks. While small units of land-based forces and individual aircraft will encounter situations in which their on-scene commanders will have to act on their own initiative, the same will not be true for naval forces. Sea-based air and missile strikes will be closely controlled, and naval fleet commanders will rarely find themselves able to fully exercise initiative.

THE VERY HUMAN tendency to centralize—to control—continues to manifest itself in commanders. New communication and computer technologies have led the American military to refine the concept of command and control to a new level, known as C⁴I: command, control, communications, computers, and intelligence. There can be no doubt that the ever more technologically sophisticated command and control systems of the Western nations in the early twenty-first century enhance fighting power when employed against less technologically advanced states. The conflicts in which the United States became involved after the Persian Gulf War of 1991—against Serbia in 1999, Afghanistan in 2002, and Iraq in 2003—demonstrated that the deck remains stacked in the American military's favor.

Copernicus is the code name for one of the navy's most recent efforts to develop an effective computer-based C⁴I system. Ideally, Copernicus would allow every level of command to share video, voice, and data, not only by integrating the requisite systems and allowing for faster and greater flow of information, but also by assigning priorities and managing that flow in terms of both what is sent and who receives it. The system would also, ideally, be fully interoperable with other service systems, such as the U.S. Air Force's Horizon, the U.S. Army's Digitized Battlefield, and the joint Global Command & Control System.

Perhaps the foremost spokesman for Copernicus was retired U.S. Navy Vice Admiral Jerry O. Tuttle. In January 1998, at a conference at the Naval Postgraduate School in Monterey, California, Tuttle remarked: "Once, the battlespace was determined by the distance one could sense, detect and identify targets, and the range of one's weapons. The long lance of our arsenal of modern weapons—whose accuracy is independent of range—expands the battlespace to global dimensions. Our country's heroes' horizons necessarily have expanded from the next trench to a vast global perspective. There should be a continuum of education, from commissioning to retirement, including interactive education while deployed. This will create a whole new dimension to the meaning of the expression 'self paced.'"[32]

Despite the obvious attractions and very real advantages of such systems, some commentators pointed out potential drawbacks. Army Lieutenant Colonel Steven J. Fox, in an essay entitled "Unintended Consequences of Joint Digitization," argued that such systems could undermine the command hierarchy, blur the distinctions between the various levels of warfare, decrease local command prerogatives, and increase the "fragility of the force." He warned that the "military services could be entering into a new era of electronic micro-management."[33]

Thus the terms "decentralization" and "initiative" remained current for the U.S. Navy, and more broadly for the American military. *Joint Warfare of the U.S. Armed Forces,* published in 1991 shortly after the end of the Gulf War, stressed the "importance" of a flexible command structure. *Joint Pub 1,* as the manual was known, noted: "A clearly understood aim (commander's intent) enables subordinates to exercise initiative and flexibility while pursuing the commander's goals and priorities." Fittingly, *Joint Pub 1* used a naval example to illustrate the point, quoting battle orders drawn up in 1986 by Vice Admiral Henry C. Mustin III, then commander of the U.S. Second Fleet: "The key to the concept is simple: centralized planning and decentralized execution . . . The basic requirement of decentralized operations in general war is preplanned response in accordance with commonly understood doctrine. Lord Nelson did not win at Trafalgar because he had a great plan . . . He won because his subordinate commanders thoroughly understood that plan and their place in it well in advance of planned execution."[34]

U.S. Navy publications likewise voiced an institutional commitment to decentralization comparable to that evident in the service before and during the Second World War. In a series of publications the short-lived Naval Doctrine Command (NDC) used historical examples to illustrate the importance of "initiative" and "decentralization." *Naval Warfare,* the first in a series of NDC doctrinal manuals, noted: "Decisive action requires unity of effort . . . Rapid action, on the other had, requires a large degree of decentralization, giving those closest to the problem the freedom to solve it. To reconcile these seemingly contradictory requirements, we use our understanding of the main effort and a tool called the commander's intent."[35]

The sixth publication in the NDC series, *Naval Command and Control (NDP 6),* provided a more detailed discussion and explicit call for decentralization. After laying out the two fundamental approaches to command and control, namely centralized and decentralized, it emphasized that "detailed control" does not "normally work well in a rapidly changing situation . . . Therefore, it is not the preferred method of control under conditions of great uncertainty and time constraints." *NDP 6* stressed the advantages of a more decentralized approach: "Unity of effort is not attained by conformity imposed from above, but grows instead from spontaneous cooperation among all the elements of the force. By decentralizing decision making authority, we seek to heighten the tempo of operations and improve the force's ability to deal with rapidly changing situations. Moreover, because it relies on implicit understanding of mission requirements, mission control is much less vulnerable to disruption than detailed control."[36]

As the U.S. Navy prepared to enter the twenty-first century, it once again returned to basics and embraced the importance of doctrine combined with decentralized command and control. The lessons of the last half-century suggest that in the future those concepts will be challenged and undermined by civilian authorities, the demands of "jointness," or the advent of new technology. The historical record is replete with evidence that a communications network in place is a network that will be used, and on occasion abused. Nevertheless, the revival of the principle of "the initiative of the subordinate" within the navy, and the existence of its counterparts in both joint and other service doctrine, is an indication of institutional health, and a reason for hope.

CONCLUSION

The Crucial Paradox of Knowledge

$\mathcal{T}$HE HISTORY of naval command and control since the sixteenth century makes evident several truths. One is that the natural tendency of most commanders has been, and always will be, to control, to centralize; and yet the decentralization of command functions by senior officers commanding units led by well-trained and well-indoctrinated personnel generates greater fighting power by allowing subordinates the leeway to act on their own initiative when conditions warrant such action. Another is that decentralization is not always appropriate and is no guarantor of victory. Lastly, technological advances in communications, whatever their nature, will never eliminate the uncertainty associated with the "fog of war."

The fog of war is more a literary attempt at explanation than a definition of a concept. It can be, for a commander, considered synonymous with uncertainty—"imperfect correspondence between information and environment."[1] Under the pressures imposed by circumstances, most particularly time, a commander is forced to make myriad decisions on the basis of incomplete information.

The fog of war, viewed as uncertainty, is a concept that conforms to modern scientific thought, for example, Heisenberg's principle. A commander can no more know the position, condition, strength, and intentions of all enemy units than the scientist can pinpoint the exact location, speed, and direction of movement of subatomic particles. As finite creatures, humans face what Jacob Bronowski termed "the crucial paradox of knowledge." "Year by year we devise more precise instruments with which to observe nature. And when we look at the observations, we are discomfited to see that they are still fuzzy, and we feel that they are as un-

319

certain as ever. We seem to be running after a goal that lurches away from us to infinity every time we come within sight of it."[2]

That has certainly been true for the history of naval warfare. Just as most commanders in Nelson's day viewed numerary flag systems as the panacea for their problems of command and control, later generations of naval officers viewed the radio, telecommunications, or digital technologies as the answers to their dilemmas. But they all found themselves "discomfited," despite major technological advances.

Why? The same technology that appeared to offer solutions to the puzzles of command simultaneously altered, often for the worse, the nature of the situations confronting a commander. In the age of sail it was not uncommon for the crew to be piped to dinner when lookouts sighted the enemy fleet because the approach to battle, as at Trafalgar, could take hours. While Nelson's communications were primitive, the pressures of decisionmaking he faced were relatively mild.[3] By comparison, Commodore Arleigh Burke, on a U.S. Navy destroyer at Kula Gulf in the southwest Pacific in March 1943, hesitated for only ninety seconds and nearly lost his ship. Even though the means of communication at Burke's disposal were vastly superior to those available in the age of sail, the same technology that had equipped navies with radios had so changed the tempo of naval warfare that Burke was no better off than Sir Horatio. Like Nelson, Burke deduced that there was "no time in battle to give orders" and chose instead to rely on personal doctrine and the initiative of his subordinates.[4]

As Bronowski implied, scientific and technological advances do not so much fix reality as allow us to explore it, to extend the horizon of our knowledge. The astronomer who develops a more powerful telescope better fixes the position of a known star, but discovers at the same time many more stars whose existence had been unknown. Commanders served by today's technology receive much more data, but at the same time the increasing complexity of warfare leaves just as much if not more information beyond their grasp.

Simply put, uncertainty is not a measurable amount of unknown information; rather, it is part of the human condition, a reality of life with which our minds grapple every day. Fortunately, our thought processes work in such a fashion that we are able to make sensible decisions without complete information. We spend our entire lives functioning within a fog of uncertainty. As Michael S. Gazzaniga demonstrated, "believing is what we humans do best." Despite our best efforts and suppositions, humans usually establish not analytic, but belief structures.[5]

Uncertainty is also a precondition of warfare. In the absence of uncertainty, there would be no conflict. Martin Van Creveld has written:

> As in any game, where the outcome of a war can be calculated in advance, fighting does not make sense since it can neither serve as a test nor be experienced as fun. Such a situation permits armed conflict to be replaced by a computer; indeed . . . one reason why low-intensity conflict is taking over from war and pushing the latter into complex environments is precisely because simpler ones are beginning to be dominated by computers.[6]

In the early twenty-first century the scientific community understands that decisionmaking is based on selected available information. If the human mind functioned as a purely analytical calculating machine, the computer would have already dispossessed us. The machine as it acquires more information functions more slowly, but the brain works faster. The ability of the human mind to learn, and to focus, is what keeps it ahead of the computer, keeps computer scientists busily at work on artificial intelligence, and ensures that people are the central element in warfare.

The proposition that the best way to control veteran subordinates is not to try is counterintuitive. Over the centuries navies, far more than armies, have employed decentralized approaches. Until the late nineteenth century admiralties had no choice at the strategic and operational levels of war but to trust to the initiative of subordinates operating on distant stations. But when new technological means of control became available, naval officers were just as eager as their foot-slogging brethren to adopt more centralized schemes of command. Only a handful of commanders, of whom Nelson is the best example, were willing to entrust their professional fates to their subordinates. Even fewer navies have formally embraced decentralization as official doctrine.[7]

There exists an evident tendency in some contemporary naval circles to view communications and information technology as the answer to the problems of command and the means by which the fog of war can be dissipated. The ability to micromanage subunits is often considered a "force enhancer."[8] That is why so many naval officers look to systems such as Copernicus to fulfill that promise. But the same expectations were held of flag signals late in the eighteenth century and of the radio in the years between the world wars.

Nelson understood that the fog of war was not a cloud of uncertainty that could be whisked away if only the appropriate communicative means were at hand, but an element inherent to warfare as to life itself: an element as resistant to the dissipatory efforts of commanders as real fog was to the blows of a sword. That element, like fog, could protectively enshroud a force led by men prepared to make decisions on their own within a tactical framework provided by their superior.

Nelson's philosophy of command has much in common with the underlying assumptions of chaos theory, a branch of science that emerged in the late twentieth century. James Gleick, whose book popularized the theory, wrote that patterns of chaos forecasting are inexact and yet remain within bounds, in what he termed "an orderly disorder."[9] Similarly, Nelson, while he sought disorder in battle, strove to contain it within the personal tactical doctrine he imparted to his subordinates. "On occasions we must sometimes have a regular confusion," he wrote in 1801, "and that apparent confusion must be the most regular method which could be pursued on the occasion."[10]

But history also demonstrates that decentralization is not suitable for all navies at all times. Suffren's attempts to decentralize failed primarily because he lacked the experienced and confident subordinates necessary to make the system work. Moreover, in a modern world shadowed by the threat of catastrophic nuclear escalation, restrictive rules of engagement and micromanagement may well be justified. Nor does decentralization guarantee success. The Japanese relied upon rather decentralized command and control and yet lost the Second World War. And as Nimitz learned at Leyte Gulf, even a decentralized system staffed by commanders of Halsey's caliber could commit grievous errors.

And yet the victories of the decentralizers over the past several centuries suggest that in battle commanders blessed with capable, well-trained and well-indoctrinated men and women ought not to expect the latest communicative technology to ensure triumph, but should rely instead, as much as reasonably possible, on the talents, judgment, and initiative of their subordinates. Despite major advances in technology, wars are still fought by people, and finding the best means to exploit their talents remains central to the realization of victory.

Notes

Prologue: A Regular Confusion

1. Log of the *Zealous,* 1 Aug. 1798, T. Sturges Jackson, ed., *Logs of the Great Sea Fights, 1794–1805,* 2 vols. (London: Navy Records Society, 1899–1900), 2:12–13; Samuel Hood to Viscount Hood, 10 Aug. 1798, ibid., 20. The French fleet actually consisted of only thirteen ships of the line and four frigates. The number following a ship's name denotes the number of cannon carried by the vessel, although it should be used as a comparative measurement of strength rather than an exact count.

2. G. J. Marcus, *The Age of Nelson: The Royal Navy, 1793–1815* (New York: Viking, 1971), 130, 129. Oliver Warner, *Nelson's Battles* (New York: Macmillan, 1965), 58.

3. Piers Mackesy, *Statesmen at War: The Strategy of Overthrow, 1798–1799* (London: Longman Group, 1974), 41. Dundas to Spencer, 10 Sept. 1798, *Private Papers of George, Second Earl Spencer: First Lord of the Admiralty, 1794–1801,* ed. Julian S. Corbett and Herbert S. Richmond, 4 vols. (London: Navy Records Society, 1913–1924), 2:463. Spencer to Dundas, 23 Sept. 1798, ibid., 469–70. Nelson had become a national hero after the battle of Cape St. Vincent on 14 Feb. 1797; see Chapter 6.

4. Spencer to St. Vincent, 16 Sept. 1798, Spencer, *Private Papers,* 2:459, 460. On British strategy and the impact of Nelson's failure and his subsequent victory, see Mackesy, *Statesmen at War,* chs. 1–3; A. B. Rodger, *The War of the Second Coalition, 1798–1801: A Strategic Commentary* (Oxford: Clarendon Press, 1964), chs. 1–5. When news of Nelson's victory at Aboukir Bay reached Constantinople, the Turks immediately notified the Russians that their fleet could pass through the straits, and a few days later, on 9 September, Turkey declared war on France.

5. Warner, *Nelson's Battles,* 62.

6. Ibid.

7. Marcus, *Age of Nelson*, 131. The log times for the battle of the Nile are notoriously inconsistent. For example, according to British logs, the French ship of the line *l'Orient* exploded as early as 2137, by the log of the *Swiftsure*, or as late as 2330, by the log of the *Orion*. See editor's introductory note, Jackson, *Logs*, 2:5.

8. O. Troude, *Batailles navales de la France*, 4 vols. (Paris: Challamel Ainé, 1867–1868), 3:95, 96–97, 91; Louis Antoine Fauvelet de Bourrienne, *Memoirs of Napoleon Bonaparte*, ed. R. W. Phipps (New York: Scribner, 1891–1892), 1:147.

9. At St. Lucia in 1778 an anchored British fleet held off a vastly superior French force. At St. Kitts in 1782 an anchored British fleet repulsed a superior French fleet. See Piers Mackesy, *The War for America, 1775–1783* (Cambridge, Mass.: Harvard University Press, 1965), 229–32, 455–56; Alfred Thayer Mahan, *The Influence of Sea Power upon History, 1660–1783*, 12th ed. (Boston: Little, Brown, 1918), 364–67, 473–76.

10. Many of Brueys's ships were in poor shape. Some had previously been condemned. They were poorly armed and woefully undermanned. *Le Tonnant*, for example, had sailed from Toulon with 400 men in a ship that should have had a crew of 866. Troude, *Batailles navales*, 3:91.

11. August Fournier, *Napoleon the First: A Biography*, ed. Edward Gaylord Bourne (New York: Henry Holt, 1903), 133. But, as Rodger points out in *War of the Second Coalition*, 59, Brueys clearly linked his assertion of impregnability to Bonaparte's ability to set up batteries ashore that could cover both ends of the French line. A pair of guns were positioned on Aboukir Island, but the promised 40-gun heavy battery never materialized.

12. The standard ship of the line drew about 30 feet, or 5 fathoms.

13. Oliver Warner, *The Battle of the Nile* (New York: Macmillan, 1960), 56. Berry's account is in *The Dispatches and Letters of Vice Admiral Lord Nelson*, ed. Nicholas Harris Nicolas (London: H. Colburn, 1845), 3:48–56.

14. Warner, *Battle of the Nile*, 73. For Nelson's signals see Jackson, *Logs*, 2:56–57; Brian Tunstall, *Naval Warfare in the Age of Sail: The Evolution of Fighting Tactics, 1650–1815*, ed. Nicholas Tracy (Annapolis: Naval Institute Press, 1990), 226. Several of Nelson's captains, understanding his probable mode of attack, had already prepared their ships to anchor with springs. Jackson, *Logs*, 2:12–13, 62.

15. The ships leading the French line, which appeared to Nelson to be the van, were actually the rear division of the fleet. Thus French accounts often discuss the inability of the van to succor the rear, whereas British accounts discuss the failure of the rear to aid the van.

16. Troude, *Batailles navales*, 3:97. Berry, in Nelson, *Dispatches and Letters*, 3:48–56; Marcus, *Age of Nelson*, 132.

17. Jackson, *Logs*, 2:22.

18. Warner, *Battle of the Nile,* 92.

19. Troude, *Batailles navales,* 3:98–99. Villeneuve quoted in Jackson, *Logs,* 2:77–79.

20. Quoted in Warner, *Battle of the Nile,* 87–88. This colorful anecdote may be apocryphal. According to French accounts, Brueys died earlier, at about 1930, when a ball ripped through his thigh and nearly cut him in two. He did remain on the quarterdeck until his death.

21. Jackson, *Logs,* 2:44.

22. Ibid., 95. Nelson's note of Berry's reported conversation with Howe, in Howe to Nelson, 3 Oct. 1798, *Dispatches and Letters,* 3:84. Warner, *Battle of the Nile,* 121.

23. For overviews see Norman Hampson, *The Enlightenment* (New York: Penguin, 1968); Ernst Cassirer, *The Philosophy of the Enlightenment* (Boston: Beacon, 1965); Carl L. Becker, *The Heavenly City of the Eighteenth-Century Philosophers* (New Haven: Yale University Press, 1932).

24. On French advances and their impact on the British see Tunstall, *Naval Warfare.*

25. John D. Steinbruner, *The Cybernetic Theory of Decision: New Dimensions of Political Analysis* (Princeton: Princeton University Press, 1974), 109.

26. Sam Slick: Thomas Chandler Haliburton, quoted in William Henry Fitchet, *Nelson and His Captains: Sketches of Famous Seamen* (London: Smith, Elder, 1902), at www.aboutnelson.co.uk/characterstudy.htm. Nelson to William Locker, 9 Feb. 1799, *Dispatches and Letters,* 3:260. Steinbruner defines the cybernetic paradigm as one in which the decisionmaker "makes no calculations of outcome and simply monitors certain information channels via some decision rule." *Cybernetic Theory,* 109. A "decision rule" may have earlier been adopted as a result of an analytic process. But whereas in an analytic paradigm an analytic method is followed throughout the decisionmaking process, in the cybernetic paradigm the previously adopted "decision rule," rather than a true analytic operation, is used to reach decisions.

27. See Nelson's 1803 tactical memorandum in Julian S. Corbett, ed., *Fighting Instructions, 1530–1816* (London: Navy Records Society, 1905), 313–16.

28. Nelson to Lady Hamilton, 1 Oct. 1805, *Dispatches and Letters,* 7:60–61.

29. Berry's narrative in Nelson, *Dispatches and Letters,* 3:48–56. Nelson to Howe, ibid., 3:230–31.

30. Nelson-Keats conversation, ibid., 7:241n. Nelson to Troubridge, 29 Mar. 1801, in John Knox Laughton, ed., *The Naval Miscellany* (London: Navy Records Society, 1902), 1:424–25.

31. U.S. Department of Defense, *Dictionary of Military and Associated Terms* (Washington: Government Printing Office, 1989), 77.

32. Carl von Clausewitz, *On War,* ed. and trans. Michael Howard and Peter Paret (Princeton: Princeton University Press, 1989), 117–21.

33. Martin Van Creveld, *Command in War* (Cambridge, Mass.: Harvard University Press, 1985), 274.

34. Department of Defense, *Dictionary*, 77. U.S. Department of the Navy, *Sound Military Decision* (Newport, R.I.: Naval War College, 1942). Author's interview with Admiral Arleigh A. Burke, 27 May 1986.

35. Mahan, *Influence of Sea Power upon History*, vi.

36. John Francis Guilmartin Jr., *Gunpowder and Galleys: Changing Technology and Mediterranean Warfare at Sea in the Sixteenth Century* (London: Cambridge University Press, 1974).

37. Department of the Navy, *Naval Doctrine Publication 6: Naval Command and Control* (Washington: Department of the Navy, 1995), 5.

1. Land Warfare Afloat: Before 1650

1. Thucydides, *The Peloponnesian War* (Baltimore: Penguin, 1954), 21. See Chester G. Starr, *The Influence of Sea Power on Ancient History* (New York: Oxford University Press, 1989), 3–6.

2. See Guilmartin, *Gunpowder and Galleys*, 194–220; John H. Pryor, *Geography, Technology, and War: Studies in the Maritime History of the Mediterranean, 649–1571* (Cambridge: Cambridge University Press, 1992), 57–86, 25–57.

3. John Noble Wilford, *The Mapmakers: The Story of the Great Pioneers in Cartography from Antiquity to the Space Age* (New York: Vintage, 1982), 22–23, 25–33; Lionel Casson, *The Ancient Mariners: Seafarers and Sea Fighters of the Mediterranean in Ancient Times*, 2d ed. (Princeton: Princeton University Press, 1991), 158.

4. Casson, *Ancient Mariners*, 23, 124, 114–15, 195. References to coast pilots can be found as early as the mid-fourth century BC.

5. See G. J. Marcus, *The Conquest of the North Atlantic* (New York: Oxford University Press, 1981), 100–18; E. G. R. Taylor, *The Haven-Finding Art: A History of Navigation from Odysseus to Captain Cook* (London: Hollis and Carter, 1956), 3–32. Greek and Roman ships generally stayed in port between October and April. Despite advances over the next thousand years, in the eleventh and twelfth centuries Christian and Muslim ships in the Mediterranean still stayed in port between November and March. Pryor, *Geography, Technology, and War*, 88. Northern sailors likewise remained ashore in the fall and winter. Marcus, *Conquest of the North Atlantic*, 101.

6. Casson, *Ancient Mariners*, 178. Pryor, *Geography, Technology, and War*, 153–59, 193–92, 193–96. Marcus, *Conquest of the North Atlantic*, 126, 161–62.

7. Frederic C. Lane, "The Economic Meaning of the Invention of the Compass," *American Historical Review* 68 (April 1963): 605–17. Carlo M. Cipolla, *Guns, Sails, and Empires: Technological Innovation and the Early Phases of European Expansion, 1400–1700* (New York: Minerva, 1965), 76n.

8. Casson, *Ancient Mariners*, 202–06. On the capabilities of ancient sea

power see Anthony Papalas, "Polycrates of Samos and the First Greek Trireme Fleet," *Mariner's Mirror* 85 (Feb. 1999): 10–11, 18n.

9. Pryor, *Geography, Technology, and War*, 85.

10. Fernand Braudel, *Civilization and Capitalism, 15th–18th Century*, vol. 2: *The Wheels of Commerce* (New York: Harper and Row, 1979), 361.

11. Guilmartin, *Gunpowder and Galleys*, 62. Marcus, *Conquest of the North Atlantic*, 94–95.

12. Cipolla, *Guns, Sails, and Empires*, 77–79; Pryor, *Geography, Technology, and War*, 39–43; Fernand Braudel, *Civilization and Capitalism, 15th–18th Century*, vol. 1: *The Structures of Everyday Life: The Limits of the Possible* (New York: Harper and Row, 1979), 402–405.

13. William Laird Clowes, *The Royal Navy: A History from the Earliest Times to the Present* (London: Sampson Low, Marston, 1897–1903), 1:101, 143–44, 265, 346–47. In the Red Sea in the spring of 1517, well-handled Ottoman galleys defeated a Portuguese squadron at Jiddah. Guilmartin, *Gunpowder and Galleys*, 7–15.

14. Cipolla, *Guns, Sails, and Empires*, 81–82. Clowes, *Royal Navy*, 409.

15. Guilmartin, *Gunpowder and Galleys*, 175, 273; Cipolla, *Guns, Sails, and Empires*, 41–45. Under Queen Elizabeth I the English crown established export controls to limit the outflow of both iron cannon and the technology to produce them. Cipolla, ibid., 45.

16. See C. R. Boxer, *Four Centuries of Portuguese Expansion, 1415–1825* (Berkeley: University of California Press, 1969).

17. Frederick Charles Danvers, *The Portuguese in India: Being a History of the Rise and Decline of Their Eastern Empire*, 2 vols. (London: W. H. Allen, 1894), 1:139–41. Clark G. Reynolds, *Command of the Sea: The History and Strategy of Maritime Empires* (New York: William Morrow, 1974), 127–34.

18. Stanford J. Shaw, *History of the Ottoman Empire and Modern Turkey*, vol. 1: *Empire of the Gazis: The Rise and Decline of the Ottoman Empire, 1280–1808* (Cambridge: Cambridge University Press, 1976), 83, 99.

19. D'Albuquerque and other governor general quoted in Cipolla, *Guns, Sails, and Empires*, 137. Ibid., 138. Guilmartin, *Gunpowder and Galleys*, 257.

20. Most long-range imperial projects in the Indian Ocean were undertaken by government-sponsored private companies, the most famous of which is the Honourable John Company—England's East India Company. English, French, and Dutch companies raised their own money, their own armies, and their own navies, and established their own governmental centers in the Indian Ocean. It could not have been otherwise.

21. Francis Bacon, "Of the True Greatness of Kingdoms and Estates," in *The Essays, Colors of Good and Evil, & Advancement of Learning* (London: Macmillan, 1925), 77–78.

22. Ibid., 78. My emphasis.

23. John G. B. Hutchins, *The American Maritime Industries and Public Policy, 1789–1914: An Economic History* (Cambridge, Mass.: Harvard University Press, 1941), 3.

24. Garrett Mattingly, *The Armada* (Boston: Houghton Mifflin, 1987), 81.

25. Ibid., 75–77.

26. Ibid., 78.

27. David Howarth, *The Voyage of the Armada: The Spanish Story* (New York: Penguin, 1981), 41.

28. Ibid., 64–66. Colin Martin and Geoffrey Parker, *The Spanish Armada* (New York: Norton, 1988), 148.

29. Howarth, *Voyage of the Armada,* 157–58. Mattingly, *Armada,* 321–22.

30. Mattingly, *Armada,* 201. Julian S. Corbett, *Drake and the Tudor Navy: With a History of the Rise of England as a Maritime Power,* 2 vols. (New York: Burt Franklin, n.d.), 1:252–53.

31. E.g., the epic Greek naval victory over the Persians at Salamis in 480 BC was decided principally by the mêlée. William Ledyard Rodgers, *Greek and Roman Naval Warfare: A Study of Strategy, Tactics, and Ship Design from Salamis (480 B.C.) to Actium (31 B.C.)* (Annapolis: Naval Institute Press, 1964), 92.

32. See Michael Lewis, *England's Sea-Officers: The Story of the Naval Profession* (London: George Allen and Unwin, 1939), 17–51.

33. Corbett, *Drake and the Tudor Navy,* 1:385.

34. Jean Froissart, *The Chronicle of Froissart,* trans. John Bourchier, 6 vols. (New York: AMS Press, 1967): 1:147–48.

35. Corbett, *Fighting Instructions,* 3–13.

36. Ibid., 5, 12.

37. Diego Garcia de Palacio, *Nautical Instruction: A.D. 1587,* trans. J. Bankston (Bisbee, Ariz.: Terrenate, 1988), 28. For a contemporary Spanish naval manual, see ibid., 151–58. English tactics against the Armada bear some similarity to those employed by Reiter cavalry during the Thirty Years' War.

38. Howarth, *Voyage of the Armada,* 97–98. Quotation from Mattingly, *Armada,* 216–17.

39. Corbett, *Fighting Instructions,* 50–52.

40. Russell F. Weigley, *The Age of Battles: The Quest for Decisive Warfare from Breitenfeld to Waterloo* (Bloomington: Indiana University Press, 1991), 131. Quotation from W. G. Perrin, ed., *Boteler's Dialogues* (London: Navy Records Society, 1929), 307.

2. The Anglo-Dutch Wars

1. Because of inconclusive accounts, the numbers of ships present in encounters of the Anglo-Dutch Wars are approximate.

2. C. R. Boxer, *The Dutch Seaborne Empire: 1600–1800* (New York: Knopf,

1965), 27. Jill Lisk, *The Struggle for Supremacy in the Baltic, 1600–1725* (London: University of London Press, 1967), 17–23. On Anglo-Dutch hostility see Bernard Capp, *Cromwell's Navy: The Fleet and the English Revolution, 1648–1660* (Oxford: Clarendon Press, 1989), 73–78; Herbert Richmond, *The Navy as an Instrument of Policy, 1558–1727* (Cambridge: Cambridge University Press, 1953), 95–102. On Amboyna see Clowes, *Royal Navy,* 2:27; Brian Gardner, *The East India Company: A History* (New York: Dorset, 1971), 38–40.

3. Charles Wilson, *Profit and Power: A Study of England and the Dutch Wars* (London: Longmans, Green, 1957), 52–53. Boxer, *Dutch Seaborne Empire,* 91.

4. See Clowes, *Royal Navy,* 2:144–48; *The Letters of Robert Blake,* ed. J. R. Powell (Greenwich: Navy Records Society, 1937), 158–59. According to some accounts, Tromp, as he sailed eastward, learned from a dispatch boat of the earlier English attack on the Channel convoy. See Francis Vere, *Salt in Their Blood: The Lives of the Famous Dutch Admirals* (London: Cassell, 1955), 66. Other accounts attribute Tromp's reversal of course to a wayward English shot across a Dutch bow that took off the arm of a seaman. See Jacob de Liefde, *The Great Dutch Admirals,* 4th ed. (London: Strahan, n.d.), 88.

5. Jaap R. Bruijn, *The Dutch Navy of the Seventeenth and Eighteenth Centuries* (Columbia: University of South Carolina Press, 1993), 70.

6. Granville Penn, *Memorials of the Professional Life and Times of Sir William Penn, Knt.: Admiral and General of the Fleet, during the Interregnum; Admiral, and Commissioner of the Admiralty and the Navy, after the Restoration, 1644–1670,* 2 vols. (London: James Duncan, 1833) 1:446–50. Clowes, *Royal Navy,* 2:166–70; Vere, *Salt in Their Blood,* 78.

7. Clowes, *Royal Navy,* 2:170; Richmond, *Navy as an Instrument of Policy,* 110–112.

8. Richmond, *Navy as an Instrument of Policy,* 108–109, considers the directive to Tromp to both damage the English fleet and escort the convoy a strategic mistake.

9. Roger Beadon, *Robert Blake: Sometime Commanding All the Fleets and Naval Forces of England* (London: Edward Arnold, 1935), 164–68.

10. Ibid., 112–14; Capp, *Cromwell's Navy,* 79–80.

11. Quotation from Samuel Rawson Gardiner and C. T. Atkinson, eds., *Letters and Papers Relating to the First Dutch War,* 6 vols. (Greenwich: Navy Records Society, 1899–1930), 4:165. From reports by Tromp and other Dutch commanders, the battle does not appear to have been forced on a reluctant Tromp. See ibid., 118–22, 177–86, 187–94, 194–97.

12. "In both official and unofficial reports of the actions of this time an almost superstitious reverence is shown in avoiding tactical details." Corbett, *Fighting Instructions,* 96–97. I suspect that the problem was more an inability than an unwillingness to recount details.

13. The Dutch generally had more divisions than the English. See R. E. J.

Weber, "The Introduction of the Single Line-ahead as a Battle Formation by the Dutch, 1665–1666," *Mariner's Mirror* 73 (Feb. 1987): 7–8. The army officers commanding the English fleet are often referred to by their army ranks, for example, General Monck. They are also sometimes listed as generals-at-sea, or by equivalent naval rank, such as admiral. The rank associated with the squadron organization described here is thus idealized.

14. Corbett, *Fighting Instructions,* 89, 91.

15. On tactics see ibid., 81–90; Clowes, *Royal Navy,* 2:151–52; Bruijn, *Dutch Navy,* 70–71.

16. Even dreadnoughts had to fire their guns broadside to maximize their firepower. Only the development of effective surface-to-surface missiles beginning in the 1960s solved the problem of movement and combat in naval warfare.

17. Tunstall, *Naval Warfare,* 18–19, 19n; Corbett, *Fighting Instructions,* 95–96.

18. *The Journal of Maarten Harpertszoon Tromp, Anno 1639,* ed. and trans. C. R. Boxer (Cambridge: Cambridge University Press, 1930), 209.

19. Ibid., 60–68. Weber, "Introduction of the Single Line-ahead," 8. Michael Lewis, *The Navy of Britain: A Historical Portrait* (London: George Allen and Unwin, 1949), 449. Geoffrey Parker, *The Military Revolution: Military Innovation and the Rise of the West, 1500–1800* (Cambridge: Cambridge University Press, 1989), 100, citing Boxer, states that it was at the Downs that the line ahead was first used in European waters. But Boxer is clear that the Dutch used it at Dunkirk.

20. Corbett, *Fighting Instructions,* 95; Tunstall, *Naval Warfare,* 19. For the instructions see Gardiner, *First Dutch War,* 4:262–73; my emphasis.

21. Gardiner, *First Dutch War,* 4:216. The surviving ships from the Mediterranean squadron reached England in May.

22. Gardiner, *First Dutch War,* 4:296, 299–302, 317–18.

23. This account is drawn principally from Tromp's, and also from others published in Gardiner, ibid., 5:21–24, 82–85, and in Clowes, *Royal Navy,* 2:186–89. Wind and course directions are approximate. The wind blew generally from the north, at times from the northwest, and at other times from the northeast.

24. Tunstall, *Naval Warfare,* 19–21. Gardiner, *First Dutch War,* 5:83–84.

25. E.g., "The victory off the Gabbard was decisive." Capp, *Cromwell's Navy,* 82.

26. For details see Clowes, *Royal Navy,* 2:193–200; Tunstall, *Naval Warfare,* 20–21.

27. On Cromwell's policies see Capp, *Cromwell's Navy,* 85–114.

28. Richmond, *Navy as an Instrument of Policy,* 140–49.

29. On the Dutch naval system, with its five independent admiralties, see Bruijn, *Dutch Navy,* 29–39, 75–82.

30. On Tromp's linear tactics see Gardiner, *First Dutch War,* 5:20; Bruijn, *Dutch Navy,* 71–72. De Guiche quoted in Corbett, *Fighting Instructions,* 118–19.

31. Tunstall, *Naval Warfare*, 36.

32. Ibid.

33. Corbett, *Fighting Instructions*, 122–28.

34. Weigley, *Age of Battles*, 145–47.

35. Corbett, *Fighting Instructions*, 134–35. Tunstall, *Naval Warfare*, 23–24.

36. Tunstall, *Naval Warfare*, 22.

37. *The Journal of Edward Mountagu, First Earl of Sandwich: Admiral and General at Sea, 1659–1665*, ed. R. C. Anderson (Greenwich: Navy Records Society, 1929), 222.

38. Ibid., 224–29; F. R. Harris, *The Life of Edward Mountagu, K. G., First Earl of Sandwich, 1625–1672*, 2 vols. (London: John Murray, 1912), 1:298–309.

39. Corbett, *Fighting Instructions*, 115; Clowes, *Royal Navy*, 2:265; Richard Ollard, *Pepys: A Biography* (New York: Holt, Rinehart and Winston, 1974), 138.

40. Corbett, *Fighting Instructions*, 134–35. Tunstall, *Naval Warfare*, 23, doubts that any such division existed.

41. Richmond, *Navy as an Instrument of Policy*, 160–62.

42. Quoted in Mahan, *Influence of Sea Power upon History*, 130.

43. Clowes, *Royal Navy*, 2:268–77; Mahan, *Influence of Sea Power upon History*, 117–26. George Edinger, *Rupert of the Rhine: The Pirate Prince* (London: Hutchinson, 1936), 247.

44. Corbett, *Fighting Instructions*, 129–30.

45. Ibid., 130n. Tunstall, *Naval Warfare*, 26.

46. Corbett, *Fighting Instructions*, 146–49. Corbett dated these instructions to 1672. Tunstall and others have determined that they were issued in 1666, shortly before the St. James's Day battle. Tunstall, *Naval Warfare*, 29–30n.

47. Clowes, *Royal Navy*, 2:281–83; P. Blok, *The Life of Admiral de Ruyter* (London: Ernest Benn, 1933), 238–51, discusses de Ruyter's anger at Tromp's actions.

48. Ollard, *Pepys*, 155, 159, 158–62; Clowes, *Royal Navy*, 2:286–89; Richmond, *Navy as an Instrument of Policy*, 163–67.

49. Bruijn, *Dutch Navy*, 87–88; Clowes, *Royal Navy*, 2:288–96; Ollard, *Pepys*, 158–70.

50. Richmond, *Navy as an Instrument of Policy*, 168–70; Ollard, *Pepys*, 206–207.

51. Clowes, *Royal Navy*, 2:441–44; Ollard, *Pepys*, 206.

52. See Carl J. Ekberg, *The Failure of Louis XIV's Dutch War* (Chapel Hill: University of North Carolina Press, 1979), 171–72.

53. Bruijn, *Dutch Navy*, 88–89.

54. Tunstall, *Naval Warfare*, 32; Corbett, *Fighting Instructions*, 146–48.

55. According to Clowes, *Royal Navy*, 322, Louis XIV sent Estrées to the Bastille for two years. See also Andrew Trout, *Jean-Baptiste Colbert* (Boston: Twayne, 1978), 146; Ekberg, *Failure of Louis XIV's Dutch War*, 163–68. Colbert advised Estrées to "change his style." Inès Murat, *Colbert* (Charlottesville: Uni-

versity Press of Virginia, 1984), 177. The difficulties of multinational operations affect all military services, not just navies. NATO, for example, has had to work diligently to provide common doctrine and communications methods and equipment for its forces, be they air, land, or sea.

56. Mahan, *Influence of Sea Power upon History,* 116. Reynolds, *Command of the Sea,* 182.

57. Weigley, *Age of Battles,* 145–47. Raoul Castex was among the first to link the indecisiveness of eighteenth-century naval warfare to developments in the final decades of the preceding century. See Castex, *Les idées militaires de la marine du XVIIIᵐᵉ siècle: de Ruyter à Suffren* (Paris: L. Fournier, 1911), 9–28.

58. Tunstall, *Naval Warfare,* 19. For brief biographies of the three men see Geoffrey Ridsdill Smith and Margaret Toynbee, *Leaders of the Civil Wars, 1642–1648* (Kineton: Roundwood, 1977), 1–2, 16–17, 42–43.

59. On the evolution of tactics see Hans Delbrück, *History of the Art of Warfare,* vol. 3: *The Dawn of Modern Warfare,* trans. Walter J. Renfroe, Jr. (Lincoln: University of Nebraska Press, 1990), 269–85. See also David Chandler, *Marlborough as Military Commander,* 91–93; Chandler, *The Campaigns of Napoleon* (New York: Macmillan, 1966), 344–50; Gunther E. Rothenberg, *The Art of Warfare in the Age of Napoleon* (London: B. T. Batsford, 1977), 67–70.

60. Liddell Hart quoted in Robert Debs Heinl Jr., *Dictionary of Military and Naval Quotations* (Annapolis: United States Naval Institute, 1966), 208.

61. Colin S. Gray, *The Leverage of Sea Power: The Strategic Advantage of Navies in War* (New York: Free Press, 1992). J. Holland Rose, writing in 1927, advanced the view that the problem was less with tactics or strategy as such than with the nature of warfare. Rose, *The Indecisiveness of Modern War and Other Essays,* reprint ed. (Port Washington, N.Y.: Kennikat, 1968), 1–28.

62. Weigley, *Age of Battles,* 132. Bruijn, *Dutch Navy,* 40, 218.

63. Extracts from Smith's work appear in Penn, *Sir William Penn,* 1:541–47.

3. At the Dawn of the Enlightenment

1. Blok, *Admiral De Ruyter,* 377–81. On the three battles see Mahan, *Influence of Sea Power upon History,* 160–66; Jacques Mordal, *Vingt-cinq siècles de guerre sur mer* (Paris: Robert Laffont, 1959), 97–99.

2. Quoted in Trout, *Colbert,* 147.

3. Mahan, *Influence of Sea Power upon History,* 70–74; Weigley, *Age of Battles,* 155; Tunstall, *Naval Warfare,* 5–6; Reynolds, *Command of the Sea,* 177–78; Murat, *Colbert,* 129–50, 171–96; Trout, *Colbert,* 135–78. And see Geoffrey Symcox, *The Crisis of French Sea Power, 1688–1697: From the Guerre D'Escadre to the Guerre de Course* (The Hague: Martinus Nijhoff, 1974).

4. Mordal, *Vingt-cinq siècles,* 102. Tunstall, *Naval Warfare,* 48. For French tactics see Symcox, *Crisis of French Sea Power,* 55–67.

5. Tunstall, *Naval Warfare,* 48.

6. Ibid., 49, 48.

7. Clowes, *Royal Navy,* 2:326.

8. J. R. Tanner, *Samuel Pepys and the Royal Navy* (Cambridge: Cambridge University Press, 1920), 57–79.

9. Corbett, *Fighting Instructions,* 164–72.

10. Ollard, *Pepys,* 300. Clowes, *Royal Navy,* 2:325–26.

11. Tunstall, *Naval Warfare,* 50.

12. Symcox, *Crisis of French Sea Power,* 72–78.

13. Ibid., 88–89. Robin Ranger, "The Anglo-French Wars, 1689–1815," in Colin S. Gray and Roger W. Barnett, eds., *Seapower and Strategy* (Annapolis: Naval Institute Press, 1989), 165.

14. Herbert Richmond, *Statesmen and Sea Power* (Oxford: Clarendon Press, 1946), 61.

15. Ibid., 61–65.

16. Symcox, *Crisis of French Sea Power,* 84.

17. Ibid., 91–93. Richmond, *Navy as an Instrument of Policy,* 215. William was in Ireland at the time.

18. Mordal, *Vingt-cinq siècles,* 103–106; Clowes, *Royal Navy,* 2:333–44; Tunstall, *Naval Warfare,* 53–54; Mahan, *Influence of Sea Power upon History,* 182–84.

19. Richmond, *Navy as an Instrument of Policy,* 218–19, and Mahan, *Influence of Sea Power upon History,* 184–85, attribute Tourville's failure to take fuller advantage of his victory as evidence of lack of strategic acumen; some French historians attribute it to sickness that swept the French fleet not long after the battle. See Mordal, *Vingt-cinq siècles,* 106–107.

20. Quoted in Symcox, *Crisis of French Sea Power,* 68.

21. Tunstall, *Naval Warfare,* 50–51. See also R. C. Anderson, "Two New Sets of Sailing and Fighting Instructions," *Mariner's Mirror* 6 (May 1920): 130–35. Anderson suggests that the instructions were issued either in late 1690, after Beachy Head, or as early as June 1689. Tunstall (50) notes that Torrington's defense of his conduct at Beachy Head indicates that he was "still using the Duke of York's book of 1672–73." Thus the instructions were most likely issued after Beachy Head.

22. Corbett, *Fighting Instructions,* 188–94, 187.

23. Ibid., 149.

24. Mordal, *Vingt-cinq siècles,* 108.

25. On Tourville's strategy see Symcox, *Crisis of French Sea Power,* 107–16.

26. Ibid., 117–18.

27. Mahan, *Influence of Sea Power upon History,* 189. Clowes, *Royal Navy,* 2:348. In a note Mahan acknowledges that the story may not be entirely accurate.

28. Symcox, *Crisis of French Sea Power,* 120, 121. Mordal, *Vingt-cinq siècles,* 108; Richmond, *Navy as an Instrument of Policy,* 229.

29. On the battle see Mahan, *Influence of Sea Power upon History*, 187–91; Clowes, *Royal Navy*, 2:347–56; Richmond, *Navy as an Instrument of Policy*, 229–31; Mordal, *Vingt-cinq siècles*, 108–20.

30. Mahan, *Influence of Sea Power upon History*, 188–91.

31. Symcox, *Crisis of French Sea Power*, 123–28.

32. Mahan, *Influence of Sea Power upon History*, 59.

33. Clowes, *Royal Navy*, 2:358–60.

34. The full title of Hoste's treatise, in the fashion of the time, was *L'Art des armées navales ou traité des evolutions navales, qui contient des regles utiles aux officiers généraux, et particuliers d'une armée navales; avec des examples itez de ce qui s'est passé de considérable sur la mer depuis cinquante ans.* The work is often cited, e.g. by Mahan and Clowes, as a primary source on the battles of the Anglo-Dutch Wars. On Hoste's work see Corbett, *Fighting Instructions*, 179–85; Tunstall, *Naval Warfare*, 59–64; S. S. and Mary L. Robison, *A History of Naval Tactics from 1530 to 1930: The Evolution of Tactical Maxims* (Annapolis: Naval Institute Press, 1942), 215–24.

35. Becker, *Heavenly City*, 34, 135. Frederick Leslie Robertson, *The Evolution of Naval Armament* (London: Harold T. Storey, 1968), 37. Hoste's two books were often printed and bound together. Tunstall, *Naval Warfare*, 59.

36. Michael Roberts, *The Military Revolution, 1560–1660* (Belfast: Marjory Boyd, 1956). Azar Gat, *The Origins of Military Thought from the Enlightenment to Clausewitz* (Oxford: Clarendon Press, 1989), 26.

37. Weigley, *Age of Battles*, 159.

38. Clowes, *Royal Navy*, 2:368–73.

39. Ibid., 377–79; Julian S. Corbett, *England in the Mediterranean: A Study of the Rise and Influence of British Power within the Straits, 1603–1713* (London: Longmans, Green, 1904), 2:213–19; J. H. Owen, *War at Sea under Queen Anne, 1702–1708* (Cambridge: Cambridge University Press, 1938), 71–82; *The Journal of Sir George Rooke, Admiral of the Fleet, 1700–1702*, ed. Oscar Browning (Greenwich: Navy Records Society, 1897), 210–12.

40. Rooke, *Journal*, 228–34; Clowes, *Royal Navy*, 2:380–385; Owen, *War at Sea under Queen Anne*, 83–86; Corbett, *England in the Mediterranean*, 2:221–25.

41. On Rooke's instructions see Corbett, *England in the Mediterranean*, 2:202; Richmond, *Navy as an Instrument of Policy*, 288. Marlborough quoted in Corbett, 2:301.

42. On the inquiry see Rooke, *Journal*, 241–52.

43. Churchill, *Marlborough*, 2:207–208.

44. Corbett, *England in the Mediterranean*, 2:242, 238–44; Richmond, *Navy as an Instrument of Policy*, 300–304; Mahan, *Influence of Sea Power upon History*, 209–210.

45. Corbett, *England in the Mediterranean*, 2:254–56.

46. Clowes, *Royal Navy*, 2:391–96; Richmond, *Navy as an Instrument of Policy*, 304–306; Owen, *War at Sea under Queen Anne*, 90–92.

47. Clowes, *Royal Navy*, 2: 396–404; Mahan, *Influence of Sea Power upon His-*

tory, 210–211; Tunstall, *Naval Warfare,* 66–67. Allied losses totaled about 2,700 killed and wounded; French about 3,000.

48. Tunstall, *Naval Warfare,* 66–67.

49. Clowes, *Royal Navy,* 2:405; Tunstall, *Naval Warfare,* 67–68; Stephen Martin Leake, *The Life of Sir John Leake, Rear-Admiral of Great Britain,* 2 vols., ed. Geoffrey Callender (Greenwich: Navy Records Society, 1920), 1:258–62.

50. Corbett, *England in the Mediterranean,* 2:286–87.

51. See Leake, *Life of Sir John Leake,* 2:273–78, 296; Corbett, *England in the Mediterranean,* 2:302–308; Clowes, *Royal Navy,* 2:412–14.

52. Mahan, *Influence of Sea Power upon History,* 211.

53. Shovell quoted in Richmond, *Navy as an Instrument of Policy,* 202.

54. Leake, *Life of Sir John Leake,* 1:257–258.

55. Mahan, *Influence of Sea Power upon History,* 237.

56. Richmond, *Navy as an Instrument of Policy,* 382–84; Clowes, *Royal Navy,* 3:30–38; Mahan, *Influence of Sea Power upon History,* 236–38; Tunstall, *Naval Warfare,* 68–69.

57. Mahan, *Influence of Sea Power upon History,* 237.

58. Quoted in Tunstall, *Naval Warfare,* 68.

59. Ibid., 69–72, ch. 2 title, 73–74.

4. The Conundrum of the Line Ahead

1. Quoted in Tunstall, *Naval Warfare,* 90.

2. Corbett, *Fighting Instructions,* 195. See Ruddock F. Mackay, *Admiral Hawke* (Oxford: Clarendon Press, 1965), 182.

3. See Herbert W. Richmond, *The Navy in the War of 1739–48,* 3 vols. (Cambridge: Cambridge University Press, 1920), 1:59–72, 151–78, 197–220.

4. Ibid., 172–75, 177. Clowes, *Royal Navy,* 3:83; Richmond, *Navy in the War of 1739–48,* 1:197.

5. The French contingent included sixteen ships of the line, and the Spanish twelve. The British fleet also included five 50-gun and two 40-gun ships. Mathews's fleet thus mounted 2,080 guns, the Franco-Spanish fleet only 1,822. Clowes, *Royal Navy,* 3:97n. For the confusion in the British fleet see Mackay, *Hawke,* 25–26.

6. Tunstall, *Naval Warfare,* 85. Richmond, *Navy in the War of 1739–48,* 2:10–13; Clowes, *Royal Navy,* 3:94–95.

7. See Richmond, *Navy in the War of 1739–48,* 2:20–51; Clowes, *Royal Navy,* 3:96–102; Tunstall, *Naval Warfare,* 86–88; Mahan, *Influence of Sea Power upon History,* 265–68; John Creswell, *British Admirals of the Eighteenth Century: Tactics in Battle* (Hamden, Conn.: Archon, 1972), 66–76; G. Lacour-Gayet, *La Marine militaire de la France sous le règne de Louis XV,* 2d ed. (Paris: Librairie Ancienne Honoré Champion, 1910), 150–54.

8. A flag captain was the commander of the admiral's flagship, not to be

confused with the "first captain" or "captain of the fleet," who served as an admiral's proto–chief of staff. Twice Mathews had sent lieutenants in small boats to get the laggards in the center division and Lestock's entire command to close up the formation. Tunstall, *Naval Warfare,* 86.

9. Richmond, *Navy in the War of 1739–48,* 2:appendix 3. Creswell, *British Admirals,* 67. Mackay, *Hawke,* 23.

10. The court found Mathews not guilty of this charge because no official regulation required any commander to issue his own instructions and signals.

11. Mahan, *Influence of Sea Power upon History,* 268.

12. Douglas Ford, *Admiral Vernon and the Navy: A Memoir and Vindication* (London: T. Fisher Unwin, 1907), 166–67. Washington's estate, Mount Vernon, is named in honor of the admiral. Tunstall, *Naval Warfare,* 79–82; Corbett, *Fighting Instructions,* 205–207, 214–16; B. McL. Ranft, ed., *The Vernon Papers* (London: Navy Records Society, 1958).

13. Vernon quoted in Tunstall, *Naval Warfare,* 80.

14. Ranft, *Vernon Papers,* 295, 290–91, 302.

15. Pamphlet quoted in Corbett, *Fighting Instructions,* 206. For example, on the eve of the battle of Toulon, the gouty Lestock, despite the cold weather, went in a small boat to Mathews's flagship, hoping to discuss the likely engagement. Mathews dismissed him.

16. Tunstall, *Naval Warfare,* 91.

17. S. W. C. Pack, *Admiral Lord Anson: The Story of Anson's Voyage and Naval Events of His Day* (London: Cassell, 1960), 153. The Western Squadron's principal responsibilities were the control of the English Channel and the blockade of the main French Atlantic fleet at Brest.

18. Ibid., 158–61; Lewis, *Navy of Britain,* 523–24; Mahan, *Influence of Sea Power upon History,* 271; Clowes, *Royal Navy,* 3:124–26; Richmond, *Navy in the War of 1739–48,* 3:86–94; Tunstall, *Naval Warfare,* 92–96; Lacour-Gayet, *La marine militaire sous le règne de Louis XV,* 179–84; Pat Crimmin, "Anson: Cape Finisterre, 1747," in Eric Grove, ed., *Great Battles of the Royal Navy: As Commemorated in the Gunroom, Britannia Royal Naval College, Dartmouth* (Annapolis: Naval Institute Press, 1994), 71–78.

19. See, e.g., Mahan, *Influence of Sea Power upon History,* 271.

20. See Richmond, *Navy in the War of 1739–48,* 3:82–86.

21. Tunstall, *Naval Warfare,* 97–98. The additional instructions were issued in either 1746 or 1747. See also Mackay, *Hawke,* 56–57.

22. See Richmond, *Navy in the War of 1739–48,* 3:101–111; Clowes, *Royal Navy,* 3:126–30; Mackay, *Hawke,* 69–88; Tunstall, *Naval Warfare,* 98–99; Mahan, *Influence of Sea Power upon History,* 272–73.

23. Tunstall, *Naval Warfare,* 91.

24. Ibid., 83.

25. Ibid., 92; Lewis, *Navy of Britain,* 538.

26. Richmond, *Navy in the War of 1739–48*, 3:191–98.

27. Ibid., 133–48; Tunstall, *Naval Warfare*, 101–103.

28. Quoted in Richmond, *Navy in the War of 1739–48*, 3:147.

29. Lewis, *Navy of Britain*, 504. Weigley, *Age of Battles*, 221.

30. Brian Tunstall, *Admiral Byng and the Loss of Minorca* (London: Philip Allan, 1928), 126.

31. Julian S. Corbett, *England in the Seven Years' War: A Study in Combined Strategy*, 2 vols. (London: Longmans, Green, 1907), 1:100–101.

32. *Augustus Hervey's Journal: Being the Intimate Account of the Life of a Captain in the Royal Navy Ashore and Afloat*, ed. David Erskine (London: William Kimber, 1954), 203–204.

33. Corbett, *England in the Seven Years' War*, 1:114n.

34. Clowes, *Royal Navy*, 3:147. Tunstall, *Admiral Byng*, 67–78. H. W. Richmond, ed., *Papers Relating to the Loss of Minorca in 1756* (Greenwich: Navy Records Society, 1913); Corbett, *England in the Seven Years' War*, 1:106–107.

35. Tunstall, *Admiral Byng*, 98–110; Corbett, *England in the Seven Years' War*, 1:107–112.

36. Tunstall, *Naval Warfare*, 108. Corbett, *Fighting Instructions*, 170–72; Creswell, *British Admirals*, 100–101; Lewis, *Navy of Britain*, 502.

37. Byng's fleet, of course, was not so divided.

38. Quoted in Tunstall, *Naval Warfare*, 110.

39. Castex, *De Ruyter à Suffren*, 53, points out that the concept of adherence to the line that led to the gap in the British line also prevented de la Galissonnière from taking advantage of the development. Lacour-Gayet, *La marine militaire sous le règne de Louis XV,* 289.

40. Corbett, *England in the Seven Years' War*, 1:124–25.

41. Ibid., 125–27. Lacour-Gayet, *La marine militaire sous le règne de Louis XV,* 301.

42. Stanley Ayling, *The Elder Pitt: Earl of Chatham* (New York: David McKay, 1976), 180, 182, 200–201.

43. Corbett, *England in the Seven Years' War*, 1:115.

44. Creswell, *British Admirals*, 94. Corbett, *England in the Seven Years' War*, 1:117. Lewis, *Navy of Britain*, 502.

45. See Tunstall, *Naval Warfare*, 104–15.

46. Quoted ibid., 106.

47. Hervey, *Journal*, 220. Mackay, *Hawke*, 180–81.

48. *The Barrington Papers: Selected from the Letters and Papers of Admiral the Hon. Samuel Barrington*, ed. D. Bonner-Smith, 2 vols. (London: Navy Records Society, 1937–1941), 1:259–60. Tunstall, *Naval Warfare*, 106. Mackay, *Hawke*, 182, 201.

49. Mackay, *Hawke*, 181–82.

50. Lacour-Gayet, *La marine militaire sous le règne de Louis XV,* 341.

51. Ibid., 342.

52. G. J. Marcus, *A Naval History of England*, vol. 1: *The Formative Centuries* (London: Longmans, 1961), 294–95; Mahan, *Influence of Sea Power upon History*, 297–98; Corbett, *England in the Seven Years' War*, 2:17–19; Weigley, *Age of Battles*, 223–29; Lacour-Gayet, *La marine militaire sous le règne de Louis XV*, 341–47; Geoffrey Marcus, *Quiberon Bay: The Campaign in Home Waters, 1759* (London: Hollis and Carter, 1960), 16–17.

53. Corbett, *England in the Seven Years' War*, 2:18–19. Mordal, *Vingt-cinq siècles*, 133. Lacour-Gayet, *La marine militaire sous le règne de Louis XV*, 345.

54. Corbett, *England in the Seven Years' War*, 2:10.

55. Ibid., 35.

56. Edward Hawke, *The Hawke Papers: A Selection, 1743–1771*, ed. Ruddock F. Mackay (London: Navy Records Society, 1990), 208.

57. Ibid., 220. On close and distant blockades, see Julian S. Corbett, *Some Principles of Maritime Strategy* (London: Longmans, Green, 1911), 185–210, esp. 191–92, regarding Hawke's approach; Wade G. Dudley, *Splintering the Wooden Wall: The British Naval Blockade of the United States, 1812–1815* (Annapolis: Naval Institute Press, 2003), chs. 1–2.

58. *Hawke Papers*, 339, 345.

59. Lacour-Gayet, *La marine militaire sous le règne de Louis XV*, 354–55.

60. Mackay, *Hawke*, 246.

61. Ibid., 248.

62. Ibid., 250.

63. Ibid., 252. Lacour-Gayet, *La marine militaire sous le règne de Louis XV*, 365.

64. Castex, *De Ruyter à Suffren*, 53. Tunstall, *Naval Warfare*, 117.

5. The Advent of Numerary Signaling Systems

1. "The Enlightenment was an attitude of mind rather than a course in science and philosophy." Hampson, *The Enlightenment*, 146. N. A. M. Rodger, *The Wooden World: An Anatomy of the Georgian Navy* (Annapolis: Naval Institute Press, 1988), 346.

2. *The Letters and Papers of Charles, Lord Barham*, ed. John Knox Laughton, 3 vols. (London: Navy Records Society, 1907–11), 1:309–313.

3. Castex, *De Ruyter à Suffren*, 98.

4. Ibid., 99, 99–107; Lacour-Gayet, *La marine militaire sous le règne de Louis XV*, 229, 230–33, 230.

5. Quoted in Castex, *De Ruyter à Suffren*, 258.

6. Tunstall, *Naval Warfare*, 123–25, 151–53. E.g., David Steel, *A System of Naval Tactics; Combining the Established Theory with General Practice, and the Particulars with the Present Practices of the British Navy* (London, 1797), includes translated selections from both Morogues and Bourdé de Villehuet.

7. Tunstall, *Naval Warfare*, 105, 117; *Barrington Papers*, 1:327–55. John Barrow, *The Life of Richard Earl Howe, K. G.: Admiral of the Fleet and General of Marines* (London: John Murray, 1838), 71. Howe's system included sixty-one day, fifteen night, and seven fog signals.

8. Tunstall, *Naval Warfare*, 127–28, 119.

9. Ibid., 126–27.

10. Ibid., 129; Julian S. Corbett, *Signals and Instructions, 1776–1794* (London: Navy Records Society, 1908), 18. Corbett, *Fighting Instructions*, 233.

11. Tunstall, *Naval Warfare*, 130–31.

12. Corbett, *Signals and Instructions*, 108–15, 114.

13. Tunstall, *Naval Warfare*, 130–31. Creswell, *British Admirals*, 86–87. *Barham Papers*, 1:xlix.

14. John A. Tilley, *The British Navy and the American Revolution* (Columbia: University of South Carolina Press, 1987), 142–45.

15. Ira D. Gruber, *The Howe Brothers and the American Revolution* (New York: Atheneum, 1972), 311–14.

16. Geoffrey M. Bennett, "The Fleet-Flagship: A Problem of Naval Command," *Journal of the Royal United Service Institute* 81 (Aug. 1936): 601–611; ibid. (Nov. 1936): 761–69; Gruber, *Howe Brothers*, 316; Tilley, *British Navy and American Revolution*, 150–51. Howe's report of 17 Aug. 1778, PRO, Admiralty 1/488, #314.

17. Clowes, *Royal Navy*, 3:398–410. Note that Charles Lord Cornwallis only surrendered 7,000 men at Yorktown.

18. Tunstall, *Naval Warfare*, 125.

19. King George III wrote to the Earl of Sandwich in May 1780: "Lord Howe has frequently told me that in action [a frigate] ought clearly to be the post of the commander." *The Private Papers of John, Earl of Sandwich, First Lord of the Admiralty, 1771–1782*, ed. G. R. Barnes and J. H. Owens, 4 vols. (London: Navy Records Society, 1932–1938), 3:212–213.

20. Mackesy, *War for America*, 104.

21. Ibid., 105.

22. Ibid., 190–92. Jonathan R. Dull, *The French Navy and American Independence: A Study of Arms and Diplomacy, 1774–1787* (Princeton: Princeton University Press, 1975), 108–12; G. Lacour-Gayet, *La marine militaire de la France sous le règne de Louis XVI* (Paris: Librairie Spéciale pour l'Histoire de la France et de ses Anciennes Provinces, 1905), 102–103.

23. Weigley, *Age of Battles*, 242. Jervis to George Jackson, 31 July 1778, in *Memoirs of Admiral the Right Honourable the Earl of St. Vincent*, ed. Jedediah Stephens Tucker, 2 vols. (London: R. Bentley, 1844), 1:67–68.

24. Mackesy, *War for America*, 229–32.

25. Clowes, *Royal Navy*, 3:433–40; Roderick Cavaliero, *Admiral Satan: The Life and Campaigns of Suffren* (London: I. B. Tauris, 1994), 38–41; Mahan, *Influence of Sea Power upon History*, 367–74; Tunstall, *Naval Warfare*, 162–64; Weigley, *Age of*

Battles, 244–46; Creswell, *British Admirals,* 132–40; Castex, *De Ruyter à Suffren,* 245–51.

26. Creswell, *British Admirals,* 139–40. Corbett, *Signals and Instructions,* 52. Clowes, *Royal Navy,* 3:440, 437–38. The toast story is true, and the officer who led it was Suffren. See Cavaliero, *Admiral Satan,* 40.

27. Weigley, *Age of Battles,* 245. Castex, *De Ruyter à Suffren,* 249–51; Mahan, *Influence of Sea Power upon History,* 370–74; Lacour-Gayet, *La marine militaire sous le règne de Louis XVI,* 201–203.

28. Corbett, *Signals and Instructions,* 20. *Barham Papers,* 1:293. In 1777 Kempenfelt published under the name Philotheorus a book of "Original Hymns and Poems." Sidney Lee, ed., *Dictionary of National Biography,* 22 vols. (New York: Macmillan, 1908–1909), 10:1283–84.

29. S. R. Shaw, "A General Staff System for the Navy?" U.S. Naval Institute *Proceedings* 77 (Aug. 1951): 824.

30. William Bell Clark and William Morgan, eds., *Naval Documents of the American Revolution,* 9 vols. to date (Washington: Naval Historical Center, 1956–), 8:484–86. Clowes, *Royal Navy,* 3:415. An "established" commodore had flag captains to look after his flagship. Commodores without flag captains were said to fly "a ten shilling pendant."

31. Clowes, *Royal Navy,* 3:341. *Barham Papers,* 1:163–64.

32. Ibid., 320–21. See also Rodger, *Wooden World,* 17–19.

33. N. A. M. Rodger believes historians have viewed Kempenfelt with too much "credulity." Rodger, *The Insatiable Earl: A Life of John Montagu, Fourth Earl of Sandwich, 1718–1792* (New York: Norton, 1994), 261. Corbett, *Signals and Instructions,* 24.

34. *Barham Papers,* 1:295. Corbett, *Signals and Instructions,* 29, 45–48.

35. *Barham Papers,* 1:301, 343, 345.

36. Ibid., 309, my emphasis.

37. Lacour-Gayet, *La marine militaire sous le règne de Louis XVI,* 231–94, termed the French effort "sorrowful." *Barham Papers,* 1:356–60; Clowes, *Royal Navy,* 3:509–510. Kempenfelt took five more ships from the convoy before he returned to port. Most of the convoy returned to Brest.

38. Corbett, *Signals and Instructions,* 43–49, 52; *Barham Papers,* 1:239. Clowes, *Royal Navy,* 3:540. Rodger, *Insatiable Earl,* 297–99, notes that the advent of coppering in the Royal Navy may have been indirectly responsible for both the disintegration of ships such as the *Royal George* and, in the next war, the mutinies of 1797. Copper sheathing of hulls, a technique advocated by Middleton, prevented the formation of marine growths that normally slowed ships and necessitated regular docking and careening. Coppered ships could be, and in times of crisis were, kept at sea for a much longer time. This placed great strain on their crews, hence the mutinies. It also meant fewer inspections of ships' hulls. Moreover, though the process was not understood at the time, the combination of iron fastenings and copper sheathing created an electrolytic corrosive effect on

the iron that may have led to the structural collapse of several ships during the final years of the American war, including the *Royal George*. The problem was ultimately solved by combining copper-iron composite bolts with the copper sheathing.

39. Barrow, *Howe*, 141.

40. *Barham Papers*, 1:330.

41. Between 1778 and 1782—five years—the British fought twenty major battles with their French, Spanish, and Dutch opponents. There had only been eight major battles during the Seven Years' War. There were seventeen fought between 1794 and 1811. While World War II involved almost continuous naval action, there were still only twenty-one major fleet engagements fought between 1939 and 1945. As for the determination of "major" engagements, I have followed Michael Sanderson, *Sea Battles: A Reference Guide* (Middletown, Conn.: Wesleyan University Press, 1971), 9–15.

42. Corbett, *Signals and Instructions*, 52–53.

43. Tunstall, *Naval Warfare*, 172. Corbett, *Signals and Instructions*, 53. Mackesy, *War for America*, 421.

44. Don Higginbotham, *The War of American Independence: Military Attitudes, Policies, and Practice, 1763–1789* (Bloomington: Indiana University Press, 1977), 380; David Curtis Skaggs, "Decision at Cap Français: Franco-Spanish Coalition Planning and the Prelude to Yorktown," in *New Interpretations in Naval History: Selected Papers from the Thirteenth Naval History Symposium*, ed. William M. McBride (Annapolis: Naval Institute Press, 1998): 23–46.

45. Corbett, *Signals and Instructions*, 251, 54. Tunstall, *Naval Warfare*, 173.

46. For the minutes of the battle see Sandwich, *Private Papers*, 4:183–86.

47. Tunstall, *Naval Warfare*, 175.

48. Tilley, *British Navy and American Revolution*, 255. Weigley, *Age of Battles*, 240. Lewis, *Navy of Britain*, 491.

49. Weigley, *Age of Battles*, 240; Tilley, *British Navy and American Revolution*, 255; Tunstall, *Naval Warfare*, 176. Mackesy, *War for America*, 424.

50. Corbett, *Signals and Instructions*, 54–55.

51. *Barham Papers*, 1:309.

52. On the strategic and operational aspects of the campaign see Mackesy, *War for America*, 420; Mahan, *Influence of Sea Power upon History*, 392.

53. David Spinney, *Rodney* (London: Allen and Unwin, 1969), 294–95, 284–88. Mackesy, *War for America*, 320; Donald Macintyre, *Admiral Rodney* (London: Peter Davies, 1962), 72–73.

54. Rodney's most recent biographer considers his reputation for prize-hunger exaggerated; Spinney, *Rodney*, 15–16. Tunstall, *Naval Warfare*, 157. Corbett, *Signals and Instructions*, 13. Morogues, like Rodney, favored concentration.

55. *Barham Papers*, 1:72. Spinney, *Rodney*, 303–304; Corbett, *Fighting Instructions*, 212–214; Corbett, *Signals and Instructions*, 13–14.

56. Spinney, *Rodney*, 294–95. Mackesy, *War for America*, 322.

57. Mackesy, *War for America*, 322–23. Tunstall, *Naval Warfare*, 164–65.

58. *Barham Papers*, 1:66.

59. Spinney contests the view; see *Rodney*, 310.

60. T. H. McGuffie, *The Siege of Gibraltar, 1779–1783* (Philadelphia: Dufour, 1965), 57–62. Spinney, *Rodney*, 317.

61. Castex, *De Ruyter à Suffren*, 79.

62. Tunstall, *Naval Warfare*, 167.

63. Ibid., 165. Corbett, *Signals and Instructions*, 186.

64. *Barham Papers*, 1:54.

65. Lewis, *Navy of Britain*, 515; Weigley, *Age of Battles*, 247. Article 12 quoted in Tunstall, *Naval Warfare*, 166.

66. Sandwich, *Private Papers*, 3:214–218.

67. Bennett, "Fleet-Flagship," 605. *The Naval Chronicle: Containing a General and Biographical History of the Royal Navy of the United Kingdom; with a Variety of Original Papers on Nautical Subjects*, 40 vols. (London: J. Gold, 1793–1818), 25:402. *Barham Papers*, 1:1.

68. *Barham Papers*, 1:156–57.

69. Spinney, *Rodney*, 329. Tunstall, *Naval Warfare*, 167. *Barham Papers*, 1:100–107. Bennett, "Fleet-Flagship," 603–10.

70. Clowes, *Royal Navy*, 3:463; Castex, *De Ruyter à Suffren*, 97. Spinney, *Rodney*, 336.

71. Sandwich, *Private Papers*, 3:212–213. Bennett, "Fleet-Flagship," 607–608. *Barham Papers*, 1:61–62.

72. Spinney, *Rodney*, 391.

73. Lacour-Gayet, *La marine militaire sous le règne de Louis XVI*, 430, says de Grasse could have avoided a battle, but Spinney, *Rodney*, 395, argues that the French were essentially cornered and could not avoid a fight.

74. Sébastien François, Vicomte Bigot de Morogues, *Tactique navale, ou, Traité des évolutions et des signaux: avec figures en taile-douce* (Paris: H. L. Guerin and L. F. Delatour, 1763), 40. Tunstall, *Naval Warfare*, 183.

75. Tunstall, *Naval Warfare*, 183; Mahan, *Influence of Sea Power upon History*, 487.

76. For Rodney's official accounts of the battle see *Letter-Books and Order-Book of George, Lord Rodney: Admiral of the White Squadron, 1780–1782*, 2 vols. (New York: New York Historical Society, 1932), 1:357–62.

77. On Clerk see Creswell, *British Admirals*, 190–95; Tunstall, *Naval Warfare*, 187–91; see also Spinney, *Rodney*, 427–28. For events on the quarterdeck of Rodney's flagship in the minutes before the British broke the line see Macintyre, *Rodney*, 232–33; Spinney, *Rodney*, 398–99; and Douglas's narrative in *Barham Papers*, 1:275–83.

78. Creswell, *British Admirals*, 171; G. Cornwallis-West, *The Life and Letters of Admiral Cornwallis* (London: Robert Holden, 1927), 122.

79. Spinney, *Rodney*, 402, 403.

80. On the battle and the controversy see Ken Breen, "Rodney: Les Saintes, 1782," in Grove, *Great Battles*, 87–94. Sandwich, *Private Papers*, 3:250–53.

81. Cornwallis-West, *Life and Letters*, 116–17.

82. *Naval Chronicle*, 25:404.

83. Nelson to Cornwallis, 30 Dec. 1804, in John Leyland, ed., *Dispatches and Letters Relating to the Blockade of Brest, 1803–1805*, 2 vols. (London: Navy Records Society, 1899–1902), 1:xvi.

84. Lacour-Gayet, *La marine militaire sous le règne de Louis XVI*, 552. Napoleon quoted in Cavaliero, *Admiral Satan*, xvii–xviii.

85. Cavaliero, *Admiral Satan*, xviii.

86. Castex, *De Ruyter à Suffren*, 212–13, 233. Cavaliero, *Admiral Satan*, 9, 15–16.

87. Castex, *De Ruyter à Suffren*, 259, 260, 235. Cavaliero, *Admiral Satan*, 18.

88. Cavaliero, *Admiral Satan*, 37–38.

89. Ibid., 60–63. Lacour-Gayet, *La marine militaire sous le règne de Louis XVI*, 516. Castex, *De Ruyter à Suffren*, 290, 312.

90. Castex, *De Ruyter à Suffren*, 258. Cavaliero, *Admiral Satan*, 258.

91. Lacour-Gayet, *La marine militaire sous le règne de Louis XVI*, 541–42.

92. Ibid., 542.

93. Cavaliero, *Admiral Satan*, 235. Bennett, "Fleet-Flagship," 609.

94. Castex, *De Ruyter à Suffren*, 329; also see 347. Cavaliero, *Admiral Satan*, 258–61.

95. *Barham Papers*, 2:371. On Patton's signaling system, "fit for use only on a cabin table," see Tunstall, *Naval Warfare*, 192–93.

6. The Zenith of the Age of Fighting Sail

1. Tunstall, *Naval Warfare*, 192–201; Corbett, *Fighting Instructions*, 252–68; Corbett, *Signals and Instructions*, 316–18.

2. Simon Schama, *Citizens: A Chronicle of the French Revolution* (New York: Vintage, 1990), 55, 60–61. William S. Cormack, *Revolution and Political Conflict in the French Navy, 1789–1794* (Cambridge: Cambridge University Press, 1995), 18–47.

3. Tunstall, *Naval Warfare*, 201–202. On the army reforms see John A. Lynn, "En Avant! The Origins of Revolutionary Attack," in Lynn, *Tools of War: Instruments, Ideas, and Institutions of Warfare, 1445–1871* (Urbana: University of Illinois Press, 1990), 157; R. R. Palmer, "Frederick the Great, Guibert, Bulow: From Dynastic to National War," in Edward Meade Earle, ed., *Makers of Modern Strategy: Military Thought from Machiavelli to Hitler* (Princeton: Princeton University Press, 1943), 62–68; Rothenberg, *Art of Warfare in the Age of Napoleon*, 22–28.

4. Joseph Martray, *La destruction de la marine française par la Révolution* (Paris:

Éditions France-Empire, 1988), 12. Cormack, *Revolution and Political Conflict,* 301; see also 1–17. Alfred T. Mahan, *The Influence of Sea Power upon the French Revolution and Empire, 1793–1812,* 2 vols. (London: Sampson Low, Marston, 1892), 1:35. Tunstall, *Naval Warfare,* 202.

    5. See J. Holland Rose, *Lord Hood and the Defence of Toulon* (Cambridge: Cambridge University Press, 1922); Mahan, *French Revolution and Empire,* 1:92.

    6. Cormack, *Revolution and Political Conflict,* 173–214. He wrote: "The defection of Toulon in 1793 was one of the greatest disasters to befall France in the whole course of the Revolutionary War." Ibid., 173, 215–41.

    7. Ibid., 242.

    8. Tunstall, *Naval Warfare,* 209.

    9. Jackson, *Logs of the Great Sea Fights,* 1:12, 32. Tunstall, *Naval Warfare,* 207; Corbett, *Fighting Instructions,* 255–59.

    10. Cormack, *Revolution and Political Conflict,* 285n.

    11. See Weigley, *Age of Battles,* 316–17.

    12. Cormack, *Revolution and Political Conflict,* 284–87. See Chris Ware, "Howe: The Glorious First of June, 1794," in Grove, *Great Battles,* 95–104; Oliver Warner, *The Glorious First of June* (New York: Macmillan, 1961); Clowes, *Royal Navy,* 4:216–240; Mahan, *French Revolution and Empire,* 1:122–61; Cormack, *Revolution and Political Conflict,* 277–86; Jackson, *Logs,* 1:1–193.

    13. Tunstall, *Naval Warfare,* 205. Lewis, *Navy of Britain,* 549.

    14. *Barham Papers,* 3:309. Corbett, *Signals and Instructions,* 317. Warner, *Glorious First of June,* 50.

    15. Barrow, *Howe,* 239. Jackson, *Logs,* 1:77–78; Warner, *Glorious First of June,* 50. Tunstall, *Naval Warfare,* 210.

    16. Barrow, *Howe,* 240–42, 246; Warner, *Glorious First of June,* 91–101. Cornwallis-West, *Life and Letters,* 272–73.

    17. Nelson, *Dispatches and Letters,* 2:369–71, 45–46; 1:494–95.

    18. Ibid., 1:67–68, 68–70, 71, 73, 2:45–46; 1:483. Alfred Thayer Mahan, *The Life of Nelson: The Embodiment of the Sea Power of Great Britain,* 2 vols. (1877; New York: Greenwood, 1968), 2:160. John M'Arthur, Hood's former secretary and later editor of the *Naval Chronicle,* published the first biography of Nelson in 1809. James Stanier Clarke and John M'Arthur, *The Life and Services of Horatio Viscount Nelson: From His Lordship's Manuscripts,* 2d ed., 3 vols. (London: Fisher, 1840).

    19. Clowes, *Royal Navy,* 4:267, 269–73.

    20. Hood, *Letters,* 104. Nelson to his wife, 1 Apr. 1795, and Nelson to William Suckling, 7 June 1795, *Dispatches and Letters,* 2:25–27, 40–41.

    21. Clowes, *Royal Navy,* 4:275–77. Nelson quoted in Marcus, *Age of Nelson,* 63. A. M. Stirling, *Pages & Portraits from the Past: Being the Private Papers of Sir William Hotham, G. C. B., Admiral of the Red,* 2 vols. (London: Herbert Jenkins, 1919), 1:80.

22. William James, *Old Oak: The Life of John Jervis, Earl of St. Vincent* (London: Longmans, Green, 1950), 60, 73, 72–73, 85.

23. Spencer, *Private Papers,* 2:73.

24. Nelson, *Dispatches and Letters,* 2:333–34. Jackson, *Logs,* 1:201; *Memoirs and Correspondence of Admiral Lord de Saumarez,* ed. John Ross, 2 vols. (London: Richard Bentley, 1838), 1:167.

25. Jackson, *Logs,* 1:210; John Drinkwater, *A Narrative of the Battle of St. Vincent: with Anecdotes of Nelson, before and after That Battle* (London: Saunders and Otley, 1840), 71; Cesáreo Fernández Duro, *Armada Española,* 9 vols. (Madrid: Sucesores de Rivadeneyra, 1895–1902), 8:92–101; "The Battle of Cape St. Vincent," *Journal of the Royal United Service Institution* 59 (Nov. 1914): 324–29.

26. Christopher Lloyd, *St. Vincent and Camperdown* (New York: Macmillan, 1963), 63–64.

27. Ibid., 49–50; James J. Tritten, "Doctrine in the Spanish Navy," in James J. Tritten and Luigi Donolo, *A Doctrine Reader: The Navies of United States, Great Britain, France, Italy, and Spain* (Newport, R.I.: Center for Naval Warfare Studies, 1995), 82–84. See also A. H. Taylor, "The Battle of Cape St. Vincent," *Mariner's Mirror* 40 (Aug. 1954): 228–30. Mercury was used in the extraction of silver from mined silver ore.

28. Duro, *Armada Española,* 8: 92–101. "Battle of Cape St. Vincent," *Journal of the Royal United Service Institution,* 334.

29. Jackson, *Logs,* 1:200–213. My references to van and rear divisions accord with their positions in battle on 14 February 1797, not their formal position within their fleets. Vice Admiral Charles Thompson's division, which fought in the rear of the British line that day, was nominally the van division. The Spanish order, too, was reversed in this battle.

30. St. Vincent, *Memoirs,* 1:256–57.

31. Steel, *A System of Naval Tactics,* 93–94.

32. See, e.g., Lewis, *Navy of Britain,* 552; Corbett, *Fighting Instructions,* 266.

33. For more on these issues see M. A. J. Palmer, "Sir John's Victory: The Battle of Cape St Vincent Reconsidered," *Mariner's Mirror* 77 (Feb. 1991): 31–46.

34. Geoffrey Bennett, *Nelson the Commander* (London: B. T. Batsford, 1972), 98; Mahan, *Life of Nelson,* 1:272; Lloyd, *St. Vincent and Camperdown,* 72; and Warner, *Nelson's Battles,* 23, all have Collingwood wearing out of line to help his friend Nelson. In fact Collingwood did not depart the line until several hours later when ordered to by Jervis.

35. Nelson, *Dispatches and Letters,* 2:340–43; 344–47. Second quotation from Drinkwater, *Narrative of St. Vincent,* 84.

36. Drinkwater, *Narrative of St. Vincent,* 77.

37. Ibid., 79.

38. Saumarez, *Memoirs and Correspondence,* 1:172–73; Lloyd, *St. Vincent and Camperdown,* 81.

39. Marcus, *Age of Nelson*, 80. Mahan, *Life of Nelson*, 1:231. Spencer, *Private Papers*, 2:95.

40. Michael A. Palmer, "Lord Nelson: Master of Command," *Naval War College Review* 41 (Winter 1988): 105–116. Nelson, *Dispatches and Letters*, 4:90–91.

41. C. S. Forester, *Lord Nelson* (Indianapolis: Bobbs-Merrill, 1926), 16.

42. Clarke and M'Arthur, *Life and Services of Nelson*, 1:23–24. Christopher Hibbert, *Nelson: A Personal History* (New York: Addison-Wesley, 1994), 15. For other biographies see Oliver Warner, *Victory: The Life of Lord Nelson* (Boston: Little, Brown, 1958); Tom Pocock, *Horatio Nelson* (New York: Knopf, 1958); David and Stephen Howarth, *Lord Nelson: The Immortal Memory* (New York: Viking, 1989); Carola Oman, *Nelson* (London: Hodder and Stoughton, 1947).

43. Gerald Jordan, "Admiral Nelson as Popular Hero: The Nation and the Navy, 1795–1805," in *New Aspects of Naval History: Selected Papers from the 5th Naval History Symposium,* ed. Department of History, U.S. Naval Academy (Baltimore: Nautical and Aviation Pub. Co. of America, 1985), 112. Nelson, *Dispatches and Letters,* 7:60–61.

44. Ibid., 7:241n.

45. Spencer, *Private Papers*, 2:178. Robert Duncan, Earl of Camperdown, *Admiral Duncan* (London: Longmans, Green, 1898), 336–37.

46. Mahan, *French Revolution and Empire*, 1:171; Bruijn, *Dutch Navy*, 211–12.

47. Spencer, *Private Papers*, 2:187–88.

48. Camperdown, *Admiral Duncan*, 191–93; Tunstall, *Naval Warfare*, 219–21.

49. Stirling, *Sir William Hotham*, 1:34–35.

50. Spencer, *Private Papers*, 2:197–99.

51. Lloyd, *St. Vincent and Camperdown,* 139, claimed that Duncan knew what he intended to do, but the logs of the battle make it obvious that he did not, as does the admiral's report to Spencer reprinted in Lloyd's book.

52. Jackson, *Logs,* 316. See Tunstall, *Naval Warfare,* 221; Lloyd, *St. Vincent and Camperdown,* 140. The diagram in Clowes, *Royal Navy,* 4:328, is far more accurate.

53. Peter Halkett, the captain of the frigate *Circe*, recalled the day as one of "dark weather . . . squally at times." Jackson, *Logs,* 1:313.

54. Ibid., 1:309–42, 317. Stirling, *Sir William Hotham,* 1:137.

55. Jackson, *Logs,* 1:317.

56. Ibid., 282–88. For Dutch reports of the battle see Camperdown, *Admiral Duncan,* 270–84.

57. Clowes, *Royal Navy,* 4:324–332.

58. Quoted in Lloyd, *St. Vincent and Camperdown,* 165.

59. Ibid., 169–71.

60. Stirling, *Sir William Hotham,* 1:139, 237. St. Vincent, *Memoirs,* 2:281–82.

61. Tunstall, *Naval Warfare,* 227–31; Corbett, *Fighting Instructions,* 268–279.

62. Jordan, "Nelson as Popular Hero," 113–14.

63. Piers Mackesy, *War without Victory: The Downfall of Pitt, 1799–1802* (Oxford: Clarendon Press, 1984), 133–35. The first league had been formed in 1780 during the American war.

64. Spencer, *Private Papers*, 3:285–86. Michael A. Palmer, *Stoddert's War: Naval Operations during the Quasi-War with France, 1798–1801* (Columbia: University of South Carolina Press, 1987), 61–62, 151–62.

65. Laughton, *Naval Miscellany*, 1:417–18. Stirling, *Sir William Hotham*, 1:258.

66. See Dudley Pope, *The Great Gamble* (New York: Simon and Schuster, 1972).

67. Jackson, *Logs*, 2:98–99, 101–103.

68. Pope, *Great Gamble*, 406.

69. Laughton, *Naval Miscellany*, 1:424–25, 414–38. Tunstall, *Naval Warfare*, 234.

70. Pope, *Great Gamble*, 404.

71. Ibid.

72. Ibid., 411, 412–13. Jackson, *Logs*, 2:119–20.

73. Jackson, *Logs*, 2:101–103.

74. Pope, *Great Gamble*, 416–417. On the truce, see ibid., 431–73; Susan Harmon, "The Serpent and the Dove: Studying Nelson's Character," *Mariner's Mirror* 75 (Feb. 1989): 43–52.

75. Pope, *Great Gamble*, 530. Mackesy, *War without Victory*, 204–205.

76. Jackson, *Logs*, 2:97.

77. Home Popham, *Telegraphic Signals; or Marine Vocabulary* (London: T. Egerton, 1803). Tunstall, *Naval Warfare*, 242–44.

78. Tunstall, *Naval Warfare*, 235–40. Audibert Ramatuelle, *Cours élémentaire de tactique navale* (Paris: Baudouin, 1802), vii.

79. Tunstall, *Naval Warfare*, 240–42; Tritten, "Doctrine in the Spanish Navy," 83–84.

80. Alan Schom, *Trafalgar: Countdown to Battle, 1803–1805* (New York: Atheneum, 1990), 1.

81. Napoleon quoted in J. Christopher Herold, *The Age of Napoleon* (New York: Dell, 1963), 209. Schom, *Countdown*, 37.

82. Schom, *Countdown*, 195–98.

83. Ibid., 97–99.

84. Ibid., 205, 203. Warner, *Nelson's Battles*, 157–58.

85. The Spanish left the bulk of their fleet behind to keep the British guessing.

86. Schom, *Countdown*, 210.

87. Warner, *Nelson's Battles*, 167.

88. Clowes, *Royal Navy*, 5:110. *Barham Papers*, 3:258–59.

89. Clowes, *Royal Navy*, 5:111–118.

90. James, *Old Oak*, 96. *Barham Papers*, 3:272.

91. Quoted in Schom, *Countdown,* 241–42.

92. Oliver Warner, *The Life and Letters of Vice-Admiral Lord Collingwood* (London: Oxford University Press, 1968), 136. Schom, *Countdown,* 242.

93. Cornwallis-West, *Life and Letters,* 484–87.

94. Clowes, *Royal Navy,* 5:119.

95. Schom, *Countdown,* 295.

96. Warner, *Collingwood,* 140.

97. Schom, *Countdown,* 302–303.

98. Ibid., 304. The count in guns was 2,568 allied to 2,148 British, an advantage of 16 percent.

99. Quoted ibid., 306.

100. Corbett, *Fighting Instructions,* 313–16. Nelson, *Dispatches and Letters,* 7:241n.

101. Warner, *Collingwood,* 144–45.

102. Corbett, *Fighting Instructions,* 316–20. Blackwood quoted in Tunstall, *Naval Warfare,* 251.

103. Tunstall, *Naval Warfare,* 253.

104. Most diagrams of the battle position the Spanish sailing toward the north. Warner, *Nelson's Battles,* 191, following the example of Rear Admiral A. H. Taylor, has the head of the allied line sailing northwest, almost directly into the wind. According to the *Victory's* log, the wind was blowing from the northwest, veering to west-northwest in the early afternoon. A close-hauled line could not be at better than north-northeast with the wind at the northwest.

105. Jackson, *Logs,* 2:149.

106. Ibid., 185.

107. See C. M. Woodhouse, *The Battle of Navarino* (Philadelphia: Dufour, 1965).

108. Jane Bouchier, *Memoir of the Life of Admiral Sir Edward Codrington,* 2 vols. (London: Longmans, Green, 1873), 1:51–52. Warner, *Collingwood,* 177; Piers Mackesy, *The War in the Mediterranean, 1803–1810* (London: Longman, Green, 1957), 100–101.

109. Woodhouse, *Navarino,* 106–107.

110. The Turkish fleet at Navarino hardly posed a tactical challenge to the British. One could plausibly argue that after Trafalgar the Royal Navy did not face another truly challenging battle until Jutland in 1916.

111. Corbett, *Fighting Instructions,* 335–42, 336–38. Palmer, "Lord Nelson," 113–14.

7. The Age of Steam through the Great War

1. Howard I. Chapelle, *The History of the American Sailing Navy: The Ships and Their Development* (New York: Norton, 1949), 478. Stephen Howarth, *To*

Shining Sea: A History of the United States Navy, 1775–1991 (New York: Random House, 1991), 120.

2. Chapelle, *American Sailing Navy,* 478.

3. Advances in the sighting of cannon were evident in the quick victory of the British 38-gun frigate *Shannon* over the comparably armed American frigate *Chesapeake* on 1 June 1813 off Boston, and in Sir Howard Douglas's treatise *Naval Gunnery* published in 1820.

4. William McElwee, *The Art of War: Waterloo to Mons* (Bloomington: Indiana University Press, 1974), 265.

5. Robert L. O'Connell, *Sacred Vessels: The Cult of the Battleship and the Rise of the U.S. Navy* (Boulder: Westview, 1991), 106–107.

6. Goodrich quoted in William N. Still Jr., *American Sea Power in the Old World: The United States Navy in European and Near Eastern Waters, 1865–1917* (Westport, Conn.: Greenwood, 1980), 13.

7. William Reynolds Braisted, *The United States Navy in the Pacific, 1897– 1909* (Austin: University of Texas Press, 1958), 24–27. On British domination of the telegraph network, see Paul M. Kennedy, "Imperial Cable Communications and Strategy, 1870–1914," *English Historical Review* 86 (Oct. 1971), 728–52.

8. Clowes, *Royal Navy,* 6:543.

9. John M. Ellicott, *The Life of John Ancrum Winslow: Rear Admiral, United States Navy* (New York: Putnam, 1902), 188–90.

10. Charles Lee Lewis, *David Glasgow Farragut,* 2 vols. (Annapolis: U.S. Naval Institute, 1941–43), 2:264. For a comparison of Nelson and Farragut, see William N. Still Jr., "David Glasgow Farragut: The Union's Nelson," in James C. Bradford, ed., *Captains of the Old Steam Navy: Makers of the American Naval Tradition, 1840–1880* (Annapolis: Naval Institute Press, 1986), 166–93.

11. Lewis, *David Glasgow Farragut,* 269; Alfred Thayer Mahan, *Admiral Farragut* (New York: Appleton, 1892), 277–78.

12. Giuseppe Fioravanzo, *A History of Naval Tactical Thought,* trans. Arthur W. Holst (Annapolis: Naval Institute Press, 1979), 118–20, 128–30.

13. Luigi Donolo, "The History of Italian Naval Doctrine," in Tritten and Donolo, *Doctrine Reader,* 102.

14. Jack Greene and Allesandro Massignani, *Ironclads at War: The Origin and Development of the Armored Warship, 1854–1891* (Conshohocken, Pa.: Combined Publishing, 1998), 235–36.

15. Lawrence Sondhaus, *The Hapsburg Empire and the Sea: Austrian Naval Policy, 1797–1866* (West Lafayette, Ind.: Purdue University Press, 1989), 255, 549.

16. John Van Duyn Southworth, *The Age of Steam: The Story of Engine-Powered Naval Warfare, 1783–1936,* 3 vols. (New York: Twayne, 1970), 3:94–95.

17. Fioravanzo, *Naval Tactical Thought,* 135–36.

18. McElwee, *Waterloo to Mons,* 257–63.

19. Ibid., 263, 271.

20. After Lissa the Imperial Japanese Navy, built up following the Meiji Restoration of 1868, adopted Western naval ideas, including ramming. The Japanese went so far as to fit ships with bamboo aprons to enable them to practice ramming. See David C. Evans and Mark R. Peattie, *Kaigun: Strategy, Tactics, and Technology in the Imperial Japanese Navy, 1887–1941* (Annapolis: Naval Institute Press, 1997), 35–36.

21. Sondhaus, *Hapsburg Naval Policy,* 256.

22. Southworth, *Age of Steam,* 116–117. Tritten, "Doctrine and Fleet Tactics in the Royal Navy," in Tritten and Donolo, *Doctrine Reader,* 21.

23. For one of Tryon's explanations of his tactical doctrine see Andrew Gordon, *The Rules of the Game: Jutland and British Naval Command* (London: John Murray, 1996), 195.

24. Ibid., 195, 620–21, 295–314.

25. S. C. M. Paine, *The Sino-Japanese War of 1894–1895: Perceptions, Power, and Primacy* (Cambridge: Cambridge University Press, 2003). Robison, *History of Naval Tactics,* 741. Evans and Peattie, *Kaigun,* 39.

26. Paine, *Sino-Japanese War,* 180. Quotation from Southworth, *Age of Steam,* 133.

27. Wayne P. Hughes, *Fleet Tactics Theory and Practice* (Annapolis: Naval Institute Press, 1986), 65–69. See also Evans and Peattie, *Kaigun,* 48. S. O. Makarov, *Discussion of Questions in Naval Tactics,* trans. John B. Bernadou (Annapolis: Naval Institute Press, 1990), 246.

28. Makarov, *Questions in Naval Tactics,* 291, 300.

29. Evans and Peattie, *Kaigun,* 50–51.

30. Julian S. Corbett, *Maritime Operations in the Russo-Japanese War, 1904–1905,* 2 vols. (Annapolis: Naval Institute Press, 1994), 1:302–309.

31. Ibid., 2:185–86, 209. See also Evans and Peattie, *Kaigun,* 116.

32. Corbett, *Russo-Japanese War,* 2:216, 231, 219–20, 223, 237.

33. Ibid., 2:239.

34. Ibid., 1:474–91, 503–24; 2:478. Evans and Peattie, *Kaigun,* 74–79. Translated extracts from Togo's battle orders are available at *www.russojapanesewar.com/instruct.html.* This excellent site is the work of the Russo-Japanese War Research Society.

35. Corbett, *Russo-Japanese War,* 2:310.

36. See A. Baudry, *The Naval Battle: Studies of the Tactical Factors* (London: Hugh Rees, 1914), 367.

37. Ibid., 200–201.

38. Rudyard Kipling, "Wireless" (1908), in *Traffics and Discoveries* (London: Macmillan, 1925), 239. Fiske quoted in Robison, *History of Naval Tactics,* 833.

39. Patrick Beesly, *Room 40: British Naval Intelligence, 1914–1918* (New York: Harcourt Brace Jovanovich, 1982), 2.

40. Ibid., 204-24.

41. Guy Hartcup, *The War of Invention: Scientific Developments, 1914-1918* (London: Brassey's, 1988), 128. Beesly, *Room 40*, 30.

42. Hartcup, *War of Invention*, 127-28.

43. Beesly, *Room 40*, 28-31.

44. Ibid., 152.

45. *The Jellicoe Papers: Selections from the Private and Official Correspondence of Admiral of the Fleet Earl Jellicoe of Scapa*, ed. A. Temple Patterson, 2 vols. (London: Navy Records Society, 1966-1968), 1:254, 253-59.

46. Quoted in Holloway H. Frost, *The Battle of Jutland* (Annapolis: U.S. Naval Institute, 1936), 126.

47. Filson Young, *With the Battle Cruisers*, reprint ed. (Annapolis: Naval Institute Press, 1986), 95-96, 33.

48. *The Beatty Papers: Selections from the Private and Official Correspondence of Admiral of the Fleet Earl Beatty*, ed. Brian McL. Ranft, 2 vols. (London: Navy Records Society, 1989-1993), 1:250, 258.

49. Ibid., 459.

50. Alfred von Tirpitz, *My Memoirs*, 2 vols. (London: Hurst and Blackett, n.d.), 1:53-54. The German official history of the Great War at sea compares Scheer's maneuvering at Jutland to Nelson's at Trafalgar. See V. E. Tarrant, *Jutland, the German Perspective: A New View of the Great Battle, 31 May 1916* (Annapolis: Naval Institute Press, 1995), 151.

51. Tirpitz, *My Memoirs*, 1:53-54; see also Gordon, *Rules of the Game*, 396. Tarrant, *Jutland, the German Perspective*, 55.

52. Ibid., 37n.

53. Arthur J. Marder, *From the Dreadnought to Scapa Flow: The Royal Navy in the Fisher Era, 1904-1919*, 5 vols. (London: Oxford University Press, 1961-1970), 3:19. Gordon, *Rules of the Game*, 355. Young, *With the Battlecruisers*, 77.

54. Gordon, *Rules of the Game*, 382. Marder, *Dreadnought to Scapa Flow*, 3:19-20; Richard Hough, *The Great War at Sea, 1914-1918* (Oxford: Oxford University Press, 1983), 270.

55. *Jellicoe Papers*, 243, 244 (my emphasis). Gordon, *Rules of the Game*, 397. It is remarkable that a commander of such a large fleet would express "hope" that his wireless sets would enable him to achieve the degree of control he believed was imperative to manage his fleet.

56. *Jellicoe Papers*, 244.

57. Hough, *Great War at Sea*, 272-73. *Beatty Papers*, 1:218, 458; Young, *With the Battlecruisers*, 117.

58. Marder, *Dreadnought to Scapa Flow*, 3:30-32. Sturdee quoted ibid., 31.

59. Hughes, *Fleet Tactics*, 81.

60. Young, *With the Battlecruisers*, 139. *Beatty Papers*, 1:457.

61. Beesly, *Room 40*, 154–46; Marder, *Dreadnought to Scapa Flow,* 3:41–44; *Jellicoe Papers,* 1:260.

62. Marder, *Dreadnought to Scapa Flow,* 3:51. Frost, *Jutland,* 155.

63. Reinhard Scheer, *Germany's High Seas Fleet* (New York: P. Smith, 1934), ch. 10.

64. Marder, *Dreadnought to Scapa Flow,* 3:61–62.

65. Ibid., 81.

66. Ibid., 85.

67. Quoted in ibid., 95.

68. Tarrant, *Jutland, the German Perspective,* 136–38.

69. Beesly, *Room 40,* 30, citing a 1934 paper by a German naval officer, Korvettenkapitän Kleikamp, entitled "Der Einfluss der Funkaufklärung auf die Seekriegsführung in der Nordsee, 1914–1918," held by the Bibliothek für Zeitgeschicte in Stuttgart. Tarrant, *Jutland, the German Perspective,* esp. 281–83.

70. N. J. M. Campbell, *Jutland: An analysis of the Fighting* (Annapolis: Naval Institute Press, 1986), 149.

71. Marder, *Dreadnought to Scapa Flow,* 3:150–51. Beesly, *Room 40,* 161. *Jellicoe Papers,* 1:260.

72. Earl Mountbatten of Burma, "The Battle of Jutland: An Appreciation Given at the Annual Jutland Dinner in H.M.S. *Warrior* on 25 May 1978," *Mariner's Mirror* 66 (May 1980): 107.

73. Ibid., 102.

8. From 1918 through the Second World War

1. See L. S. Howeth, *History of Communications-Electronics in the United States Navy* (Washington: Bureau of Ships and Office of Naval History, 1963).

2. Dudley W. Knox, "Trained Initiative and Unity of Action: The True Bases of Military Efficiency," U.S. Naval Institute *Proceedings* 39 (Mar. 1913): 42, 43, 59–60.

3. Dudley W. Knox, "The Great Lesson from Nelson for Today," ibid. 40 (Mar.–Apr. 1914): 306.

4. Dudley W. Knox, "Old Principles and Modern Applications," ibid. 40 (July–Aug. 1914): 1021.

5. Dudley W. Knox, "The Rôle of Doctrine in Naval Warfare," ibid. 41 (Mar.–Apr. 1915): 327, 333.

6. Harold J. Stark, ed., *Extracts from Books Read in Connection with War College Reading Courses* (Newport, R.I.: Naval War College, 1923).

7. William F. Halsey Papers, Speeches and Writings, 1933–1957, Container #45, 3, 4, 6–7, Library of Congress, Manuscript Division.

8. U.S. Navy, *War Instructions* (Washington: Government Printing Office, 1924), foreword.

9. Ibid., 11, 9, 84, 102. See Trent Hone, "The Evolution of Fleet Tactical Doctrine in the U.S. Navy, 1922–1941," *Journal of Military History* 67 (Oct. 2003): 1107–48.

10. U.S. Navy, *War Instructions* (1924), 25.

11. Ibid., 12, 98.

12. See Willis Joe Cato II, "Undersea Samurai: Imperial Japanese Navy Submarine Doctrine and Operations of the Second World War" (M.A. thesis, East Carolina University, 2003).

13. U.S. Navy, *War Instructions* (Washington: Government Printing Office, 1934), 93.

14. Ibid., 21, 17.

15. CINCLANT Serial #053, 21 Jan. 1941, in Julius Augustus Furer, *Administration of the Navy Department in World War II* (Washington: Naval History Division, 1959), 943–44, my emphasis.

16. Ernest J. King and Walter Muir Whitehill, *Fleet Admiral King: A Naval Record* (New York: Norton, 1952), 81, 87.

17. Quoted in Eberhard Rechtin, *The Technology of Command* (Washington: National Academy Press, 1983), 11.

18. Thomas B. Buell, *Master of Sea Power: A Biography of Fleet Admiral Ernest J. King* (Boston: Little, Brown, 1980), 131, 196, 194–98; E. B. Potter, *Nimitz* (Annapolis: Naval Institute Press, 1976), 65–66. Stephan D. Regan, *In Bitter Tempest: The Biography of Admiral Frank Jack Fletcher* (Ames: Iowa State University Press, 1994), 102–104; John B. Lundstrom, *The First Team: Pacific Naval Air Combat from Pearl Harbor to Midway* (Annapolis: Naval Institute Press, 1984), 158–59.

19. E. B. Potter, *Bull Halsey* (Annapolis: Naval Institute Press, 1985), 41, 43. Potter, *Nimitz,* 37.

20. Potter, *Nimitz,* 37–39, 43.

21. Ibid.

22. U.S. Navy, *Sound Military Decision* (Newport, R.I., 1942).

23. Ken Jones, *Destroyer Squadron 23: Combat Exploits of Arleigh Burke's Gallant Force* (Philadelphia, 1959), 125; narratives recorded by Commodore Arleigh Burke, 31 July 1945, no. 411, 6, 13; no. 411–1, 16, Washington, Naval Historical Center, Operational Archives, World War II Interviews. E. B. Potter, *Admiral Arleigh Burke* (New York: Random House, 1990), 73.

24. Burke Narratives, no. 411–1, 16. See Nelson's 1803 and 1805 tactical memoranda in Corbett, *Fighting Instructions,* 313–16, 316–20.

25. Jones, *Destroyer Squadron 23,* 267.

26. Burke Narratives, 31 July 1945, no. 411; no. 411–1, 16.

27. Ibid., no. 411–1, 13.

28. Burke interview, 27 May 1986.

29. Burke Narratives, 31 July 1945, no. 411–1, 16, 11, 17, 18.

30. Commander in Chief, U.S. Pacific Fleet, *Current Tactical Orders and Doctrine, U.S. Pacific Fleet: PAC-10* (June 1943), IV, 3–4.

31. Ibid., Section 213.

32. Quoted in Potter, *Halsey,* 279; and in Samuel Eliot Morison, *History of United States Naval Operations in World War II,* 15 vols. (Boston: Little, Brown, 1950–1962), 12:58.

33. The U.S. Navy's Third and Fifth Fleets consisted of the same ships commanded by different headquarters. Spruance commanded the ships as the Fifth Fleet during the Marianas operations, while Halsey's Third Fleet staff rested and planned for the next operation.

34. Potter, *Halsey,* 277–78.

35. Ibid., 290.

36. William F. Halsey and J. Bryan III, *Admiral Halsey's Story* (New York: McGraw-Hill, 1947), 216–17.

37. Potter, *Nimitz,* 335.

38. Potter, *Burke,* 206. Carl Solberg, *Decision and Dissent: With Halsey at Leyte Gulf* (Annapolis: Naval Institute Press, 1995), 123–26.

39. Potter, *Nimitz,* 336–37.

40. Ibid., 337.

41. Thomas J. Cutler, *The Battle of Leyte Gulf, 23–26 October 1944* (New York: HarperCollins, 1994), 221–22. "Taffys" were subgroups of task forces.

42. Potter, *Nimitz,* 340.

43. Potter, *Halsey,* 303.

44. Ibid., 303–304.

45. Peter Padfield, *Dönitz, the Last Führer: Portrait of a Nazi War Leader* (New York: Harper and Row, 1984), 86–91.

46. F. H. Hinsley, *British Intelligence in the Second World War,* abridged ed. (Cambridge: Cambridge University Press, 1993), 308.

47. Ibid.

48. Padfield, *Dönitz,* 159. Clay Blair, *Hitler's U-boat War: The Hunters, 1939–1942* (New York: Random House, 1996), 425.

49. Jürgen Rohwer, *The Critical Convoy Battles of March 1943: The Battle for HX.229/SC122* (Annapolis: Naval Institute Press, 1977), 198.

50. Hinsley, *British Intelligence,* 307, 309.

51. Padfield, *Dönitz,* 165, 171–80. Karl Dönitz, *Memoirs: Ten Years and Twenty Days* (Annapolis: Naval Institute Press, 1990), 341. Blair, *Hitler's U-boat War,* 425, 426.

52. Donolo, "History of Italian Naval Doctrine," in Tritten and Donolo, *Doctrine Reader,* 112–15.

53. Marc'Antonio Bragadin and Giuseppe Fioravanzo, *The Italian Navy in World War II,* trans. Gale Hoffman (Annapolis: Naval Institute Press, 1957), 12.

54. Andrew Browne Cunningham, *A Sailor's Odyssey: The Autobiography of*

Admiral of the Fleet Viscount Cunningham of Hyndhope (London: Hutchinson, 1951), 190. James J. Sadkovich, *The Italian Navy in World War II* (Westport, Conn.: Greenwood, 1994), 10, 10n. Bragadin and Fioravanzo, *Italian Navy*, 12.

55. Quoted in S. W. C. Pack, *Cunningham the Commander* (London: B. T. Batsford, 1974), 277. Cunningham, *Sailor's Odyssey*, 231–32.

56. *The Cunningham Papers: Selections from the Private and Official Correspondence of Admiral of the Fleet Viscount Cunningham of Hyndhope,* ed. Michael Simpson, vol. 1: *The Mediterranean Fleet, 1939–1942* (Brookfield, Vt.: Ashgate/ Navy Records Society, 1999), 299, 464; Philip Vian, *Action This Day: A War Memoir* (London: Frederick Muller, 1960), 86–92. Cunningham, *Sailor's Odyssey*, 452, 453.

57. Cunningham, *Sailor's Odyssey*, 161, 178.

58. Pack, *Cunningham the Commander*, 5. Oliver Warner, *Admiral of the Fleet: Cunningham of Hyndhope, The Battle for the Mediterranean* (Athens: Ohio University Press, 1967), 110, 111.

59. Erich Raeder, *My Life,* trans. Henry W. Drexel (Annapolis: Naval Institute Press, 1960).

60. Sadkovich, *Italian Navy*, 125.

61. Bragadin and Fioravanzo, *Italian Navy*, 84. F. W. Winterbotham, *The Ultra Secret* (New York: Harper and Row, 1974), 66; Sadkovich, *Italian Navy*, 126–27. Bragadin, writing in the 1950s, two decades before the release of "the Ultra Secret," suspected that some form of "signal intelligence" had alerted Cunningham to the Italian sortie, because the British Alexandria fleet left port before the Sunderland flying boat that sighted the Italians made its report. See Bragadin and Fioravanzo, *Italian Navy*, 99.

62. Cunningham, *Sailor's Odyssey*, 326.

63. Sadkovich, *Italian Navy*, 127.

64. Bragadin and Fioravanzo, *Italian Navy*, 86.

65. Sadkovich, *Italian Navy*, 127.

66. *Cunningham Papers*, 325.

67. Bragadin and Fioravanzo, *Italian Navy*, 88, 89.

68. Bragadin and Fioravanzo, *Italian Navy*, 319, 91; Sadkovich, *Italian Navy*, 129.

69. Bragadin and Fioravanzo, *Italian Navy*, 90–91.

70. *Cunningham Papers*, 320.

71. Ibid., 321.

72. Pack, *Cunningham the Commander*, 149.

73. *Cunningham Papers*, 472–73.

9. The Cold War and Beyond

1. Stefan T. Possony, "The Vindication of Sea Power," U.S. Naval Institute *Proceedings* 71 (Sept. 1945): 1033–43.

2. See William H. Hessler, "The Carrier Task Force in World War II," U.S. Naval Institute *Proceedings* 71 (Nov. 1945): 1271–81.

3. Martin Van Creveld, *Fighting Power: German and U.S. Army Performance, 1939–1995* (Westport, Conn.: Greenwood, 1982). The JTIDS turned out to be a $600 million boondoggle. See "JTIDS—Diary of a $600 Million Pentagon Fiasco," *Washington Post,* 11 May 1986, D1. C. Kenneth Allard, *Command, Control, and the Common Defense* (New Haven: Yale University Press, 1990), 130–33.

4. See Jeffrey G. Barlow, *Revolt of the Admirals: The Fight for Naval Aviation, 1945–1950* (Washington, DC: Naval Historical Center, 1994); Michael A. Palmer, *Origins of the Maritime Strategy: The Development of American Naval Strategy, 1945–1955* (Annapolis, Maryland: Naval Institute Press, 1991).

5. Van Creveld, *Fighting Power.*

6. Paul Bracken, *The Command and Control of Nuclear Forces* (New Haven: Yale University Press, 1983), 180–81.

7. Ibid., 180, ch. 6.

8. U.S. Navy, *Principles and Applications of Naval Warfare: United States Fleets, USF 1* (Washington: Office of the Chief of Naval Operations, 1947), paragraphs 212, 365.

9. John C. Kim and Eugen I. Muehldorf, *Naval Shipboard Communications Systems* (Englewood Cliffs, N.J.: Prentice Hall, 1995), 1–2, 31–33. Norman Friedman, "C³ at Sea," U.S. Naval Institute *Proceedings* 103 (May 1977): 126.

10. Roger W. Barnett and William M. Carpenter, *Strategic Forecast: U.S. Navy in the Year 2000; Phase II: Policy, Strategy and Technology in Global Competition* (Arlington, Va.: SRI International, 1985), 95.

11. Norman Friedman, *The Naval Institute Guide to World Naval Weapons Systems* (Annapolis: Naval Institute Press, 1989), 30–33. Michael Tucker, "DARPA's SCP: Toward the Automation of War?" *Journal of Defense and Diplomacy* 4 (Feb. 1986): 14–17.

12. Norman Friedman, "The *Vincennes* Incident," U.S. Naval Institute *Proceedings* 115 (May 1989): 72–79; William M. Fogarty, *Investigation Report: Formal Investigation into the Circumstances Surrounding the Downing of Iran Air Flight 655 on 3 July 1988* (Washington: Department of Defense, 1988). *Aviation Week and Space Technology,* 22 July 1991, 60–61.

13. *Christian Science Monitor,* 28 May 1986, 1.

14. Milan Vego, *Soviet Naval Tactics* (Annapolis: Naval Institute Press, 1992), 70–71, 52, 63.

15. Norman Polmar, "Soviet C³: An Overview," *Signal* 39 (Dec. 1984): 33. Roger Beaumont, "The Soviet Command Structure: The Three Headed Serpent," ibid., 41.

16. Vego, *Soviet Naval Tactics,* 353, 354. Norman Friedman, "Soviet Naval Command and Control," *Signal* 39 (Dec. 1984): 55; see also Charles Dick, "Soviet C³ Philosophy: The Challenge of Contemporary Warfare," ibid.

17. For a fictional view of Soviet and Western naval forces in a conventional war see Michael A. Palmer, *The War That Never Was* (New York: I-Books, 2003).

18. James A. Winnefeld and Dana J. Johnson, *Joint Air Operations: Pursuit of Unity in Command and Control, 1942–1991* (Annapolis: Naval Institute Press, 1993), 43.

19. James A. Field Jr., *History of United States Naval Operations, Korea* (Washington: Government Printing Office, 1962), 387.

20. Winnefeld and Johnson, *Joint Air Operations,* 50.

21. Ibid., 63.

22. Edward J. Marolda and Oscar P. Fitzgerald, *The United States Navy and the Vietnam Conflict,* vol. 2: *From Military Assistance to Combat, 1959–1965* (Washington: Naval Historical Center, 1986), 386, 445–46, 501, 500.

23. Mark Clodfelter, *The Limits of Air Power: The American Bombing of North Vietnam* (New York: Free Press, 1989), 84.

24. John B. Nichols and Barrett Tillman, *On Yankee Station: The Naval Air War over Vietnam* (Annapolis: Naval Institute Press, 1987), 26.

25. For a tongue-in-cheek view see Michael A. Palmer, "If Nelson Spoke German?" *Military Review* 69 (Jan. 1989): 98–99.

26. This account is drawn from Ronald O'Rourke, "Gulf Ops," U.S. Naval Institute *Proceedings* 115 (May 1989): 44–47; Bud Langston and Don Bringle, "Operation Praying Mantis: The Air View," ibid., 54–65; J. B. Perkins III, "Operation Praying Mantis: The Surface View," ibid., 66–70; John H. Admire, "A Report on the Gulf," *Marine Corps Gazette* 72 (Dec. 1988): 56–61; William M. Rakow, "Marines in the Gulf—1988," ibid., 62–68; Hans S. Pawlisch, "Operation Praying Mantis," *VFW Magazine* (Jan. 1989): 34–37; Michael A. Palmer, *On Course to Desert Storm* (Washington: Naval Historical Center, 1992), appendix A, "Operation Praying Mantis," by Hans S. Pawlisch, 141–46; Michael A. Palmer, *Guardians of the Gulf: A History of America's Expanding Role in the Persian Gulf, 1833–1992* (New York: Free Press, 1992), 138–44; and discussions with participants.

27. According to Crowe, "We had intercepted their [the Iranians'] attack orders." William J. Crowe Jr. with David Chanoff, *The Line of Fire: From Washington to the Gulf, the Politics and Battles of the New Military* (New York: Simon and Schuster, 1993), 202.

28. Interview with Anthony A. Less, "Mideast Perspective," *Wings of Gold* 15 (Spring 1990): 50–52.

29. Crowe, *Line of Fire,* 202.

30. Colonel Brian E. Wages, USAF, "End of Tour Report as Air Force Liaison Officer to Commander, US Naval Force, Central Command (COMUSNAVCENT/AFLO)," 5 Mar. 1991, copy in the author's possession.

31. Winnefeld and Johnson, *Joint Air Operations,* 139. Wages, "End of Tour Report."

32. The record of the conference and Tuttle's remarks can be found at *web.nps.navy.mil/FutureWarrior.*

33. Steven J. Fox, "Unintended Consequences of Joint Digitization," in *Sun Tzu Art of War in Information Warfare,* ed. Robert E. Neilson (Washington: National Defense University, 1997), *www.ndu.edu/inss/siws/cont.html.*

34. U.S. Joint Chiefs of Staff, *Joint Warfare of the U.S. Armed Forces* (Washington: National Defense University Press, 1991), 36.

35. U.S. Navy, *Naval Doctrine Publication 1: Naval Warfare* (Norfolk, Va.: Naval Doctrine Command, 1994), 38.

36. U.S. Navy, *Naval Doctrine Publication 6: Naval Command and Control* (Norfolk, Va.: Naval Doctrine Command, 1995), 26, 27.

Conclusion: The Crucial Paradox of Knowledge

1. Steinbruner, *Cybernetic Theory,* 16.

2. Jacob Bronowski, *The Ascent of Man* (Boston: Little, Brown, 1973), 356.

3. At Trafalgar the fleets came into action about six hours after the initial sightings.

4. Michael A. Palmer, "Burke and Nelson: Decentralized Style of Command," U.S. Naval Institute *Proceedings* 117 (July 1991): 58–59.

5. Michael S. Gazzaniga, *The Social Brain: Discovering the Networks of the Mind* (New York: Basic Books, 1985), 3.

6. Martin Van Creveld, *The Transformation of War* (New York: Free Press, 1991), 171, 173.

7. The Japanese navy allowed its commanders to operate in a decentralized fashion. Yamamoto, for example, did not interfere with Admiral Nagumo's command of the carrier striking force at Midway. Great Britain's Royal Navy operated in a decentralized fashion during the Falklands War; see Sandy Woodward and Patrick Robinson, *One Hundred Days: The Memoirs of the Falklands Battle Group Commander* (Annapolis: Naval Institute Press, 1992), 98–99, 150–51, 300–301, 316–17.

8. Roger A. Beaumont, "The Paradoxes of C³," in James H. Buck and Lawrence J. Korb, eds., *Military Leadership* (Beverly Hills: Sage, 1981), 115–38.

9. James Gleick, *Chaos: Making a New Science* (New York: Penguin Books, 1987), 15.

10. Nelson to Troubridge, 29 March 1801, in John Knox Laughton, ed., *The Naval Miscellany* (London: Navy Records Society, 1902), 1:424–25.

Acknowledgments

$\mathcal{T}$HE GENESIS of this book was my realization that the reason Sir
John Jervis did not signal the rear of his fleet to wear on 14 February
1797 at the battle of Cape St. Vincent was not that he committed an
error of judgment; but rather that the requisite number did not exist
in the signal book. Historians had managed to overlook this fact for
nearly two centuries. What other realities of command had they missed, I
wondered. And so I set out to write a history of naval command and
control.

Over the years, many people have contributed to the completion of
this work. I offer special thanks to the staffs of the Navy Department Library in Washington and the Joyner Library of East Carolina University
in Greenville, especially the latter's interlibrary loan personnel. I also
wish to thank the staffs of the Madison Room of the Library of Congress, the Davis Library at the University of North Carolina at Chapel
Hill, the Duke University Library, and the Historical Society of Pennsylvania.

William N. Still, Jr., to whom this work is dedicated, Frank Uhlig,
Peter Swartz, James Tritten, Edward J. Marolda, William S. Dudley, G.
Gordon Bowen-Hassel, Ronald Spector, David Skaggs, Craig Symonds,
and Carl Swanson, friends and colleagues all, read several or all of the
chapters. Darren Poupore, my former graduate assistant, helped with
some aspects of the research. W. Roger Biles, the chair of my department
in 1997, found the resources to allow me to focus on completing the first
draft of the manuscript. My dean, W. Keats Sparrow, kept pushing me to
finish. Fritz Heinzen, who is also my literary agent, read the manuscript

several times. I also offer special thanks to the patient Joyce Seltzer, the world's best editor. My son and daughter, Ryan and Lisa, put up with a father who was all too often an absentee parent. And finally, I thank my loving wife, Carol, who has always been patient and supportive.

To all, my sincere thanks.

Index

Downs, battle of the, 39-41, 44
Drake, Francis Samuel, 152, 154
Dreadnought, 212, 226
Dreadnoughts. *See* Battleships
Duff, Robert, 117-119
Duilio, 212
Duncan, Adam, 180-186, 348n51
Duncan, Henry, 135
Dundas, Henry, 2-3
Dungeness, battle of, 42-44
Dunkirk, battle of, 45-46
Duquesne, Abraham, 67-68
Dutch East India Company, 39-40, 329n20

Eagle, 135
Edward III, 35
Egypt, 1-4, 19, 27, 207-208
Eisenhower, Dwight, 262
Elephant, 189-191
Elizabeth, 149
Elizabeth I, 30, 35-36, 329n15
Empress Augusta Bay, battle of, 265
England. *See* Britain
English Channel, 40-44, 56, 59, 70-71, 75-78, 82, 338n17
English East India Company, 39-40, 329n20
Enigma encoding machines, 276-277, 285, 291
Enterprise, 261, 310-312
Eratosthenes, 20
Ericsson, John, 210-211
Essex, 121
Estaing, comte d' (Charles-Hector Théodat), 128-134, 147, 157, 159
Estrées, Jean d', 61, 79
Euryalus, 202-204
Evan-Thomas, Hugh, 244-245
Excellent, 172, 174, 176

Falklands War, 360n7
Farragut, David Glasgow, 217-218, 227, 231
Field, James A., Jr., 305-306

First captains, 135-136, 338n8
Fisher, William W., 282
Fiske, Bradley, 232
Flag captains, 135, 337n8, 342n30
Flag officers, 44-45, 56, 83, 135-136, 229, 242, 258
Flagships, 44-45, 52, 54, 56, 59, 89, 94-95, 123, 143, 150-151, 186, 238, 263-264, 274, 337n8, 342n30
Foley, Thomas, 7-8, 191, 242
Forester, C. S., 178
Formidable (1782), 153
Formidable (1941), 285-289, 291
Four Days' Battle, 56-59
Fowke, Thomas, 106
Fox, Steven J., 317
France, 17, 51, 210-211, 216, 232, 280, 283; in Napoleonic wars, 1-14, 163-209, 325n1, 326nn7,9-11,15, 327n20, 360n3; early navy of, 24, 26, 35; in Anglo-Dutch wars, 56, 59-62; in War of the League of Augsburg, 67-80, 89, 335nn19,21; in War of the Spanish Succession, 81-88; in War of the Austrian Succession, 92-96, 99-103, 337n5, 338n15; in Seven Years' War, 105-109, 111-121, 125, 339n39; during peace following Seven Years' War, 123-126; and American Revolution, 128-134, 136-145, 147-161, 344nn73,77
François, 24
Franklin, 9-10
French Revolution, 164-165, 346n6
Friedman, Norman, 301, 304
Friedrich der Grosse, 247-248
Fulton, Robert, 210

Gabbard Shoal, battle of, 47-49, 51-52, 62
Galatea, 244
Galissonnière, marquis de la (Roland-Michel Barin), 107-108, 158, 339n39
Galleys, 20, 22-25, 34, 38, 329n13
Gama, Vasco da, 25

Numerary signaling systems, 38, 103,
125-126, 136, 138, 163, 320

Océan, 158
Oldendorf, Jesse B., 272
Ollard, Richard, 70
Onslow, Richard, 181-184, 188
Operation Desert Storm, 314-316
Operation Praying Mantis, 309-314
Operations, naval, 30-34, 255, 321; in
Anglo-Dutch wars, 50, 65; in War of
the Austrian Succession, 102; in
Seven Years' War, 113; in American
Revolution, 157, 160-161; in Napole-
onic wars, 193; and technology, 213-
216, 231-232; in World War I, 234,
237, 250-251; in World War II, 292-
293; in Korean War, 305-306; in
Vietnam war, 307; in Persian Gulf
wars, 315
Orange, Prince of. *See* William III
Orde, John, 196
Orient, 9-12, 326n7
Oriente, 172, 174
Orion (1798), 3, 8-10, 171-172, 177, 207,
326n7
Orion (1941), 288
Orvilliers, comte d' (Louis Guillouet),
131-132
Ottoman Empire, 3, 22, 24-25, 27, 34,
207-208, 216, 223, 232, 325n4,
329n13, 350n110
Ozawa, Jisaburo, 268, 270-272

*PAC-10: Current Tactical Orders and Doc-
trine*, 265-266
Paixhans, Henri-Joseph, 210
Paixhans guns, 211
Palestro, 220, 222
Palliser, Hugh, 131
Parker, Geoffrey, 32-33
Parker, Hyde, 134, 148, 187-192
Parker, William, 171-172, 174, 176
Parma, duca di (Alessandro Farnese),
30-33

Patton, Philip, 161-162
Paul I, 187, 192
Pavillon, chevalier du (Jean-François de
Cheyron), 125-126, 164
Pearl Harbor, attack on, 260, 292
Penn, William, 42, 47
Penny, Taylor, 154
Pepys, Samuel, 69-70
Persano, Carlo Pellion di, 219-223, 226
Persian Gulf wars, 294, 302, 304, 308-
316
Persians, 27, 330n31
Peuple Souverain, 10
Peyton, Edward, 103
Peyton, John, 9
Philip II, 30-32, 37, 71, 76, 82, 113, 195
Philippines, 215, 226-227, 260, 266-275
Piracy, 21, 49, 68
Pitt, William (the Elder), 110
Pitt, William (the Younger), 2-3, 187,
195
Poder, 96, 100
Pointis, baron de (Jean-Bernard
Desjeans), 85, 87
Pola, 287, 289-290
Polmar, Norman, 304
Pope, Dudley, 189-190
Popham, Home, 192-193, 206
Porto Praya, battle of, 159
Portugal, 25-28, 50, 65, 86, 116, 329n13
Possony, Stefan T., 295
Potter, E. B., 261-262
Preble, George, 216
Pridham-Whippell, H. D., 286, 288,
290
Prince George, 171-172
Princess Louisa, 108
Princess Royal, 148
Princeton, 269, 271
Prince of Wales, 198, 201
Professionalism, naval, 65-66, 80, 124-
125
Providien, battle of, 161
Prussia, 113, 164, 187, 194
Ptolemy, Claudius, 20